Celebrity and the Feminist Blockbuster

Anthea Taylor

Celebrity and the Feminist Blockbuster

Anthea Taylor
Department of Gender and Cultural Studies
University of Sydney
Sydney, Australia

ISBN 978-1-137-37333-5 (hardcover)   ISBN 978-1-137-37334-2   (eBook)
ISBN 978-1-349-67699-6 (softcover)
DOI 10.1057/978-1-137-37334-2

Library of Congress Control Number: 2016956393

© The Editor(s) (if applicable) and The Author(s) 2016, First softcover printing 2019
The author(s) has/have asserted their right(s) to be identified as the author(s) of this work in accordance with the Copyright, Designs and Patents Act 1988.
This work is subject to copyright. All rights are solely and exclusively licensed by the Publisher, whether the whole or part of the material is concerned, specifically the rights of translation, reprinting, reuse of illustrations, recitation, broadcasting, reproduction on microfilms or in any other physical way, and transmission or information storage and retrieval, electronic adaptation, computer software, or by similar or dissimilar methodology now known or hereafter developed.
The use of general descriptive names, registered names, trademarks, service marks, etc. in this publication does not imply, even in the absence of a specific statement, that such names are exempt from the relevant protective laws and regulations and therefore free for general use.
The publisher, the authors and the editors are safe to assume that the advice and information in this book are believed to be true and accurate at the date of publication. Neither the publisher nor the authors or the editors give a warranty, express or implied, with respect to the material contained herein or for any errors or omissions that may have been made.

Cover illustration: © GeorgePeters / Getty Images
Cover design by Fatima Jamadar

Printed on acid-free paper

This Palgrave Macmillan imprint is published by Springer Nature
The registered company is Macmillan Publishers Ltd.
The registered company address is: The Campus, 4 Crinan Street, London, N1 9XW, United Kingdom

For Amelie Sara Taylor

Acknowledgements

Much primary material for this book was found in archives, especially in the US. The Schlesinger Library at Radcliffe's Institute for Advanced Study, Harvard University and the Sophia Smith Collection at Smith College were invaluable resources and I thank the staff at both institutions for their support. The School of Historical and Philosophical Inquiry at the University of Sydney provided funding for that research trip. At the University of Melbourne, archivist Katrina Dean and her team helped me to navigate the relatively newly acquired Germaine Greer archive.

Material upon which some of these chapters are based has been previously published, including in *Feminist Media Studies* and *Celebrity Studies*: '"Blockbuster" celebrity feminism', *Celebrity Studies*, (2014) 5:1–2, 75–78, Hamad, H., Taylor, A. (2015); 'Feminism and contemporary celebrity culture', *Celebrity Studies*, 6(1), 124–127; 'Germaine Greer's adaptable celebrity: Feminism, unruliness, and humour on the British small screen' (2014) *Feminist Media Studies*, 14.5: 759–774. I also drew upon material from *Single Women in Popular Culture* (2012, also published by Palgrave Macmillan) for the chapter on Helen Gurley Brown. I thank the editors of these journals, as well as Palgrave Macmillan, for their permission to draw upon that material here.

I also wish to thank all those involved in the 'Intervening Media' workshop at RMIT in Barcelona in 2015 for their thoughtful feedback in the

---

The original version of this book was revised. An erratum to this book can be found at DOI http://dx.doi.org/10.1057/978-1-137-37334-2

final stages of this project: Mark Andrejevic, Jack Bratich, Nick Couldry, Olivier Driessens, Tania Lewis, Graeme Turner, and Zala Volcic. Big thanks also to Alifa Bandali and Kate O'Halloran, who both generously offered to read chapter drafts and provided valuable comments; I look forward to returning the favour. I am also grateful to Marg Henderson for her astute feedback in the final stages of drafting.

Thanks must go to Felicity Plester, Commissioning Editor at Palgrave Macmillan, who has been an enthusiastic supporter of my work not just for this book but for my previous one too. Thanks also to Sophie Auld for her assistance during the production phase.

This book was contracted while I was a Postdoctoral Research Fellow in the Centre for Critical and Cultural Studies at the University of Queensland. Accordingly, I wish to offer thanks to my former colleagues for their encouragement, friendship, and the community we all formed not just in the Forgan Smith Tower but beyond. And especially to Graeme Turner for always being such a generous mentor and friend. For his unwavering support, intellectual engagement and guidance over many years, and specifically for providing insightful feedback on drafts of each of the following chapters, I am truly grateful.

My heartfelt thanks go to my extraordinarily supportive partner, Eoin O'Sullivan, for all the love and laughter. And to my family, Owen, Kirsty, Isabella, Olivia, and Amelie, and especially to my parents, Rose and Maurice, who have always unconditionally supported and believed in me and this book has been no exception. My youngest niece had not entered this world when I dedicated an earlier book to her sisters so this one is for you, Millie.

Contents

1 Introduction   1

2 'Blockbuster' Feminism and Celebrification   25

Part I   The 1960s/1970s Blockbuster and
Ongoing Feminist Stardom   59

3 Helen Gurley Brown: Prototypical Celebrity Feminism,
Cultural Intermediaries, and Agency   63

4 Betty Friedan: The 'Mother' of Feminism, Self-fashioning,
and the Celebrity Mystique   93

5 Germaine Greer: 'The Star Feminism Had to Have',
Unruliness, and Adaptable Celebrity   127

Part II The New Bestsellers, Online Media, and Branding Feminism in the Twenty-first Century — 161

6 Naomi Wolf: Twitter and the Transformation of a 'Third wave' Celebrity — 165

7 Sheryl Sandberg and Roxane Gay: The Limits and Possibilities of Contemporary Blockbuster Feminism — 197

8 Amy Poehler and Lena Dunham: Celebrity Memoirs, Comedy, and Digital Activism — 235

9 Conclusion: The Future of Celebrity Feminism—Contemporary Celebrity Culture, the Blockbuster, and Feminist Star Studies — 271

Erratum to: Celebrity and the Feminist Blockbuster — E1

Index — 301

CHAPTER 1

Introduction

Feminism has always had its celebrities, a situation that has historically caused much anxiety. Within the women's liberation movement, the making, and marketing, of 'media stars' was, as Martha Shelley's comments suggest, believed to be thoroughly inconsistent with the goals and anti-hierarchical principles of second wave feminism: 'These media stars, carefully coiffed and lathered with foundation makeup, claim to represent all women. In actuality, they are ripping all women off ... If large numbers of women are going to passively depend on a few stars to liberate them, instead of getting themselves together to do it, the movement will surely fail' (cited in Gever 2003, p. 84). Such women, in their commodification of feminism, were routinely dismissed as 'selling out' the movement, selfishly privileging the individual over the collective, and, as Shelley argued, potentially jeopardizing the success of the women's movement itself. During feminism's second wave, such charges were most commonly levelled against the author of bestselling feminist non-fiction, who was implicated in mainstream commercial publishing ventures (as opposed to ostensibly more politically sound feminist presses).[1]

In 1971, Germaine Greer, long known for her own work in artfully cultivating a star feminist persona, made clear the role of the 'feminist blockbuster' in the celebrification of certain women over others:

> Now that Women's Liberation has become a subject upon which each publishing house must bring forth its book ... the struggle for the liberation of women is being mistaken for yet another battle of the books. Each

publishing house backs its own expertise to identify the eventual bible of the women's movement, characterizing it as a religious cult in which one publisher will corner the credibility market, sending the world's women rushing like lemmings after a book. *The hapless authoresses of the books in question find themselves projected into the roles of cult leaders, gurus of helpless mewing multitudes* ... (in Murray 2004, p. 179, my emphasis)

One of the biggest problems with Greer's statement above, apart from its positioning of readers as 'lemmings', is its characterization of fame as something *done* to reluctant, passive feminist authors. Greer, however, is not alone in making this somewhat disingenuous assumption, which is predicated on the disavowal of feminist agency in the celebrification process, and which underestimates the power of bestselling feminist works of non-fiction, such as her own, in reaching large audiences of women who may not have otherwise engaged with feminism. 'Blockbuster' feminist authors like Greer, and Helen Gurley Brown and Betty Friedan before her, and Naomi Wolf, Roxane Gay, Sheryl Sandberg, Amy Poehler, and Lena Dunham after her, are all women who have actively worked to shape our understandings of Western feminism, in some cases over many decades. With the assistance of various cultural intermediaries, they have all laboured to establish and maintain a public feminist persona, as well as putting their celebrity capital to what could be broadly considered 'feminist' uses.

As the public embodiment of feminism, such women have come to mediate what this complex social movement means in the popular imaginary. Celebrity feminism, as I have previously argued, is itself an internally variegated phenomenon but it appears that, historically, the most visible form of celebrity feminist has been the popular non-fiction author (Tuchman 1978; Taylor 2008, 2010). For Shane Rowlands and Margaret Henderson (1996), a 'feminist blockbuster' is a bestselling, skilfully marketed, often contentious popular feminist book, with a heavily celebrified author; and to this I would add that the blockbuster is a text that endures. While readership figures, through bestseller lists such as those offered by the *New York Times*, on which all these books have appeared, are a useful gauge of cultural impact, it is also significant that such publications receive extensive media coverage and engagement, thereby reaching a much broader audience than their *actual* readers. But in addition to their success as commodities and wider cultural visibility, Sandra Lilburn et al. have suggested 'what all these books [feminist blockbusters] have in common is an author who functions as a public persona, a celebrity—who has the capacity to create a space for public debate on feminism' (2000, p. 343). The authors analyzed here certainly have created, and worked to sustain, such a discursive space. Rather than being 'well known for their well-knownness' (Boorstin 1971, p. 97), in Chris Rojek's (2001) typology they can be classified 'achieved celebrities', in that their renown is, at least initially, predicated on one specific achievement: the publication of a bestselling feminist work of non-fiction.

As myriad feminist scholars have made clear, the field of representation matters politically, in terms of shaping our understandings of gender as well as feminism itself (Dow 1996; Gill 2007; Griffin 2015). Popular cultural texts, in which I include the blockbuster and media representations of its authors, work to inform whether, how, and to what extent women come to engage with feminism, making sustained analysis of them and the political and cultural work they do vital. While many women celebrities over the past few years, including Emma Watson and Beyoncé, have eagerly claimed an identification with feminism, my definition of celebrity feminism does not encompass such figures. For me, as I will further outline in Chap. 2, a celebrity feminist is someone whose fame is the product of their public feminist enunciative practices; that is, they are famous *because* of their feminism. In this definition, the feminist blockbuster author reigns supreme, even in the twenty-first century.

Asserting that celebrity has always been a significant resource for feminism, here I have two key goals: to understand how these books and their authors shape the kinds of feminism that come to circulate in the mediasphere, and how their celebrity feminism works, and develops, as a 'performative practice' (Marwick and boyd 2011) across various sites and platforms, in ways that are not in any simple sense homologous with other forms of fame. As I argue throughout, the function of these women in actively keeping feminism alive in the mainstream cultural imaginary cannot be overstated. Through them, certain stories—including histories—come to stand for feminism. Whatever we think of this metonymic slippage, it is undoubtedly part of feminism's conditions of possibility in mainstream media and popular culture, and has been since at least the early 1960s. Blockbusters, as commercially successful forms of feminism, are evidence of what has been called 'the mainstreaming of feminism'[2] but while this commodification has often been viewed as solely negative, here I seek to provide a more nuanced analysis. By challenging critical and popular narratives about celebrity feminism's essential failings, I am interested in laying bare the possibilities, alongside the much-canvassed limitations, of making select women publicly visible as authoritative feminists.

Rather than being 'unspeakable' (Tasker and Negra 2007, p. 3), feminism is arguably now more visible than it ever has been, in no small part due to new media, but also because of the myriad ways in which it has been incorporated into popular culture more broadly. This has not, however, led to the demise of the feminist blockbuster as a resonant cultural form. Blockbusters, as I will demonstrate, remain part of what Claire Hemmings calls the dominant 'feminist grammar' in the public sphere; here I recognize that there is much at stake, not just in the kinds of 'feminist storytelling' they privilege but in who is able to tell these stories (2011, p. 1).[3] Although individual chapters will of course offer a brief analysis of each blockbuster and consider the regimes of value in which they became implicated, this study is not primarily focused on the formal aspects of these books, or even literary reception processes. Rather, its central preoccupation is what these blockbusters helped make possible: the celebrification of their feminist authors, and what that celebrification made possible in feminist terms. That is, how they—these books, as well as representations and self-representations of the women who penned them—have worked to shape the 'public identity'[4] of Western feminism, in some cases over many decades, popularizing feminism and rendering it accessible for women into whose lives it may not otherwise have flowed. Here I am interested in the kinds of feminist stories that are (able to be) told, as well as the kinds of feminist politics that are performed, promoted, and enabled by the celebrification of these authors.

In engaging with texts from the early 1960s to the present I seek to map the changing contours of the feminist blockbuster, as well as of feminist fame itself. What are we to make of the fact that, despite post-feminist proclamations of the redundancy of feminist critique (McRobbie 2009), particular iconic feminists continue to culturally reverberate and new feminist non-fictional books become bestsellers? The relatively recent development of 'celebrity studies' as a field of critical inquiry provides the opportunity to review the contribution of these women to public understandings of modern feminism, as well as the processes of celebrity-making itself. This book, therefore, makes an important contribution to what Sarah Projanksy has recently dubbed 'feminist star studies' (2014), but while her deployment of this phrase signals feminist scholarship preoccupied with stardom, my work doubles its meaning to apply it to the feminist study of distinctly feminist stars; stars that, I argue, are inextricably tied to the blockbuster form and its associated promotional apparatus.

Celebrity feminism, including in its blockbuster variant, continues to be disdainfully characterized as 'faux feminism' (McRobbie 2009; hooks 2013). But rather than dismissing the feminism embodied by these authors in favour of 'some real authentic feminism which is "elsewhere"' (Brunsdon 1997, p. 101; Wicke 1994), that exists outside popular culture, I suggest that participation in the networks of celebrity in and of itself can be conceptualized as a feminist practice, not as something distinct from or extraneous to other forms of feminist activism. However, as Su Holmes and Diane Negra tell us, the 'forms and functions of female celebrity' (2011; see also Jermyn and Holmes 2015) have been markedly under-examined within the booming critical industry that is celebrity studies. Indeed, as Brenda Weber also notes, gender is 'infrequently considered … an important modality in the theorization of celebrity' (2012, p. 15). In keeping with this gendered elision, feminist figures have also received short critical shrift, with this being the first book-length study on celebrity feminism. However, celebrity studies does provide valuable critical tools through which to interrogate public subjectivity (Marshall 1997; Rojek 2001; Turner 2014), including the public subjectivity of so-called 'blockbuster' feminists.

Drawing upon recent work in this field, I hope to intervene in ongoing debates about 'celebritization'—the kinds of cultural and social changes associated with increased attention to celebrity—and 'celebrification'—the process via which an individual is transformed into a celebrity, including through her own labour (Driessens 2013b; van Krieken 2012). Blockbuster celebrity is important, I would argue, due to its crucial, and overtly political, role in working to shape how Western feminism has been publicly constructed: 'Clearly feminists have been, and continue to be, reflexive in their approaches to media, and the strategic symbolic work they have done in this area is a critical (and under-researched) part of the story of feminism's public identity' (Barker-Plummer 2010, p. 172). Feminist blockbusters and their authors have been, and remain, a vital part of this 'symbolic work'.

'Authors', as Joe Moran notes, 'actively negotiate their own celebrity rather than having it imposed upon them' (2000, p. 10). Such non-fictional triumphs would not have achieved their remarkable success had it not been for their authors' extensive labour and persona-building.[5] In terms of celebrification, I am especially interested in the question of agency in the establishment and maintenance of a public feminist persona. They each, as is common for women writers, 'became involved in an active relationship with their own fame' (Hammill 2007, p. 15). Therefore, in considering why and how these voices come to be privileged over others, the agency exercised by all these figures is central—an agency which of course must be recognized as 'situated', operating 'alongside and even within structural forces and constraints' (York 2013b, p. 1339; Moran 2000). However, in none of these cases do I argue that there is an authentic, unmediated feminist identity lurking beneath these public performances—such a distinction is untenable. But it is possible to locate apparent instances of persona-building by each of the authors, as well as a pronounced degree of publicly expressed self-reflexivity about their own celebrification. Despite the changing nature of the blockbuster form, celebrity, and media culture more widely, they are all authors not just of various forms of cultural production but of *themselves*, and I will take up this other form of 'authorship' in each chapter.

In regard to feminism, especially, it is often presumed that the 'turn to celebrity' is a relatively recent phenomenon, isolated to the past few decades in particular (Cameron 1999). However, as I work to show throughout, it is vital we recognize that 'celebrity feminism was there from the beginning, and depends for its success on media-savvy individual subjects' (Sheridan et al. 2006, p. 34). Celebrity for writers, too, including for women writers, has a much longer history than is sometimes conceded (Moran 2000; Glass 2004; Hammill 2007; Mole 2007; York 2007, 2013a; Galow 2010; Weber 2012). Similarly, developments in information and communication technologies are commonly presumed to have provided hitherto unavailable opportunities for celebrities to be active in their own persona construction and management. For example, Alice Marwick argues that through the technological affordances of social media, celebrity is now something people *do* rather than something they *are* (2016, p. 334). Although I agree with this sentiment as it fruitfully contests assumptions about celebrity as 'the property of specific individuals' (Turner et al. 2000, p. 11), I argue throughout that it is not only recently that celebrity can be seen to function in this way and that the blockbuster celebrity feminist—who seeks to 'do' this celebrity for particular political purposes—allows us to think further about celebrity as a process or, as Marwick remarks with danah boyd, as 'a performative practice' (2011). That is, as something that feminists *do* for decidedly political ends.

In the contemporary context of ubiquitous self-branding, Angela McRobbie suggests that a 'more branded and personalized feminism has surfaced in recent years and which comes immediately attached to certain names and careers. Feminists speaking out become immediately identifiable. Feminism is now a heavily named or signature activity, where in the past the "collective" sufficed' (2015, p. 133). However, rather than presuming that feminism has only become a 'signature activity' in the twenty-first century, this study uses the figure of the blockbuster feminist author to show how such mechanisms of self-branding have long been integral to public feminist performances—and adds that we should not presume that this is inevitably limiting to feminism.

Although a number of these women were by no means 'one-book wonders' (Mitchell 1997, p. 12), in each chapter I begin by underscoring the formative role played by the initial blockbusters in their establishment as feminist stars.[6] The publication of these blockbusters permitted them a media visibility, and authority, not granted to other women, and which in turn permitted them access to other mediated spaces such as television news and current affairs programmes, as well as various types of print, and, in the more recent examples, online media. Therefore, while all the women spotlighted in my analysis have penned bestselling works of nonfiction that—to varying degrees—can be considered feminist, they often parlay this initial celebrity capital into other forms, genres, and discursive spaces. Accordingly, while their celebrity may have started with the appearance of their first 'blockbuster', it certainly did not end there, and indeed grew, shifted, and transformed, as both feminism and the mediasphere themselves changed over time.

While much recent critical attention focuses on the fleeting nature of celebrity—such as reality television stars—a number of the women discussed in this book are, in contrast, remarkable in terms of their longevity in the public arena. Their very continued recognizability, not just as feminist writers but as female public figures, is in many ways unprecedented. In the case of those whose fame has endured—Brown, Friedan, Greer, and Wolf—I am most interested in their own role in its maintenance and in effecting its transformation over the years: 'As commodities, celebrities are the real embodiment of a more abstract kind of capital—attention' (van Krieken 2012, p. 54; Driessens 2013a). What did these feminists do with such attention capital, and how did they ensure its sustainability? This is a question with which I engage here, especially in Part I.

All of these women have been chosen due to the commercial success and cultural resonance of their blockbusters, and their immense, sustained media visibility, especially relative to other feminists. It is significant that all these authors have publicly identified as feminist, and this self-identification becomes especially important in the case of women like Brown, who initially may not have been associated with second wave feminism. Despite presumptions of generational cohesion, the type of feminism they construct in their blockbusters, and in their subsequent public performances as celebrity feminists, is by no means uniform; instead, in and through them different forms of feminism co-exist. For example, Betty Friedan's project was fundamentally a liberal one, centred on achieving 'equality' for women in the public sphere, while for Greer such a reformist aim was decidedly unambitious and would do little to actually liberate women from the demands of the normative femininity being imposed by patriarchy, or to destabilize the structural factors putting them in a subordinate position. Further, the relationship of all these authors to the women's movement or organized feminism itself differs, depending upon their own subjectivities and cultural and historical context, as does how they publicly position themselves in relation to dominant narratives of Anglo-American feminist history.

Indicative more of the limitations of celebrity when it comes to public constructions of feminism, there have also been several (anti-) feminist celebrities who have produced bestselling works of non-fiction and who have similarly worked to shape popular understandings of feminism, especially in the 1990s—with the most notable being Camilla Paglia (1990), Christina Hoff Sommers (1994), Katie Roiphe (1993), and Rene Denfeld (1995). However, while such figures may represent a cautionary tale for arguments around the political potentiality of celebrity for feminism, they have already been the subject of much previous analysis, particularly relating to 'third wave' feminism. Further, the authority granted them has not been commensurate with that enjoyed by the women featured here, and they do not continue to resonate in the same way. Nevertheless, I do briefly engage with these figures when I consider 1990s blockbuster feminist, Naomi Wolf.

THE SPECIFICITIES OF BLOCKBUSTER CELEBRITY FEMINISM

While it is now common to suggest that professionals in fields other than those traditionally associated with celebrity are increasingly being subject to the same kinds of celebrity logics and celebrification processes, this study, as mentioned, underscores that this is not an entirely new phenomenon. First, however, in order to come to terms with the question of what can be constituted as 'celebrity feminism', it is necessary to provide a broader definition of celebrity itself. There are of course many ways of conceptualizing celebrity. Sean Redmond (2014, p. 5) describes the celebrity as 'a person whose name, image, lifestyle, and opinions carry cultural and economic worth' (see also Wernick 1991; Rein et al. 1997, p. 15). That is, celebrities are those who, in addition to generating profit across a range of fields, accrue 'attention capital' via 'self-promotion and exposure management' (Rojek 2014, p. 456; see also van Krieken 2012; Gunter 2014). When it comes to the women featured here, these comments are certainly applicable and critically valuable. However, there are important ways in which the celebrity of feminists differs from that of those in other fields. Among other variations, the women featured in this book, particularly in its earliest chapters, sought not merely to publicize themselves and their books (although they did do that too) but to publicize *feminism* itself.

Although there are inevitably some similarities across the cultural field when it comes to celebrity, Graeme Turner (2014, p. 17) urges us to be mindful that 'what constitutes celebrity in one cultural domain may be quite different in another'. Similarly, as Rein et al. argue, 'Every field, no matter how visible or how obscure, produces its own celebrities' (1997, p. 85). It is the specificities of the field of blockbuster celebrity feminism that concern me here; that is, I seek to underscore that celebrity feminism is a distinct form of renown that cannot, in any simple way, be seen as homologous with other forms, particularly given that the key role of its author is to mediate public understandings of feminism. Through their blockbusters and subsequent media interventions, these authors, for the most part, are seeking to persuade readers/viewers of the necessity of feminist modes of knowing and being, making celebrity feminism inherently political. Moreover, I emphasize that even within the field of the blockbuster feminist, fame is 'performed in different keys' (York 2007, p. 4). Here, then, I seek to develop a deeper understanding of 'blockbuster celebrity feminism', as well as discussing the not inconsiderable limitations of this specific mode of public, and political, subjectivity.

Through the aggregation of a series of case studies, I seek to determine what is distinctive about this form of renown, as well as where/how it, simultaneously, and perhaps inevitably, reinscribes certain logics of wider celebrity culture. The timeframe, of fifty years or so, also enables me to track how the 'mechanisms available and used for garnering attention [as a feminist] have altered' (Gamson 2007, p. 142). However, this is no simple narrative of progress; feminist critics have highlighted the tensions and limitations of such stories (Hemmings 2011). Rather, here I seek to map some continuities in terms of how public feminist personas are produced and consumed (including how they are challenged, as at times they are), as well as the different pathways that celebrity feminists may have taken in the twenty-first century, given that celebrity culture, media more broadly, and feminism itself have all changed dramatically over the fifty-year period with which I am concerned.[7]

Methodologically I employ a combination of archival research and textual analysis, the former only being available in the case of the three figures dealt with in Chaps. 3, 4, and 5. Given that archives are selective repositories, sometimes shaped by these figures themselves, the material available therein is by no means consistent and hence the degree to which I draw upon them necessarily varies. Furthermore, given that star texts are intertextual (Ellcessor 2012; see also Dyer 1979; Marshall 1997), this study covers various media platforms and genres of representation and self-presentation, including authorial profiles, interviews, reviews in newspapers and magazines, the books themselves, subsequent publications (including autobiographies), television appearances, and different types of new media.

In terms of context, this study is focused on Western celebrity feminism, something that must be taken into account. Anders Ohlsson et al. argue that we need to maintain some sense of 'geographical differentiation', especially when it comes to authors, 'since the scope of influence of literary celebrities may vary quite considerably' (2014, p. 33). This point could be extrapolated to all forms of celebrity, including feminist authors. It important, therefore, that I am referring to the role of these women in specific contexts (and even within which their level of celebrity and cultural legitimacy can be seen to vary). While most of these blockbusters, with the exception of *The Female Eunuch*, were initially published in the United States, they were subsequently released internationally, each secured large readerships and received extensive media coverage elsewhere, including in the United Kingdom and Australia (from where I write), often on the occasion of promotional tours by their authors. Therefore, here I move between media coverage and texts produced in these three contexts. Throughout I am conscious, however, not just that a very different story may be told about celebrity feminism in different socio-political contexts, but that the privileging of these women relies upon rendering invisible others—something that needs to be problematized without completely dismissing the political possibilities of the celebrity zone for feminism (Wicke 1994).

The question 'What is celebrity feminism?' is necessarily complicated by the fact that there is not (nor ever was) a singular feminism, either conceptually or practically in terms of lived experiences or activisms. Though feminism is indeed a highly contested signifier, attempts to stabilize its meanings abound in public discourse—in large part through its blockbuster celebrities. Furthermore, feminism, as many scholars have argued over the past few decades (Dow 1996; Lumby 1997; Lilburn et al. 2000; Henderson 2006; Hollows and Moseley 2006; Taylor 2008), has become an integral part of the media landscape and its meanings have, of course, altered according to the discursive context in which it is invoked. And if it is difficult, or perhaps impossible, to impose definitional closure on feminism, then likewise it is impossible to say there is one singular mode of being a feminist celebrity—or rather 'doing' celebrity feminism. Nonetheless, what I do identify as crucial in all these instances is the active role of these women in deploying celebrity for particular feminist purposes. That is, that celebrification is not something simply done to unwitting and unwilling feminist authors, as per Greer's earlier comments, but an ongoing process that requires their labour and active intervention.

Given that celebrities are 'both labour and the thing that labour produces' (Dyer 1986, p. 5), this attention to the celebrities themselves will throughout be balanced by a consideration of the network of professional individuals involved in the complicated processes of constructing and sustaining celebrity. As Rojek reminds us, following Pierre Bourdieu, celebrity depends upon 'the expert intervention of cultural intermediaries' (2014, p. 458; Bourdieu 1993), attempting to cultivate—even pre-publication— a 'buzz' around the text and its author (Thompson 2010). Accordingly, in various chapters, and to differing degrees, I will engage with the central role of 'cultural intermediaries' in the construction and maintenance of blockbuster celebrity feminism. Audiences, too, by consuming these books, engaging with coverage of these authors, participating in public dialogue about them, or by being fans, are crucial to this celebrification process. Here, while only marginally attending to the role of these actors, I am fully aware that celebrity requires affective investment (Grossberg 1992) from them for its sustenance.

Structure and Chapter Outlines

Though these case studies can be read as self-contained, they are unified in a number of crucial ways. First, because they each enrich our understanding of the media–feminism relationship at different temporal junctures, not to mention the evolution of celebrity culture itself; second, because they each reveal strategies for negotiating the celebrity zone as a feminist; and finally, analyzing them together enables a mapping of the shifting terrain of celebrity feminism—from the early 1960s to 2015. Covering such a period, too, will allow consideration of ongoing debates over feminist 'waves' as well as postfeminism and its often troublesome politics.

The first part of this book focuses mainly on women who initially came to public prominence in the 1960s and 1970s but who have remained central in public contestations over the meanings of feminism (including in two cases post-mortem); women who, to varying degrees, came to be associated with feminism's second wave. These are women whose renown has endured. However, given that 'it would be naïve to expect celebrity cultures to be identical in form in widely differing times and places' (Morgan, in Lawrenson-Woods 2015, p. 14), I am also interested in more recently authorized feminist voices and in changes in blockbuster celebrity feminism over time. In Part II of the book, therefore, I consider some more recent forms of the blockbuster and the women who have authored them, as a way of mapping some changes in the establishment of feminist fame and the role of the blockbuster in informing popular understandings of feminism.

Chapter 2 locates this study within a number of key fields, including celebrity studies and feminist media and cultural studies. It demonstrates how celebrity has historically caused feminist activists and critics much unease, and links such discomfort to broader critiques of the mainstream media and the governing assumption that it necessarily works to undermine or contaminate a feminism that exists beyond or outside of the media or popular culture (Wicke 1994; Brunsdon 1997). This chapter, therefore, troubles the dominant critical narrative about the inevitable limitations of 'media mediated' (Murray 2004) feminism, as well as engaging with debates about star labour and agency. It argues that these authors' public performances, in a paratextual sense, work to delimit the meanings of their bestsellers (and thus of feminism itself) in significant ways (Genette 1997). Moreover, it outlines some of the key differences between the fame attached to feminism and other forms of renown, and situates the proceeding analysis in relevant debates about collective memory and the always-interested processes of publicly historicizing feminism. It also considers the form of the feminist blockbuster, which, while having changed somewhat, remains one of the key ways of making feminism accessible to a wide audience.

While 'the power of individual celebrities is often fragile and ephemeral' (Drake and Miah 2010, p. 60), the three women examined in the first part of this work—Helen Gurley Brown, Betty Friedan, and Germaine Greer— are remarkable for their longevity as highly visible feminists in the Western mediasphere. Their first blockbusters (for they each published further, if less successful, works of feminist non-fiction)—*Sex and the Single Girl* (1962), *The Feminine Mystique* (1963), and *The Female Eunuch* (1970) respectively[8]—have each remained in print; been translated into several languages; and have been reissued, often appearing with revised introductions or additional contextualizing essays, several times since their initial publication in the 1960s and 1970s. To varying extents, they are each still invoked in popular attempts to frame and historicize feminism in particular ways, as well as being repackaged for a new generation (as was most obviously the case with Brown being figured as responsible for Candace Bushnell's and subsequently HBO's *Sex and the City*).

In each chapter, I start by engaging with their blockbuster and the author's initial celebrification immediately following its publication (and in some cases preceding it, through pre-publicity), then move on to how this renown has been sustained—in, at times, quite diverse ways. I also use the ongoing celebrity feminism of these women to destabilize 'wave'-centric narratives; rather than relegate them to the second wave of feminism, and thereby preclude an examination of how and why they continue to *matter* culturally as well as politically, I argue that they each exceed their association with this particular temporal marker and accordingly trouble the generational frame through which feminism has been commonly understood in public discourse.

While these three women and their literary texts, to varying degrees, have been subject to scholarly attention, an in-depth focus on the processes of their celebrification has been lacking. Nor has there been any concerted critical effort to track the kinds of feminisms made possible by their celebrification. What is feminism allowed to be in and through these elevated women and their individualized narratives? What story does this celebrification tell about the media–feminism nexus over time? In terms of the diverse case studies that constitute this work, I begin my analysis in the early 1960s, before the resurgence of feminist activism that came to be dubbed the second wave, starting with two bestselling texts, from 1962 (*Sex and the Single Girl*) and 1963 (*The Feminine Mystique*). These are both texts that—in vastly different ways—came to underline and contest the gendered assumptions that worked to delimit how it was possible to be, as a woman, in the middle of the twentieth century.

The first celebrity feminist I examine is perhaps not one of those who, in regard to modern feminism and how it has been constructed in and through various media sites, immediately comes to mind. That is, Helen Gurley Brown has been, and for some remains, at best a liminal figure in feminist history and, at worst, is not conceived of as feminist at all. However, rather than reinforcing such border policing around an 'authentic' feminism and its Others, this chapter positions *Sex and the Single Girl* (1962) and its flamboyant author within a wider tradition of popular feminism and in this regard continues a critical agenda commenced by Jennifer Scanlon (2009a, b, c, see also Le Masurier 2007; Genz 2009). In 'Helen Gurley Brown: Prototypical Celebrity Feminism, Cultural Intermediaries, and Agency', drawing on the extensive archival material available in the Sophia Smith collection, I emphasize the labour that Brown and various industry professionals invested in establishing her enduring celebrity. Here, as elsewhere, I am able to destabilize the idea that it has only been relatively recently that authors and publishers—including of books articulating feminist positions—have actively worked to cultivate a star persona capable of generating immense exchange value and attention capital. This chapter demonstrates how Brown ensured that her particular brand of feminism (even if not publicly framed as such until much later) received as wide an audience as possible, indeed as all blockbusters authors have done.

The subsequent chapter focuses on a figure whose relation to feminism and the women's liberation movement in the United States has been much less precarious; though that does not mean it has been unproblematic or uncontested. Indeed, Betty Friedan's 1963 blockbuster, *The Feminine Mystique*, looms large to this day in popular media engagement with feminism and its modern history. This fourth chapter, 'Betty Friedan: The 'Mother' of Feminism, Self-fashioning, and the Celebrity Mystique', looks at how the figure of Friedan—and the blockbuster bearing her signature—was produced and reproduced over many decades. In addition to authorial profiles and interviews, and the kind of feminist self that Friedan performed therein, it examines literary attempts by the author to delimit the way her celebrity sign was being made to mean, including through her memoir, *Life So Far* (2000). This chapter considers how Friedan actively worked to shape a number of key myths about herself and her blockbuster, through interviews, her own journalistic pieces, and life writing—largely with success. In particular, it is concerned with Friedan's role in shaping collective memory around feminism, primarily through her repeated attempts to position herself and her liberal feminism at the centre of popular narratives about second wave feminism and its origins.

One of the most iconic feminists, especially in terms of her enduring visibility, is Germaine Greer, originally from Australia. Greer's 1970 blockbuster, *The Female Eunuch*, has also been figured as a classic popular feminist text (although in the academy she has been viewed much more ambivalently, if considered at all; Taylor et al. 2016). In Chap. 5, 'Germaine Greer: "The Star Feminism Had to Have", Unruliness, and Adaptable Celebrity', I am most concerned with Greer's self-reflexivity around her fame as well as how she has adapted her public persona for new media formats, especially via television, and new audiences. Her strategic recognition of the possibilities of mainstream media for feminist purposes has meant that, for nearly five decades, she has sustained the publicity initially yielded by *The Female Eunuch*, being active not just as a media source but as a journalistic actor and highly sought-after television performer. In keeping with my interest in how women like Brown, Friedan, and Greer have maintained their renown, and adapted it for an altered political and representational climate, a large part of this chapter will focus on her comedic performances on British lifestyle and variety television, the site wherein she is now most visible and into which she strategically inserts feminist critique. In such spaces, she continues to perform as the 'unruly woman', a subjectivity that is especially significant in terms of the ageing female (celebrity) body.

In the second part of this book I will discuss whether, in relation to feminism, the non-fictional blockbuster does the same kinds of cultural work it has since its modern inception, as well as identifying some of the changing features of the blockbuster (both in terms of genre and its marketing) and the kind of celebrity figures who now author them. Is the blockbuster still the key vehicle for feminist celebrification? Do these women inform popular understandings of feminism in the way their predecessors and their blockbusters patently did, and still do? Taking up these questions in the final chapters, therefore, I analyze how a number of contemporary bestselling books, not necessarily written by those seeking to recruit women to feminism (though they certainly sometimes do have such a goal), have recently been marketed as beginning new conversations about what it means to be a woman in neoliberal postfeminist times. Given the contemporary political environment, the women examined in this section are not seen to represent a nascent social movement or original set of ideas and practices in the way their blockbuster predecessors were, thereby resulting in differences both in terms of celebrity production and consumption; I will attend to these differences throughout.

While, with the exception of Naomi Wolf, the women featured in Part II are all relative newcomers to feminist stardom, their emergence in a context of rapid technological, as well as broader socio-political, shifts requires a reassessment of how blockbuster celebrity feminism is now constituted and sustained in ways that are both consistent with and divergent from the way it was for women whose public feminist careers have spanned in excess of four decades. What has 'convergence culture' (Jenkins 2006) done to the blockbuster, its production and its consumption, as well as to contemporary celebrity feminism more broadly? Are blockbuster celebrity feminists still important given that anyone can ostensibly be celebrified (as per 'micro', 'ordinary', or 'DIY' celebrity)? In many ways, feminism and contests over its meanings are now hyper-visible, not least because of new media. These chapters underline how celebrity feminists are using these newly available platforms, in different ways, to reach audiences—including but not limited to book-promoting efforts. I concur that 'as media changes, so does celebrity' (Marwick 2016, p. 333), but I am also interested in the continuities, in terms of celebrity feminist labour, especially in ensuring the success of their blockbusters. Like Brown, Friedan, and Greer, the women examined in Part II can be seen as active agents in their own celebrification, with online media exposing their attempts to help shape the meanings of their public personas, and indeed their blockbusters. Moreover, in a number of instances, and like their predecessors, twenty-first century blockbuster celebrity feminists move beyond the blockbuster form to different kinds of media intervention, and often online activist initiatives, which nonetheless are reliant upon the capital they accrued through the publication of their bestsellers.

Chapter 6 focuses on 'third wave' feminism's most well-known representative, Naomi Wolf. But in addition to engaging with her third wave texts, *The Beauty Myth* (1990) and *Fire with Fire* (1993), and their roles in her initial celebrification, in this chapter I turn my attention to Wolf's most recent feminist blockbuster, *Vagina: A New Biography* (2012). In doing so, I am able to illustrate how Wolf's feminism, and indeed her celebrity, has changed markedly since the publication of her first blockbuster, not least because of new media. The publication of *Vagina* also provides the opportunity to consider how the authority of celebrity feminists is by no means uncontested, nor is it static. Given that the book was widely criticized for its biological essentialism and new age rhetoric, here I argue that Wolf turns to social media to effectively rewrite the book's reception, as well as buttress her own flailing celebrity. Through an examination of her Twitter practice, this chapter demonstrates how new media now function as another means through which celebrity feminists can work to intervene in the public meanings of their own persona, work, and feminism—especially when their authority is under strain in other discursive spaces. In the remaining chapters I build further upon these themes.

In Chap. 7, 'Sheryl Sandberg and Roxane Gay: The Limits and Possibilities of Contemporary Blockbuster Feminism', I continue this focus on how the feminist blockbuster, as well as the celebrity of its authors, may have shifted in the twenty-first century. Through this chapter, focusing on Sandberg's *Lean In* (2013) and Gay's *Bad Feminist* (2014), I am preoccupied with how the new blockbuster operates at the confluence of postfeminist and neoliberal logics and rhetorics, while demonstrating that more progressive alternatives based upon intersectional feminism are also becoming bestsellers. The contemporary blockbuster, accordingly, is certainly not homogeneous and, in terms of politics, can be seen to diverge considerably. In the case of Sandberg I consider how she extends the 'Lean In' brand, exploring how she deploys her blockbuster celebrity capital to develop a series of political initiatives and campaigns that are predicated on the individualistic, 'post-race' form of feminism pursued through her blockbuster. The example of Gay enables me to further explore the role of new media in the genesis, not just of feminist fame, but of the blockbuster itself; through it, I also examine questions about the role of self-branding in the neoliberal academy, as well as how she works to contest the post-race discourses mobilized by Sandberg. Although celebrity feminism has always been cross-platform, these two authors also provide the opportunity to expand upon the role new media play in the constitution and maintenance of blockbuster feminist celebrity, with varying effects.

In Chap. 8, the last of my blockbuster case studies, I argue that the women examined therein—Amy Poehler and Lena Dunham—represent the mid-point between the forms of celebrity feminism embodied by Brown, Friedan, Greer, Wolf, Sandberg, and Gay (all women whose feminism is the source of their fame) and those women considered in the conclusion, who have achieved stardom through their performance in a particular field, and then come to publicly claim a relation to feminism. That is, Poehler and Dunham are not simply celebrities who decided to add feminism to their 'brand'; rather it has always been central to their various forms of cultural production and practice, and is thereby integral to their renown. Furthermore, both memoir and humour have long been important to feminist politics and the critique at its core, and, in terms of their 2014 bestsellers, *Yes Please* and *Not That Kind of Girl* respectively, Poehler and Dunham have each produced autobiographical narratives heavily steeped in their comedic practice. In each case, while their blockbuster memoirs worked to sustain their feminist celebrity in important ways, they represent only one part of the equation. Accordingly, engaging with Poehler's *Smart Girls* and Dunham's *Lenny* e-newsletter, here I argue that, in addition to literary works, celebrities are increasingly deploying new media to shape public conversations around feminism.

While I was writing this book the terrain of feminism and celebrity culture shifted dramatically. Suddenly, it appeared, celebrities from various fields were eager to publicly identify with feminism; it became a form of social capital they could use to help shift the meanings of their celebrity signs. This identification—or in some cases, disidentification—was newsworthy, with myriad news reports, especially online, devoting much space to this issue throughout 2014 and 2015 (Hamad and Taylor 2015), suggesting that the issues with which I am preoccupied here are becoming relevant across an increasingly wider field. Moreover, what has been labelled 'fourth wave' feminism has come to flourish in/through digital culture, purportedly providing more discursive spaces within which to problematize the kinds of voices being privileged in the mainstream media. Accordingly, in the conclusion, 'The Future of Celebrity Feminism: Celebrity Culture, the Blockbuster, and Feminist Star Studies', I take up some of these issues while yet arguing for the maintenance of a distinction between women whose feminism is the *source* of their fame—exemplified most clearly by the blockbuster authors that make up my study—and those whose celebrification is predicated on their 'achieved celebrity' in other fields (predominantly entertainment like music or film). Despite these new forms of connection between feminism and celebrity culture, I argue that the feminist blockbuster remains one of the key ways in which feminist discourse comes to reach a wider audience and through which debate around feminism comes to be publicly staged. Finally, I point to some further ways in which we can attempt to come to terms with the complexity of the intersection between celebrity culture and feminism, and the ideological and cultural work it does, including through future empirical research that takes both celebrities and audiences as subjects in an attempt to gain a deeper, multi-faceted understanding of the social as well as the broader political function of celebrity feminism.

Notes

1. For a detailed analysis of the perceived opposition between feminist and commercial publishing, see Murray (2004).
2. In her study of *Ms.*, Amy Farrell makes this claim of the magazine (1998, p. 2).
3. That is not to say there that these two realms are entirely separable; nevertheless, the academy at best has had an ambivalent relation to these books and their authors, with the women featured in Part I having been largely omitted from second wave anthologies, while their presence in academic histories of the second wave varies considerably.
4. I am indebted to van Zoonen (1992) for this term, which she uses in her analysis of media representations of the Dutch women's movement.
5. Marshall has even argued we need a new field, persona studies, to address these issues, especially in terms of agency. As he notes, 'Persona allows us to explore the masks of identity as they are both constructed by our elaborate media and communication systems and enacted by individuals with a degree of intention and agency' (Marshall 2013, pp. 371–2).
6. Like Lorraine York (2007, p. 7), in her study of Canadian literary celebrity: 'I wanted examples of writers whose fame, no matter what Hollywoodised forms it might subsequently have assumed, derived from their labour as writers of books.'
7. For a critical analysis of these changes, see Turner's *Reinventing the Media* (2016).
8. Of course, the other most enduring celebrity feminist, who even recently appeared on an episode of television court drama, *The Good Wife*, is Gloria Steinem. I have opted not to include Steinem in Part I, as, while her fame is undoubtedly a product of her feminism, her popular non-fictional work emerged subsequent to her having already attained a great deal of renown, and thus was not central to

her preliminary celebrification. That said, I do acknowledge that Steinem's prolonged media visibility and celebrity feminism, including through her establishment of *Ms.* and her various works of nonfiction, including her recently published memoir, *My Life on the Road* (2015), is worthy of further critical attention. For an analysis of Steinem and American television, see Bonnie Dow's *Watching Women's Liberation* (2014).

References

Barker-Plummer, B. (2010) 'News and Feminism: A Historic Dialog', *Journalism and Communication Monographs*, 12.3/4: 145–203

Boorstin, D. (1971) *The Image: A Guide to Pseudo Events in America*, New York: Atheneum

Bourdieu, P. (1993) *The Field of Cultural Production*, Cambridge: Polity

Brown, H.G. (1962/2003) *Sex and the Single Girl*, New York: Barricade Books

Brunsdon, C. (1997) *Screen Tastes*, London: Routledge

Cameron, D. (1999) 'The Price of Fame', *Trouble and Strife*, Issue 39, accessed via http://www.troubleandstrife.org/articles/issue-39/the-price-of-fame/

Denfeld, R. (1995) *The New Victorians: A Young Woman's Challenge to the Old Feminist Order*, New York: Grand Central Publishing

Dow, B. (1996) *Prime Time Feminism: Television, Media Culture and the Women's Movement Since 1970s*, Philadelphia: University of Pennsylvania Press

——— (2014) *Watching Women's Liberation, 1970: Feminism's Pivotal Year on the Network News*, Chicago: University of Illinois Press

Drake, P. & Miah, A. (2010) 'The Cultural Politics of Celebrity', *Cultural Politics*, 6.1: 49–64

Driessens, O. (2013a) 'Celebrity Capital: Redefining celebrity Using Field Theory', *Theory and Society*, 42: 543–560

——— (2013b) 'The celebritization of society and culture: Understanding the structural dynamics of celebrity culture', *International Journal of Cultural Studies*, 16.6: 641–657

Dunham, L. (2014) *Not That Kind of Girl*, New York: Random House

Dyer, R. (1979) *Stars*, London: British Film Institute

——— (1986) *Heavenly Bodies: Film Stars and Society*, London: British Film Institute

Ellcessor, E. (2012) 'Tweeting@feliciaday: Online Social Media, Convergence, and Subcultural Stardom', *Cinema Journal*, 51.2: 46–66

Farrell, A.E. (1998) *Yours in Sisterhood: Ms Magazine and the Promise of Popular Feminism*, Chapel Hill: University of North Carolina Press

Friedan, B. (1963/1992) *The Feminine Mystique*, London: Penguin
Galow, T. (2010) 'Literary Modernism in the Age of Celebrity', *Modernism/Modernity*, 17.2: 313–329
Gamson, J. (2007) 'The Assembly Line of Greatness', in S. Holmes & S. Redmond eds. *Stardom and Celebrity: A Reader*, London: Sage, pp. 141–155
Gay, R. (2014) *Bad Feminist: Essays*, New York: Harper
Genette, G. (1997) *Paratexts: Thresholds of Interpretation*, Cambridge: Cambridge University Press
Genz, S. (2009) *Postfemininities in Popular Culture*, Basingstoke: Palgrave Macmillan
Gever, M. (2003) *Entertaining Lesbians: Celebrity, Sexuality, and Self-Invention*, New York: Routledge
Gill, R. (2007) 'Postfeminist Media Culture: Elements of A Sensibility', *European Journal of Cultural Studies*, 10.2: 147–66
Glass, L. (2004) *Authors, Inc.: Literary Celebrity in the Modern United States, 1880–1980*, New York: New York University Press
Greer, G. (1970/1993) *The Female Eunuch*, London: Flamigo
Griffin, P. (2015) *Popular Culture, Political Economy and The Death of Feminism*, London: Routledge
Grossberg, L. (1992) 'Is there a fan in the house? The Affective Sensibility of Fandom', in L. Lewis ed. *The Adoring Audience: Fan Culture and Popular Media*, London: Routledge, pp. 50–68
Gunter, B. (2014) *Celebrity Capital*, London: Bloomsbury Academic
Hammill, F. (2007) *Women's Literary Celebrity Between the Wars*, Austin: University of Texas Press
Hamad, H. & Taylor, A. (2015) 'Feminism and Contemporary Celebrity Culture', *Celebrity Studies*, 6.1: 124–127
Hemmings, C. (2011) *Why Stories Matter: The Political Grammar of Feminist Theory*, Durham: Duke University Press
Henderson, M. (2006) *Marking Feminist Times: Remembering the Longest Revolution in Australia*, Bern: Peter Lang
Hollows, J. & Moseley, R. (2006) 'Introduction', in J. Hollows & R. Moseley eds. *Feminism in Popular Culture*, London: Berg, pp. 1–22
Holmes, S. & Negra, D. eds (2011) *In the Limelight and Under the Microscope: Forms and Functions of Female Celebrity*, London: Continuum
hooks, b. (2013) 'Dig Deep: Beyond Lean In', 28 October, *The Feminist Wire*, accessed via http://www.thefeministwire.com/2013/10/17973/
Jenkins, H. (2006) *Convergence Culture: Where Old and New Media Collide*, New York: New York University Press
Jermyn, D. & Holmes, S. (2015) 'Introduction: A Timely Intervention—Unravelling the Gender/Age/Celebrity Matrix', in D. Jermyn & S. Holmes eds. *Women, Celebrity and Cultures of Ageing*, Basingstoke: Palgrave Macmillan, pp. 1–10

Le Masurier, M. (2007) 'My Other, My Self', *Australian Feminist Studies*, 22.53: 191–211

Lilburn, S., Magarey, S. & Sheridan, S. (2000) 'Celebrity Feminism as Synthesis: Germaine Greer, *The Female Eunuch* and the Australian Print Media', *Continuum*, 14.3: 335–348

Lumby, C. (1997) *Bad Girls: The Media, Sex and Feminism in the 1990s*, St Leonards: Allen & Unwin

Marshall, P.D. (1997) *Celebrity and Power*, Minneapolis: University of Minnesota Press

—— (2013) 'Personifying Agency: The Public–Persona–Place–Issue Continuum', *Celebrity Studies*, 4.3: 369–371

McRobbie, A. (2009) *The Aftermath of Feminism*, London: Sage

—— (2015) 'Notes on the Perfect: Competitive Femininity in Neoliberal Times', *Australian Feminist Studies*, 30.83: 3–20

Marwick, A.E. (2016) 'You May Know Me from YouTube (Micro-)Celebrity in Social Media', in P.D. Marshall & S. Redmond eds. *A Companion to Celebrity*, London: Wiley Blackwell, pp. 333–350

Marwick, A. & boyd, d. (2011) 'To See and Be Seen: Celebrity Practice on Twitter', *Convergence*, 17.2: 139–158

Mitchell, S. (1997) *Icons, Saints and Divas: Intimate Conversations with Women Who Changed the World*, Sydney: Harper Collins

Mole, T. (2007) *Byron's Romantic Literary Celebrity: Industrial Culture and the Hermeneutic of Intimacy*, Basingstoke: Palgrave Macmillan

Moran, J. (2000) *Star Authors: Literary Celebrity in America*, London: Pluto

Murray, S. (2004) *Mixed Media: Feminist Presses and Publishing Politics*, London: Pluto

Ohlsson, A. Forslid, T. & Steiner, A. (2014) 'Literary Celebrity Reconsidered', *Celebrity Studies*, 5.1–2: 32–44

Paglia, C. (1990) *Sexual Personae: Art and Decadence from Nefertiti to Emily Dickinson*, New Haven: Yale University Press

Poehler, A. (2014) *Yes Please*, London: Picador

Projansky, S. (2014) *Spectacular Girls: Media Fascination and Celebrity Culture*, New York: New York University Press

Redmond, S. (2014) *Celebrity and the Media*, Basingstoke: Palgrave Macmillan

Rein, I., Kotler, P. & Stoller, M. (1997) *High Visibility: The Making and Marketing of Professionals into Celebrities*, New York: NTC

Roiphe, K. (1993) *The Morning After: Sex, Fear and Feminism*, New York: Bayback Books

Rojek, C. (2001) *Celebrity*, London: Reaktion

—— (2014) 'Niccolo Machiavelli, Cultural Intermediaries and the Category of Achieved Celebrity', *Celebrity Studies*, 5.4: 455–468

Rowlands, S. & Henderson, M. (1996) 'Damned Bores and Slick Sisters: The Selling of Blockbuster Feminism in Australia', *Australian Feminist Studies*, 11.23: 9–16

Sandberg, S. (2013) *Lean In: Women, Work, and The Will to Lead*, London: WH Allen

Scanlon, J. (2009a) *Bad Girls Go Everywhere*, Oxford: Oxford University Press

——— (2009b) 'Sensationalist Literature or Expert Advice?' *Feminist Media Studies*, 9.1: 1–15

——— (2009c) 'Sexy from the Start: Anticipatory Elements of Second Wave Feminism', *Women's Studies*, 38.2: 127–150

Sheridan, S., Magarey, S. & Lilburn, S. (2006) 'Feminism in the News', in J. Hollows & R. Moseley eds. *Feminism in Popular Culture*, Oxford: Berg, pp. 25–40

Sommers, C. Hoff (1994), *Who Stole Feminism? How Women Have Betrayed Women*, New York: Simon and Schuster

Steinem, G. (2015) *My Life on the Road*, London: Oneworld

Tasker, Y. & Negra, D. eds. (2007) 'Introduction', in *Interrogating Postfeminism: Gender and the Politics of Popular Culture*, Durham: Duke University Press, pp. 1–26

Taylor, A. (2008) *Mediating Australian Feminism: Rereading the First Stone Media Event*, Oxford: Peter Lang

——— (2010) 'Celebrity (Post)feminism, the Sixties Feminist Blockbuster and Down with Love', *The Sixties: A Journal of Politics, History and Culture*, 3.1: 79–96

Taylor, A. with Dever, M. & Adkins, L. (2016) 'Greer Now: Editorial', *Australian Feminist Studies*, 31.87: 1–6

Thompson, J.B. (2010) *Merchants of Culture: The Publishing Business in the Twenty First Century*, London: Polity

Tuchman, G. (1978) *Making News: A Study of the Construction of Reality*, New York: The Free Press

Turner, G. (2014) *Understanding Celebrity*, London: Sage

——— (2016) *Re-inventing the Media*, London: Routledge

Turner, G., Marshall, P.D. & Bonner, F. (2000) *Fame Games: The Production of Celebrity in Australia*, Cambridge: Cambridge University Press

Van Krieken, R. (2012) *Celebrity Society*, New York: Routledge

Van Zoonen, L. (1992) 'The Women's Movement and Constructing a Public Identity', *European Journal of Communication*, 7.4: 453–476

Weber, B. (2012) *Women and Literary Celebrity in the Nineteenth Century: The Translantic Production of Fame and Gender*, Farnham: Ashgate

Wernick, A. (1991) *Promotional Culture: Advertising, Ideology and Symbolic Expression*, London: Sage

Wicke, J. (1994) 'Celebrity Material: Materialist Feminism and the Culture of Celebrity', *South Atlantic Quarterly*, 93.4: 751–778
Wolf, N. (1990) *The Beauty Myth*, London: Virago
―――― (1993) *Fire with Fire: The New Female Power and How It Will Change the 21st Century*, London: Chatto and Windus
―――― (2012) *Vagina: A New Biography*, London: Virago
Woods, F. (2015) 'Girls Talk: Authorship and Authenticity in the Reception of Lena Dunham's Girls', *Critical Studies in Television*, 10.2: 37–54
York, L. (2007) *Literary Celebrity in Canada*, Toronto: University of Toronto Press
―――― (2013a) *Margaret Atwood and the Labour of Literary Celebrity*, Toronto: University of Toronto Press
―――― (2013b) 'Star Turn: The Challenges of Theorizing Celebrity Agency', *The Journal of Popular Culture*, 46.6: 1330–1347

CHAPTER 2

'Blockbuster' Feminism and Celebrification

INTRODUCTION

Despite the ambivalence towards celebrity identified in the Introduction, it has always been central in delimiting the kinds of feminisms, as well as feminist histories, that have become visible in the Western mediasphere. The 'celebrity zone' is indeed, as Jennifer Wicke persuasively argued over twenty years ago, the 'material culture in which we have our being as feminists' (1994, p. 776), and this is even more the case in our current climate, where the meanings of feminism are more highly contested than ever. How, therefore, might we define 'celebrity feminism' as the first step to better understanding its cultural and political function? Like other 'modalities of renown' (Newbury 2000, p. 282), celebrity feminism is a complex, heterogeneous, evolving phenomenon that necessitates a more careful, nuanced critical approach (Taylor 2008).

The women featured in Part I have each worked—and in many cases, still work—to mediate what comes to constitute feminism in the popular imaginary: 'It is a mixture of all these different faces represented in the media-sphere that makes up the popular memory of feminism for the broad public of men and women' (Sheridan et al. 2006, p. 38). However, as I argue, the role of the blockbuster in shaping popular understandings of feminism has not diminished in the so-called postfeminist era. Feminism remains in the public consciousness largely through these individual high-profile women, rather than events or issues (Pearce 2004). They have, therefore, been central in constructing, publicizing, and popularizing, feminism(s). Such women, those who have been called 'feminism's big girls' (Henderson 2006), exemplify the specific intersection of feminism and celebrity that I label 'blockbuster celebrity feminism'.

In the case of Brown, Friedan, and Greer it is not just these women as celebrities but also their blockbusters that remain publicly visible and that continue to shape certain narratives about feminism and its history. That is not to suggest that the cultural legitimacy they are granted is commensurate. Inevitably, given that celebrity is essentially hierarchical, some feminists are of course more famous than others: 'Similar to other power resources, celebrity is distributed unequally' (Driessens 2013b, p. 643). Moreover, I do not focus on these women to reify them and their stories, but instead to show how the stories that have been told about feminism are inextricable from their individual stories as figures of renown, even if at times contested: 'The celebrity zone of my analysis has nothing to do with role models or exemplary "feminists", whoever they may be; instead, it is a space for registering and refracting the current material conditions under which feminism is partly practiced' (Wicke 1994, p. 765). Here, I am concerned with both such conditions and such practices.

Celebrity, of course, is fundamentally bound up in questions of authority and thereby power. Through the complicated operations of celebrity, certain speakers are granted not only the ability to speak but also to have such speech legitimized (Taylor 2008, p. 105). That is, as David Marshall (1997, p. x) suggests: 'Celebrity status confers on the person a certain discursive power: within society, the celebrity is a voice above others, a voice that is channelled into the media systems as being legitimately significant.'. Therefore, as he argues, the celebrity is an important ideological and epistemological 'player' in public discourse (Marshall 1997, p. 19), not least in terms of the ways in which Western feminism's public identity has been constituted. In *Stars* (1979), one of the earliest studies of fame, Richard Dyer argued that such figures are important as they enable us to ask questions around *personhood* or selfhood, helping us to negotiate the contradictions of modern subjectivity (Marshall 1997; Rojek 2001). These celebrity feminists add another layer to this, insofar as they permit us to ask questions not just around gendered subjectivity and the tensions of being gendered feminine but of what it might mean to identify as a politicized woman and especially a feminist. Therefore, celebrity feminism can be seen, in Ruth Barcan's terms, as a distinct 'modality of public personhood' (2000, p. 145), and we need to rethink how we theorize it—especially in light of historical, political, and technological changes that make this critical work more urgent. First, it is necessary to engage with previous feminist scholarship on celebrity.

Feminist Critiques of Celebrity and the Media

We can classify blockbuster feminist texts as forms of 'popular feminism', when such a term signals the ways in which feminism is 'translated' for a wider audience of women who may not otherwise engage with it (Le Masurier 2007, 2010). However, feminism found, or rather constructed, in popular media forms such as blockbusters has been routinely condemned, as has the intersection of feminism and celebrity itself. As Elaine Showalter (2001) notes, 'feminism, like other social movements, has always been uneasy about the morality of personal fame'. To understand this sense of anxiety, or at least to contextualize it, we need to engage with feminist critiques of the mainstream media and its appropriation of feminism, for it is a general suspicion or distrust of what the media 'do' to an ostensibly unmediated feminism that undergirds much academic dismissal of celebrity feminists and the cultural work they do. It is not just a disdain for celebrity that has marred such assessments but the fact that such texts are 'popular' and are thereby deemed 'inauthentic' (a position long critiqued by cultural studies). In particular, it is their commercial viability that most creates a sense of unease. Imelda Whelehan identifies this anxiety well when she suggests, of the 'feminist [fictional] bestseller': 'The phrase feels awkward, even treacherous, particularly when we apply it to groundbreaking non-fiction texts such as Kate Millett's *Sexual Politics* or Germaine Greer's *The Female Eunuch*, because the fact that individual women could make a great deal of money out of their feminist convictions caused controversy within the Women's Movement at the time' (2005, p. 2). Such a comment is indicative of the troublesome politics/profit antithesis, in terms of feminist book publishing, mobilized by feminists during the second wave in particular (Murray 2004).

The academy, too, has had a difficult relationship with these popular texts, which are seen to work in opposition to the more intellectually rigorous and politically 'pure' form of feminist discourse ostensibly offered therein; worryingly, such an assumption further cements the 'ordinary' woman/academic feminist dichotomy upon which many popular denunciations have been based (Brunsdon 1997; Hollows and Moseley 2006).

Such an opposition is neither desirable nor in itself sustainable, given the extent to which feminist theorizing itself takes place—and indeed has always taken place—outside the privileged space of the academy: 'Theory takes multiple forms and often transpires in unlikely places' (Siegel 1997, p. 71; see also King 1994). Nevertheless, within much feminist scholarship, the academy/popular seems to be a recalcitrant binary.

As I have previously argued (2008), there is a long history of condemning the mainstream media as inherently patriarchal and thereby anti-feminist. The idea that feminists are misrepresented, distorted or stereotyped in the media has historically dominated criticism (Faludi 1991; Rhode 1995; Huddy 1997; Norris 1997; Lind and Salo 2002; Hall and Rodriguez 2003) and continues to be invoked (Dean 2010; Mendes 2011, 2015). Kaitlynn Mendes, for example, in an otherwise astute analysis of the Slut Walk movement, argues that there continues to be an erasure of feminism in mainstream news, with feminism's utility put into question through 'the continual insistence that it is dead, redundant, and passé' (2015, p. 230). Such a critical narrative has gained considerable traction over a number of decades, where, among other things, the press's appropriation of feminism is figured in terms of a logic of 'domestication' (Dean 2010) or recuperation (Macdonald 1995). That is, rather than acknowledging media's role in the construction of feminism, it is thought that a pre-existing form of it is lamentably altered, becoming effectively 'contaminated' by and through its engagements with mainstream media. Such an assumption is, however, unsustainable, given that feminism 'is an impure, porous public discourse' and does not exist in any unadulterated form outside its media representations (Felski 2000, p. 201; Sheridan et al. 2006). As Hollows and Moseley (2006, p. 11) argue, 'underpinning many discussions of popular feminism is the assumption that there is a better "unpopular" form of feminism [usually either an academic or activist form]'. Celebrity feminism, especially, has been the subject of such judgements.

However, alongside this work that continues to see feminism as having been always already damaged or diluted by its interactions with the mainstream media there have been attempts to rethink, and reaffirm the importance of, this relationship. That is, over the past decade or so a number of critics have sought to shift the focus from 'negative images' of feminists to a more nuanced, complex theorization of how feminism is constituted in and through various sites of media culture. In relation to figures of public renown, however, this nuance continues to be absent from critical conversation.[1] Before considering some of that scholarship, it is necessary to further examine how feminists, during the second wave especially, conceptualized the mainstream media and their celebrification of select women over others.

In contrast to liberal feminists like Steinem or Friedan, who sought to tailor their message to fit the mainstream news agenda and priorities, during the 1970s radical feminists unsurprisingly viewed mainstream media culture as 'little more than the handmaiden and voice of the establishment power structure' (Hole and Levine, in Dow 2014, p. 9). In such a context, as Barker-Plummer observes, 'any kind of celebrity or notoriety became suspect' (2010, p. 162; see also Echols 1989). For example, a member of the second wave activist group, Radicalesbians, identifies this disdain: 'We saw star tripping as an evil that the group had to avoid at all costs' (Jay in Barker-Plummer 2010, p. 163). As Patricia Bradley underscores, feminist publications themselves became preoccupied with the question of how the mainstream media's elevation of certain figures as representative of the women's movement could work as a way of undercutting or even depoliticizing the movement as well as eliding its diversity (Gever 2003). Publications like *off our backs*, she notes, feared that the media would demand a single leader to speak on behalf of the heterogenous movement, define feminism through her individual actions, and ultimately 'discredit her personal life rather than dealing with her politics'—which, she observes, so notoriously happened to Kate Millett (Bradley 2003, p. 75).

However, such a position did not stand unchallenged. In 1976 Jo Freeman wrote a piece in *Ms.* magazine about the propensity for what she calls feminist 'trashing' within the women's liberation movement: 'I have been watching for years with increasing dismay as the Movement consciously destroys anyone within it who stands out in any way.' As she implies, it arises, effectively, out of a discomfort with women's power, and especially the power *over* other women that this elevation symbolizes. As Freeman (1976) observes:

> To do something significant, to be recognized, to achieve, is to imply that one is 'making it off other women's oppression' or that one thinks oneself better than other women …The quest for 'leaderlessness' that the Movement so prizes has more frequently become an attempt to tear down those women who show leadership qualities, than to develop such qualities in those who don't.

While Freeman is referring to the question of leadership more broadly, her comments are certainly relevant to the elevation of feminist stars in the mediasphere.

It was not just in the 1970s, however, that the disdain for celebrity circulated. In the context of millennial 'postfeminism', fears about the commodification of feminism, including through the celebrification of individual women, seem to be gathering more traction (McRobbie 2013)—as my conclusion explores. Given the ascendancy of postfeminist logics, such a narrative tells us, feminists were right to be wary of the popularization and mediatization of feminism. For example, in *Reclaiming the F Word*, Redfern and Aune challenge the idea that the high visibility of celebrity feminists is a mark of progress, arguing that 'the problem with this is the assumption that feminism's success necessitates having one or two media figureheads … This is as misguided now as it was in the 1970s' (2013, p. 218). They continue, 'in today's celebrity-obsessed culture it's significant that most feminists are unconcerned with fame' (Redfern and Aune 2013, p. 218). Redfern and Aune celebrate this supposed lack of interest, reinscribing the notion that a feminism not implicated in systems of celebrity and commodification is morally and politically superior to those that more blatantly exhibit this investment (see also hooks 1994; Hammer 2000). Most importantly, such critiques fail to concede that popular feminism, including through blockbuster authors, represents a key (if not *the* key) way that many women come to access various forms of feminism (Hollows and Moseley 2006).

The stories that I reveal here around individual celebrity feminists over a long period of time serve to complicate such reductive arguments about the inherent limitations of feminist engagement with the media (Taylor 2008; see also Henderson 2006). Nonetheless, as Bonnie Dow notes, such assumptions persist in scholarship on feminism–media interactions, especially those focusing on the second wave: 'The established narrative holds that national media functioned primarily as feminism's enemy and not its ally in its early period' (2014, p. 4). Other feminist media and communications scholars have similarly argued the need for greater complexity in how we theorize the feminism–media nexus, especially in terms of feminist active engagement. For example, underscoring the symbiotic relationship of feminism and mainstream media, Bernadette Barker-Plummer (2010, p. 147) has convincingly argued: 'Feminists were not only "covered" by news, they were actively involved, if not always successfully, as strategists in this interaction …' As she continues, such media history has rarely been taken into account, 'perhaps because it complicates our oversimplified narratives of the "misogynous media" that (deterministically) marginalized feminism' (2010, p. 149; see also Farrell 1998; Henderson 2006; Sheridan et al. 2006; Le Masurier 2007, 2010). Building upon Barker-Plummer's insights, I would suggest that this, in part, is why there has been such little critical engagement with feminist celebrity; because it actually *requires* that such a seductive, enduring narrative be complicated. Here, therefore, I offer not an examination of how 'passive' feminists have been represented in various media platforms but shift the focus to how these celebrity feminists have been actively engaged in the process of constructing feminism—largely through the process of constructing themselves.

While much of the criticism outlined above demonstrates that the authority afforded 'celebrity feminists' has sat uncomfortably with many feminists, Jennifer Wicke's 'Celebrity Material: Materialist Feminism and the Culture of Celebrity' attempts to recuperate the feminist celebrity. She suggests that feminist engagement with this 'celebrity zone'—the public space where feminism is 'in most active cultural play' (1994, p. 757)—needs to be taken seriously by feminist critics. Most valuably, she cautions feminists against dismissing the celebrity zone on the grounds that it offers 'corrupt', 'inauthentic' images of feminism: 'Things look very different, though, if the celebrity sphere is not immediately vilified as a realm of ideological ruin or relegated to aberrant or merely "popular" practices' (Wicke 1994, p. 758).[2] Such assumptions, reinscribed in contemporary critiques of celebrity, work to foreclose recognition of the possibilities of celebrity for feminism, and also fail to account for the changing contours of blockbuster celebrity feminism and the emergent media platforms upon which it has come to rely.

Nonetheless, as I have noted, Wicke (1994, p. 758) 'does acknowledge the tensions in celebrity feminism, viewing this zone (like the broader relationship between feminism and media culture) as simultaneously productive and unproductive for feminism' (Taylor 2008, p. 109). In particular, blockbuster celebrity has appropriately been criticized on the grounds of its stark whiteness, heterosexuality, and class privilege (hooks 1994), something I take up further in Chap. 7. It is this emphasis on both the limits and the possibilities of celebrity feminism that characterizes my approach in this book. Here, as Wenche Ommundsen has done with literary celebrity, I seek to offer 'a more complex and sympathetic reading' (2007, p. 248) of celebrity feminism, especially in terms of its blockbuster variant. That said, one of the issues that must be addressed, when thinking through how—and perhaps with more difficulty, why—the select women in this study have been celebrified, and thereby come to be seen as 'representative' of feminism, is that of unevenly distributed authority.

Who Speaks? The Exclusions of Celebrity Feminism

A study of this nature, which seeks to understand the functions and effects of how certain feminists have been celebrified, must engage with debates both around authority and those around how feminism is made to mean within the modern mediasphere. What are the discursive and ideological processes via which some women are granted the authority to speak on/ for/about feminism? How can such authorizations be troubled or criticized without invoking a singular or more 'legitimate' feminism/feminist that should be publicly represented? What is feminist speech and, therefore, what makes a feminist speaker? Any attempt to come to terms with modern feminism and its celebritization must grapple with such fraught questions.

The question of speaking 'as a feminist', and especially speaking for others, has preoccupied many scholars over the past few decades (Alcoff 1991; Gunew 1993; Hekman 1999; Moreton-Robinson 2000), invoking attendant questions such as: which feminism, and whose feminism? Authorizing one set of speakers obviously entails the elision of others. In this vein, I was once asked whether my focus on these hyper-visible, immensely privileged authors, could in effect buttress their authorization, and thereby potentially work to further mask the heterogeneity of feminists, especially in relation to race, class, and sexuality. In this way, could a study concentrating on these prominent women perpetuate the 'symbolic annihilation' (Tuchman 1978) of the enormous diversity among feminist women? On the contrary, it seems to me that underscoring the processes of authorization, and in particular the overwhelming whiteness and heteronormativity of mainstream feminism, as effects of power, can help in imagining ways in which this elevation of a fairly homogeneous group of women might be otherwise. That is, shining a light on these deeply ideological processes of celebrification may enable us to think through how celebrity feminism might become a more inclusive mode of public subjectivity and, how, following Hemming's (2011) exhortation, we might learn to tell these dominant narratives of feminism differently, in and through different voices.

Informed by poststructuralism and increased consciousness of intersectionality, the critique of identity politics means we need to recognize that there is no one, singular, authentic way of 'doing feminism, being feminist' (Heywood and Drake 1997), and therefore judging particular elevated women on the grounds that they fail to effectively 'represent' feminism is complicated by both the problem of representation more broadly, as well as the impossibility of there being a unified, fixed form of feminism. Relatedly, while it may be difficult to define what constitutes a 'feminist' text, we can identify texts that have been marketed as feminist, and positioned in public discourse as representative (in spite of all the limitations of such a gesture). That is, this book is concerned with the varied social and political uses to which such texts are put (Lauret 1994), and the role of their authors in such a process. However, in feminist criticism, the blockbuster—in terms of literary techniques, marketing, paratexts, or its author—has not been granted the critical attention it deserves. This book, in addition to reconceptualizing feminist celebrity as a mode of renown that simultaneously complicates and reinscribes certain representational and presentational logics, seeks to help remedy this elision by focusing on the public careers of such texts—largely through their authors, who have been so central to the way they, and thereby feminism more broadly, have publicly come to mean.

Feminism and Popular Non-fiction

The field of literary production and print culture more broadly has always been central to feminism's attempts to make itself available, and desirable, to a broad audience. As Astrid Henry remarks: 'Texts have helped to spread feminist ideas since the beginning of the U.S. women's movement—from suffragist newspapers in the nineteenth century to mimeographed manifestos of the late 1960s to bestselling feminist books in all eras' (2014, p. 172). From Mary Wollstonecraft's *A Vindication on the Rights of Woman* (1792), Virginia Woolf's *A Room of One's Own* (1929), and Simone de Beauvoir's *The Second Sex* (1949), and in addition to alternative print forms,[3] popular feminist non-fiction has long performed vital political and cultural work. In particular, the transformative power of literary texts, which have been seen to give women the tools to effectively 'read' both texts and the everyday through a feminist lens, has always been important in terms of refiguring patriarchal imaginaries as well as envisioning alternatives (Hogeland 1998).

Although some have dismissed such texts on the grounds of their commercialization, seeing politics and profit as antithetical (Murray 2004), feminist blockbusters have represented an important form of discursive politics or activism (Young 1997; Maddison 2013), during the second wave and beyond. Rather than privileging forms of activism that seek policy or other reformist changes at the level of the state, 'cultural activism and discursive political engagement should also be recognised as important and valid activism in and of themselves. Feminist discourse has been powerful in changing women's expectations for their lives' (Maddison 2013, p. 51). As discursive forms with such a wide reach, the blockbuster's political potentialities should not be downplayed: 'Language acts—including published writing—could play a crucial part in bringing about individual and collective change' (Young 1997, p. 25). While there has been much celebration about the internet now functioning in such a way (Shaw 2013), (some) women's greater participation in new media has not displaced the commercial viability or the apparent cultural resonances of the feminist blockbuster and its authors. Indeed, it continues to evolve as new forms, and indeed new markets, come into being—something to which I turn my attention in the final chapters especially.

Bestselling books about feminism often work to precipitate public debate and, whatever we think of their politics, serve to open up a space for intense discursive struggles over its meanings (Lilburn et al. 2000; Taylor 2008), making such popular texts and the debates they spark 'important to the survival of feminist politics' (Whelehan 2000, p. 88). However, compared to fictional texts, the role of popular non-fiction in coming to shape what comes to be made available publicly as feminism has been the subject of much less critical attention.[4] In terms of literary celebrity, moreover, it is common to presume that the author of non-fiction 'will not attract the star status that fiction authors do' and will 'have a more limited shelf-life than fiction stars' (Look 1999, p. 28). The women analyzed in Part I, especially, represent a challenge to the idea that the celebrity status of fictional writers will far outstrip that of their counterparts working in a form that purports (however problematically) to represent the 'real'; their chosen form does, however, work to mediate their public personas in ways that can be seen as different from those of authors of fiction, as I will explore. Furthermore, while authors of fiction become implicated in debates about 'literary value and cultural hierarchy' (Hammill 2007, p. 16; Moran 2000), blockbusters' authors instead have been assessed primarily in terms of their cultural value and the kinds of feminism they articulate, both through their books and subsequent public performances.

The role of the mainstream media in attributing value and helping to constitute literary reputations has been well established (Turner 1993,

1996; Carter and Ferres 2001). In terms of the meaning-making process in which such texts become implicated, Stanley Fish's well-known work, which refigures literary interpretation, reminds us that 'all objects are made and not found, and … they are made by interpretive strategies we set in motion' (cited in Templin 1995, p. 9; see also Radway 1984; Fish 1980; Felski 1989). It is axiomatic within literary and cultural studies, therefore, that texts are not hermetically sealed but made to mean in particular ways, within various contexts, for specific cultural and ideological purposes. Furthermore, we have learnt from Roland Barthes (1967) and Michel Foucault (1969) that the author is one of the key ways of delimiting how a literary text comes to signify. Celebrity culture ensures that the author remains central to the processes of interpretation in which their text becomes enmeshed, not least in selling the feminist blockbuster.

Constituting the Feminist Blockbuster

Since I am arguing that the most highly visible feminist is the blockbuster author, including in the present, it is incumbent upon me to flesh out precisely what is meant by my usage of this term, as well as its positioning in feminist literary and cultural studies. In relation to non-fictional literary work, I take this term—'feminist blockbuster'—from Shane Rowlands and Margaret Henderson (1996). For them, the feminist blockbuster's constitutive elements include: its semi-sensationalistic mode; the pronounced role of the author in marketing the text; its 'media-friendly' nature, which makes it open to media appropriation and depoliticization; and, finally, its 'bestseller' status (Taylor 2008, p. 28). For Henderson and Rowlands, the 'feminist blockbuster' represents the inherent limitations of the commercialization of feminism. However, as critics such as Beverley Skeggs (1997; see also Bulbeck 1997; Dux and Simic 2008) have shown through empirical work, for those not actively involved in feminist politics, knowledge of modern feminism is textually mediated through media and popular culture, including 'feminist blockbusters' and their celebrity authors: 'For the mainstream publishing industry has not been a neutral medium for the communication of feminist ideas, but has *crucially* mediated those ideas through its commissioning, packaging and marketing of feminist texts' (Murray 2004, p. 168, original emphasis). Such books and their authors are able to capture the attention of large audiences, and are able to stay firmly in the public imaginary in ways that are not possible with more ephemeral communicative forms, like new media.

Politically, the blockbuster is by no means homogeneous, and each author embodies a specific form of feminism, from those that fail to considerably disrupt the status quo to those that articulate a more radical, utopian vision. Generically, the key features of the feminist blockbuster are that they use a combination of 'authenticating anecdotes' (Pearce 2004) as well as other relevant scholarly or popular work. The degree to which the authorial 'I' intervenes varies, with many of the blockbusters considered in the latter chapters functioning more like memoirs. Overall, feminist blockbusters seek to persuade readers of the validity of their critique of gender relations and limiting patriarchal assumptions around femininity, and indeed masculinity. Roxane Gay proffers this definition of the feminist novel, which is also useful in terms of non-fiction: '[it] illuminates some aspect of the female condition and/or offers some kind of imperative for change and/or makes a bold or unapologetic political statement in the best interests of women' (2014, p. 46; see also Felski 1989, p. 14). While certainly not wishing to provide a singular definition of the blockbuster, Gay's comments are useful for thinking through its political uses. Moreover, although each case study will commence with a brief textual analysis of the blockbuster in question, here I am less interested in the formal elements of the books than the ways in which they are made to mean in the extensive media attention directed towards them; that is, particular texts are brought into being in and through public talk around them and, more significantly for my purposes, their authors (Bourdieu 1993).

Following Simone Murray (2004), here 'blockbuster' signals those non-fictional works which have been in the top ten on the bestseller lists in the year of their initial production. The *New York Times* and *Publishers Weekly* are the two 'most watched' (Miller 2000); all of the books dealt with here have appeared, at some stage of their public career, on the *New York Times* bestseller list, and in the majority of cases at number one. But what makes a blockbuster? Why do some books remain in print and others fall into obscurity? John Thompson refers to extensive work that publishers focus on, in terms of marketing and promotion, 'big books' (2010, pp. 187–8). Such 'big books', I argue, are the primary vehicle through which feminism's 'big girls' (Henderson 2006) have been publicly anointed to speak on its behalf. These non-fictional bestsellers, like their fictional counterparts, are implicated in multi-pronged strategies, often initiated at the publisher level, to create, as Thompson tells us, a 'buzz' around them even prior to their arrival on the bookshelves. Central to this process, and indeed to the celebrification of authors, is what has been called the book's 'epitext'.

In his work *Paratexts: A Theory of Interpretation*, Gerard Genette argues 'the paratext is what enables a text to become a book and to be offered as such to its readers, and, more generally, to the public' (1997, p. 1). An integral part of the paratext, and its attempt to delimit a text's signifying capacity, is what he calls the 'epitext'. In his account, the 'epitext' represents those elements of the paratext which are not 'materially appended' to it; so, in contrast to book covers, blurbs, author's notes, testimonials, and so on, which appear as part of the actual printed work, the epitext includes material like reviews, authorial interviews, and promotional material (Genette 1997, p. 344). Celebrity culture, then, contributes significantly to the blockbuster's epitext (Taylor 2007). These public performances outside the text, of course, come to affect how it is interpreted in important ways—and indeed how and if it is consumed at all; therefore in each chapter I consider various aspects of paratextuality, including the publisher's and the author's epitext. Publishers and authors, however, are not alone in the celebrifying process, and the role of journalists as well as other 'cultural intermediaries' (Bourdieu 1993), like publicists and photographers, in mediating this (self-)construction is also crucial, as I will argue. While there are some similarities with other forms of fame, especially those emerging from the literary field, here I also demonstrate that we need to acknowledge the specificities of celebrity feminism.

CELEBRITY FEMINISM AS A DISTINCT MODE OF RENOWN

From the earliest scholarly works, much has been made within celebrity studies of the ways in which fans or followers of celebrities search for the extraordinary made ordinary (Dyer 1979). Similarly, for Graeme Turner, a public figure becomes a celebrity when 'media interest is transferred from reporting on their public role (such as their specific achievements in politics or sport) to investigating the details of their private lives' (2014, p. 8). For the most part, Turner's observation seems easily substantiated. But I want to ask here: to what extent can such claims be mapped onto the celebrity feminist? Though these authors are not vigorously pursued by paparazzi, their profiles in newspapers and magazines often function as forms of biographical writing, seeking to establish why a particular author may have produced a particular type of feminist text. In this sense, as I will discuss further shortly, their life narrative becomes imbued with an explanatory power, as Roland Barthes (1967) famously remarked has always been the case with authors. That said, in other media texts it is predominantly her words, not her life, which garner interest and produce discussion/debate. Moreover, given that, in feminist terms, the 'personal is political', this shift from interest in public activities to private life should not necessarily be viewed as limiting, and indeed can, in the case of celebrity feminists, be seen as a key strategy in their attempts to politicize gendered inequities. In individual chapters, therefore, I will be seeking to test Turner's assertion that a shift from the public to the private is constitutive of celebrity feminism. Here, though, it is necessarily to clarify my definition of this term.

There are, I would suggest, broadly two ways that feminism and celebrity can be explicitly seen to intersect: through celebrity feminists and through celebrities who are or come to publicly identify as feminist, with the blockbuster author being representative of the former. Whether we agree with their specific 'brand', their feminist enunciative practice—through the publication, circulation, and public debate around their blockbuster—is the primary reason for their celebrification. That is, their publicly articulated feminism is the very reason for their fame. In the case of the latter, celebrities often deploy the capital afforded by this status to publicly articulate various political positions, including those that can be broadly considered feminist. However, important though such contributions to public discourse may be, I would not designate such voices 'celebrity feminists' as their renown stems from, and is maintained by, something other than their public feminist discursive practices.[5] That said, towards the end of the book, I will consider how public contests around the meanings of feminism are increasingly being staged in and through the wider circuits of celebrity.

As McCurdy (2013, p. 311) has argued of celebrified environmental activists, there is some 'conceptual utility' in differentiating between celebrities who have developed into activists and activists who have been celebrified. For McCurdy, it is about a difference in emphasis. Celebrities who use their existing celebrity capital for activist purposes are defined as '*celebrity* activists', while activists whose notoriety stems primarily from this activism are 'celebrity *activists*' (McCurdy 2013, p. 311, original emphasis). Similarly, as implied above, we could suggest that with regard to this project, the emphasis is on celebrity *feminists* rather than on *celebrity* feminists. Given that celebrity feminism is a distinct representational and presentational form, then, we must ask different questions of it than other modes of renown, particularly in terms of the public conversations around feminism it precipitates.

Although claims have been made for the recognition of literary celebrity as a 'distinct brand of fame' (Ommundsen 2007, p. 245), I would suggest the specificities of blockbuster celebrity feminism also warrant such a claim (2014b). Feminists are clearly celebrified in a fundamentally different way to their counterparts in film, music, or even sport and politics. The celebrity feminist has an overtly political function and purpose, and is not generally, or at least not to the same degree, subject to attempts to satisfy voracious appetites for insights into her personal life or the same kinds of affective investments from audiences as other forms.[6] That is, similar to the politician-as-celebrity (Higgins and Drake 2006, p. 87), the audience, as well as the media industries, make different demands of the celebrity feminist than of other forms—making it difficult to position celebrity feminism as homologous with other modes of stardom. While by no means homogeneous in terms of how they embody this blockbuster celebrity feminism, they also serve a different cultural and political function, with different effects (and indeed affects).

It will be clear, therefore, that I am not primarily reading these women through either the critical prisms of literary celebrity or political celebrity; blockbuster celebrity feminism, I want to suggest, simultaneously incorporates aspects of, and exceeds, both these ways of theorizing public subjectivity. That said, some discussion of both these forms, and how scholarship in these areas may or may not be illuminating for these case studies, is necessary here. Literary theorists and authors, like feminists, have commonly viewed celebrity with suspicion—the former built upon assumptions about aesthetics and the intrinsic value of literature as art, the latter more explicitly concerned about the political implications of direct engagement with the marketplace (Frow and English 2006). As Ommundsen argues: 'A writer, it is implied, has no business courting celebrity: in order to serve the cause of literature he [sic] must maintain a position separate from the grubby practices of politics or commercialised culture' (2007, p. 245). We can see here how such critiques occupy very similar terrain to those mounted by feminists discussed earlier. However, these feminist writers, like literary celebrities more broadly, cannot exist 'outside the promotional loop' (Moran 2000, p. 67). As Tomlinson argues: 'Authors may differ according to *how* they are promoted and distributed, but not *whether* they are promoted or distributed' (2005, p. 114, original emphasis).

Writers have always been subject to public attempts to delimit the meanings of their literary productions, especially through journalistic attempts to read biographically. As Turner (1993, p. 132) argues: 'journalists are confirmed reflectionists and doggedly attempt to identify the writer's work with their lives'; of course when the work is generically positioned as non-fiction, this gesture becomes even more pronounced and appears almost commonsensical. While actors can be seen to play characters in their primary art form, television, film, theatre, and so on, with their public persona being nonetheless performed in interviews or on publicity tours, there is still perceived to be a division between the two. In the case of the non-fiction author, this distinction is extinguished. These authors, and the journalists who participate in their celebrification, represent 'themselves not only in the narrative proper, but also in interviews and public discourse as literally identical to the "I" of the narratives' (Lakoff 2001, p. 35; see also English and Frow 2006). For Lynne Pearce, women's, and especially feminist, writing is invariably read publicly through what she dubs a 'biomythological context' (2004).

Pearce tells us that 'media reporting of feminist texts has, since the 1970s, insisted on a biographical—or, indeed, biomythological— "context" to the work, *whether or not*, and this is the pertinent point here, the text itself contains autobiographical elements and/or uses a first-person pronoun' (2004, p. 24, original emphasis). Many of these books, too, draw explicitly upon autobiographical strategies, making such conflation even more assured. This conflation is perhaps unsurprising in terms of popular works of non-fiction, like the feminist blockbuster, where it is not so much that a slippage occurs between 'author' and 'narrator' in media discourse, but that no such distinction is ever posited in the first instance (Taylor 2008), either in the text or its paratext. While there may have been more success in terms of debunking the intentional fallacy when publicly discussing fictional texts, authors who have penned works of an explicitly non-fictional bent are—despite the author's purported 'death'—still routinely called upon to help us unlock the text's truths (Barthes 1967; Foucault 1969). These writers, then, work to help provide interpretive strategies through which their texts—and thereby their feminism—can be readily 'deciphered'. As celebrities, they are key to the public interpretation of these blockbusters and concomitantly of feminism. And with the acceleration and proliferation of celebrity, the author's central position as the privileged 'locus of meaning' (Barthes 1967) has never been more assured.

Given the perpetual slippage between narrator and the person who wrote the blockbuster, it is possible to view the celebrity feminist non-fictional author as similar to the television personality who—as James Bennett (2011) has convincingly argued—is often seen to just be 'themselves' on the small screen; that is, there is an assumption that the 'front stage' and the 'back stage' personas are largely indistinguishable (Goffman 1959). Indeed, it seems that the non-fiction author has been largely overlooked in studies of literary celebrity; I would suggest on the same grounds as the television personality. In this way, the blockbuster author is part of a larger cohort of public individuals whose actual self and celebrity self are perceived to be indistinguishable—a persistent rhetorical slippage which requires a more nuanced critical vocabulary around celebrity than has hitherto been mobilized in relation to the forms of stardom that have tended to feature most prominently in celebrity studies (actors, musicians, and so on). As Bennett notes, because of this slippage, the labour that goes into the production of a celebrity persona goes largely unrecognized in the case of the television personality, a point also applicable to the blockbuster celebrity feminist. Given their role as essentially political figures, it is also necessary to engage with some scholarship around the celebritization of politics.

Despite its longer history, the 'celebritization of politics' is a widely written about, and sometimes lamented, modern phenomenon; others have emphasized its potentialities, especially in terms of engaging audiences (Drake and Higgins 2006; Street 2012; Wheeler 2013). That politicians are now required to use the same tools of marketing and self-presentation, and models of fan interaction and intimacy traditionally associated with those in entertainment fields, is unquestionable. Although 'even the non-politically active celebrity is legible politically', as Biressi and Nunn incisively observe (2013, p. 98), the celebrity feminist is an explicitly political figure. However, celebrity feminists exist outside the two dominant ways of theorizing the interrelationship (indeed inextricability) of politics and celebrity. Mark Wheeler, drawing upon John Street (2004), deploys the distinction between 'CP1s', 'celebrity politicians who have incorporated the principles of fame for electoral achievement' and 'CP2s', described as 'politicized celebrities who have become activists in their own right'

(2013, p. 3). It is clear neither categorization can be readily mapped onto the feminist-as-celebrity, and especially onto the specific form I am tracking here.

These blockbuster celebrity feminists do not necessarily engage in politics in the manner implied by these classifications but rather largely perform their (celebrity) politics beyond traditional political structures. Not only does such a classificatory system obscure the possibility of writing-as-activism (something upon which feminism has always relied), it also fails to consider the diffuse nature of politics, and that these celebrity feminists can and do perform politically, even when appearing on television or when they use Twitter to circulate feminist critique or to raise awareness of particular political issues relevant to women (as Naomi Wolf and Roxane Gay do). That is, cultural politics should never be seen in opposition to 'real' politics (Giroux 2000). Moreover, in contrast to those celebrities who come to intervene in politics, such as U2's Bono or Angelina Jolie, celebrity feminism is a product of prior interventions into the broadly conceived political realm. That is, the celebrity feminist is not merely a celebrity who has been politicized but a political figure who has been celebrified, itself an important distinction which again underscores the need for critics to attend to the specificities of celebrity feminism as a modality of renown (Taylor 2014a).

Celebrity or Fame? A Gendered Distinction

Some critics have attempted to maintain a distinction between fame and celebrity, usually presuming that the former relates to renown being a product of exceptional talent or ability, and the latter having little to do with an individual's aptitude in a given field.[7] In such analyses, there is an implicit hierarchy—fame is privileged over celebrity as that which is earned and thereby warranted, while, in such renderings, celebrity becomes the province of those whose visibility is seen as less deserved and often ephemeral (as in the case of reality television stars) against the longevity of 'achieved' celebrity. Moreover, as Brenda Weber emphasizes, the fame/celebrity distinction is problematic, in gendered terms. As she argues, 'fame stands for the high, celebrity for the low' (2012, p. 18); and, of course, many critics have shown how the former has been historically gendered masculine and the latter feminine, and, in the case of fame/celebrity, these assumptions are thoroughly reinscribed. She continues that this divide is shot through with gendered and class distinctions: 'Fame marks aspiration; celebrity brands ambition. Fame indicates valor; celebrity stains scandal' (2012, p. 18). For Weber, apart from the boundary being porous, choosing to deploy the terms interchangeably represents an important critical and political strategy 'to problematize the gender bias that stands at the heart of the fame/celebrity distinction' (2012, p. 18). Being sympathetic to Weber's reading of the gendered implications of this division, I too will move between these two loaded terms.

As Weber further demonstrates in her study of women writers, one thing that is repeatedly occluded is the agency of these individuals in their own celebrification, and, indeed, when it is conceded it is deplored. The public uneasiness with women's fame identified by Weber and others enables us to locate the disdain for feminist celebrity in a longer tradition of seeing fame and women as problematic. That is, women's agency in seeking fame has historically been met with disapproval. As Weber argues of nineteenth-century women writers: 'If a woman were passive in her celebrity (it simply came to her without her bidding), she could be forgiven her fame. But if she schemed and plotted to achieve her fame, the avarice for celebrity was a scathing social stigma' (2012, p. 18). If she were the 'done to', rather than the 'doer', then this fame could be recuperated. As Virginia Woolf remarks, 'publicity for women is detestable' (cited in Weber 2012, pp. 16–17), and it seems that, when it comes to the blockbuster celebrity feminist, this value-laden assumption persists.

While of course claims regarding the need for 'impression management' (Goffman 1959) are not new, nor solely applicable to those in the public spotlight, even among feminist critics there has been an obvious hesitancy around conceding women's agency in relation to celebrity culture. Even within feminist scholarship it is common to conceptualize celebrification as something *done to* select, reluctant women. Whelehan's comments are indicative in this regard: 'Feminism, leadership as it has always been, never satisfied the public's thirst for figureheads and spokespeople, and therefore the media made figureheads for themselves …' (2000, p. 78). Such assumptions of feminist passivity are in themselves problematic but are also one of the other reasons—along with the denigration of those who *are* conversely seen to actively welcome celebrification—why a more comprehensive understanding of feminism and political star-making has not yet been produced. That is, becoming and remaining a celebrity feminist has not been coded a feminist *practice*—something I hope to challenge here.

Industry, Agency, and the Celebrity Feminist

As many scholars have posited, celebrity is not the property or possession of individuals but an ongoing, labour-intensive process (Marshall 1997; Marwick and boyd 2011; Turner 2014). Rather than seeing 'celebrities as arising organically from the populace', it is impossible to ignore that 'celebrity is an industry like many others' (Gamson 2007, p. 148). As Gamson notes in *Claims to Fame*, 'celebrity-making' is essentially a 'commercial enterprise, made up of highly developed and institutionally linked professions and sub-industries such as public relations, entertainment law, celebrity journalism and photography, grooming and training, managing and agenting, novelty sales' (1994, p. 64). Similarly, P.D. Marshall notes that 'It takes effort to be famous' (2007, p. 647; see also Turner et al. 2000). Given the vast array of industry professionals implicated in its creation and maintenance, celebrity is best conceptualized as 'a collective affair' (Glass 2016, p. 44). The celebrity thereby needs to be made and remade in a multi-faceted process in which a wide range of players, not least the author herself, are engaged.

Lorraine York (2013b) has recently explored how agency has been an unexamined factor in studies of celebrity, where the critical gaze has overwhelmingly tended to rest on the industry's role in persona production. Since I am hoping that this study will intervene in these debates, it is worth engaging with them here. As York argues in 'Star Gazing: The Challenges of Theorizing Celebrity Agency' (2013b, p. 1333), scholarship in celebrity studies has been marred by a production/consumption dualism, which effectively leaves 'celebrity agency stranded in its interstices'. That is, critics have sought to come to terms with the manufacture of celebrity, attending to celebrity as an industry, or—conversely—have privileged the active meaning-making in which audiences engage around celebrity. For example, David Shumway cites Denise Scott Brown's study of fame and architecture: 'stardom is something done to a star by others. Stars cannot create themselves' (2000, p. 87). While this acknowledgement that industry professionals, and indeed audiences, are integral to the celebrification process is sound, Scott's comments are indicative of the over-reliance on production and consumption mapped by York. This deprivation of agency is especially troublesome in feminist terms.

Following work on literary celebrity, therefore, one of the core premises underpinning this study is 'that authors actively negotiate their own celebrity rather than having it imposed upon them' (Moran 2000, p. 10;

Hammill 2007; York 2007, 2013a). The labour of celebrity feminists is crucial here. As Rosemary Coombe (2007, p. 726) suggests, 'Clearly, individual labour is necessary if the person is to have value ... but it is not usually sufficient for the creation of public value', not least because this value relies upon specific affective investments from audiences. That said, while consumption and fandom is vitally important to celebrity studies, 'it is worth finding out the various possibilities and cultural positionings open to that often ironically silenced agent, the celebrity' (York 2013b, p. 1346; see also Hammill 2007). As York conjectures, literary scholars have been more open to this way of theorizing celebrity and the individuals who become implicated in it than those who focus on other forms.

In addition to York's work, I will draw upon other scholarship that seeks to challenge the production/consumption focus she identifies. For example, drawing attention to their attempts to shape their celebrity signs, Barry King notes that stars are 'individuals engaged in constantly re-negotiating the terms of their engagement with public life' (2003, p. 52); he refers to this process as acting 'autographically'. As professional authors, these women arguably possess skills uniquely fitted to such a self-presentational project. Here, I am less concerned with whether these women could control their public images, and thus their feminisms, than their apparent *attempts* to do so. Like Tanya Serisier (2013) in her analysis of controversial radical feminist Andrea Dworkin, I am interested in the ways in which these women invent *themselves* as feminist icons, not just in their writing (Serisier's focus) but in the context of other public performances like newspaper or television interviews, or—in the later cases—via social media. All these celebrity performances constitute important forms of feminist creative labour, and indeed 'emotion work' (Nunn and Biressi 2010), which are too often overlooked.

Feminism and Star Labour

Although of course no one, including the feminist blockbuster author, can entirely delimit the ways her own celebrity sign comes to mean, or exercise full control over her public image, there are moments we can identify a complicated two-way flow between the figure being celebrified and the industries credited with that celebrification. That is, they are by no means the 'hapless authoresses' portrayed by Greer. Throughout this work, therefore, I am especially interested in moments where the celebrity's agency is rendered visible, and each chapter will locate and foreground such moments. This focus is attuned to the idea that celebrity is a performative practice (Marwick and boyd 2011; see also Marshall 2007). As Marwick and boyd argue, stars are best conceptualized as 'celebrity practitioners', a moniker which underscores the work involved in its maintenance (2011, p. 140). As part of this focus on the labour of individual feminist stars, I also engage with self-reflexive commentary on their own celebrification, where these celebrities explicitly reflect upon their own renown including sometimes, and often rather disingenuously, disavowing the systemic and discursive processes responsible for their visibility. The women in this study, like those examined in York's study of Canadian literary celebrity, 'have given voice to sceptical treatments of celebrity culture while participating to varying degrees in that culture' (2007, p. 30). This is a paradox of which they were all too aware, as my analysis will show.

Give the methodological limitations of textual analysis in terms of ascertaining how these women partook, and in some instances continue to partake, in the arduous processes of persona-making, what I seek here are textual traces of this labour. Such traces can be found in their own published works and in media interviews, but also in less publicly accessible sites, such as personal papers and especially letters. Memoirs, too, can be singled out as discursive instances where the blockbuster author can be seen to actively intervene in the construction of her own blockbuster author sign. Concerned as it is, then, with illuminating the labour in which these feminist authors have been engaged, in terms of the maintenance of their celebrity and the construction of particular celebrity personas, this study draws upon archival material where it is available—especially in the case of those older celebrities who have amassed extensive archives which are now held at universities both in Australia and in the United States.

In the case of Brown, Friedan, and Greer, archival documents from publishers and literary agents, as well as authors themselves, give some sense of the expansive promotional networks in which all these women were (and in some cases, still are) thoroughly implicated. Archives are, of course, selective, arranged in particular ways, and this arrangement and strategic inclusion (and thus exclusion) of specific material works to circumscribe the kinds of academic uses to which it can be put (York 2013a, p. 19). The archive—especially when sold to an institution prior to the celebrity's death—is shaped by the author, representing another obvious attempt to control the public meanings of their lives, their texts, and their public selves. Archives need to be conceptualized, therefore, as 'contested sites of power … dynamic technologies of rule which actually *create* the histories and social relations they ostensibly only *describe*' (Schwartz and Cook 2002, p. 7, original emphasis). With this caveat in mind, these archives enable the telling of a particular story about feminism, in and through these particular women and their personal and public subjectivities.[8] The materials found therein, moreover, are by no means consistent, so the extent to which I draw upon them differs in individual chapters. Though the same kind of material is not yet available for women like Wolf or Gay, there are other ways to gauge the extent to which they assiduously work to manufacture particular public selves or seek to act 'autographically' (King 2003), most notably through their online presence as well as through their published writing.

Accordingly, texts of 'self-fashioning', like autobiographies, letters, and interviews (Hammill 2007, p. 15), are integral to the process of celebrification—including that of feminist blockbuster authors. In various chapters, I will be attentive to both 'authorized' and 'unauthorized' life stories; the former signifies those in which the celebrity has willingly participated, either through themselves writing an autobiographical text or by agreeing to take part in biographical narratives such as documentaries and television, magazine, or newspaper interviews (Biressi and Nunn 2013, p. 94). Even such 'authorized' narratives are effectively 'collaboratively produced' and are in many ways economically driven as they seek to secure viewers and readers for this 'life story' product (Biressi and Nunn 2013, p. 95). Conversely, unauthorized biographical texts include any attempt to construct a life narrative without the direct involvement of the celebrity in question. While Biressi and Nunn are primarily interested in the former as 'narratives of individuation', their comment that such narratives 'are doubly loaded when their protagonist invests in their own narration' (2013, p. 95) is prescient here. Moreover, as John Rodden (2007) argues, writers commonly use interviews 'as a performance space for authorial orchestration and self-promotion', something I will explore to varying degrees in the coming chapters. This study, accordingly, is organized around both representation and self-representation, and the tensions that often exist between them, including in the field of new media.

Although the development of new media is said to have resulted in the escalation of celebrity culture, as Weber argues, 'in the centuries before our own, celebrity was experienced with no lesser intensity' (2012,

p. 15). Similarly, as Thomas notes (2014, p. 244), 'contemporary discourses on fame emphasise newness and change, often at the expense of making somewhat unfashionable connections with the past'. Therefore, it is important to not overplay the 'newness' of the contemporary operations of celebrity.[9] What we may find useful in platforms such as Twitter, for example, is how 'the site, its usage and its content, renders historical negotiations around the construction and presentation of stardom visible' (Thomas 2014, p. 243). That is, such processes of self-representation are not in the least innovative but, through new media, they are now publicly discernable. In particular, the (self-)labour and branding that many see as being associated with new media is, as many of these figures suggest, by no means a new phenomenon.

Celebrity and the 'Branding' of Feminism

The celebrity, as Turner et al. (2000) make clear in their study of the celebrity industry in Australia, is and arguably always has been, a 'brand', a fundamentally commodified self. Much work has recently been published around how women, and young girls in particular, are exhorted to make of themselves a 'brand'; this, in particular, is seen as integral to postfeminist culture. As Sarah Banet-Weiser (2012) notes, for young women this very publicly staged self-branding is in many ways constitutive of their subjectivity. Such self-branding is argued to be quintessentially postfeminist (and indeed neoliberal); it is 'privileging the individual, aligning with the focus on individualism inherent in both postfeminist and neoliberal discourses' (Keller 2015, p. 277). In her recent article, Jessalyn Keller identifies 'a larger cultural trend towards the branding of feminism' that is co-terminous with this wider, pervasive logic (2015, p. 274; Negra 2014; McRobbie 2015). Perhaps unsurprisingly, literature (both popular and academic) around the branding of feminism often tends to mobilize those familiar arguments about its commodification or, more generally, its mediatization—that it must come at the price of 'real' and certainly 'collective' politics, that its necessary focus on the individual is anathema to feminism.

However, these mechanisms of self-branding—while perhaps hitherto not as publicly visible as they are now—have always, by necessity, engulfed the celebrity, including feminist writers. Although opportunities for self-branding have multiplied as well as having become normative (Banet-Weiser 2012; Marwick 2013), an integral part of our very being in the world, especially in cyberspace, feminist authors have always been actively engaged in attempts to 'brand' themselves, their works, and their feminisms in particular ways. Moreover, as a commodity, necessarily part of the market place, the feminist blockbuster has always been thoroughly entangled with the logics of commodity capitalism (and is often dismissed on such grounds). In many ways, it is possible to conceptualize the blockbuster celebrity feminist as a kind of 'brand ambassador'—in terms of themselves, their own product, and feminism as a movement, discourse, and/or set of shifting ideas and ideals. One of their key roles, as highly visible women with discursive power, especially those in Part I, is to delimit the kinds of feminist histories that come to publicly circulate and receive cultural legitimacy.

History, 'Waves', and Celebrity

Here I will attend to the role of these celebrities in the historicization of feminism, in the constitution of cultural memory. That is, especially in terms of Part I, I examine how the privileging of their voices has worked to shape the kinds of narratives that have come to circulate about the second wave in particular. Although not herself explicitly engaging with theories of celebrity, in *Feeling Women's Liberation* (2013, p. 17), Victoria Hesford remarks that 'this process whereby some women (young, white, and middle-class) and not others are seen as political activists, feminists, and recorded as such by the national media has very real repercussions for what we know of the women's liberation movement in the present'. Through such women, as Hesford makes clear, certain narratives about feminism—as well as certain ways of being feminist—come to be privileged while others are elided.

But rather than simply reinscribing the dominant critical narrative that feminism is rendered a spent force in millennial media and popular culture especially, my work sees these celebrities—those who first came to prominence in the mid-twentieth century and those whose feminist fame is a more recent phenomenon—as central to the process of keeping feminism 'alive'. Here I am indebted to Sean Fuller and Catherine Driscoll, who draw upon Wendy Brown (2001) in service of their argument that post-feminism is a simplistic, reductive way of critically thinking through recent changes in our representational landscape. They quote Brown's argument that any political phenomenon, like feminism, remains 'alive, refusing to recede into the past, precisely to the extent that its meaning is open and ambiguous, to the extent that it remains interpreted and contested by the present, and to the extent that it disturbs settled meanings in the present' (in Fuller and Driscoll 2015, p. 253). These women are figures around whom these ongoing conversations over feminism, its complicated and messy histories, its lacunae, and its relevance, coalesce.

Following recent work on feminism and temporality (Browne 2014; Withers 2015), as well as earlier critiques of generationalism and familial metaphors (Bailey 1997; Orr 1997; Roof 1997; Siegel 1997; Henry 2004; Taylor 2008), this study also works to complicate the dominant historiographical mode when it comes to narrating feminist pasts, and indeed as a means of classifying its present. Although, of course, waves and generations are distinct, 'waves are nonetheless stuck to feminist generations, and, at times, operate in a synecdochical fashion, so much so that it becomes impossible to think feminist generations apart from waves' (Withers 2015, p. 30). Numerous scholars have problematized the 'great hegemonic model' of feminist waves (Sandoval 2000, p. 46), but this has not compromised its ubiquity—especially in the mediasphere.

While this study begins with women who were writing in the 1960s and 1970s, it maps their celebrity feminist interventions well into the twenty-first century; classifying them only as 'second wave' celebrity feminists would elide their own complicated personal histories and relationship to the women's liberation movement (in the USA especially), as well as the ongoing development not just of their celebrity signs but likewise their feminisms and how they came to be popularly framed. It would also fail to recognize how they continue to shape popular understandings of feminism in the present (and indeed, in Brown's case, how she came to resonate more in the so-called postfeminist context), not just mediate narratives of second wave history.

As Browne notes: 'The ordering of different feminisms into successive waves or phases implies that only one kind of feminism is possible at a time and, moreover, that older forms of theory and practice necessarily become obsolete as time moves on' (2014, p. 1). In contrast to succession narratives, the authors examined in Part I challenge this assertion of generational homogeneity; they have not simply been replaced by younger celebrified writers or activists but co-exist alongside them. They have not faded into the background as the eras with which they are most commonly associated ended. Instead, their ongoing media performances serve to highlight the impossibility of relegating them to specific temporal junctures; of securely locating them within a bounded time designated the 'second wave' or the 'women's liberation movement'. Like their own feminist identities, narratives about them are mobile, not static or fixed, and are put to different uses in different contexts. Moreover, the women examined in Part II rarely locate their feminism within the terms of the troublesome wave metaphor, and indeed, through establishing intergenerational commonalities and intragenerational differences, they can be seen to destabilize attempts to fix feminism along generational lines (see Roof 1997). In this way, celebrity feminism can offer a resistance to dominant ways of figuring feminism and its history. In Part I, I turn my attention to the authors of three of the most historically visible Western feminist blockbusters, *Sex and the Single Girl*, *The Feminine Mystique*, and *The Female Eunuch*, and how their authors have, over decades, maintained their renown and continued to shape public conversations around feminism.

Notes

1. In terms of popular culture, it is clear that—critically—fictional feminisms (and overwhelmingly in the past decade or so, *postfeminisms*) have come to overshadow the explicit discursive interventions staged by my objects of analysis. That is, myriad studies have been produced on how feminism has been taken up, appropriated, and reimagined in television programmes like *Buffy the Vampire Slayer*, *Sex and the City*, and more recently *Girls*. However, when it comes to *actual* feminists, studies have been comparatively scarce. Mendes (2011) is a recent exception, as is Dow's 2014 study of how feminism was televized in the USA in 1970.
2. While Wicke, writing in the mid-1990s, sees celebrity as effectively filling a gap produced by the decline of an organized women's movement in America, here I argue that the relationship between celebrity and feminism has a much longer history.
3. As Piepmeier notes, mimeographs in particular have become iconic in accounts of the second wave, 'coming to stand for all informal feminist publishing'. They were also seen as a way to enable the circulation of feminist ideas that were not popularly available: 'Because there were no books or magazines that addressed the issues they were taking on, these activists had to create and distribute their own' (Piepmeier 2009, p. 36).
4. For example, Lisa Hogeland (1998) demonstrates the importance of the 'consciousness-raising (CR) novel' to attuning women to the inequitable gendered dynamics feminism has long sought to challenge, during feminism's second wave in particular (see also Felski 1989; Lauret 1994). Similarly, Imelda Whelehan's *The Feminist*

Bestseller (2005) focuses predominantly on popular fiction, although it does briefly engage with Friedan and Brown.
5. This contradicts Wicke's (1994) position that any woman with a public profile will be 'assimilated' into the category of 'celebrity feminist'.
6. Ommundsen (2004) makes a similar point regarding literary celebrity.
7. For others, fame has a much longer history than 'celebrity', which is often seen as associated with, and changing in response to, the modern mass media (Marwick 2016).
8. Feminist archives pose particular questions, to which feminists have recently turned their attention (Eichorn 2013).
9. Su Holmes (2005), too, has made this argument around early forms of reality television and the celebrification of 'ordinary' individuals.

References

Alcoff, L. (1991) 'The Problem of Speaking for Others', *Cultural Critique*, 20: 5–32
Bailey, C. (1997) 'Making Waves and Drawing Lines: The Politics of Defining the Vicissitudes of Feminism', Hypatia, 12.3: 17–28
Banet-Weiser, S. (2012) *Autheticity, TM*, New York: New York University Press
Barcan, R. (2000) 'Home on the Range: Nudity, Celebrity, and Ordinariness in the Home Girls/Blokes Pages', *Continuum*, 14.2: 145–58
Barker-Plummer, B. (2010) 'News and Feminism: A Historic Dialog', *Journalism and Communication Monographs*, 12.3/4: 145–203
Barthes, R. (1967/1978 ed) 'The Death of Author', in *Image/Music/Text*, London: Fontana
Bennett, J. (2011) *Television Personalities: Stardom and the Small Screen*, London: Routledge
Biressi, A. & Nunn, H. (2013) *Class and Contemporary British Culture*, Basingstoke: Palgrave Macmillan
Bourdieu, P. (1993) *The Field of Cultural Production*, New York: Columbia University Press
Bradley, P. (2003) *Mass Media and the Shaping of American Feminism, 1963-1975*, Jackson: University of Mississippi Press
Brown, W. (2001) *Politics Out of History*, Princeton: Princeton University Press
Browne, V. (2014) *Feminism, Time, and Non Linear History*, Basingstoke: Palgrave Macmillan
Brunsdon, C. (1997) *Screen Tastes*, London: Routledge
Bulbeck, C. (1997) *Living Feminism: The Impact of the Women's Movement on Three Generations of Australian Women*, Cambridge: Cambridge University Press

Carter, D. & Ferres, K. (2001) 'The Public Life of Literature', in T. Bennett & D. Carter eds. *Culture in Australia*, Cambridge: Cambridge University Press, pp. 140–160

Coombe, R. (2007) 'Author(iz)ing the Celebrity: Engendering Alternative Identities', in P.D. Marshall ed. *The Celebrity Culture Reader*, London: Routledge, pp. 721–769

de Beauvoir, S. (1949/1989) *The Second Sex*, New York: Vintage

Dean, J. (2010) 'Feminism in the Papers: Contested Feminisms in the British Quality Press', *Feminist Media Studies*, 10.4: 391–407

Dow, B. (2014) *Watching Women's Liberation, 1970: Feminism's Pivotal Year on the Network News*, Chicago: University of Illinois Press

Drake, P. & Higgins, M. (2006) 'I'm a Celebrity, Get Me into Politics: The Political Celebrity and the Celebrity Politician', in S. Holmes & S. Redmond eds. *Framing Celebrity: New Directions in Celebrity Culture*, London: Routledge, pp. 88–100

Driessens, O. (2013a) 'Celebrity Capital: Redefining Celebrity Using Field Theory', *Theory and Society*, 42: 543–560

―――― (2013b) 'The celebritization of society and culture: Understanding the structural dynamics of celebrity culture', *International Journal of Cultural Studies*, 16.6: 641–657

Dux, M. & Simic, Z. (2008) *The Great Feminist Denial*, Melbourne: Melbourne University Press

Dyer, R. (1979) *Stars*, London: British Film Institute

Echols, A. (1989) *Daring to be Bad: Radical Feminism in America, 1967–1975*, Minneapolis: University of Minnesota Press

Eichorn, K. (2013) *The Archival Turn in Feminism*, Philadelphia: Temple University Press

English, J.F. & Frow, J. (2006) 'Literary Authorship and Celebrity Culture', in J.F. English ed. *A Concise Companion to Contemporary British Fiction*, Malden: Blackwell, pp. 39–57

Faludi, S. (1991) *Backlash: The Undeclared War Against American Women*, London: Vintage

Farrell, A.E. (1998) *Yours in Sisterhood: Ms Magazine and the Promise of Popular Feminism*, Chapel Hill: University of North Carolina Press

Felski, R. (1989) *Beyond Feminist Aesthetics*, Cambridge: Harvard University Press

―――― (2000) *Doing Time: Feminist Theory and Postmodern Culture*, New York: New York University Press

Fish, S. (1980) *Is There a Text in This Class? The Authority of Interpretive Communities*, Cambridge: Harvard University Press

Foucault, M. (1969/1984 ed) 'The Author Function', in P. Rainbow ed. *The Foucault Reader*, New York: Penguin, pp. 101–120

Freeman, J. (1976) 'Trashing: The Dark Side of Sisterhood', April, *Ms Magazine*, 49–51, 92–98, accessed via http://www.jofreeman.com/joreen/trashing.htm

Fuller, S. & Driscoll, C. (2015) 'HBO's Girls: Gender, Generation, and Quality Television', *Continuum*, 29.2: 253–262
Gamson, J. (1994) *Claims to Fame: Celebrity in Contemporary America*, Berkeley: University of California Press
––––––– (2007) 'The Assembly Line of Greatness', in S. Holmes & S. Redmond eds. *Stardom and Celebrity: A Reader*, London: Sage, pp. 141–155
Gay, R. (2014) 'Theses on the Feminist Novel', *Dissent*, 61.4: 45–48
Genette, G. (1997) *Paratexts: Thresholds of Interpretation*, Cambridge: Cambridge University Press
Gever, M. (2003) *Entertaining Lesbians: Celebrity, Sexuality, and Self-Invention*, New York: Routledge
Giroux, H. (2000) *Impure Acts: The Practical Politics of Cultural Studies*, London: Routledge
Glass, L. (2016) 'Brand Names: A Brief History of Literary Celebrity', in P.D. Marshall & S. Redmond eds. *A Companion to Celebrity*, London: Wiley Blackwell, pp. 39–57
Goffman, E. (1959) *The Presentation of Self in Everyday Life*, New York: Random House
Gunew, S. (1993) 'Feminism and the Politics of Irreducible Differences: Multiculturalism/Ethnicity/Race', in S. Gunew & A. Yeatman eds. *Feminism and the Politics of Difference*, St Leonards: Allen & Unwin, pp. 1–19
Hall, E.J. & Rodrigeuz, M.S. (2003) 'The Myth of Postfeminism', *Gender and Society*, 17.6: 878–902
Hammer, R. (2000) 'Antifeminists as Media Celebrities', *Review of Education, Pedagogy, and Cultural Studies*, 22.3: 207–222
Hammill, F. (2007) *Women's Literary Celebrity Between the Wars*, Austin: University of Texas Press
Hekman, S. (1999) *Feminism, Identity and Difference*, London: Psychology Press
Hemmings, C. (2011) *Why Stories Matter: The Political Grammar of Feminist Theory*, Durham: Duke University Press
Henderson, M. (2006) *Marking Feminist Times: Remembering the Longest Revolution in Australia*, Bern: Peter Lang
Henry, A. (2004) *Not My Mother's Sister: Generational Conflict and Third Wave Feminism*, Bloomington: University of Indiana Press
––––––– (2014) 'From a Mindset to a Movement: Feminism in the 1990s', in D.S. Cobble, L. Gordon, & A. Henry, *Feminism Unfinished: A Short, Surprising History*, New York: W.W. Norton, pp. 147–226
Hesford, V. (2013) *Feeling Women's Liberation*, Durham: Duke University Press
Heywood, L. & Drake, J. (1997) 'Introduction', in L. Heywood & J. Drake eds. *Third Wave Agenda: Being Feminist, Doing Feminism*, Minneapolis: Minnesota University Press, pp. 1–24
Higgins, M. & Drake, P. (2006) "I'm a Celebrity, Get Me into Politics: The Political Celebrity and the Celebrity Politician", in S. Holmes & S. Redmond

eds. *Framing Celebrity: New Directions in Celebrity Culture*, London: Routledge, pp. 87–100

Hogeland, L.M. (1998) *Feminism and Its Fictions: The Consciousness Raising Novel and the Women's Liberation Movement*, Philadelphia: University of Pennsylvania Press

Hollows, J. & Moseley, R. (2006) 'Introduction', in J. Hollows & R. Moseley eds. *Feminism in Popular Culture*, London: Berg, pp. 1–22

Holmes S. (2005) '"Starring ... Dyer?' Re-visiting star studies and contemporary celebrity culture', *Westminster Papers in Communication and Culture*, 2.2: 6–21

hooks, b. (1994) *Outlaw Culture*, New York: Routledge

Huddy, L. (1997) 'Feminism and Feminists in the News', in P. Norris ed. *Women, Politics and the Media*, Oxford: Oxford University Press, pp. 183–204

Keller, J. (2015) 'Girl Power's Last Chance? Tavi Gevinson, Feminism and Popular Media Culture', *Continuum*, 29.2: 274–285

King, B. (2003) 'Embodying an Elastic Self: The Parametrics of Contemporary Stardom', in T. Austin & M. Barker eds. *Contemporary Hollywood Stardom*, London: Hodder Education, pp. 43–61

King, K. (1994) *Theory in its Feminist Travels*, Bloomington: Indiana University Press

Lakoff, R.T. (2001) *The Language War*, Berkeley: University of California Press

Lauret, M. (1994) *Liberating Literature: Feminist Fiction in America*, New York: Routledge

Le Masurier, M. (2007) 'My Other, My Self', *Australian Feminist Studies*, 22.53: 191–211

———. (2010) 'Reading the Flesh', *Feminist Media Studies*, 11.2: 215–229

Lilburn, S., Magarey, S. & Sheridan, S. (2000) 'Celebrity Feminism as Synthesis: Germaine Greer, *The Female Eunuch* and the Australian Print Media', *Continuum*, 14.3: 335–348.

Lind, L. & Salo C. (2002) 'The Framing of Feminists and Feminism in News and Public Affairs Programs in U.S. Electronic Media', *Journal of Communication*, 52.1: 211–228

Look, H. (1999) 'The Author as Star', *Publishing Research Quarterly*, Fall: 12–29

Macdonald, M. (1995) *Representing Women: Myths of Femininity in Popular Media*, London: Bloomsbury

Maddison, S. (2013) 'Discursive Politics: Changing the Talk and Raising Expectations' in S. Maddison & M. Sawer eds. *The Women's Movement in Protest, Institutions and the Internet: Australia in Transnational Perspective*, Oxford: Routledge, pp. 37–53

Marshall, P.D. (1997) *Celebrity and Power*, Minneapolis: University of Minnesota Press

———. (2007) 'Intimately Intertwined in the Most Public Way: Celebrity and Journalism', in P.D. Marshall ed. *The Celebrity Culture Reader*, London: Routledge, pp. 315–323

Marwick, A. & boyd, d. (2011) 'To See and Be Seen: Celebrity Practice on Twitter', *Convergence*, 17.2: 139–158

Marwick, A.E. (2013) *Status Update: Celebrity, Publicity, and Branding in the Social Media Age*, New Haven: Yale University Press

———. (2016) 'You May Know Me from YouTube (Micro-)Celebrity in Social Media', in P.D. Marshall & S. Redmond eds. *A Companion to Celebrity*, London: Wiley Blackwell, pp. 333–350

McCurdy, P. (2013) 'Conceptualising Celebrity Activists: The Case of Tamsin Omond', *Celebrity Studies*, 4.3: 311–324

McRobbie, A. (2013) 'Feminism, the Family and the New Mediated Maternalism', *New Formations*, 80–81: 119–137

———. (2015) 'Notes on the Perfect: Competitive Femininity in Neoliberal Times', *Australian Feminist Studies*, 30.83: 3–20

Mendes, K. (2011) *Feminism in the News: Representations of the Women's Movement Since 1960*, Basingstoke: Palgrave Macmillan

———. (2015) 'Slutwalk, Feminism and the News', in K. Silva & K. Mendes eds. *Feminist Erasures: Challenging Backlash Culture*, Basingstoke: Palgrave Macmillan, pp. 219–234

Miller, L.J. (2000) 'The Best-Seller List as Marketing Tool and Historical Fiction', *Book History*, 3: 286–304

Moran, J. (2000) *Star Authors: Literary Celebrity in America*, London: Pluto

Moreton-Robinson, A. (2000) *Talkin' Up to the White Woman: Indigenous Women and Australian Feminism*, St Lucia: University of Queensland Press

Murray, S. (2004) *Mixed Media: Feminist Presses and Publishing Politics*, London: Pluto

Negra, D. (2014) 'Claiming Feminism: Commentary, Autobiography and Advice Literature for Women in the Recession', *Journal of Gender Studies*, 23.3: 275–286

Newbury, M. (2000) 'Celebrity Watching', *American Literary History*, 12.1: 272–283

Norris, P. ed. (1997) *Women, Politics and the Media*, Oxford: Oxford University Press

Nunn, H. & Biressi, A. (2010) '"A Trust Betrayed": Celebrity and the Work of Emotion', *Celebrity Studies*, 1.1: 49–64

Ommundsen, W. (2004) 'Sex, Soap and Sainthood: Beginning to Theorise Literary Celebrity', *JASAL*, 3: 45–56

———. (2007) 'From the Altar to the Market-Place and Back Again: Understanding Literary Celebrity', in S. Redmond & S. Holmes eds. *Stardom and Celebrity: A Reader*, London: Sage, pp. 244–256

Orr, C. (1997) 'Charting the Currents of the Third Wave', *Hypatia*, 12.3: 29–45

Pearce, L. (2004) *The Rhetorics of Feminism*, London: Routledge

Piepmeier, A. (2009) *Girl Zines: Making Media, Doing Feminism*, New York: New York University Press

Radway, J. (1984) *Reading the Romance: Women, Patriarchy, and Popular Literature*, Chapel Hill: University of North Carolina Press
Redfern, C. & Aune, K. (2013) *Reclaiming the F Word: Feminism Today*, London: ZED Books
Rhode, D. (1995) 'Media Images, Feminist Issues', *Signs*, 20.3: 685–709
Rodden, P. (2007) *Performing the Literary Interviews: How Writers Craft Their Public Selves*, Lincoln: University of Nebraska
Rojek, C. (2001) *Celebrity*, London: Reaktion
Roof, J. (1997) 'Generational Difficulties; or the Fear of a Barren History', in D. Looser & E.A. Kaplan eds. *Generations: Academic Feminists in Dialogue*, Minneapolis: University Minnesota Press, pp. 69–87
Rowlands, S. & Henderson, M. (1996) 'Damned Bores and Slick Sisters: The Selling of Blockbuster Feminism in Australia', *Australian Feminist Studies*, 11.23: 9–16
Sandoval, C. (2000) *Methodology of the Oppressed*, Minneapolis: University of Minnesota Press
Schwartz, J.M. & Cook, T. (2002) 'Archives, Records, and Power: The Making of Modern Memory', *Archival Science*, 2.1: 1–19
Scott, L. (2000) 'Market Feminism: The Case for a Paradigm Shift', in M. Catteral, P. MacLaran, & L. Stevens eds. *Marketing and Feminism: Current Issues and Research*, London: Routledge, pp. 16–38
Serisier, T. (2013) 'Who Was Andrea? Writing Oneself as a Feminist Icon', *Women: A Cultural Review*, 24.1: 26–44
Shaw, F. (2013) 'Blogging and the Women's Movement', in S. Maddison & M. Sawer eds. *The Women's Movement in Protest, Institutions and the Internet: Australia in Transnational Perspective*, Oxford: Routledge, pp. 118–131
Sheridan, S., Magarey, S. & Lilburn, S. (2006) 'Feminism in the News', in J. Hollows & R. Moseley eds. *Feminism in Popular Culture*, Oxford: Berg, pp. 25–40
Showalter, E. (2001) 'In Search of Heroines', 14 June, *The Guardian*, accessed via: https://www.theguardian.com/world/2001/jun/14/gender.uk
Siegel, D. (1997) 'Reading Between the Waves: Feminist Historiography in "Postfeminist" Moment', in L. Heywood & J. Drake eds. *Third Wave Agenda: Being Feminist, Doing Feminism*, Minneapolis: Minnesota University Press, pp. 55–82
Skeggs, B. (1997) *Becoming Respectable: Formations of Class and Gender*, London: Sage
Street, J. (2004) 'Celebrity Politicians: Popular Culture and Political Representation', *BJPIR*, 6: 435–452
———. (2012) 'Do Celebrities Politicians Matter?' *The British Journal of Politics and International Culture*, 14.3: 346–356
Taylor, A. (2007) 'Misreading Feminists/Feminists Misreading: Helen Garner, Literary Celebrity and Epitextuality', *Australian Feminist Studies*, 22.52: 73–87
———. (2008) *Mediating Australian Feminism: Rereading the First Stone Media Event*, Oxford: Peter Lang

——. (2014a) 'Germaine Greer's Adaptable Celebrity: Feminism, Unruliness, and Humour on the British Small Screen', *Feminist Media Studies*, 14.5: 759–774

——. (2014b) '"Blockbuster" Celebrity Feminism', *Celebrity Studies*, 5.1–2: 75–78

Templin, C. (1995) *Feminism and the Politics of Literary Reputation: The Example of Erica Jong*, Lawrence: University of Kansas Press

Thomas, S. (2014) 'Celebrity in the "Twitterverse": History, Authenticity and the Multiplicity of Stardom', *Celebrity Studies*, 5.3: 242–255

Thompson, J.B. (2010) *Merchants of Culture: The Publishing Business in the Twenty First Century*, London: Polity

Tomlinson, B. (2005) *Authors on Writing: Metaphors and Intellectual Labour*, Basingstoke: Palgrave Macmillan

Tuchman, G. (1978) *Making News: A Study of the Construction of Reality*, New York: The Free Press

Turner, G. (1993) 'Nationalising the Author: The Celebrity of Peter Carey', *Australian Literary Studies*, 16.2: 131–139

——. (1996) *Literature, Journalism and the Media*, Rockhampton: James Cook University

——. (2014) *Understanding Celebrity*, London: Sage

Turner, G., Marshall, P.D. & Bonner, F. (2000) *Fame Games: The Production of Celebrity in Australia*, Cambridge: Cambridge University Press

Weber, B. (2012) *Women and Literary Celebrity in the Nineteenth Century: The Translantic Production of Fame and Gender*, Farnham: Ashgate

Wheeler, M. (2013) *Celebrity Politics*, London: Polity

Whelehan, I. (2000) *Overloaded: Popular Culture and The Future of Feminism*, London: The Women's Press

——. (2005) *The Feminist Bestseller: From Sex and the Single Girl to Sex and the City*, Basingstoke: Palgrave Macmillan

Wicke, J. (1994) 'Celebrity Material: Materialist Feminism and the Culture of Celebrity', *South Atlantic Quarterly*, 93.4: 751–778

Withers, D. (2015) *Feminism, Digital Culture and the Politics of Transmission*, London: Rowman & Littlefield

Wollstonecraft, M. (1792/2004) *A Vindication on the Rights of Woman*, London: Penguin

Woolf, V. (1929/1977) *A Room of One's Own*, London: Grafton

York, L. (2007) *Literary Celebrity in Canada*, Toronto: University of Toronto Press

——. (2013a) *Margaret Atwood and the Labour of Literary Celebrity*, Toronto: University of Toronto Press

——. (2013b) 'Star Turn: The Challenges of Theorizing Celebrity Agency', *The Journal of Popular Culture*, 46.6: 1330–1347

Young, S. (1997) *Changing the Wor(l)d: Discourse, Politics and the Feminist Movement*, London: Routledge

PART I

The 1960s/1970s Blockbuster and Ongoing Feminist Stardom

In the first part of this book I offer three case studies, dealing with arguably three of the most well-known, highly visible authors of feminist non—fiction in the West. All these women are remarkable in that they continue to be invoked in public engagements with feminism, and especially in terms of the establishment of a second wave collective memory. In particular, these chapters work to foreground the agentic dimensions of celebrity feminism, disrupting the popular critical narrative that it is only in an environment of 'convergence culture' that celebrities have been able to strategically intervene in their own persona management or in the narratives of feminism that come to be privileged in mainstream media.

After decades of feminist activism and change, feminists are now seen to *be* the media (Bulbeck 1997; Curthoys 1997; Lumby 1997), however this certainly was not the case mid-century. The kinds of feminist rhetoric and ideas being publicly articulated, and embodied, by women like Brown, Friedan, and Greer were highly innovative. In the early 1970s in particular, 'the women's movement and feminist ideas were "in the news" for novelty value' (Sheridan et al. 2006, p. 26). As Sheridan et al. note, this novelty has well and truly dissipated and there are now many feminisms being constructed in and through the mediasphere (not least online). However, of the unique political and representational environment of the late 1960s and early 1970s, erstwhile celebrity feminist Kate Millett remarked: 'we were fresh meat for the media' (in Wallace 1997, p. 231). While this may account for the initial 'attention capital' accumulated by these women, how might we explain its maintenance over decades (especially given the dominant critical narrative about inevitable media hostility towards feminists)? The three women examined in this section all 'speak to the particular demands of [their] time' (Baumgardner and Richards 2003, p. 162). However, their celebrity also extends far beyond the 1960s and 1970s, when they initially produced their blockbusters. Rather than their celebrity, or indeed their feminism, having ossified, it can be seen to do new things for new audiences. Furthermore, given the marked differences in their feminisms, their public feminist personas also differ significantly—a point the following chapters will bear out.

These women, along with various cultural intermediaries, work to construct themselves as 'mediagenic authors' (Turner 1996; Moran 2000; Robinson 2013)—not just in the contemporary, purportedly more celebrity-driven context, but when their books were initially published. That they each laboured strenuously to ensure their own, and thus feminism's, visibility is a key factor that unites these three very different women. As Olivier Driessens argues, 'media visibility needs renewal and repetition, hence celebrity capital is founded on recurrent media representations; otherwise it quickly fades' (2013, p. 552). How do these women authors, and the cultural intermediaries invested in them, ensure that this does not happen? What kinds of cultural and textual spaces were made available to them, and how were they used? Most importantly here, in terms of the books' initial publication, if women were accessing feminism predominantly through these celebrities, as I argue many were, what picture of feminism would they have? Furthermore, although the authors continue to be figures of renown, they have also received challenges to their ability to speak authoritatively on/for feminism. Such moments reinforce that celebrity feminism, and the discursive power that purportedly accompanies it, needs to be continually established and re-established, and can never be taken for granted.

Given that the books considered in the first part of this volume have all remained in print to date, they are what have been described in the publishing industry as 'longsellers' (Feather and Woodbridge 2007). In the 1960s and 1970s, many women's links to the women's movement were, as Amy Farrell (1998, p. 12; see also Arrow 2007) reminds us, 'mediated through commercial texts'; while her study focuses on *Ms.* magazine, such comments are also relevant to non-fictional popular texts like feminist blockbusters. These books were crucial in the process of translating feminist ideas for a wider audience; as already noted, they all continue to be culturally visible, suggesting a resonance that few other works of non-fiction can boast. Along these lines, in a *New Yorker* article reassessing the cultural impact of *The Feminine Mystique*, Louis Menand (2013) suggests:

'In the early nineteen-sixties, books, for some reason, were bombs ... Books were always an important force in the women's movement, possibly because the book was a medium that women had relatively unobstructed access to as authors and as readers.' The work of constructing such 'bombs', however, was extensive, a process into which Helen Gurley Brown's archive provides significant insights.

References

Arrow, M. (2007) '"It has become my personal anthem": *I am Woman*, Popular Culture and 1970s Feminism', *Australian Feminist Studies*, 22.53: 213–230

Baumgardner, J. & Richards, A. (2003) 'Who's the New Gloria: The Quest for The Third Wave Super Leader', in R. Dicker & A. Piepmeir eds. *Catching a Wave: Reclaiming Feminism for the Twenty-First Century*, Boston: Northeastern University Press, pp. 159–170

Bulbeck, C. (1997) *Living Feminism: The Impact of the Women's Movement on Three Generations of Australian Women*, Cambridge: Cambridge University Press

Curthoys, A. (1997) 'Where Is Feminism Now?' in J. Mead ed. *Bodyjamming: Sexual Harassment, Feminism and Public Life*, Sydney: Vintage, pp. 189–212

Driessens, O. (2013) 'Celebrity Capital: Redefining Celebrity Using Field Theory', *Theory and Society*, 42: 543–560

Farrell, A.E. (1998) *Yours in Sisterhood: Ms Magazine and the Promise of Popular Feminism*, Chapel Hill: University of North Carolina Press

Feather, J. & Woodbridge, H. (2007) 'Bestsellers in the British Publishing Industry, 1998–2005', *Publishing Research Quarterly*, 23.3: 210–223

Lumby, C. (1997) *Bad Girls: The Media, Sex and Feminism in the 1990s*, StLeonards: Allen & Unwin

Menand, L. (2013) Books as Bombs, 24 January, *The New Yorker*, accessed via http://www.newyorker.com/magazine/2011/01/24/books-as-bombs

Moran, J. (2000) *Star Authors: Literary Celebrity in America*, London: Pluto

Robinson, D. (2013) Novel Forms and Brand New Relations: Exploring Convergence Culture and Australian Literary Celebrity, *Limina*, pp. 1–12, accessed via http://www.limina.arts.uwa.edu.au

Sheridan, S., Magarey, S. & Lilburn, S. (2006) 'Feminism in the News', in J. Hollows & R. Moseley eds. *Feminism in Popular Culture*, Oxford: Berg, pp. 25–40

Turner, G. (1996) *Literature, Journalism and the Media*, Rockhampton: James Cook University

Wallace, C. (1997) *Greer: Untamed Shrew*, Sydney: Pan Macmillan

CHAPTER 3

Helen Gurley Brown: Prototypical Celebrity Feminism, Cultural Intermediaries, and Agency

INTRODUCTION

Helen Gurley Brown's positioning in relation to feminism has always been contentious, if indeed acknowledged at all. In fact, it has only been recently that her popular books have started to be recuperated by feminist critics for their role in helping to shape public discourses around women's empowerment that now appear largely commonsensical (Genz 2009; Scanlon 2009a, b, c; Taylor 2010, 2012; Whelehan 2012). She was, as fellow celebrity feminist Lena Dunham would suggest in her own blockbuster, the 'bane' of the women's movement (2014, p. xvi). However, it is clear that her most well-known text, *Sex and the Single Girl* (1962), is a popular feminist book that addresses the question of women's sexual agency and pleasure as well as financial independence. Indeed, while debate about whether she 'empowered women to take charge of their lives or self-helped them into good old-fashioned servitude' (Luther 2012) is ongoing, modern forms of popular culture, like the television programme *Sex and the City*, are routinely seen to be indebted to Brown's individualist, liberatory philosophy. As is always the case with the feminist blockbuster, Brown was heavily active in the promotion of her book, and in circulating pro-sex discourses about single women in particular, in ways that are taken for granted now but which were unique at the time of its publication.

Drawing upon archival material from the Sophia Smith Collection, the majority of this chapter works to establish Brown as a central actor in her own persona management, along with other key 'cultural intermediaries'. While the performative aspect of (feminist) celebrity is often seen to be a particularly twenty-first century quality, here I contest dominant critical narratives about the 'newness' of self-branding (Thomas 2014) as well as—like Jennifer Scanlon—seeking to rewrite Brown into not just feminist publishing and media history but the history of modern feminism itself. Although she remains a contested figure for many feminists, this chapter considers how Brown functioned as a prototypical celebrity feminist and concludes by briefly addressing how she used this celebrity to stage feminist interventions into the mediasphere, including through her editorship of *Cosmopolitan*, over a number of years, and how she continues to reverberate in the twenty-first century. First, it is valuable to consider where Brown has been critically positioned vis-à-vis feminism.

In terms of where Brown has been situated in narratives of the American second wave, Scanlon notes that most tend to argue that Betty Friedan's *The Feminine Mystique* (see Chap. 4 this volume) was the spark that helped ignite the women's movement. Such accounts rarely 'acknowledge—never mind consider—Helen Gurley Brown' (Scanlon 2009a, p. 94). Despite the elision of Brown as a key feminist figure in academic histories of modern feminism, '*Sex and the Single Girl*, like Betty Friedan's *The Feminine Mystique*, introduced feminist thinking to millions of readers, documented both women's aspirations and their discontents, and refused to apologize for its bold demands for women' (Scanlon 2009a, p. 94). Indeed, as Scanlon emphasizes, Brown sought to broaden and effectively shift the terms of the public debate about women and liberation, focusing not on women in the domestic sphere, as Friedan had done, but by displaying an alternative mode of feminine subjectivity outside the traditional roles of wife and mother. Brown and her 'brand' of feminism, focusing on sexual empowerment, desire, agency, and financial independence, effectively complicates the wave model and the idea of a homogeneous second wave feminism that emerged in the 1960s and 1970s; the example of Brown, especially, reveals instead that there were competing feminisms circulating in and through the mediasphere (Scanlon 2009a)—including through the blockbuster form.

This chapter, and indeed my previous work on Brown (Taylor 2010, 2012), is consistent with the feminist recuperation pursued by Scanlon (and others since; Genz 2010), largely by placing Brown—as an agentic figure whose celebrity practice can be seen as distinctly feminist—at its centre. Building upon the idea that the savvy Brown 'successfully manipulated the power of media culture' for feminist ends (Scanlon 2009b, p. 2), this case study provides some significant insights into the blockbuster as a vehicle for feminist celebrification, as well as the role of the individual author in ensuring her book's, and indeed her own, ongoing viability as a commodity. Initially, it is necessary to engage with Brown's blockbuster and the kind of innovative feminism it offered readers in the early 1960s.

Sex and the Single Girl as a Feminist Blockbuster

Sex and the Single Girl was published in May 1962; within its first three weeks it had sold over 2 million copies; and by July it appeared on the *New York Times* bestseller list (where it remained for seven months) as well as those published by *Time*, the *Los Angeles Times* (Douglas 1994, p. 68; Scanlon 2009a, p. 58), and the *New York Post*, where it was also serialized. When it originally circulated, it was not explicitly identified as a 'feminist' text, though its indebtedness to feminism is patent. How then did it and its flamboyant author contribute to the construction of feminism's public identity, as I argue here? Although it does not actually invoke the term feminism, *Sex and the Single Girl* can be considered a form of 'popular feminism' in the sense defined by Le Masurier: 'Popular feminism encompasses the exploration, translation and making of women's [and sexual] liberation for ordinary women in some examples of popular media' (2010, p. 218; see also Hollows and Moseley 2006). Without doubt, the audience of *Sex and The Single Girl* would have been women who were unlikely otherwise to have come into contact with feminist ideas or discourses. With it, then, Brown effectively 'translated' sexual liberation for a broad audience of women, as Le Masurier has argued is the case with women's magazines, and thereby she helped inform how feminism came to mean in the popular imaginary. Accordingly, the bestselling *Sex and the Single Girl* can easily be identified as a 'feminist blockbuster'. Moreover, in 1962 America, 'the nation's readers and pundits could barely stop talking about it' (Scanlon 2009a, p. 58), and in this sense it fulfils what has been identified as one of the constitutive elements of the feminist blockbuster (Lilburn et al. 2000; Taylor 2008): that it precipitates intense public debate and discursive contestation around gender and feminism itself. The fact that people could not 'stop talking about it' was, however, no mere accident, but was rather the product of an orchestrated campaign by Brown and her publishers to ensure that the book—and, even more importantly for my purposes, its author and her feminist brand—remained firmly in the media spotlight over many decades.

Like many feminist blockbusters, especially those considered here in chapters 6-8, *Sex and the Single Girl* is in many ways a form of memoir. In a television interview conducted by fellow celebrity feminist Gloria Steinem, Brown is insistent about this, while also drawing attention to how controversial her book was, given its frankness about women's sexuality: 'When I got around to writing "Sex and the Single Girl", I could only write about what I knew and I had had a number of men in life before David—he knew that—it was what I knew. I wrote about what I knew. I didn't realize until later how upset everyone was going to be.'[1] As Pearce (2004) has underscored, the use of personal experience as an authorizing discourse has always been common in feminist non-fictional texts, and Brown's blockbuster is no exception. In fact, her authority to speak is largely predicated upon the strategies she had personally deployed as a single woman. As Scanlon notes: 'Her claim to fame was neither a degree nor a pedigree; she simply spoke from experience' (2009b, p. 8).

In this regard, Brown's autobiographical voice is strong in her newspaper and magazine articles, as well as her 'manuals' for the single girl. In addition to *Having It All* (1982), itself a form of memoir that deploys similar rhetorical strategies to her earlier works, she published an autobiography in 2000 (*I'm Wild Again: Snippets from My Life and a Few Brazen Thoughts*). Along with her editorials and other journalistic pieces, she continued to publish works of non-fiction throughout her life (though, as is characteristic of this form, none would attain the 'blockbuster' status of her non-fictional debut). These include: *Outrageous Opinions* (1967), *The Single Girl's Cookbook* (1969), *Sex and the New Single Girl* (1970), *The Late Show: A Practical, Semiwild Survival Guide for Every Woman in Her Prime Or Approaching It* (1994), *The Writer's Rules: The Power of Positive Prose—How to Create It and Get It Published* (1998), and *Dear Pussycat: Mash Notes and Missives from the Desk of Cosmopolitan's Legendary Editor* (2004). Given that Brown's renown is so deeply implicated in the publication of her first book, it is worthwhile to briefly consider the book, its rhetorical strategies, and its politics.

Prior to the period of intense activism around women's rights that became known as the second wave of feminism in the late 1960s and early 1970s, the question of women's liberation was, albeit perhaps more obliquely than in the radical feminist tracts that came to characterize the movement, receiving public attention (Taylor 2010). With *Sex and the Single Girl* (1962), Brown differed from others engaging in feminist critique at the time: 'In order to pursue the ideal of equality, feminists in the early 1960s were keen to abolish markers of difference—such as femininity...' (Genz 2009, p. 38). In Brown's framework, femininity was definitely not conceptualized as a form of victimization, as it was for other writers, including Friedan (Genz 2009; see also Scanlon 2009a). Rather than rejecting behaviours and appearances traditionally coded 'feminine', she suggested women strategically use them to their advantage, in both the public and the private spheres–especially if they were single.

For Brown, the single woman, in particular, was believed to require advice on how to live a more fulfilled, and in many ways (sexually) empowered, life. She apparently faced unique dilemmas, both personal and professional, that necessitated friendly yet authoritative intervention. Although feminists have criticized her approach as 'insufficiently collective', heterosexist, and infantilizing (Scanlon 2009a, p. 78), Brown's book clearly helped to contest dominant ways of circumscribing femininity. However, in contrast to later, more radical feminist writing, the strategies she advocated were micro-political and, as Whelehan argues, Brown's blockbuster 'encourages women to fight in their corner as individuals rather than encourage any more radical social challenges' (2005, p. 29). In this regard, it is a clear antecedent of later feminist blockbusters considered here, such as Sheryl Sandberg's *Lean In*.

Brown's two most well-known books, *Sex and the Single Girl* (1962) and *Sex and the Office*[2] (1964), are nevertheless remarkable for their views on women's sexual agency and desire—especially given that even uttering the word 'sex' on television was highly controversial at the time (Scanlon 2009a, p. 88). As David Allyn remarks, 'Brown packaged sexual liberalism for early-sixties America as only an advertising copywriter could' (2000, p. 19). With Brown's popular feminist texts in the early 1960s, the single woman morphed from dowdy, asexual spinster to a pleasure-seeking, unabashedly sexual subject. Contra dominant discourses, there was nothing undesirable about the single girl in Brown's account. As a British reviewer put it during Brown's UK book tour, the purpose of Brown's book 'is to point out that the unmarried girl is not a failure' (*Evening Chronicle*, 5 November, 1964).[3] But while, as some critics have recently emphasized (Genz 2009; Scanlon 2009a), Brown's assertions about women's sexual agency are laudable, the end game was still to find and secure a mate; the single girl of her popular texts would conceivably, at some point, 'settle down'. The single girl, for Brown, might choose to enjoy this transitory state but she would never choose to indefinitely embrace this liminality. Nonetheless, 'the single woman', Brown argues,

> far from being a creature to be pitied and patronized, is emerging as the newest glamour girl of our times. She is engaging because she lives by her wits. She supports herself. She has had to sharpen her personality and mental resources to a glitter in order to survive in a competitive world and the sharpening looks good. Economically she is a dream. She is not a parasite, a dependent, a scrounger, a sponger or a bum. She is a giver, not a taker, a winner and not a loser. (1962/2003, pp. 5–6)

Here, she draws attention to the single girl as an important consumer category, economically independent and agentic. Brown was entirely cognizant of her own pivotal role in bringing the 'single girl' subject position into being; as she remarks in a letter to Letty Cottin: 'The more I think about it the more it seems to me we are defining and bringing into focus a new kind of person' (30 April 1962). This 'new person', therefore, would require expert guidance on how to navigate the murky terrain of inequitable gender relations, and to use all the capital she had at hand—be it social, educational, or corporeal—to position herself at a distinct advantage.

Sex and the Single Girl is, therefore, a form of self-help book; as one reviewer remarked, the book is 'a manual of sorts for sexy spinsters' (Fimrite 1962). Covering everything from recipes for the single girl's dinner parties, make-up tips, where to meet men, financial advice, through to how to 'manage' an affair with a married man, Brown notes: 'It's a practical book which deals with the everyday problems of the single girl' (in Buchwald 1962). For Brown, however, the single girl's identity predominantly comes from her positioning in the workplace not, like previous generations of women, the home (Radner 1999, p. 12). 'A job', she tells readers, 'gives a single woman something to *be*' (Brown 2003, p. 89, original emphasis), and, unlike married women, 'A single woman is known for what she does rather than whom she belongs to' (Brown 2003, p. 89). Unlike the 'unhappy housewives' Friedan was soon to identify, Brown's single girls were not defined solely relation to men (or, relatedly, children) but had a freedom that eluded their married sisters; however, largely ignoring differences between women as well as systemic factors, in many ways she overstates their ability to fully control their destiny.

Nevertheless, 'Brown's often witty, and indeed *risqué* for the time of its production, narrative voice confides in her readers... She speaks from the other side: she was the single girl of/to whom she speaks but, with a sigh of relief, married in her late thirties. Brown buttresses her observations and instructions with tales of her own successful enactment of these life-altering strategies; the book clearly implies that its author can be trusted because she has *lived* it' (Taylor 2010, p. 81). She was, therefore, the personal embodiment of her brand of feminism. Her narrative voice ensured her positioning as 'both expert and friend', and the book's advice contrasted markedly with that being doled out to women through outlets like *Ladies Home Journal* (Scanlon 2009a, pp. 86–7). Seeking to normalize women's desire, for both sex and an autonomous identity, her affirmation of singleness as a viable way of being in the world clearly struck a chord in her implied readers. As Geis notes in a memo to their sales team, 'Letters are pouring in from women who say that this book has done more for them than a psychoanalysis, that it makes them proud of being single' (26 June 1962; see also Alexander 1963).[4] Therefore, her book resonated with single women readers, who seemed to appreciate Brown's legitimation of their 'Single Girl' identities.[5] Such public affirmation seems even more remarkable now, given the ongoing, and indeed intensified, pathologization and regulation of women's singleness (Taylor 2012).

In terms of historical context, Brown's blockbuster appeared around the time the contraceptive pill was becoming more widely available and the so-called 'sexual revolution'[6] was burgeoning, with women's sexuality becoming detached from reproduction and recognized as not confined to the marital boudoir: 'Theoretically, a "nice" single girl has no sex life. What nonsense! She has a better sex life than most of her married friends. She need never be bored with one man per lifetime. Her choice of partners is endless and they seek *her*' (Brown 2003, p. 7, original emphasis). Sex for women, like a living space solely their own (Brown 2003, p. 119), within *Sex and the Single Girl* is seen as one of life's essentials, and Brown even provides a chapter devoted to schooling readers in 'How to be Sexy' (Chap. 4). As she remarked in a promotional interview, 'I don't think the single girl should suffer for having a normal libido' (in Buchwald 1962). In its emphasis on the liberatory aspects of female sexuality, Brown's blockbuster, perhaps surprisingly, actually has much in common with Greer's later work. And as was often the case with the feminist blockbuster, early reviews reveal that the book had a polarizing effect. A number of reviewers were concerned about its potential impact on sexual morality, while others deemed it, both in terms of the writing style and content, 'pedestrian at best' (Scanlon 2009a, p. 91). For example, L. Kirsch in the *Los Angeles Times* branded it 'as tasteless a book as I have read' and, because of its recommendation that women effectively manipulate the men in their lives, he criticized what he believed to be its contemptuous attitude towards men (in Alexander 1963). In contrast, some commentators applauded 'the book's liberating effect on readers' (Scanlon 2009a, p. 91), and a number of journalists reported on Brown's inundation by fan mail and letters from single women seeking advice from the author (Buchwald 1962; *New York Post*, 11 November 1962, p. 16; Alexander 1963). As Brown noted, single women readers remarked on her book's authenticity: 'Yes, yes, someone should have done this before. This is how it really is' (in Berman 1962).

Through both her non-fiction and decades-long editorship of *Cosmopolitan*, Brown is now seen to have influenced public conceptualizations of women, sexuality, and feminism itself in important ways.[7] *Sex and the Single Girl*, however, did not simply organically emerge as a feminist blockbuster; much labour, including on the part of the author herself, was expended to ensure that Brown's form of feminism would reach as wide an audience as possible—and, no less important to its author, that it would also be a lucrative project. The next section, accordingly, will establish how the book and its feminist author as media celebrity were effectively brought into being through various promotional strategies and initiatives.

Manufacturing a Blockbuster, Manufacturing a (Feminist) Star

As noted in the previous chapter, throughout this work I seek to underscore the star agency of these specific feminists. However, 'celebrities are [not] the sole authors of their own images, free to present whatever they want' but rather are reliant upon a network of professionals (Williams 2007, p. 120; Turner 2014). Letters between Brown and her publisher reveal a dynamic, collaborative relationship in which all parties were self-reflexive actors working to ensure the book's, and concomitantly its author's, success (and, in the process, expose a larger audience to her valorization of women's singleness). As Brown herself assured publisher Bernard Geis, 'we three [Brown and her husband David Brown] continue to be a team and that our stake in you and yours in me is unassailable both on the basis of enlightened self-interest and genuine affection and esteem' (10 January 1963). As part of what Geis would later refer to as 'Operation Brown–Geis' (Geis to Brown, 16 April 1963), this 'team' would exchange ideas, suggestions, and strategies to capitalize on and develop the Brown brand and ensure the public circulation of her (for some, controversial) feminism (Scanlon 2009a).

The letters of Bernard Geis and Letty Cottin suggest that Brown's publisher was zealous in the book's—and indeed the author's—promotion: 'We have a special interest in keeping SEX AND THE SINGLE GIRL in the public mind and eye' (Geis to Jim Russell, 19 November 1962). In this section, drawing upon Brown's archival material from the Sophia Smith Collection, as well as Scanlon's work, I will emphasize how these figures functioned as 'cultural intermediaries', who strenuously worked, in tandem with the author herself, to ensure Brown's viability as a (feminist) public persona. This material problematizes the critical presumption, outlined in the previous chapter, that feminists have merely been passive victims of celebrification; rather, well before the era of convergence culture, they can be seen to have successfully intervened in the construction and management of their own celebrity signs. Here I challenge these narratives, arguing that the feminist celebrity has always functioned as an agentic figure—a point that I will develop in each of the subsequent case studies.

As many scholars have argued, the cultivation and maintenance of celebrity is big business (Gamson 1994; Turner 2014). In terms of book publishing, the network involved in ensuring an author becomes a celebrity includes the publisher themselves, literary agents, marketing representatives, and, not least, the author herself. Brown provides an especially useful case study into these mutually beneficial relationships. Cultural intermediaries, in Pierre Bourdieu's (1993) sense, are seen as the bridge between production and consumption. Bourdieu, Rojek tells us, 'aims to underline the socially constructed character of celebrity status'. To do so, 'Bourdieu maintains that artistic practice and association are indissolubly enmeshed with a field of changing balance of power relationships in which cultural intermediaries are understood to be central' (2014, pp. 457–8). In such a framework, cultural intermediaries can be seen as 'star-makers who take it upon themselves to determine sound methods for engineering renown …' (Rojek 2014, p. 466). The correspondence between Brown (and her husband) and staff at Bernard Geis and Associates certainly provides insight into such calculated 'methods', but also shows that the author herself played a crucial a role in 'engineering such renown'. In this way, they demonstrate that the strategies and tactics she encouraged her single girls to adopt, both personally and professionally, to ensure their success were also deployed by the author herself.

As noted above, books that become bestsellers are heavily reliant upon an extensive network of professionals to help create a 'buzz' (Thompson 2010) around the text, especially pre-publication. As Claude Martin (1996) notes of bestsellers and the unique promotional environment around them:

> The marketing of bestsellers is different from that of other books. They receive special treatment, more copies are printed, promotional budgets are higher, authors are pushed onto the television stage, free copies are given to journalists in liberal quantities, bookstores are advised of the author's appearances on television and are supplied with displays or posters … Each of these features aims to create a social and media event, to foster a 'bestseller atmosphere' around the book. They weld together links of production and distribution of a book, establishing confidence in the performance of a book.

Consistent with these comments, letters between staff at Geis and Brown reveal that pre-publicity efforts around the book were extensive, and included its widespread serialization.[8] The tactic they favoured, as Cottin makes clear, was the '"*Everybody* is talking about SEX AND THE SINGLE GIRL" approach', which included endorsements and testimonials from Hollywood celebrities like Joan Crawford (14 March 1962, Cottin to Brown, original emphasis).

In 1962, the 3 June issue of *American Weekly*, a Sunday supplement carried by newspapers including the *Los Angeles Herald Examiner*, *San Francisco Examiner*, and the *Seattle Times*, consisted solely of extracts from the book and advertising material.[9] As Cottin wrote: 'This is completely unprecedented and demonstrates the exceptional appeal they believe this book offers the nation's women' (to Brown, 26 April 1962). The deal, which *Publishers Weekly* (1962) reported to be worth 'tens of thousands of dollars', also included teaser-style advertisements in the ten papers to be run three days before the supplement was issued, while the supplement itself featured an announcement regarding the upcoming edition which included a picture of its author as well as the book jacket. Newspaper delivery trucks also featured advertisements and radio and television[10] stations ran announcements of the upcoming issue. It was billed as 'A complete issue devoted to a digest of a sure-fire best seller'. The serialization itself received media coverage and was credited with rendering the book's *risqué* material acceptable, effectively normalizing its content. As Brown told the *New York Post*: 'When I first came to New York to publicize my book, the book was considered taboo and there were certain television shows I couldn't appear on.' After its serialization, she continued, 'it became apparent that the book was truthful and done with taste. Now I can make my appearance on any program I please' (in *New York Post*, 11 November 1962, p. 16). Following the edition, Geis also paid for a large advertisement, encouraging readers to follow up by purchasing the book, which the ad declared 'the book that made publishing history'.[11] All these promotional efforts serve to illustrate that 'the selling of a book has happened long before it reaches the bookshop' (Gardiner 2000, p. 66). And, of course, the author's public persona is central to this process, and additional commodities related to the initial product represent a common means of extending the author's visibility.

As van Krieken (2012, p. 54) argues, 'The economic network around the celebrity is extensive, restricted only by the imagination of the celebrity and their management.' There were a number of lucrative spin-offs, including a record—'Lessons in Love'—a cookbook, and a Hollywood movie; indicative of his role as a key cultural intermediary, Brown's husband, David, secured all these deals (Scanlon 2009a). As he wrote, 'the book has become an industry in itself'.[12] He even investigated the possibility of a Monopoly-style board game (David Brown to James Shea, 17 December 1963) and a musical based on the book (Lucy Kroll to Browns, 4 January 1963), which they decided to shelve pending the Warner Brothers movie deal. Helping to raise the book's public profile even further, its film adaptation, starring Natalie Wood as the single sex expert 'Dr Brown' and Tony Curtis as the cad she reluctantly falls for, appeared in 1964:[13] 'In selling the rights Brown had achieved what she wanted from the adaptation—an extension of brand Brown' (Whelehan 2012, p. 6).

Such cross-platform initiatives make clear that 'marketing and public relations plainly dominate in the pursuit and management of public attention for profit' (Meyer and Gamson 1995, p. 184). While seeking 'public attention for profit' has been seen as antithetical to feminism, such attention ensured that feminism, or ideas broadly consistent with it, became accessible to a wide audience. In addition to targeted advance copies and advertisements in major newspapers and magazines, including the *New York Sunday Times Book Review*, *Esquire*, *Cosmopolitan*, *Mademoiselle*, *Redbook*, and the *Los Angeles Sunday Examiner* (Memo from Geis to sales group, 26 June 1962), the carefully orchestrated promotional strategies around the book included an extensive book tour, spanning radio, television, and newspaper interviews, as well as signings in local bookstores, starting with Chicago on 18 May, and followed by New York from 21 May, where Brown appeared on the *Tonight Show*, with similar tours in Los Angeles and San Francisco to follow in June.[14] Brown featured on over thirty television and radio programmes in the year of the book's publication (Scanlon 2009b, p. 1). Schedules contained in the Sophia Smith Collection reveal just how gruelling these promotional activities were,[15] as well as how its author responded to them.

Collaborative Feminist Star-Makers

On delicate sheets of pink paper, Brown's typed letters to her publisher, Bernard Geis, and her marketing representative, Letty Cottin (Director of Promotion at Geis),[16] exhibit a clear consciousness of the need to strategize to ensure the book's commercial success—and secure her own (and thus feminism's) visibility. While scholars have previously drawn upon these letters, especially Scanlon, none have yet done so through the conceptual lens supplied by celebrity studies and its critical emphasis upon the construction of public personhood. Throughout 1962 and 1963, Geis and Cottin regularly wrote to Brown, not simply to keep her informed about the myriad promotional initiatives but to seek her opinion on and response to their plans; letters are commonly dated just days apart, especially those between Cottin and Brown. Although the letters' rhetorical strategies could themselves be subject to sustained analysis, what is most illuminating about them, for my purposes, is the level of collaboration around not just the book's promotion but its author's. Furthermore, they explicitly invoke the rhetoric of stardom and fame-building; that is, they were all clearly 'agents in the reputation-making process' (Templin 1995, p. 12). Before the book's publication Brown was to write to Geis: 'I know you are not in business to develop girl writer personalities …' (5 March 1962). However, this turned out to be very far from the truth; this was precisely Geis's 'business', and his role in establishing Brown's renown has been underscored by various commentators (Didion 1965; Scanlon 2009a; Whelehan 2012), but Cottin played an equally crucial part in this process.

Brown and Cottin's letters have an exceptionally affectionate tone, often ending with 'love' and/or kisses, and intimate salutations, and commonly range between three and six pages. In addition to this clear sense of mutual affection is evidence of their commitment to a singular goal. As Cottin explicitly makes clear in a letter to Brown, 'we have one common objective: to make SEX AND THE SINGLE GIRL and Helen Gurley Brown the most famous eight words in America' (8 November 1962). Indicative of just how active the author was in the promotional strategies around her book, a letter from Cottin to the author dated 14 March 1962 commences: 'Hark: The time has come to go to your cerebral file cabinet and pull out the folder containing your promotional thinking cap.'[17] Brown was not simply provided with a promotional plan which she was then expected to obediently follow. On the contrary, she was one of the key architects of the multi-pronged strategy that would help guarantee that the book's controversial position was widely disseminated (Scanlon 2009a). With a professional background in advertising, Brown herself recognized: 'It's *such* an exploitable subject' (to Cottin, 26 March 1962 original emphasis), and set out to 'exploit' it she certainly did. She regularly sent Cottin lists of industry representatives and relevant personalities to whom copies of the book should be sent in the hope of endorsement or further advertising possibilities, as well as having copies of the book circulated among secretaries at various agencies (Brown to Cottin, 10 April 1962).

This correspondence also reveals an orchestrated attempt at censorship: 'A little bit of censorship in the right place won't hurt' (Cottin to Brown, 14 March 1962). As Scanlon remarks, 'both Letty Cottin and Helen Gurley Brown proved relentless in their [promotional] efforts and conspired on another strategy to capitalize on the controversial sexiness of the book and its title: a book ban' (2009a, p. 89). Though the US ban itself did not eventuate (it was later banned in the Republic of Ireland as well as Spain), these letters are indicative of the degree of careful planning and attempted (though in many respects always impossible) management of the book's reception. Although they also often involved David Brown, the collaboration between Cottin and Brown arguably invokes the kinds of collectivist feminist practices that Cottin would later implement as co-founding editor of *Ms.* magazine. Clearly committed to what would later become known as 'consciousness-raising', both Brown and Cottin (like all the women here) were well aware that they had to 'generally play the system in order to get feminist messages to mass audiences of women' (Scanlon 2009b, p. 12).

In response to the pre-publication *American Weekly* edition devoted solely to sections of her book, Brown writes to Cottin: 'What a coup the American Weekly issue is! I guess we've just got a very promotable subject ... Lots has been written about single women before but only in the shuffle-them-under-the-rug sort of way' (27 April 1962). Here Brown exhibits an awareness of the innovative narrative that she is seeking to sell, and it is clear that her attempt to refigure women's singleness was in itself a feminist project. She also suggests that various agents be enlisted to promote the book, providing Cottin with a list of names she remarks: 'Now, Letty, the next three people are all high-powered agents who, while they can't exactly publicise the book are all capable of yapping about it quite a bit' (27 April 1962). This public discourse, or 'yapping', about the book is central to keeping it quite literally in circulation (Foucault 1969; Mills 1998), something of which Brown is acutely aware.

There is no doubt that the author was at the centre of this campaign, and, as is always the case with blockbuster feminists, author and narrator were persistently conflated. For example, Cottin suggests that newspapers like the *New York Times* should be approached about an article focusing on Brown, underscoring that her personal life narrative is central to the book's commercial viability:

> Seriously, you are that *rara avis*—an agency copywriter turned author who draws her literary material from her personel [sic] agency experience. Obviously the legions of single women working in the huge agencies as secretaries, clerks, traffic department gal fridays, etc., will be fascinated with a book whose research virtually eminates [sic] from their real life experiences. (original emphasis, 14 March 1962)

Consistent with this emphasis on Brown herself, and the book's testimonial aspects, promotional material sent out to booksellers included a photograph, a press release, a biographical portrait of the author, and a book blurb (see letter from Cottin to Brown, 30 March 1962). Such images, taken by professional photographers, work to conflate the identity of author and text, and serve to 'literally circulate the author' (Gardiner 2000, p. 260). Through the pre-packaging of the press release, 'publicists decrease the uncertainty of coverage content', effectively offering 'the celebrity in a standardized, controlled, packaged form' (Gamson 1994, pp. 87, 93; see also Turner 2014, 2016). These promotional efforts, and the money that would have been invested in them, suggest that Geis was indeed committed to ensuring the book's—and, more saliently here, its author's—'pre-publication visibility' (Gardiner 2000, p. 66). Although Genette (1997) effectively dismisses the publisher's epitext, which includes the kind of promotional material outlined above, Gardiner argues that it is as central to the meanings given to a literary work as other aspects of its paratext (2000, p. 274)–especially when, as in the case of Brown, it foregrounds the author.

The multi-pronged, author-centric, promotional campaign does appear to have been a success, especially given that the book came to be represented on a number of bestseller lists, including number one on the *New York Times'* coveted list. Reporting on its appearance on such lists, Cottin astutely observes: 'In much the same way that money breeds money, bestseller listings breed bestseller behavior so this should be self-nourishing' (to Brown, 25 July 1962). The appellation 'bestseller' signifies a form of value that undeniably works to inform future consumer behaviour. Although the bestseller list and its methodology may be questionable, as Miller reminds us in her discussion of the *New York Times* list, it is important in terms of enhancing the book's future commercial success:

> While the ability of the *Times* list to reflect accurately which books are the country's top sellers is dubious, its ability to *sell* books is unquestionably tremendous ... once a book makes the *Times* list, the achievement is trumpeted in all further promotional material, the book is sought out by readers who habitually read best-sellers, and it is given special treatment by retailers. In their print and broadcast advertisements, publishers make the best-selling status of a book its most notable feature. Indeed, if the promotional machine was not already on before a title made the list, it soon goes into full force in order to capitalize on the book's apparent mass-market appeal. (2000, p. 294)

As Miller implies, the invocation of the *Times* bestseller status becomes an important part of the book's paratext, acting as a marker of the work's value as it does with all the blockbusters examined here. Along with Brown's own extensive efforts (Scanlon 2009a), such success was clearly the result of the labour of the key cultural intermediaries I have been discussing.

Brown and these intermediaries were interested in 'anything to spread the name and fame of HGB and Sex' (to Geis, 8 December 1962). These letters make it clear that the process of cultivating renown was one they explicitly discussed, and indeed was a goal that both author and publisher actively sought; one initiative that they discussed as potentially boosting both her profile and book sales was her syndication as a weekly columnist (Geis to David Brown, 16 August 1962). Following negotiations by all these key actors, Brown's 'Woman Alone' syndicated column appeared in around 75 US newspapers between 1963 and 1965 (Hunt 2012, p. 134; Scanlon 2009a).[18] This extended her reach well beyond the readers of her book; and she herself noted that it gave her 'several million readers over whom I exert some influence' (in Hunt 2012, p. 134). Indeed, like the other books examined here, *Sex and the Single Girl* ensured that her innovative, feminist refiguration of women's singleness could be extended into other popular forms, including women's magazines, whose implied readers were arguably the same as those of her blockbuster.

As Graeme Turner (2014, p. 156) contends, 'When we conceptualise celebrity as something to be professionally managed, as well as discursively deconstructed, we think about it differently.' Likewise, when we conceptualize it as something to be actively performed (as well as 'managed') by the individual who is celebrified, we are also able to think about it in new ways. The case of Brown complicates the argument, critiqued in Chap. 2 of this volume, that celebrity is externally *done to* a veridical individual who can be readily separated from the self being constructed via the discourses of celebrity.[19] This conceptual shift, from the processes of celebrification being viewed as externally imposed and grudgingly endured by reluctant individuals to being seen as an integral part of their creative persona-building labour, is necessary if we are to reposition celebrity feminists as active agents. In Brown's case, such labour did not go publicly unnoticed. As Joan Didion (1965) pondered, 'What is it like to be the little princess, the woman who has fulfilled the whispered promise of her own books and of all the advertisements, the girl to whom things happen? It is hard work.' This observation is an important one in terms of celebrification, for rarely is such labour so publicly laid bare. It was also recognized by Geis himself, who attributed the book's success, in part, to Brown's own promotional labour: 'We couldn't be more tickled with the way the book is rolling, *nor the way in which you are accelerating its happy progress!*' (Geis to Brown, 9 July 1962, emphasis added). Her fame, too, and her role in her own success, was also the subject of media coverage; for example, eliding the role of those who co-produced 'Brown', in *Life* magazine she takes full responsibility for the 'fame, money, and success the book has brought. "It's me, me, me! That's what's so heady about it", she crows' (Alexander 1963). These letters reveal, however, that celebrification also had its limitations for this blockbuster author.

The Toll of Celebrity

In her article in the *Saturday Evening Post*, which covers Brown's *Sex and the Office* book tour, Didion offers a 'day-in-the-life' style narrative of Brown's frenetic promotional activities and presciently remarks:

> To talk to Helen Brown in the waning days of the 13-week promotional tour of the United States and England was to talk to a very tired woman indeed, a woman weary of flirting with disc jockeys, tired of parrying insults and charming interviewers and fighting for a five-minute spot here and a guest appearance there, exhausted by writing her syndicated column in airports on typewriters borrowed from her press agents and by waking up in different time zones ... (Didion 1965)

This idea that celebrity culture takes a large, not least physical and psychological, toll on those reliant upon it is one commonly invoked (Rojek 2001; Moran 2000), including by blockbuster authors. As Gamson (2006, p. 718) argues, 'Celebrities are manufactured as attention-getting bodies, a process complicated but not negated by the fact that celebrities are human beings.' The letters examined throughout this chapter, while of course acts of self-construction, provide unique insight into these complications.

Brown herself is also candid about the personal toll of celebrification. Discursively positioning herself as somewhat of a victim, she confesses to Geis: 'when you are a new writer and are sent on a promotion trip it's like winning a contest and the prize is a trip around the world! Then apparently after you become/successful writer [sic] the aspects of promotion change subtly and it's more like a duty than a glamour binge' (10 October 1962). Given that scant attention has been given to how celebrities have experienced and interpreted their fame, with the focus instead being on 'fans and celebrity watchers' (Marwick 2013, p. 148), these letters offer significant insights into Brown's perspective on the pressures, and drawbacks, of celebrification. In this letter, although conceding the value of her promotional duties, she can be seen to push back against the demands being placed upon her by the publishers: 'The more promotion we do the better it is for *me* of course—we're all in this—however I vaguely resent that it is simply assumed a few more days will be fine' (original emphasis). Although Brown here acknowledges the collaborative process of fame-building, and its collective benefits, she is careful to position herself firmly at the centre of this endeavour. She also explicitly, and strategically, draws attention to her own status as a valuable commodity to the publishing company: 'I am something of a little *star* now! I make a lot of money for us' (original emphasis). Brown recognizes, then, that as a celebrity she is a 'financial asset to those who stand to gain from [her] commercialisation' (Turner 2014, p. 37). In this way, 'the development of a celebrity's public persona is … a serious business' (Turner 2014, p. 37). Here she seeks to leverage this celebrity capital for some more agency in decisions about the length and scope of her book tours; she attempts to use her value to the publishing company to wrestle back some control over her own publicity schedule, and is successful in this endeavour.[21]

These letters also reveal that Brown does not experience any of the discomfort with her own commodification that appeared to dog other feminists; for the 'Brown' that emerges from these epistolary texts, there are no moral or ethical issues with monetizing her own particular version of women's empowerment, and, unlike Greer, she does not frame publicity as a necessary evil. Indeed, it is an integral part of her putting her feminist philosophy into practice. Brown is acutely aware of, and indeed celebrates, her own marketability and profitability; as she unabashedly boasts to Didion (1965): 'They can't put me off by hinting I write to make money … I love money. And I'm promotable. Some people aren't …' The politics/commerce tension simply does not exist for Brown as it has for other feminists (Murray 2004), and she is aware of how central her own public persona is to her book's commercial success—as well as herself as a viable commodity. As Turner (2014, p. 37) notes, the celebrity's 'personal objective is most likely to be the construction of a viable career through the astute distribution and regulation of their celebrity-commodity'. This is clearly something that Brown and those dependent on her marketability for their own commercial success (predominantly her publishers) factored in as they planned her myriad interventions into the market.

What these letters elucidate is the fundamentally collaborative nature of celebrity-making—as labour in which a number of actors, with varying degrees of literal and affective investment in Brown and her controversial text, are engaged. In addition to her own efforts, Geis, Cottin, and her husband David[22] were all committed to ensuring the book's, and the author's, cultural visibility across a number of media platforms—be it television, women's magazines, newspapers, or radio. Geis and his staff held the firm view that 'marketing a book must, by necessity, be a multimedia event' (Scanlon 2009a, p. 88). This mounts a challenge to the idea that only in the present does the promotional apparatus surrounding bestselling books cross a myriad of media platforms.

These letters also suggest how securing discursive spaces in which Brown could speak, and thereby in which her critique of various assumptions underpinning normative femininity could circulate, such as syndicated columns, did not simply organically occur but was the product of active intervention by these key cultural intermediaries. That is, recognizing the celebrity as a co-creation, they make clear that 'fame does not advance by accretion, but by design' (Rojek 2011, p. 15)—something of which Brown (and her husband) appeared acutely aware. In terms of Brown herself, they function to destabilize dominant narratives around women's lack of agency in celebrity networks. In particular, they work to fracture the assumption that women generally, and feminists specifically, only became actors in the construction of their 'brands' in the twenty-first century (where, although the emergence of new media has seen opportunities for self-branding expand, the persona management tactics remain the same as for earlier forms of stardom (Thomas 2014)). On the contrary, through archival material, this section has shown not just that celebrification is processual, but that the labour of celebrity has been something in which women—including the blockbuster feminist author—have been productively implicated in over many decades, and with long-lasting effects. It has also revealed that discomfort about celebrification certainly did not haunt all feminists who were in the public spotlight. In the concluding section, underscoring Brown's ongoing cultural reverberations, I build upon this analysis to briefly consider how Brown's 'single girl' morphed into the 'Cosmo girl', how the celebrity author transformed into the celebrity editor, as well as considering the implications of this move for popular (and indeed post-) feminism.

Brown's Fame Post-*Sex and the Single Girl*

It appears that Brown's active attempts to ensure that she herself, and her consumer-friendly feminism, would continue to publicly circulate were remarkably successful. Through various platforms, and initiatives outlined above, 'Gurley Brown was a media entrepreneur' (Landers 2010, p. 222); in much the same way as later celebrities, including Lena Dunham, 'She and husband David wanted to create a long-term career for her that would outlast the temporary fame' (Landers 2010, p. 222). Accordingly, in 1965, Brown assumed editorship of floundering women's magazine,

Cosmopolitan: 'In the process of transforming *Cosmopolitan* from a failing title into a flourishing one, she also created millions of devotees known as Cosmo Girls' (Hunt 2012, p. 130). With this new position, Brown's media visibility was secured and she continued to appear on television as well as in various news sites. That is, while *Sex and the Single Girl* was key to her initial stardom, she—like all the blockbuster authors examined here—parlayed this attention capital into a different kind of publishing venture and her name value helped secure her the role.

To give a sense of the magazine's consistency with Brown's blockbuster, it has been said that *Cosmo* was effectively *Sex and the Single Girl* transformed into magazine form (Hunt 2012). As Hunt notes, 'Brown understood her audience: those millions of women who had purchased *Sex and the Single Girl*, read her column, showed up for her book signings, and wrote her letters seeking advice' (2012, p. 134). Profiles of her emphasize that she modelled the behaviour she advocated for women. Brown was, therefore, seen to personally embody the 'Cosmo girl's' key characteristics (Hunt 2012, p. 134), which themselves mirrored those of her blockbuster's 'Single Girl': independent, resourceful, personally and professionally successful, and—most of all—sexually agentic. As she observed, reinscribing the 'mouseburger' persona of her blockbuster, 'I still identify with my girl—the one who's doing it herself. The one who's a little behind, lacking in education, beauty, wealth or great emotional security' (in Hunt 2012, p. 134). Although a detailed textual analysis of *Cosmopolitan* under Brown's tenure is outside the scope of this book, it is important to note that the magazine was largely an extension of her blockbuster, which itself had helped create an audience with which *Cosmopolitan*'s feminist 'message' would resonate. As she served as editor-in-chief for 32 years, Brown's often controversial feminism continued to shape the magazine, and its (and its star editor's) role in translating women's and sexual liberation for a large audience of women should not be underestimated. And while her 'Gurley Girl' feminism was not the form commonly associated with the women's liberation movement, 'Brown's agenda continued to exist side by side with more radical forms of feminism, only to reemerge in full force, decades later, as something called the third wave' (Scanlon 2009a, p. 111). As Scanlon suggests, Brown's celebration of women's sexuality, valorization of consumption, her apparent reconciliation of feminism and femininity, and the pleasures afforded by the latter, is reinscribed in much third wave writing (Henry 2004). Therefore, in the 1990s and 2000s, Brown's feminism came to receive a renewed type of cultural legitimation, not least because of the way single women were being represented across various televisual sites.

In 2003, Brown's blockbuster and its sequel were republished, tapping into a new generation of readers who had been exposed to her ideas through a different popular culture text: HBO's *Sex and the City* (1998–2004). Given the intensity of audience affective investment in that programme, Brown's fame received a significant boost, and she came to be refigured as the ultimate postfeminist heroine. As Genz (2010, p. 147) argues, 'Brown's core ideas—in particular, her belief in feminine/sexual power—are appealing to a late-twentieth-century female audience that celebrates the freedoms of single life and the material independence afforded by their jobs.' The book's paratext, especially its front cover, gives some insight here: 'Before there was *Sex and the City* there was …'. The cover image, featuring a cartoon portrait of a woman consuming a cocktail (presumably a Cosmopolitan), also makes explicit this link to *Sex and the City* as well as chick lit novels, whose heroines are likewise indebted to Brown's writing. The book's inside jacket cover continues to make this link, even including a quotation from Kim Cattrall (who played Samantha Jones, perhaps the *Sex and the City* character who appears most indebted to Brown's sexually emancipatory philosophy) which explicitly ties Brown to the series' four protagonists. The back-cover blurb, too, is noteworthy in terms of the assumptions it makes about the book, its author, and the salience of her arguments for a 'postfeminist' audience: 'It's been over 40 years since Helen Gurley Brown's *Sex and the Single Girl* sent Shockwaves through American culture. How times have changed, or have they?'[23]

The 2003 edition, and its follow up, *Sex and the Office*, published by Barricade Books, also included a new introduction from Brown, explaining why the book was thought suitable for republication at that particular juncture: 'The book caused something of a commotion at the time of its original publication in 1962. Through the years women have come up to me in restaurants, at airports, on the street, to tell me the book changed their lives (for the better) so why not republish?' (Brown 2003, p. xi). Blockbuster authors commonly make claims regarding their book's transformative effect on readers, as subsequent chapters on Friedan and Greer will also demonstrate. As Brown further notes, the book, however, was not subject to revision given that 'many of the basics do hold up' (2003, p. xi). Here, she underscores the ongoing cultural resonance of her initially quite provocative text, and the trope of her being 'ahead of her time' is regularly mobilized in media engagements with this figure—including post-mortem in the myriad obituaries following her death in 2012.

Celebrity feminism, like any other form of renown, is necessarily exclusionary—not least through the remembrance of certain figures as renowned feminists: 'After death, only some figures achieve and sustain fame, and only some figures spark negotiation of their posthumous legacy' (Jensen 2005, p. xxi). That Brown's death was so extensively covered, that her feminism was largely celebrated therein, and that her feminist 'legacy' was revisited, reveals much about the durability of her fame as well as the resonance of her blockbuster feminism. The majority of obituaries invoked *Sex and the Single Girl* as a ground-breaking popular feminist book. Overwhelmingly, while acknowledging that she has been a contentious figure for many feminists, commemorative texts reposition Brown firmly within modern feminism, with a number crediting her with inciting 'a revolution in the daily lives of women' (Stewart 2012; see also Abraham 2012), and another characterizing her as 'the essence of a feminist', a pioneering figure who paved the feminist way for contemporary women (Childs 2012). However, her emphasis on the 'politics of personal advancement' (Fox 2012), as one obituary writer put it, meant that she has largely been seen in opposition to the collectivist politics of the second wave. For some, there is a sense that she was temporally misplaced; in this vein, that she and her feminism are more appropriate to the current, purportedly postfeminist context, is a common implication (Hughes 2012; Olen 2012; Wilson 2012). Rather than feminism's symbolic death being reinscribed (Hawkesworth 2004; Reger 2012) in these popular narratives about a literal feminist death, these obituaries use Brown's passing to offer compelling narratives about her contribution to understandings of women as agentic, entrepreneurial subjects. She becomes, therefore, in these popular rewritings, the perfect feminist for neoliberal times (Taylor 2016). Such texts further illustrate her, and her feminism's, popular recuperation in the twenty-first century, as well as demonstrating that she remains important to public debate on the meanings around feminism—as all these blockbuster authors do.

Conclusion

As I have shown here, Brown—alongside key cultural intermediaries—was central in creating her celebrity sign, and with lasting effects. Rather than this simply being a gesture of self-promotion, it is important to remember that Brown concomitantly was promoting a particular feminist critique of the normative assumptions around femininity, arguing that women were entitled to freedom of sexual expression as well as independence through full participation in the public sphere. Both in her blockbuster and in subsequent media performances, her own experiences were central to the authorization of this vision, and—like the other authors examined in this book—publicly Brown was largely positioned (and positioned herself) as an extension of her sassy narrator. Moreover, this chapter has demonstrated that the feminist persona-construction and active self-branding said to be a unique feature of the current environment is something in which blockbuster authors have always been engaged, a point further developed in subsequent chapters on Friedan and Greer.

While Brown's status as a representative feminist figure has been highly contested—or often completely elided—through her blockbuster and its affirmation of singleness as a viable way of being in the world for women, she was clearly a pioneering figure in bringing women's attention to how stymied their lives might be *otherwise*. Her status as a key celebrity feminist has been retrospectively attributed, both in scholarly and journalistic writing, and it has been in the contemporary, so-called postfeminist representational environment that this rewriting has been most pronounced. Nevertheless, her celebrity feminism endures, while the subjectivity she endorsed for women, and herself embodied, informs many contemporary televisual representations, especially of single women. Brown, and the key tenets of her blockbuster, have been taken up and effectively repurposed for the 'postfeminist' era—thus further suggesting their ongoing cultural reverberations.

As Scanlon (2009a, p. 95) remarks, despite the differences in their publicly articulated philosophies, Friedan and Brown shared a central aim: 'the desire to achieve not only fame but fortune as popular, even populist writers'. Such goals, as argued in Chap. 2, have been figured not only as unfeminist but unfeminine. That is, 'fame' and 'fortune' are coded as things neither feminists nor women more broadly should covet. Although these twin desires united them, Friedan appeared contemptuous of Brown's approach, reportedly dubbing her liberatory philosophy 'obscene and horrible' (cited in Oulette 1999, p. 361). That said, the books overlap in their emphasis on 'individual transformation over and above social transformation' (Whelehan 2005, p. 31), and in their authors' belief that they could 'could assist women in their search for a more rewarding way of living a woman's life' (Scanlon 2009a, p. 95). In the next chapter, building upon the work in this chapter on agency and self-presentation, I examine the figure of Betty Friedan, whose *The Feminine Mystique* was published the year after Brown's bestseller and has been seen as central to the history of American feminism in ways that (until quite recently) have eluded Brown.

Notes

1. This material was found in Gloria Steinem's archives, also part of the Sophia Smith Collection at Smith College. GS.SSC.102.13.
2. *Sex and the Office* by no means replicated the success of Brown's earlier work. As her husband noted in a letter to Geis, 'Like the rest of us, she is depressed by the failure of SATO to become airborne. She will not be first or last author to have written a bestseller and come a cropper with a sequel, however worthy' (15 November, 1964, HGB-SSC.22).
3. Coverage of Brown during this tour was extensive and largely sympathetic; see HGB.SSC.21.4B. This may have been the result of her assessment of the British as having 'a natural and uninhibited attitude which makes them the sexiest in the world' (in *The Sun*, 20 October 1964).
4. All archival material and letters subsequently cited comes from Folder 19 of the Helen Gurley Brown archives in the Sophia Smith Collection, Smith College, unless otherwise stated.
5. Though there is no scope to do so here, an exploration of these letters from readers would help to flesh out the kinds of affective investment that readers were making in this text—and indeed its author.
6. Feminist response to the sexual revolution was, unsurprisingly, ambivalent (see Jeffreys 1985/1990).
7. Hilary Radner (2010) has reconceptualized Brown's impact on modern popular culture, through what she calls 'neo-feminism', see 'Chap. 2: Neo-Feminism and the Rise of the Single Girl'.
8. It was also serialized internationally, including in the UK (*Women's Sunday Mirror*) and Australia (*Women's Weekly*), as well as Japan and South Africa (Cottin to Brown, 19 December 1962).
9. See letter from Cottin to Brown outlining the deal, 4 April 1962. HGB-SSC.22.
10. Joan Didion met Helen Gurley Brown while she was on her promotional tour for *Sex and the Office* (Nilsson 2012). In the *Saturday Evening Post*, Didion credits Brown's myriad television appearances with ensuring the book's commercial success: 'Through such talk shows [*Girl Talk, Count Marco, Long John Nebel*] she has sold almost two and a half million copies of two books' (Didion 1965).
11. HGB-SSC.21, SASG clippings, *Publishers Weekly*, May 1962.
12. David Brown to James Shea, 17 December 1963, HGB-SSC. 20.2B.

13. A revisioning of that film, *Down with Love* (2004, Peyton Reed), representing a further fictionalization of Brown, was released in 2004. The film was replete with multiple intertextual allusions, including through the casting of Renée Zellweger, who had played the quintessential single girl in the form of Bridget Jones, in the lead role (see Taylor 2010).
14. HGB-SSC.21, SASG clippings, *Publishers Weekly*, May 1962.
15. See, in particular, HGB-SSC.20.2B, which contains these schedules.
16. Cottin was to go on to help found the feminist magazine, *Ms.*, with Gloria Steinem.
17. HGB-SSC.10.10.
18. For a more detailed analysis of these columns, see Scanlon (2009a, pp. 118–21).
19. Brown was pro-active, and regularly sent press material and books to journalists and those who might be able to promote her. Such strategies are detailed in Brown to Cottin, 2 May 1962 and 12 July 1962. As she notes: 'Helping in any way I can to promote the book is constantly on my mind…'I'm making a speech to a bunch of college ladies and will of course bludgeon them to the bookstore' (26 March 1962, to Cottin).
20. The Sophia Smith Collection also contains complete tour schedules, which substantiate this intensely paced tour.
21. Following Brown's letter regarding her schedule, Geis wrote to David Brown: 'I feel pretty obtuse for not realizing until now that, along with her other wonderful qualities, Helen is also human. It is obvious that she has been overburdened to an unreasonable degree, and I'm afraid that BGA has been the chief offender. You are perfectly right to curb matters with a firm hand' (12 October 1962). Such a response (while directed at Brown's husband as opposed to the author herself) reveals the characteristic level of respectful negotiation between the employees of Geis publishing and the Browns.
22. Brown herself foregrounds her husband's ongoing role in the manufacture and maintenance of her fame and thus her commercial success, as she notes: 'It is he who hustles me off to all my promotional dates and keeps me making new ones over my dead body' (Brown to Geis, 10 October 1962). See also Scanlon (2009a, p. 60).
23. 'Celetoid', Carrie Bradshaw, the narrator of *Sex and the City*, has even been seen as 'an updated Helen Gurley Brown' (Scanlon

2009c, p. 145). In Chris Rojek's (2001) framework, 'celetoids' include fictional characters who have been celebrified, effectively taking on a life of their own. As I argue in *Single Women in Popular Culture* (2012), figures like Carrie Bradshaw are continually invoked in news coverage about single women as if she were a 'real' person as opposed to a fictional character.

References

Abraham, A. (2012) 'Media Worlds Pay Tribute After Legendary Cosmopolitan Editor', Helen Gurley Brown, dies at the age of 90', 14 August, *The Daily Mail*, accessed via http://www.dailymail.co.uk/femail/article-2187889/Media-world-pays-tribute-legendary-Cosmopolitan-editor-Helen-Gurley-Brown-dies-age-90.html

Alexander, S. (1963) 'Singular Girl's Success', *Life*, March, accessed via Helen Gurley Brown Archives, the Sophia Smith Collection. HGB-SSC.21.5c

Berman, A. (1962) 'Married Life Pleases Author of Sex and the Single Girl', 15 June, *New York Post*, accessed via Helen Gurley Brown Archives, the Sophia Smith Collection. HGB-SSC.21.5c

Bourdieu, P. (1993) *The Field of Cultural Production*, New York: Columbia University Press

Brown, H.G. (1962/2003) *Sex and the Single Girl*, New York: Barricade Books

——— (1964/2003) *Sex and the Office*, New York: Barricade Books

——— (1967) *Outrageous Opinions*, New York: Geis and Associates

——— (1969) *The Single Girl's Cookbook*, New York: Geis and Associates

——— (1970) *Sex and the New Single Girl*, New York: Geis and Associates

——— (1982) *Having it All: Love, Success, Sex, Money Even If You're Starting With Nothing*, New York: Simon and Schuster

——— (1994) *The Late Show: A Practical, Semiwild Survival Guide for Every Woman in Her Prime Or Approaching It*, New York: William Morrow and Co

——— (1998) *The Writer's Rules: The Power Of Positive Prose-how To Create It And Get It Published*, New York: William Morrow and Co

——— (2000) *I'm Wild Again: Snippets from My Life and a Few Brazen Thoughts*, New York: St Martin's Press

——— (2004) *Dear Pussycat: Mash Notes and Missives from the Desk of Cosmopolitan's Legendary Editor*, New York: St Martin's Press

Buchwald, A. (1962) 'Sex and the Single Girl', 5 November, *The Minneapolis Star*, accessed via Helen Gurley Brown Archives, the Sophia Smith Collection. HGB.SSC.21.5c

Childs, M. (2012) 'Helen Gurley Brown Helen Gurley Brown: Bestselling author and editor of Cosmopolitan', *The Independent*, 15 August, accessed via http://

www.independent.co.uk/news/obituaries/helen-gurley-brown-bestselling-author-and-editor-of-cosmopolitan-8046747.html
Didion, J. (1965/2012) 'Bosses Make Lousy Lovers', 30 January, *Saturday Evening Post*, reprinted 13 August, accessed via http://www.saturdayeveningpost.com/2012/08/13/archives/helen-gurley-brown.html
Douglas, S. (1994) *Where the Girls are: Growing Up Female with the Mass Media*, New York: Penguin
Dunham, L. (2014) *Not That Kind of Girl*, New York: Random House
Fimrite, R. (1962) 'The Single Girl's Expert on Sex', July 6, *San Francisco Chronicle*, accessed via Helen Gurley Brown Archives, the Sophia Smith Collection. HGB.SSC.21.5c
Foucault, M. (1969/1984 ed) 'The Author Function', in P. Rainbow ed. *The Foucault Reader*, New York: Penguin, pp. 101–120
Fox, M. (2012) Gave "Single Girl" a Life in Full (Sex, Sex, Sex)', *The New York Times*, 13 August, accessed via http://www.nytimes.com/2012/08/14/business/media/helen-gurley-brown-who-gave-cosmopolitan-its-purr-is-dead-at-90.html?pagewanted=all&_r=0
Gardiner, J. (2000) '"What is an author?": Contemporary Publishing Discourse and the Author Figure', *Publishing Research Quarterly*, Spring: 63–76
Gamson, J. (1994) *Claims to Fame: Celebrity in Contemporary America*, Berkeley: University of California Press
—— (2006) 'The Negotiated Celebration', in P.D. Marshall ed. *The Celebrity Culture Reader*, London: Routledge, pp. 698–720
'Geis Book to Have Entire Issue of 'American Weekly'' (1962), May, *Publishers Weekly*, accessed via Helen Gurley Brown Archives, the Sophia Smith Collection. HGB.SSC. 21.4B
Genz, S. (2009) *Postfemininities in Popular Culture*, Basingstoke: Palgrave Macmillan
—— (2010) 'Singled Out: Postfeminism's "New Woman" and the Dilemma of Having It All', *Journal of Popular Culture*, 43.1: 97–119
Genette, G. (1997) *Paratexts: Thresholds of Interpretation*, Cambridge: Cambridge University Press
Hawkesworth, M. (2004) 'The Semiotics of Premature Burial: Feminism in a Postfeminist Age', *Signs*, 29.4: 961–985
Helen Gurley Brown Papers (1932–2012), Sophia Smith Collection, Smith College, Northampton, U.S.A.
Henry, A. (2004) *Not My Mother's Sister: Generational Conflict and Third Wave Feminism*, Bloomington: University of Indiana Press
Hollows, J. & Moseley, R. (2006), 'Introduction', in J. Hollows & R. Moseley eds. *Feminism in Popular Culture*, London: Berg, pp. 1–22
Hughes, S. (2012) 'Helen Gurley Brown: How to Have it All', *The Guardian*, 15 August, accessed via http://www.theguardian.com/lifeandstyle/2012/aug/14/helen-gurley-brown-cosmopolitan-sex

Hunt, P.D. (2012) 'Editing Desire, Working Girl Wisdom, and Cupcakeable Goodness', *Journalism History*, 38.3: 130–141

Jensen, J. (2005) 'Introduction: On Fandom, Celebrity, and Mediation: Posthumous Possibilities', in J. Jensen & S. Jones eds. *Afterlife as Afterimage: Understanding Posthumous Fame*, New York: Peter Lang, pp. xv–xxiii

Jeffreys, S. (1985/1990 ed) *Anticlimax: A Feminist Perspective on the Sexuality Revolution*, London: The Women's Press

Landers, J. (2010) *The Improbable First Century of Cosmopolitan Magazine*, Columbia: University of Missouri Press

Le Masurier, M. (2010) 'Reading the Flesh', *Feminist Media Studies*, 11.2: 215–229

Lilburn, S., Magarey, S. & Sheridan, S. (2000) 'Celebrity Feminism as Synthesis: Germaine Greer, *The Female Eunuch* and the Australian Print Media', *Continuum*, 14.3: 335–348

Luther, C. (2012) 'Helen Gurley Brown: 1922–2012', 14 August, *Chicago Tribune*

Martin, C. (1996) 'Production, Content, and Uses of Bestselling Books in Quebec', *Canadian Journal of Communication*, 21.4, accessed via http://www.cjconline.ca/index.php/journal/article/view/958/864

Marwick, A.E. (2013) *Status Update: Celebrity, Publicity, and Branding in the Social Media Age*, New Haven: Yale University Press

Meyer, D. & Gamson, J. (1995) 'The Challenge of Cultural Elites: Celebrity and Social Movements', *Sociological Inquiry*, 65.2: 181–206

Miller, L.J. (2000) 'The Best-Seller List as Marketing Tool and Historical Fiction', *Book History*, 3: 286–304

Mills, S. (1998) *Discourse*, London: Routledge

Moran, J. (2000) *Star Authors: Literary Celebrity in America*, London: Pluto

Murray, S. (2004) *Mixed Media: Feminist Presses and Publishing Politics*, London: Pluto

Nilsson, J. (2012) 'Sex in the '60s: Remembering Helen Gurley Brown', *Saturday Evening Post*, accessed via http://www.saturdayeveningpost.com/2012/08/13/archives/helen-gurley-brown.html

Olen, H. (2012) 'Helen Gurley Brown and the Failures of Do Me Feminism', 14 August, *Forbes Magazine*, accessed via http://www.forbes.com/sites/helaineolen/2012/08/14/helen-gurley-brown-and-the-failure-of-dome-feminism/

Oulette, L. (1999) 'Inventing the Cosmo Girl: Class Identity and Girl-Style American Dreams', *Media, Culture and Society*, 21: 359–383

Pearce, L. (2004) *The Rhetorics of Feminism*, London: Routledge

Radner, H. (1999) 'Introduction: Queering the Girl', in H. Radner & M. Luckett eds. *Swinging Single: Representing Sexuality in the 1960s*, Minneapolis: University of Minnesota Press, pp. 1–35

—— (2010) *Neo-Feminist Cinema: Girly Films, Chick Flicks and Consumer Culture*, New York: Routledge

Reger, J. (2012) *Everywhere and Nowhere: Contemporary Feminism in the United States*, New York: Oxford University Press

Rojek, C. (2001) *Celebrity*, London: Reaktion Books

——— (2011) *Fame Attack*, London: Bloomsbury
——— (2014) 'Niccolo Machiavelli, Cultural Intermediaries and the Category of Achieved Celebrity', *Celebrity Studies*, 5.4: 455–468
Scanlon, J. (2009a) *Bad Girls Go Everywhere: The Life of Helen Gurley Brown*, Oxford: Oxford University Press
——— (2009b) 'Sensationalist Literature or Expert Advice?' *Feminist Media Studies*, 9.1: 1–15
——— (2009c) 'Sexy from the Start: Anticipatory Elements of Second Wave Feminism', *Women's Studies*, 38.2: 127–150
Sex and the City (1998–2004), Television series. HBO: USA
'Single Girl Author Begins New Chapter', 11 November, *New York Post*, p. 16, accessed via Helen Gurley Brown Archives, the Sophia Smith Collection. 21.5c
Stewart, E. (2012) 'The Cosmo Girl's Legacy', *Sydney Morning Herald*, 15 August, accessed via http://www.dailylife.com.au/news-and-views/dl-culture/the-cosmo-girl-legacy-20120815-247f9.html
Taylor, A. (2008) *Mediating Australian Feminism: Rereading the First Stone Media Event*, Oxford: Peter Lang
——— (2010) 'Celebrity (Post)feminism, the Sixties Feminist Blockbuster and *Down with Love*', *The Sixties: A Journal of Politics, History and Culture*, 3.1: 79–96
——— (2012) *Single Women in Popular Culture: The Limits of Postfeminism*, Basingstoke: Palgrave Macmillan
——— (2016) 'Post-mortem Celebrity Feminism: Collective Memory, 'Legacy', and the Obituaries of Betty Friedan and Helen Gurley Brown', unpublished conference paper presented at the Celebrity Studies Conference, University of Amsterdam, 28th–30th June
Templin, C. (1995) *Feminism and the Politics of Literary Reputation: The Example of Erica Jong*, Lawrence: University of Kansas Press
Thomas, S. (2014) 'Celebrity in the "Twitterverse": History, Authenticity and the Multiplicity of Stardom', *Celebrity Studies*, 5.3: 242–255
Thompson, J.B. (2010) *Merchants of Culture: The Publishing Business in the Twenty First Century*, London: Polity
Turner, G. (2014) *Understanding Celebrity*, London: Sage
Turner, G. (2016) 'Celebrity, Participation, and The Public', in P.D. Marshall & S. Redmond eds., *A Companion to Celebrity*, London: Wiley Blackwell, pp. 83–97
Van Krieken, R. (2012) *Celebrity Society*, New York: Routledge
Whelehan, I. (2005) *The Feminist Bestseller: From Sex and the Single Girl to Sex and the City*, Basingstoke: Palgrave Macmillan
——— (2012) 'Sexing the Single Girl: Adapting Helen Gurley Brown Without Reading Her Book', pp. 1–12, accessed via https://oer.utas.edu.au/d2l/lor/viewer/viewFile.d2lfile/6606/63/Sex%20and%20the%20Single%20Girl%20York.pdf

Williams, R. (2007) 'From Beyond Control to in Control: Investigating Drew Barrymore's Agency/Authorship', in S. Holmes & S. Redmond eds. *Stardom and Celebrity: A Reader*, London: Sage, pp. 111–125

Wilson, C. (2012) 'Helen Gurley Brown Made 'Cosmopolitan' More Than a Magazine', 13 August, *USA Today*, accessed via http://usatoday30.usatoday.com/life/people/obit/story/2011-08-02/helen-gurley-brown-cosmopolitan-dies-at-90/57039456/1

CHAPTER 4

Betty Friedan: The 'Mother' of Feminism, Self-fashioning, and the Celebrity Mystique

INTRODUCTION

Betty Friedan's popular text, *The Feminine Mystique* (1963), is often publicly framed as the catalyst for the modern women's movement, and such a trope is recurrent in all media engagements with this iconic feminist. As fellow blockbuster celebrity Germaine Greer observed, its publication marked 'the beginning of the second feminist wave' and, in the generationalism that mars popular accounts of feminism, Friedan is routinely, and problematically, figured as its 'Mother' (Henry 2004, p. 68). Her treatise on the malaise that was engulfing the 'happy housewife heroines' of the 1950s and 1960s, *The Feminine Mystique* (1963), brought to the fore what she dubbed 'the problem with no name'. Friedan's book came to circulate widely, not least because of its author's marketing savvy and active interventions into the mediasphere at a time when other feminists thought it better to eschew it (Bradley 2003, p. 5; Siegel 2007). Augmented by her position as founder of the National Organization for Women in 1966,[1] Friedan remained a key public feminist figure throughout her life, and indeed she continues to be newsworthy. Her celebrity endures post-mortem as the extensive media coverage of the 2013 fiftieth anniversary of her blockbuster attests; countless journalistic pieces on Friedan and her book's 'legacy' appeared in Australia, the UK and the USA (Bastow 2013; McDonagh 2013; Warner 2013; Ziesler 2013).[2] Therefore, like the other authors in Part I, *The Feminine Mystique* and its author's brand of feminism continue to culturally reverberate.

Fame, including in the case of blockbuster feminists, must be recognized as 'the by-product of historical circumstances, biographical representations and media portraits' (Weber 2012, p. 35). In this chapter, accordingly, following a brief consideration of *The Feminine Mystique* itself, I focus on three forms of representation and self-representation through which the figure of 'Friedan' has been constructed over fifty years: authorial profiles and interviews; her own journalistic pieces; and her memoir. The star is, as Christine Gledhill reminds us (drawing upon Richard Dyer), 'an intertextual construct produced across a range of media and cultural practices' (1991, p. xii), and attending to these different forms will allow me to map this often complicated process, especially as it relates to feminist politics. Women like Friedan, and the others examined in Part I of this book, moved feminism away from being just an abstraction. As Henderson remarks, 'feminist "stars" or the movement's "big names" are the legitimate modes of figuring feminism in the media, and hence come to act as metonyms for, and personifications of, the women's movement' (2008, p. 172). They are themselves, however, as I argue throughout, integral to this personification. As embodiments of feminism, these figures have shaped—and continue to shape—our emotional responses to the women's movement, and to feminism more broadly (Hesford 2013), making an interrogation of the political and affective work they do vital to understanding how feminism comes to publicly circulate and resonate.

Of the three women examined in Part I, Friedan is the figure most clearly and regularly seen to be synonymous with feminism's second wave, in the USA especially. She was positioned as a spokesperson for the women's liberation movement in ways that Brown and Greer simply were not, and she continues to be invoked in mainstream media's attempts to historicize and produce a cultural memory around modern feminism. As Hirsch and Smith (2002, p. 5) note, 'Always mediated, cultural memory is the product of fragmentary personal and collective experiences articulated through technologies and media that shape even as they transmit memory'. In this vein, Betty Friedan, over many decades, worked to circulate a narrative that positioned her firmly at the centre of the modern American women's movement; this origin story, which ensured that liberal feminism came to metonymically stand in for feminism as a whole, has been central to her celebrity. As Katie King reminds us, 'origin stories about the women's movement are interested stories, all of them' (1994, p. 214). They are told in specific ways, for particular personal and ideological purposes, and it is always vital to ask who is doing the 'telling' and what is her position (Friedman 1995)? Like Brown and Greer, Friedan's blockbuster was merely the beginning of her ongoing life project to help shape public understandings of feminism, and she too produced a number of subsequent works of feminist non-fiction, including *It Changed My Life* (1976), *The Second Stage* (1981), *The Fountain of Age* (1993), *Beyond Gender: The New Politics of Work and Family* (1997), and *Life So Far* (2000). And as was the case with the other authors, although receiving pronounced media coverage on the back of their author's existing celebrity, such publications failed to reverberate in the way *The Feminine Mystique* did.

Media desire for insights into Friedan's life, as a celebrity feminist, enabled her to further politicize the personal, weaving her own experiences into a critique of normative femininity and the gendered public/private divide. In interviews she routinely draws upon, or rather constructs, her own life narrative to shore up her authority to speak about these tensions, mobilizing what Lynne Pearce calls 'authenticating anecdotes' (2004); for example: 'the life I lived enabled me to write *The Feminine Mystique*' (in Lamb 1993, p. 134). Of course, through such comments she seeks to bring into being a certain 'Friedan' rather than simply representing an unmediated, 'authentic' self.[3] That is, much labour, including by Friedan herself, went into constructing this narrative and into crafting a public persona that would resonate with her target audience. In this chapter, I am especially interested in these public acts of self-fashioning, and how they result in particular mediated forms of second wave feminism. Here I unpack the discursive processes via which Friedan worked to constitute *herself* as simultaneously an 'exceptional woman',[4] who, in this case, was at the very epicentre of the modern American women's movement, and an 'ordinary', discontented American housewife, mapping the centrality of these interlocking narratives in her celebrification. Before doing so, it is necessary to briefly engage with the text that apparently had such a powerful impact on its author and its millions of readers.

THE PROBLEM WITH NO NAME: READING *THE FEMININE MYSTIQUE*

Betty Friedan's polemical work on 'the problem with no name', *The Feminine Mystique* (1963), was a key text—as she repeatedly tells audiences—in the resurgence of American feminism in the 1960s. The book's first edition reportedly sold 1.4 million copies, and remained on the *New York Times* bestseller list for nearly two years (Knight 1997). Despite

Friedan's critique of women's magazines and their role in the maintenance of the feminine mystique, in January and February 1963 *McCall's* and *Ladies Home Journal* both published excerpts from the book. Serialization was key to the book's success, as it was for Brown's, enabling it to reach its preferred addressees: the unhappy housewives of America. In marketing the book, her publisher, Norton, sought to ensure its characterization as a transformative text: '*The Feminine Mystique* would appear to epitomise the feminist "instrumental text", being the first to be emblazoned with the epithet "This book changes lives", a slogan that is virtually synonymous with second wave feminism' (Dearey 2006). Extensive pre-publicity also pursued this angle, with memos from Norton's sales department to booksellers revealing concerted attempts to position the book as a highly coveted bestseller.[5] As with all blockbusters, meta-commentary around the controversy it sparked was pronounced: 'Hardly had the book left the presses than the controversy raged. Cocktail parties turned into debating teams' (Cook 1964). Her bestselling treatise made a significant impact on the American cultural imaginary, and indeed beyond, and was one of the first modern feminist 'blockbusters': 'In the canon of post-war feminist works it sits somewhat isolated, and somewhat incongruously, midway between *The Second Sex* and the outpouring of texts and tracts later on' (Bowlby 1987, p. 61). As one of only a few bestselling feminist texts published in the early 1960s (including *Sex and the Single Girl*), *The Feminine Mystique*'s public impact was unrivalled, arguably until Kate Millett's *Sexual Politics* and Greer's *The Female Eunuch* in 1970.

As in de Beauvoir's work, in Friedan's analysis of women's subjectivity in 1950s and 1960s suburban America, being 'feminine' was found to be a form of constraint that rendered many women deeply unhappy. The 'problem', as she emphasizes, was that assumptions about what constituted 'legitimate' femininity were limiting the way it was possible for women to be in the world. She sought to emphasize that the problem lay not in individual women but in the feminine ideal that they were expected to embody. 'The Feminine Mystique' is the term she coined to describe women's deep dissatisfaction with the prescriptive gender roles to which women in post-war America were expected to adhere. As she argues of the problem which she purports to name:

> The problem lay buried, unspoken, for many years in the minds of American women. It was a strange stirring, a sense of dissatisfaction, a yearning that women suffered in the middle of the twentieth century in the United States.

Each suburban wife struggled with it alone. As she made the beds, shopped for groceries, matched slipcover material, ate peanut butter sandwiches with her children, chauffeured Cub Scouts and Brownies, lay beside her husband at night—she was afraid to ask even of herself the silent question—'Is this all?' (1963/1992, p. 13)

Women had thoroughly internalized the mystique, and she sought to awaken them from their stupor: '*The Feminine Mystique* exposes the internal and psychological dilemmas of suburban housewives who are not realizing their full potential and suffer from an internalized sense of limitation' (Genz 2009, p. 43). For Friedan, however, women could transcend the 'false consciousness' that kept them hostage to the mystique, including through changes to education policies and opportunities for greater workforce participation. In her blockbuster's final sentence, Friedan confidently pronounces, 'the time is at hand when the voices of the feminine mystique can no longer drown out the inner voice that is driving women on to become complete' (1963, p. 331). The discovery of this 'voice', she argues, would result in the complete emancipation of women. Given that Friedan believed that the 'cause of women's oppression was an internalised and self-limiting blockage', a position she publicly reiterated well beyond her initial blockbuster (Siegel 2007, p. 78), little wonder Sheryl Sandberg's later tract, placing the emphasis on the recalibration of individual women, came to be so often compared to Friedan's.

Interspersed with academic literature, including from within psychology and anthropology, and data collated from her interviewees, were Friedan's own autobiographical vignettes, said to be the source of the book's appeal to readers (and they are also central to her celebrification): 'The personal asides in *The Feminine Mystique* conform to the conventions of the genre of sin and redemption: I was once like you but now I have seen the light—and you can follow my example' (Wolfe 1999). In this respect, it appears to do similar work to the 'consciousness-raising' novel (Hogeland 1998). Indeed, given the foregrounding of the narrator's voice, some critics have even referred to it as a 'work of collective and individual women's life writing', a form of 'auto/biography' rather than the social scientific study it at times sets itself up to be, productively shifting between the 'I/we' to secure readerly identification (Dearey 2006).

Although immensely popular with readers, *The Feminine Mystique* has not been without its critics. In and through allegations of an orchestrated conspiracy by the culture industries, as well as government, to keep women ideologically enslaved to the 'mystique', Friedan echoes Frankfurt School rhetoric, especially when it comes to the role of advertising agencies in the mystique's maintenance (Knight 1997, p. 44). While this trope of conspiracy may have rendered the book problematic, Knight also sees it as central to subsequent American popular feminist non-fiction, including Susan Faludi's *Backlash* and Naomi Wolf's *The Beauty Myth*. Another key limitation of the book identified by various feminist critics is its discursive construction of the figure of the 'housewife' as that which must be transcended for liberation to be achieved: 'The awkward opposition between feminism and the housewife played out in a number of paradigmatic second wave texts [here they include Friedan and Greer's blockbusters] which indicate that whatever else she might be, the feminist subject is *not a house wife*' (Munford and Waters 2013, p. 73, original emphasis). In this respect, Friedan is seen to have played a central role in firmly positioning feminism in the popular imagination as 'an anti-housewife phenomenon' (Scanlon 2009a, p. 102; Lloyd and Johnson 1999; Hollows 2000). In the contemporary context, as Munford and Waters note, it is ironic that the 'happy housewife' has been recuperated and is central to what they dub the 'postfeminist mystique', in which the housewife has made a 'spectacular return'.[6] Moreover, bell hooks, as Munford and Waters (2013, p. 75) note, critiqued Friedan's text on the grounds that it privileges white, middle-class, heterosexual women, an elision that, she suggests, had an enduring effect on the tenor and direction of the women's movement itself.

Despite its rhetorical and political limitations, Friedan's blockbuster clearly had an impact and early reviews were largely sympathetic. In fact, fellow celebrity feminist Helen Gurley Brown was one of the earliest reviewers, and she used Friedan's book to effectively reiterate the position of her own blockbuster:

> What I've gleaned from the book is that a woman who either by choice or circumstance has *not* enveloped herself in domesticity may have 'unwittingly' worked out a better life for herself than her married friends! Whether I've got Mrs. Friedan's message straight or not, I think you'll enjoy 'The Feminine Mystique'.[7]

Moreover, Friedan herself, in interviews, invoked the way the book was resonating with its targeted audience, American housewives: 'Women are so delighted to know there is nothing wrong with them' (in Cook 1964; see also Coontz 2012). This positioning of Friedan as women's knowing saviour was to characterize much media coverage of the book; she allegedly spoke from experience and, for her readers, she was 'just like us', thereby providing the sense of ordinariness and intimacy upon which celebrity, and affective investment from fans, relies. The book, as Whelehan notes, featured 'personal testimony' to help support its argument, as its author 'casts herself most definitely as one of those who left a promising future in higher education to start a family, and, as a mother of small children, now wonders if this is all there is' (2005, p. 31). It was such 'casting' that arguably facilitated her lifelong celebrification as a feminist who changes lives.

'Everything I Know Has Come from My Own Experience': The Celebrification of Friedan

Friedan[8] is known for openly embracing celebrity, lacking any of the ambivalence publicly expressed by Greer and Steinem, something that was integral to her blockbuster's success. Rather than seeing a tension between feminism and commercial success,[9] Friedan, like Brown, was actively involved in the promotion of her blockbuster. In interviews it was common for her to draw attention to her agency in this process: 'I knew the book was big but it had to be promoted' (in Wilkes 1970, p. 31) and, given that third party industry professionals are always central to the maintenance of celebrity (Turner 2014), she reportedly 'eventually browbeat[10] Norton [her publisher] into paying a freelance publicist …' who organized book tours[11] and myriad television appearances. As Stephanie Coontz (2012) argues, though, this appears to be a calculated attempt to attribute the book's success solely to Friedan's promotional labour, and effectively attempts to write Norton's publicity department out of the history of the book's public career.[12]

Nonetheless, like all blockbuster authors, Friedan's image was clearly central to the book's promotion; for example, as part of the publisher's epitext, one flyer featured a side-on portrait of the author, above which the following question was posed: 'What kind of woman are you?' Options included: 'frantic cook, chauffeur, smothered mother'. The flyer reassured readers that Friedan, through her blockbuster, could help provide the answer.[13] In 1963, at the time of book's initial publication, there was a newspaper strike in the USA, making television and radio outlets—and the author herself—even more crucial in the book's promotion. Friedan's central role in the success of the book is evidenced by figures from *Publishers Weekly* magazine in 1963, which noted that sales dramatically increased following Friedan's 'personal appearances on television and radio' (cited in Murray 2004, p. 175). Here, then, there is a direct correlation between authorial public performances and the book's commercial success.

With the establishment of the National Organization for Women in 1966, as well as the ongoing reverberations of her blockbuster, Friedan secured her positioning within the American media as the women's movement's key representative, though not without contestation. As her homophobic comments about lesbian feminists as the 'lavender menace' indicate, she would come to be a controversial figure for other movement activists, enabling the media to reinscribe the melodramatic trope of a 'catfight' between feminists, dramatizing the conflict upon which news discourse thrives (Douglas 1994). Throughout her public career, and especially during the second wave, Friedan positioned herself as speaking from and to the 'mainstream', a gesture that necessarily rendered her a problematic figure for those less interested in reformism than radical social upheaval (Siegel 2007). Coverage of her disagreements with other prominent feminists, most notably Gloria Steinem, was pronounced throughout the 1970s (Carmody 1972a, b). She was seen to be pro-men, whom she dubbed women's 'fellow victim' (Wilkes 1970), and particularly pro-family, as well as being more pragmatic than her radical feminist sisters, facilitating interviews and articles in *Life*, *The New York Times Magazine*, *Working Woman*, *Newsday*, *TV Guide*, *Family Circle*, and *Esquire*.

Myriad television appearances (on *Merv Griffith*, *Girl Talk*, *David Frost*) were not only about selling books—and herself as commodity—they were about *selling* her specific 'brand' of feminism. Similarly, drawing upon the attention capital accumulated since *The Feminine Mystique*'s publication, and consistent with her desire to speak to women who were not yet convinced of feminism and its necessity (1976, p. 188), between 1971 and 1974 Friedan wrote a regular column for *McCall's Magazine*. 'Betty Friedan's Notebook' covered topics such as marriage and its relevance, the impact of feminism on men, women and orgasms, and 'female chauvinism', all of which were written in the first person, and in a style reminiscent of her blockbuster. Functioning effectively as forms of life writing, further positioning her feminism as emerging from her own experiences, the columns represented a vital form of self-representation for the blockbuster author, and markedly extended her reach.[14]

Crafting a Public Self: Authorial Profiles, Interviews, and Life Writing

For the remainder of this chapter my focus will be the narratives that Friedan, with the help of journalists as cultural intermediaries, would construct about the book, its genesis, its feminism, and her positioning within the women's movement. These include authorial profiles and interviews, confessional articles by Friedan, and her memoir, *Life So Far*. As throughout this book, my focus will be on the self-representational strategies deployed by Friedan herself. If we deem star agency to be the regulation and circulation of a particular public persona, as Rebecca Williams argues (2007, p. 119), then it is clear that Friedan seeks to exercise such control. As Horowitz claims, in order to secure readerly identification Friedan effectively reinvents herself in both the drafting and promotion of her blockbuster, being very 'careful about her autobiographical revelations and how she connected her past to her present' (1998, p. 2).[15] This reinvention continued as the book and its author embarked on their public careers.

As Stephanie Coontz similarly argues, 'a number of myths about the origins and impact of *The Feminine Mystique* have been perpetuated over the years, including by Friedan herself' (2012, p. 107). As both Horowitz and Coontz make clear, the two key 'myths' that came to circulate were that Friedan's feminism emerged from her own position as suburban wife and mother, as opposed to any political commitments, and that she was single-handedly responsible for the resurgence of feminist activism that came to be dubbed the second wave: 'the myth that Betty Friedan did it alone, with a little help from Gloria Steinem' (Kerber 2002, p. 94). Along with the idea that her feminist celebrification required great personal sacrifice, these are 'myths' that Friedan herself worked to substantiate, especially in her journalistic and autobiographical writing. The other key narrative in which 'Friedan' becomes implicated relates to the book's life-altering capacity. In this regard, the trope 'it changed my life', also the name of Friedan's second work of non-fiction (1976), is one that both Friedan and journalists/interviewers invoke throughout her five-decades-long public career, and one that persists after death, resurfacing in virtually all of her obituaries. The creation and certainly the perpetuation of such personalized myths and core tropes are an important part of Friedan's celebrification.

Ordinary/Extraordinary Feminism

Authorial profiles 'can act as a platform for "staged celebrity" where celebrity is achieved through the projection and performance of the subject's life in a biographical narrative' (Lawrenson-Woods 2014, p. 15). Of course, forms of life writing by the celebrity herself also intervene in the process of 'staging' her own celebrity, and ensuring that such narratives are desirable in readerly terms (Rojek 2001). Authorial profiles, as well as these self-representations, can be seen as central to this process, enabling a particular narrative, not just about Friedan but about the women's movement, to come to the fore. However, texts such as interviews, reviews or author profiles need to be recognized within a broader economy of publicity and promotion (Moran 2000; Tomlinson 2005). Furthermore, authorial interviews and profiles necessarily work to inform how readers engage with that writer's work, and cannot merely be conceptualized as 'secondary' to the literary text; readers often first encounter it/ its author through interviews or other forms of public performance, thus 'inaugurating a relationship rather different from that established subsequent to reading the author's text' (Tomlinson 2005, p. 122). As with all blockbuster authors, such public narratives would necessarily feed back into interpretations of Friedan's text, and of the kind of feminism it was advocating. In addition to publicly performing her feminist identity, the blockbuster celebrity, through epitextual forms such as interviews, seeks to delimit both the meanings of her own text and of feminism in a wider sense (whether readers accept these meanings is another question).

Although of course interviews are shaped in certain ways by the interviewer, who mediates the self-construction their subject seeks to offer, effectively co-creating 'Friedan', they can be used to supplement an analysis of her own self-narration in other forms (Young 2004, p. 4), and it is indeed possible to identify some core strategies of self-representation and recurrent tropes across these diverse textual sites—especially that of the ordinary, extraordinary Friedan. In one of the earliest works on stardom, Dyer (1979) makes the claim that celebrity is marked by this paradox of ordinariness and extraordinariness. Friedan's star text, like those of all celebrities if we are to follow Dyer, is produced out of these tensions between the ordinary and the exceptional. Both these myths are encompassed in this quotation from an article on its thirtieth publication anniversary. In 'Feminism Turns 30', Nicholas Lemann's (1992) *GQ* byline reads: 'It's now three decades since a certain housewife wrote *The*

Feminine Mystique, a book that simply changed the world.' The perpetual oscillation between these two positions is central to the establishment and maintenance of 'Friedan' as a renowned feminist speaker, and one in whom readers can affectively invest. Rather than the professional being displaced by a focus on the personal, as is argued to commonly be the case with celebrity (Turner 2014), in profiles and interviews there is an interweaving of her professional and personal identities throughout.

Furthermore, the texts that I consider in this section can be seen as representative of the celebrity confessional mode, wherein celebrities are often self-reflexive about the 'business' of fame as well as about their lives pre-celebrification: 'Such a confession(s) can include reference to their humble beginnings; the troubles, hardships and corruption they have faced along their journey to fame; who they really are beneath their fame gown; and how alike they are to the people who [buy their books]' (Redmond 2008, p. 110). The confessional is also a promotional technique used to further commodify and brand an individual (Redmond 2008, p. 110), which in the case of an autobiography becomes a literal commodity. While there are important factors distinguishing celebrity feminists from other forms, the centrality of 'personal truths' (Friedan 2000, p. 106; 130) to Friedan's feminist writing means that her public persona regularly slips—or rather falls deliberately—into such a revelatory mode. Rather than being concerned about media interest in her private identity, Friedan used the desire for details about her own history to help personalize her feminist politics, and thus to engage women audiences.

As I have noted, as for many other feminist writers, Friedan's personal voice was central to much of her writing, and it was also central to the discursive construction of this ordinary/extraordinary Friedan. For example, in the introduction to her collection of articles, essays, and speeches, *It Changed My Life*, published in 1976, she reflects on her blockbuster's genesis: 'In a certain sense it was almost accidental—coincidental—that I wrote *The Feminine Mystique*, and in another sense my whole life had prepared me to write that book; all the pieces of my own life came together for the first time in the writing of it' (Friedan 1976, p. 6). Here she recruits her past to construct a narrative about the inevitability of her blockbuster and thus her fame. Similarly, she subsequently outlines her parents' marriage and the effect of growing up in an environment of palpable dissatisfaction, and how it informed the position she would later take in her book. She continues, mining her own life for evidence of the enslavement of women, 'But above all, what brought me to consciousness was the fact that—with all my high powered education and brilliant promise as a future psychologist or journalist—I too embraced and lived that feminine mystique' (Friedan 1976, p. 6). However, this narrative about 'an apolitical suburban housewife' (Coontz 2012, p. 142) has not gone unquestioned, and has been recognized as a calculated self-presentational strategy deployed by Friedan to increase her blockbuster's appeal. Nonetheless, as the next sections show, it was central to establishing the author's 'ordinariness' while her exceptionality as the 'mother' of feminism was simultaneously underscored.

Profiling the 'Mother' of Feminism

Throughout her public career, both Friedan and those at least partially responsible for her ongoing celebrification, such as journalists, have attributed the beginnings of the modern women's movement to her. While such origin stories, as I will show, are problematic due to the artificial closure they seek to effect, and the teleological assumptions they make about the linearity of history, they feature heavily in media coverage of Friedan, as well as in her own writings. For example: 'Friedan will stand in history as an initiator of the "second wave" of feminism and as one who has never wavered in fidelity to its larger vision' (French 1983, p. 73).

It was not just journalists making such claims but Friedan herself, who was repeatedly quoted on her integral role in the development of second wave feminism. As she told one interviewer, 'I have a continuing commitment to the women's movement—after all, I helped start it ...' (in Gottlieb 1983, p. 53). Given her persistent reliance on this trope, it is perhaps not surprising that in one interview she was dubbed 'The Mother Superior of Women's Lib' (Wilkes 1970). Consistent with her figuration as modern feminism's 'Mother', Friedan repeatedly asserted that she was responsible for the 1960s/1970s apparent 'rebirth' of the movement towards women's liberation, a claim that journalists largely reinscribed without question. For example, in the *New York Times*, Deirdre Carmody (1972a) described Friedan as having given 'birth to the women's liberation movement nine years earlier'. Even in 2000, a book review of her memoir declared: 'She is truly the mother of us all' (Steiner 2000), while this maternal trope was also common in obituaries (Woo 2006).

The deployment of generational tropes and familial metaphors has long been recognized as having been central in delimiting popular ways of figuring feminist history (Siegel 1997; Henry 2004; Taylor 2008). This discursive positioning of Friedan has significant implications for the way feminism's history can be told as well as how its future can be imagined. Such familial positioning and generational logic also 'imports ideologies of property' (Roof 1997, p. 72). In this instance, a claim to ownership is implicit in the idea that Friedan is responsible for the women's movement, which works to buttress her authority to speak on its behalf. Problematically, as I have observed, such 'proprietorial discourse situates feminism as a fixed body of knowledge and practices, rather than something which is perpetually in process' (Taylor 2008, p. 198). Nonetheless, throughout her career, Friedan, especially through her blockbuster text, is said to have precipitated intense social, cultural, and political shifts across the USA. Positioning the book as a cultural flashpoint, she remarks: '*The Feminine Mystique* was the beginning of it all. It made people conscious of what millions of women were feeling ... people still stop me in the street and tell me where they were when they read it' (in Suplee 1983, p. 61; see also Sheff 1992). Here, she draws attention to readerly affective investments while also, in the self-reflexivity that is common for blockbuster authors, underscoring her own fame.

This trope of a life-changing book, and implicitly a life-changing author, was ubiquitous throughout Friedan's public career (Tornabene 1971; Friedan 1976, 1983; Walton 1981; French 1983), and she strategically used the book's resonance with readers to help secure her authority. Its repeated invocation effectively serves to write alternative histories of the women's movement out of popular memory, and problematically celebrates one individual over the collective. As Roberta Pearson notes, 'some representations erase signs of contestation and temporarily halt history, establishing a set of unquestioned, frozen, and abstracted "facts"' (2014, p. 192). This celebrifying narrative—that Friedan, via *The Feminine Mystique*, was solely responsible for the women's liberation movement—became a largely uncontested truth-claim, reanimated at various moments, including in commemorative texts like publication anniversaries and obituaries. On the book's thirtieth anniversary one journalist remarked, 'Modern feminism began with one person: Betty Friedan' (Lemann 1992, p. 221). Similarly, in the myriad obituaries published in 2006, almost without exception Friedan was seen to have 'sparked feminism's second wave' (Sweet 2006; see also Coultan 2006; Sullivan 2006); 'single handedly revived the feminist movement' (Jong in Goldstein 2006); and 'helped to inaugurate what we call second wave feminism' (Butler in Goldstein 2006). In relation to feminism, such origin tales are deeply problematic at the best of times (King 1994), but during grief their affective charge intensifies considerably. That Friedan's post-mortem celebrity sign was consistent with the self she herself had attempted to craft over many decades, through various discursive forms, suggests that acts of self-presentation by celebrities are indeed central in the process of reputation building—even after death.

As in *The Feminine Mystique* itself, and in a further attempt to establish her 'ordinariness', in authorial profiles Friedan's feminism is framed as being a response to her mother's stymied life: 'Like so many women, she wanted above all to avoid her mother's misery, her mother's life, and attempted to do this by renouncing her mother's values' (French 1983, pp. 64–5). In addition, overwhelmingly in interviews, as well as in her later memoir, her own experience of marriage is used as evidence of the mystique she had catalogued. For example, deploying the authority of experience, Friedan herself renders a portrait of married life that firmly positions her as one of her implied readers: a miserable, suburban housewife:

> Carl's vision of a wife was one who stayed home and cooked and played with the children. And one who did not compete. I was not that wife ... My trips into the real world to do the interviews and visit editors in New York was the difference between Betty Friedan in a mental institution or out. (Wilkes 1970, p. 16)

Here, as is common, Friedan establishes her own sense of dissatisfaction, herself embodying the discontentment she had mapped in her bestseller, and thereby seeks to secure audience engagement. However, mediated as it is by language and memory, 'experience', including that recounted by Friedan, 'is already an interpretation of the past and of our place in a culturally and historically specific present' (Smith and Watson 2010, p. 31). Nonetheless, as autobiographical acts, in these interviews Friedan positions herself as 'a uniquely qualified authority' (Smith and Watson 2010, p. 31), one who lives, and has lived, her feminism.

In many of these interviews, Friedan's public success invariably results in personal failure but it also enables a sense of self-sacrifice on the part of Friedan, thus rendering her a sympathetic character in the public imaginary. The trope of the selfless feminist toiler is evident in many authorial profiles: 'She worked tirelessly, literally day and night: she lobbied, she organised, she raised funds. She drew hundreds of women from across the country into a ferment of activity' (French 1983, p. 68). This narrative of commendable feminist self-sacrifice, which detaches her from the collectivist politics of the women's movement, is also evident in the following quotation: 'I've been at work trying to liberate every woman in this country, and I'm not yet liberated, I've not fulfilled myself' (in Wilkes 1970, p. 21). The implication, here, of course, is that Friedan has exerted so much energy attempting to effect change in the lives of other women that she has neglected to focus on her own transformation; feminist stardom has come at a grave cost. This is the 'complication' that prevents her from living a fulfilled life. As Nunn and Biressi argue of celebrity interviews, in an effort to foster intimacy, 'These quasi-therapeutic spaces often prompt celebrity performances which identify the complication or "dysfunction" immanent in the celebrity life story; that which prevents the individual from being successful, fulfilled, happy or intimate despite all appearances of a triumphant life' (2010, p. 45). Accordingly, confessions and performed intimacy are central to sustaining renown, including in the case of this blockbuster celebrity feminist. But this characterization is also consistent with the narrative that she is at the heart of American feminism, once again obscuring the fact that her liberal feminism is just one among many different forms; it also demonstrates the inextricability of her professional and personal selves.

As Christine Geraghty argues, 'women are particularly likely to be seen as celebrities whose working life is of less interest than their personal life' (2000, p. 187). Literary celebrities, too, are often represented in ways that disconnect them from their work, rendering the media personality of more value than the text from which their renown derives (Turner 1996, p. 9). Blockbuster celebrity feminists, however, complicate this, I would argue, not only because their literary selves and their public selves are seen to be indistinguishable, but because insights into their private selves/lives are generally only invoked to help make sense of their literary texts and, concomitantly, their feminisms. In Friedan's case, her personal life does not eclipse her professional one, but the former is granted an explanatory power in terms of the latter (Barthes 1967), and indeed the origins of her blockbuster are located in the remembrances offered in these interviews. For example, Friedan draws attention to her own inability to negotiate the competing demands of personal and professional identities, something with which women readers could presumably identify. In this way, she represents—as celebrities always do—a 'significant nodal point of articulation between the social and the personal' (Rojek 2001, p. 16). Of her rejection of a fellowship after her college boyfriend gave her an ultimatum, Friedan notes: 'It was the kind of either-or-situation that is my constant burden in life; either I pursue my career or I sublimate my wishes to man' (in Wilkes 1970, p. 15). This is a tension that continues to play out, especially in the contemporary postfeminist discourse around 'having it all'. Though it was

Brown (1982) who coined this fraught phrase, Friedan's public narrative of self was clearly reliant upon it too.

Moreover, indicative of Friedan's ongoing reverberations, the negotiation of the tensions between the public/private spheres has come to stand for feminism in the twenty-first century, where debates about 'opting out' and 'retreatism' (Negra 2009; Vavrus 2007) are rehearsed in various sites of media culture, leading to claims about the failure of feminism as a political project. Such discourses are firmly rooted not just in Friedan's blockbuster but in the feminism she came to publicly embody as a celebrity. In the same interview, she confesses her desire for a fuller life, alongside a fear that she is not representative of her own feminist politics: 'Right now, my biggest desire is to slow down, to stop being the prime example of the either-or kind of life I oppose, the career-love choice. I want both ... No more either-or any more. I don't want to go to bed alone until the revolution is over' (in Wilkes 1970, p. 24). This was a personalized rendering of the kind of feminism she would go on to pursue even more vigorously, especially with the publication of *The Second Stage* (1981), where she moved away from her original position to argue that feminists needed to re-embrace the familial and the private sphere rather than subordinating it to the public in an effort to achieve gender equality. In it, she argued that the problem that needed 'naming' was now feminism itself: 'We have to break through our own feminist mystique now and move into the second stage, no longer against men but with them' (Friedan 1981).

Writing for the *Chicago Tribune Magazine* in the wake of its publication, Margaret Walton positions Friedan as having personally attempted to negotiate the competing demands of the public and private spheres— and as having failed. Here, she asserts a dissonance between these two aspects of Friedan's persona: 'Betty Friedan became that new class of Superwomen. I can do it all! Write books, lead movements, and still raise children. That sort of thing. But even as the public persona was crusading in a strident, demagogic, slightly mad fashion, the private persona was having a rough time. Friedan's marriage crumbled, she never cooked anymore, and the new apartment was a mess' (Walton 1981, p. 40; see also Tornabene 1971, p. 31). In this way, Friedan's argument about women's ability to 'have it all' is compromised by her own experiences, and thereby so is feminism as a project; if its leading proponent does not personally exemplify the liberation she advocates, how viable could it be? As publicity for *The Second Stage*, such interviews created a sense that the new phase of feminism being advocated by Friedan was a clear necessity. This interview, produced in the early 1980s, also needs to be read in light of the backlash against feminism catalogued by Faludi[16] (1991), with the coding of Friedan as miserable, implicitly because of feminism, being consistent with narratives about scores of women left discontented by feminism's unrealistic goals. Moreover, that feminism itself becomes equated with successfully negotiating the competing demands of the public/private spheres further suggests how different understandings of feminism were obscured by a focus on the liberal Friedan, and further demonstrates how she shaped (and continues to shape) public conversations around feminism. In the next section, I engage with Friedan's memoir insofar as it can be seen as an attempt to control her own celebrity sign and with it the meanings of modern feminism itself—a strategy she can be seen to put into place throughout her career, with varying degrees of success.

Memoir, Feminism, and Celebrity Self-fashioning

In 2000, six years before her death, Friedan published her autobiography. In line with the notion that she uses the memoir form to offer an 'authentic', deeply personal account of the women's movement, a review in *Time* magazine observes: 'Friedan gives us the fullest, most candid account of her experience in the vortex of that revolution, and the toll it took on her personal life' (Blackman 2000). For stars, it has been argued, 'the autobiographical narrative denounces all possible competing forms; its purpose is to answer the false stories circulated by the media' (Amossy 1986, p. 679). In this case, Friedan seeks to rewrite the biographical narratives that were starting to gather some traction; she even explicitly suggests that the purpose of her memoir was to 'set the record straight' (2000, p. 14). These claims to truth, however, cannot simply be taken for granted, and are complicated by the fact that the autobiographer is never an unconstrained actor but one who takes up a variety of available subject positions and in effect brings into being, as opposed to merely expresses, the self of which they write and whose 'truth' they purport to express (Smith and Watson 2010). Given that writing deemed autobiographical is, in effect, 'an intersubjective process' between the narrator and her reader, any notion of a singular, stable 'truth' is in itself always impossible (Smith and Watson 2010, p. 13). Nonetheless, in autobiographical genres, narrators do seek to persuade readers that their portrayal of events/people is authoritative (Smith and Watson 2010, p. 7), a notion that is often central to their marketing and to establishing them as viable commodities. For Couser

(2011), memoir is important not for what it *is* but for what it *does*. What, therefore, does *Life So Far: A Memoir* do, in terms of its author's celebrity and in terms of the feminist public identity and history that it privileges?

The memoir is becoming an increasingly significant literary form for the celebrity, and it is common to position it as offering a kind of unfettered access not permitted by other media forms: 'While celebrity interviews and reality media appearances can be edited and misappropriated, the autobiographical product is more controllable' (Bell 2011, p. 207). This comment, while not taking account of the active meaning-making of readers, emphasizes how celebrities are able to exercise more agency over some forms and genres than others, perhaps none more so than texts which are explicitly constituted as autobiographical. Such control, of course, either over one's image or one's text, is never entirely possible, given that there are always moments 'when the semiotics of a given text break loose from both authorial intention and corporate handling' (Wicke, in English and Frow 2006, p. 44). Notwithstanding the performative nature of autobiographical subjectivity (Cosslett 2000; Smith and Watson 2010), that the 'I' is produced as opposed to merely expressed in/through language, we can attribute some 'situated agency' (Moran 2000) to Friedan, who throughout deploys a recurrent set of tropes about her book, its impact, and the women's movement, and her role in them all. Friedan uses this memoir to show that, far from simply being an 'ascribed' or 'accidental' celebrity (Rojek 2001), she is an achieved one, who laboured strenuously on behalf of feminism and, more broadly, women.

Autobiographical texts by figures of renown stage a 'collision between private interiority and public exteriority' (Glass 2004, p. 8); this, of course, is the tension constitutive of modern celebrity, as theorists like Dyer and others have outlined. In *Life So Far*, Friedan attempts to depict, initially, an 'ordinary' woman (housewife, mother) who did 'extraordinary' things. As shown in the previous section, this ordinary/extraordinary dialetic has long been seen to be at the heart of celebrity culture and our investment in it (Dyer 1979). Around the time Friedan's memoir appeared, the desire for these types of narratives was becoming more pronounced, despite claims of a lamentable, pervasive ahistoricism. As Rita Felski notes, 'the current explosion of women's texts exploring issues of memory, time, tradition, and change all seem at odds with the bland assertion that "we" live in a post-historical era' (2000, p. 145). Feminist life writing came to be especially prominent in the 1990s, as anniversaries of particular events and the publication of key texts from the second wave came to be publicly marked (Ion 1998; Henderson 2006; Taylor 2008). Such personalized versions of public histories, performing as they did a destabilization of public/private borders, worked both to contest the impartiality of historical narrative and to provide women readers with an empathetic voice that resonated with their own experience.

In the history of the women's movement that she offers readers through her personalized narrative, Friedan is contributing to cultural memory around feminism, as she had done earlier through various media interventions. As Gillian Whitlock argues, in terms of memory production, 'autobiographic writings are among the most powerful forms' (cited in Henderson 2006, p. 61). As someone who is authorized to speak on feminism's behalf, including of its history, Friedan's textual remembrances will be granted the status of 'truth' and be folded into public ways of historicizing feminism. Among popular attempts to construct feminist history, Catherine Orr's questions are relevant to Friedan's personal history *as* movement history position: 'How is the second wave being historicised? How is that history being circulated (or perhaps not circulated)? What are the functions to which this history is being put?' (1997, p. 42). In the case of Friedan, such history was being put to use to help secure her positioning as iconic feminist and to circulate a narrative of irrevocable feminist progress (Hemmings 2011).

Life So Far is a linear text, tracing the beginnings of Friedan's exceptionality through to her more recent activism, including the much-publicized disputes with other feminists, and the development of her later publications. Initially, however, she provides a justification for the text that readers are about to consume. The memoir's first paragraph makes it clear that the author is seeking to intervene in how her life is being discursively constituted; rather than allowing others to write her life, and thereby proffer a particular 'Friedan' with which she might disagree or whom she may fail to recognize, she asserts that she was motivated to offer her own autobiographical narrative. She tells readers that, as a forward thinker, she was a reluctant life writer:

> I never intended to write a memoir about my so-called life. First of all, a memoir usually signals the end of a person's career or profession, and I'm still going strong. Second, I think looking backward is boring. I'd rather spend my time looking forward. But my hand was forced, really, when my family and friends and colleagues, past and present, told me a few years ago

that they were being contacted for interviews for books *other* people were writing about *my* life. Well, really. (Friedan 2000, p. 13, original emphasis)

Outraged that biographers would seek to render her life meaningful, here it is clear that she seeks to exert some control over her own life narrative, and with it her broader public persona. Friedan here invokes criticism often levelled at celebrity: that construction of the self within the terms of its dominant discourses necessarily results in distortion and misrepresentation of a 'real' self (Moran 2000; Rojek 2001). Noting that such 'unauthorized biographies' were 'false, mistaken, sensational and trivializing' (Friedan 2000, p. 14), she purports to offer unmediated access to the authentic 'Friedan', an assumption upon which both the celebrity and life writing industries thrive.

Much of the memoir rehearses incidents she already narrated in *It Changed My Life*: the genesis and reception of her blockbuster, including its effects upon her marriage; the establishment of NOW; intramural feminist battles, where she of course is positioned as the moderate and 'reasonable' feminist who was coming under attack from a radical fringe ('I wanted the movement to speak to and for the mainstream' [2000, p. 222]); and what she deemed to be other significant life events such as her meetings with Indira Ghandi and the Pope, and her attendance at the controversial International Women's Conference in Mexico in 1975. Such 'exceptional woman' narratives seek to place their authors at the centre of social movements like feminism, a problematic gesture given the women's movement basis in collectivism (Henderson 2008). Most importantly, in terms of the autobiographical mode's centrality in the celebrification process, the 'Friedan' who emerges from *Life So Far*, published in 2000, is one firmly at the centre not just of the American women's liberation movement but who, with the publication of her blockbuster, is responsible for alleged revolutionary shifts in the gendered organization of social life:

> I guess there was a rekindled interest toward the end of the millennium in the revolutionary book I wrote in the sixties—*The Feminine Mystique*—and the subsequent women's movement I helped start that changed the face of women's history. Over the countless years people have asked me 'What made you do it?' And I never could answer that question. Because I never set out to start a women's revolution. I never planned it. It just *happened*, I would say, by some miracle of convergence of my life and history, serendipity, one thing leading to another. (Friedan 2000, p. 13, original emphasis)

Such claims regarding the role of her book in 'chang[ing] women's lives, chang[ing] history' (2000, p. 106) and being responsible for 'starting a revolution' (2000, p. 135) and the women's movement itself (2000, p. 163) are made repeatedly in *Life So Far*, as they are in other public textual sites.

Like writers of other forms of memoir, Friedan seeks to construct a specific past (and present) feminist self, and this idea of a subject to whom things *just happened* is invoked throughout her public commentary. Yet it sits uneasily against a competing assumption that she actively worked to bring second wave feminism into being. That is, although at times in the narrative Friedan attempts to discursively position herself as being caught up in historical forces, elsewhere in the text the authorial 'I' makes much greater claims to agency. For example, the title of Chap. 7 unambiguously indicates that this will be an origin story foregrounding the author: 'Starting the Women's Movement' (2000, p. 164). Such a claim, and the responsibility it implies, makes clear that this will be an especially interested history, as memoirs necessarily are (Couser 2011). That is, 'remembering has a politics' (Smith and Watson 2010, p. 24).

Despite her apparent disdain for the processes of celebrification above, she suggests that her renown enabled her to achieve feminist goals. Dubbing a small network of Washington bureaucrats the 'underground', she notes: 'That "underground" of women maneuvered me into place all right, recognizing that I, famous for writing a controversial book about women, could do publicly what they could only do underground: organize a women's movement' (Friedan 2000, p. 165). Here, Friedan locates her celebrity capital, garnered through the publication of *The Feminine Mystique*, as crucial to the foundation of the women's movement. Again, undermining the collectivist politics of second wave feminism, Friedan proffers a 'spectacle of the individual as maker of historical change' (Henderson 2008, p. 175). Moreover, like other celebrity authors, here, and indeed throughout her public career, she 'deliberately enacts her own celebrity by exaggerating her impact' (Hammill 2007, p. 2).

Friedan also suggests that the success of her blockbuster made clear that there was an audience, eagerly anticipating an organized women's movement—something that she would dutifully and selflessly offer them: 'I knew there were women out there, waiting. Over three million copies of *The Feminine Mystique* had been sold and I was still getting all these letters telling me "it changed my life"' (Friedan 2000, p. 179). Such women, she implies, simply needed an author like her to facilitate their feminist awakening. Although Friedan does appear to overplay such correspondence, reader letters, not just from women in the USA but a number from both urban and rural Australia, held in the Schlesinger Library at Radcliffe, confirm these assertions about the book's transformative role.[17] However, placing herself at the centre of social transformation, Friedan arguably overstates the gains of the second wave, and NOW especially, and also fails to take account of how not all women have benefited equally from the policy or legislative changes she maps, as well as how these changes are themselves contestable and revocable. Thereby she exhibits little sense of the necessity for ongoing feminist activism—hers is very much a tale of the past (Henderson 2008; Taylor 2009).

In asserting remarkable societal transformations, Friedan implies that she and her peers were indeed successful in 'finishing' the feminist project initiated by the suffragettes but that the mystique effectively dulled:

> At the century's end, understanding how the women's movement transformed our whole society, I see as then … that we were accepting the challenge history was giving us to take up that unfinished revolution for women's equality that the suffragists had carried forward, but that had nearly sputtered out in those years of feminine mystique. (2000, p. 175)

It is clear here that, with *Life So Far*, Friedan tells a particular tale, for very specific ideological, personal, and affective purposes. However, as Dana Heller argues, 'origin stories' such as Friedan's effectively work to obscure 'feminism's historical lack of ideological coherence' (1997, pp. 309–10) and also metonymically substitute this particular narrative of one celebrity feminist for the whole—itself a common strategy in popular feminist writing using a historiographical mode (Siegel 1997, p. 59), in which I would include Friedan's memoir. Such narratives posit this one interested story as *the* story of the American women's movement and in doing so not only foreclose the possibility of alternative modes of telling but also the possibility of conceptualizing feminist pasts themselves as 'partial stories with no beginning and no end' (Roof 1997, p. 68; Taylor 2009).

Throughout her memoir, Friedan mobilizes what Hemmings (2011) refers to as a 'narrative of progress', one of the dominant ways of figuring feminism in both popular and academic contexts. Feminist historians have long problematized such assumptions about irrevocable feminist progress, especially as they fail to take account of how tenuous such 'gains' can be. However, Friedan exhibits no sense of precarity: 'what used to be the feminist agenda is now an everyday reality. The way women look at themselves, the way other people look at women, is completely different, *completely different* than it was thirty years ago' (2000, pp. 374–5, original emphasis). Here, she also fails to take account of the very specific subject to have benefited from the 'major transformative force' she identifies. Her account also reduces myriad feminisms to the liberal vision she pursued. In this 'fantasy of retrospection' (Kavka 2001, p. x), the heterogeneity of the American second wave is elided by what Kavka deems a 'trick of memory'. In this regard, the narrativization of feminist pasts by 'those who were there' must always be seen to have been formed 'through the blindnesses and forgetting that characterise memory' (Kaplan 1997, p. 13; Taylor 2009). The other problem with memory is the kind of remembrances that come to be privileged; 'memory remains suspect and partial, with only the few, furthermore, given the opportunity to narrate their memories in published texts' (Segal 2009, p. 121). Friedan's ability— as a celebrity feminist, recurrently positioned and positioning herself as one of feminism's key drivers—to authoritatively tell the tale of second wave feminist history has gone remarkably unchallenged in the mediasphere.

Friedan's memoir, therefore, is not simply seeking to discursively construct a particular personal history/identity, it is also an attempt to shape the history and public identity of the women's movement and feminism more broadly. Celebrity and the legitimation of particular voices in relation to feminist history is part of a broader cultural 'battle over feminism's place in popular memory' (Heller 2002, p. 87; Henderson 2006). As well as functioning as an autobiography, Friedan's book is also an especially interested history of a social movement. Of course, the biggest problem with history as narrativized by Friedan is its elisions: 'This version of the origins of Second Wave history is not sufficient in telling the story of multiracial feminism' (Thompson 2002, p. 338). Underlining the politics of how second wave feminist history has been constructed, feminist scholars have worked to contest the dominant idea that 'women of color feminists emerged in reaction to (and therefore later than) white feminism' (Thompson 2002, p. 338). However, Friedan's narrative buttresses what Sandoval (2000) calls 'hegemonic feminism', one that seeks to privilege white feminism as the originary, and indeed only, manifestation of women's activism during the second wave. The celebrification of women like Friedan is thereby central to this process of obscuring other ways of figuring the feminist past, and it serves to downplay the centrality of collectivist struggles in which diverse actors were engaged (Henderson 2006, pp. 152–3). But rather than dismissing her memoir outright as the product of a fading celebrity feminist seeking to reassert her relevance in a postfeminist context, Friedan's 'self-coding' can be seen as 'a strategic use of celebrity: attempting to keep feminist memory alive, appealing, and comprehensible to a broad range of women in a context saturated by celebrity discourse and identities' (Henderson 2008, p. 174). This is a more productive reading than is generally offered of the capacity of both celebrity and memoir to be enlisted for feminist purposes.

Of celebrity autobiographies, Amossy writes: 'Instead of an image built by others, she is now a narrator capable of shaping herself and mastering the meaning of her own life' (1986, p. 681). Characterized by this gesture of 'reclamation', the celebrity autobiography purports to provide access to the 'real' which is never, and can never, be fully granted; this is no less the case in the autobiographies of feminist blockbuster stars. However, all texts are made as part of a broader social process, and what readers do with these narratives cannot be known from a textual analysis. That said, through the recurrence of a number of key tropes about Friedan and the text responsible for her celebrification, there is a degree of consistency in her public persona and the feminism she embodies. Furthermore, the narrative Friedan constructed for herself continues to be reinscribed, even post-mortem (Taylor 2016).

Conclusion

As with the other blockbusters examined here, Friedan-as-celebrity became integral to *The Feminine Mystique*'s ongoing success and cultural visibility. As I have shown, through an analysis of various genres of representation and self-representation, her status as an iconic feminist relied heavily upon her own carefully crafted performances. As Tanya Serisier argues of controversial radical feminist Andrea Dworkin, 'Her larger-than-life status was not simply imposed upon her, but one that she wrote for herself' (2013, p. 43). And although there is no guarantee with regard to how such self-inscription will be read, this makes it no less important. In casting herself as an 'ordinary' American woman, while at once underscoring how exceptional her book and her cultural reverberations were, Friedan positioned herself as the personification of the modern women's movement. Through these narratives, and Friedan's ongoing media visibility, liberal feminism comes to be substituted for the whole of second wave feminist activism, a common slippage in popular histories of feminism, which ensures that discourses of equality come to displace more radical attempts to undermine hetero-patriarchal social relations and associated gendered assumptions.

Friedan's 'legacy' (itself a troublesome term) lies in what feminism is now allowed to be publicly—primarily an equality discourse, although celebrity feminists like Greer and Gay continue in their efforts to publicly reimagine feminism as a more radical project (see Chaps. 5 and 7 respectively). In terms of shaping popular understandings of feminism, Friedan's influence is evident in ongoing public debates about the 'double shift', childcare and the need for altered domestic arrangements, and tensions between the still often conflicting subject positions of mother and worker—something that preoccupies Sheryl Sandberg in her 2013 blockbuster, *Lean In*, a text whose debt to Friedan's is clear. That feminism is simply a project towards gender 'equality' has itself become a commonsensical assumption—not least because of the feminism embodied by blockbuster authors like Friedan. Moreover, in this chapter I have considered how the celebrity feminist is the figure through which the historicization of feminism is mediated and, in this instance, through which the possibility of feminism as an unfinished project is foreclosed. It has also mapped how Friedan herself sought to offer an origin story of the second wave, in which she was crucial. It seems, too, that this partial history is one firmly rooted in the popular imaginary. In the next chapter, I move on to another figure who likewise came, not unproblematically, to publicly personify feminism in the 1970s and beyond: Germaine Greer. As a feminist who renounces the search for 'equality' as inadequate, and who persistently underscores that the liberation of women remains incomplete, she ensures that a feminism that runs counter to Friedan's narrative of progress continues to circulate. In particular, Greer has proven remarkable in terms of how she has adapted her celebrity feminism to accord with shifting environments and indeed media platforms, and it is to the strategies she has deployed to ensure this ongoing visibility that I now turn.

Notes

1. While Friedan's role as a founding member of the National Organization for Women (NOW) certainly worked to augment her status as celebrity feminist, here, given my overall concern with the blockbuster, I will not be reflecting upon media coverage focusing on this role. Nonetheless, it is worth mentioning that, even in news media consideration of NOW, Friedan's text is often used to buttress her authority as a feminist speaker.

2. Even on what would have been her 95th birthday, there were celebrations of her contribution to the refiguration of modern gender relations (Brill 2016).
3. As James Bennett (2011) argues of television personalities, although in their performances they are commonly seen to just 'be themselves', this is nonetheless a construction which should be interrogated as such.
4. In her 2013 study of Andrea Dworkin, Tanya Serisier similarly focuses on how this radical feminist worked to craft her public persona.
5. In particular, Norton's Sales Manager, Eugene P. Healy, seems to play an especially active role in making the book visible prior to its official publication date. For example, he wrote to booksellers across the USA with excerpts to pique their interest, confidently proclaiming: 'We believe the sales potential of THE FEMININE MYSTIQUE to be enormous.' Another memo from the Norton Sales Department (also in Healy's name), titled 'Memorandum to Boston Booksellers' (18 February 1963), underscores Friedan's increasing celebrity capital, which he directly correlates with increased demand for the book:

   > Betty Friedan, author of THE FEMININE MYSTIQUE, will be interviewed on WNAC-TV on Sunday afternoon, February 24th, at 3 o'clock. On Monday, the 25th, she will deliver a lecture for the Harvard Graduate School of Education. In preparation for these appearances, I strongly recommend that you give prominent display space to the stock you now have on hand and that you reorder now to make sure you do not run out of stock. (Betty Friedan Papers (Box 54, Folder 668), Schlesinger Library, Radcliffe Institute, Harvard University.)

   A further undated memo from the Norton Sales Department, which presumably would have been circulated among booksellers, notes that the book 'is one of the most controversial and intelligently discussed books we have ever published. Published on February 19th it is already in its 3rd printing.' Offering a series of testimonials, the memo—once more signed Eugene P. Healy—concludes: 'Mrs Friedan has appeared on a number of network TV and radio programs to talk about her book—and many more of these appearances are scheduled' (Betty Friedan Papers (Box 54, Folder 669), Schlesinger Library, Radcliffe Institute, Harvard University). Such promotional material can be seen, in many ways, to be performative—working actively to bring *The Feminine Mystique* into being as a bestseller.

6. For an extensive analysis of postfeminist media culture's ambivalent relation to the housewife, as to feminism itself, see Munford and Water's (2013, chapter 4): 'Haunted Housewives and the Postfeminist Mystique'.
7. It appeared in the *California Examiner* as 'Girl on her Own: No Man? Maybe It's a Blessing!' (3 June 1963), as well as in the *Boston Evening Traveller* (1 July 1963) (Betty Friedan Papers (Box 54, Folder 669), Schlesinger Library, Radcliffe Institute, Harvard University).
8. The quote in the subheading is from Friedan (1976, p. 191).
9. See Murray (2004) for a critique of how such anti-commercialism has operated in regard to feminist publishing in particular.
10. Although Friedan suggests, in *Life So Far*, that 'it was Carl who persuaded them to hire an outside publicist and send me on a publicity tour' (2000, p. 140).
11. Friedan would argue that 'author tours were relatively unknown at the time' (2000, p. 141). Such a claim, however, is undermined by the example of Brown.
12. Coontz (2012) argues that there is little evidence that the publisher did not heavily invest in promotional strategies around the book, and indeed my own archival research reveals extensive prepublicity initiatives on the part of Norton.
13. 'Temple Emanu-El Sisterhood flyer', October 1963. (Betty Friedan Papers (MC 575, Box 2, Folder 79), Schlesinger Library, Radcliffe Institute, Harvard University), accessed via https://schlesingerlibrary.omeka.net/items/show/48.
14. A number of the columns are reprinted in *It Changed My Life* (Friedan 1976).
15. Horowitz argues that Friedan downplayed her leftist and union history in order to help craft a narrative of empathy with readers.
16. In her chapter, 'Betty Friedan: Revisionism as Marketing Tool', Faludi sees Friedan as part of a wider coterie of feminist 'recanters' (in which she includes Greer and Susan Brownmiller), when from the mid-1980s a number of celebrity feminists, whose 'moment under the camera lights', she argues, 'had long since passed, sought to reclaim centre stage'—predominantly through renouncing their earlier feminist positions (1991, p. 352).
17. Friedan discusses these letters in 'Angry Letters, Relieved Letters', in *It Changed My Life*. Personal letters of gratitude include many

deeply confessional pieces. Myriad letters in the Betty Friedan papers held at the Schlesinger Archives, Radcliffe Institute for Advanced Studies at Harvard University, articulate the readers' sense of indebtedness. They also routinely figure the book as articulating that which they have themselves long felt (Betty Friedan Papers (MC 668, Box 54, Folders 697–715), Schlesinger Library, Radcliffe Institute, Harvard University).

References

Amossy, R. (1986) 'Autobiographies of Movie Stars: Presentation of Self and Its Strategies', *Poetics Today*, 7.4: 673–703

Barthes, R. (1967/1977) 'The Death of the Author', *Image/Music/Text*, Oxford: Blackwell

Bastow, C. (2013) 'Re-reading The Feminine Mystique', 7 March, *Daily Life*, accessed via http://www.dailylife.com.au/news-and-views/dl-opinion/rereading-the-feminine-mystique-20130306-2fkx0.html

Bell, E. (2011) 'The Insanity Plea: Female Celebrities, Reality Media and the Psychopathology of British Pop Feminism', in S. Holmes & D. Negra eds. *In the Limelight and Under the Microscope: Forms and Functions of Female Celebrity*, London: Continuum, pp. 199–223

Bennett, J. (2011) *Television Personalities: Stardom and the Small Screen*, London: Routledge

Betty Friedan Papers (1933–2007), Schlesinger Library, Radcliffe Institute, Harvard University

Blackman, A. (2000) 'The Friedan Mystique', 1 May, *Time Magazine*, accessed via http://content.time.com/time/subscriber/article/0,33009,996777,00.html

Bowlby, R. (1987) '"The Problem with No Name": Rereading Friedan's "The Feminine Mystique"', *Feminist Review*, 27: 61–75

Bradley, P. (2003) *Mass Media and the Shaping of American Feminism, 1963–1975*, Jackson: University of Mississippi Press

Brill, A. (2016) 'Betty Friedan, Considered', 4 February, *The Huffington Post*, accessed via http://www.huffingtonpost.com/alida-brill/betty-friedan-considered_b_9159454.html

Brown, H.G. (1982) *Having it All: Love, Success, Sex, Money – Even If You're Starting with Nothing*, New York: Simon and Schuster

Carmody, D. (1972a) 'Feminists Scored by Better', 19 July, *New York Times*, p. 43

——— (1972b) 'Feminists Rebut Friedan Charge', 20 July, *New York Times*, p. 29

Coontz, S. (2012) *A Strange Stirring: The Feminine Mystique and American Women at the Turn of the Century*, New York: Basic Books

Cook, J. (1964) '"Mystique" View Backed by Many, Author Finds', March 12, *New York Times*, p. 30

Cosslett, T. (2000) 'Matrilinieal Narratives Revisited', in T. Cosslett, C. Lurie & P. Summerfield, eds. *Feminism and Autobiography: Texts, Theories, Methods*, London: Routledge, pp. 141–153

Coultan, M. (2006) 'Friedan Lifted Lid on Suburbia's Problem that Had No Name', *Sydney Morning Herald*, 6 February, accessed via http://www.smh.com.au/news/world/friedan-lifted-lid-onsuburbias-problem-that-had-no-name/2006/02/05/1139074110070.html

Couser, M. (2011) *Memoir: An Introduction*, Oxford: Oxford University Press

Dearey, M. (2006) 'Betty Friedan: A Tribute', *Sociological Research Online*, 11.3, accessed via http://www.socresonline.org.uk/11/3/dearey.html

Douglas, S. (1994) *Where the Girls: Growing Up Female with the Mass Media*, London: Penguin

Dyer, R. (1979) *Stars*, London: British Film Institute

English, J.F. & Frow, J. (2006) 'Literary Authorship and Celebrity Culture', in J.F. English ed. *A Concise Companion to Contemporary British Fiction*, Malden: Blackwell, pp. 39–57

Faludi, S. (1991) *Backlash*, Lobdon: Vintage

Felski, R. (2000) *Doing Time: Feminist Theory and Postmodern Culture*, New York: New York University Press

French, M. (1983/2002) 'The Emancipation of Betty Friedan', in J. Sherman ed. (2002) *Interviews with Betty Friedan*, Jackson: University Press of Mississipi, pp. 64–73

Friedan, B. (1963/1992) *The Feminine Mystique*, London: Penguin

—— (1976) *It Changed My Life*, New York: Random House

—— (1981) *The Second Stage*, New York: Summit Books

—— (1983) 'Twenty Years After *The Feminine Mystique*', 27 February, *New York Times*

—— (1993) *The Fountain of Age*, London: Vintage

—— (1997) *Beyond Gender: The New Politics of Work and Family*, New York: Woodrow Wilson Centre Press

—— (2000) *Life So Far*, New York: Simon & Schuster

Friedman, S.S. (1995) 'Making History: Reflections on Feminism, Narrative and Desire', in D. Elam & R. Wiegman eds. *Feminism Beside Itself*, London: Routledge, pp. 11–53

Genz, S. (2009) *Postfemininities in Popular Culture*, Basingstoke: Palgrave Macmillan

Geraghty, C. (2000) 'Re-examining Stardom: Questions of Texts, Bodies and Performance', in C. Gledhill & L. Williams eds. *Reinventing Film Studies*, London: Arnold, pp. 183–20

Glass, L. (2004) *Authors, Inc.: Literary Celebrity in the Modern United States, 1880–1980*, New York: New York University Press

Gledhill, C. (1991) *Stardom: Industry of Desire*, London: Routledge

Goldstein, S. (2006) 'Betty Friedan's legacy', 7 February, *Salon*, accessed via http://www.salon.com/2006/02/06/remembering_friedan/
Gottlieb, P.G. (1983/2002) 'My Side: Betty Friedan', in J. Sherman ed. *Interviews with Betty Friedan*, Jackson: University Press of Mississipi, pp. 52–58
Hammill, F. (2007) *Women's Literary Celebrity Between the Wars*, Austin: University of Texas Press
Healy, E.P. (1963) 'Memorandum to Boston Booksellers', Betty Friedan Papers, Schlesinger Library, Radcliffe Institute, Harvard University, Box 668, Folder 54
——— (undated) 'Memorandum to Sales Department', Betty Friedan papers, Schlesinger Library, Radcliffe Institute of Advanced Studies, Harvard University, Box 669, Folder 54
Heller, D. (1997) 'The Anxiety of Influence: Movements, Markets, and Lesbian Feminist Generation(s)', in D. Looser & E.A. Kaplan eds. *Generations: Academic Feminists in Dialogue*, Minneapolis: University of Minnesota Press, pp. 309–326
——— (2002) 'Found Footage: Feminism Lost in Time', *Tulsa Studies in Women's Literature*, 21.1: 85–98
Hemmings, C. (2011) *Why Stories Matter: The Political Grammar of Feminist Theory*, Durham: Duke University Press
Henderson, M. (2006) *Marking Feminist Times: Remembering the Longest Revolution in Australia*, Bern: Peter Lang
——— (2008) 'The Feminine Mystique of Individualism is Powerful: Two American Feminist Memoirs in Postfeminist Times', *Auto/biography*, 23.2: 165–184
Henry, A. (2004) *Not My Mother's Sister: Generational Conflict and Third-Wave Feminism*, Bloomington: University of Indiana Press
Hesford, V. (2013) *Feeling Women's Liberation*, Durham: Duke University Press
Hirsch, M. & Smith, V. (2002) 'Feminism and Cultural Memory: An Introduction', *Signs*, 28.1: 1–19
Hogeland, L.M. (1998) *Feminism and Its Fictions: The Consciousness Raising Novel and the Women's Liberation Movement*, Philadelphia: University of Pennsylvania Press
Hollows, J. (2000) *Feminism, Femininity and Popular Culture*, Manchester: University of Manchester Press
Horowitz, D. (1998) *Betty Friedan and the Making of the Feminine Mystique*, Boston: University of Massachusetts
Ion, J. (1998) 'Unravelling our Past: Questions of Feminism, History and Memory', *Australian Feminist Studies*, 13.27: 107–116
Kaplan E.A. (1997) 'Feminism, Ageing, Changing Paradigms', in D. Looser & E.A. Kaplan eds. *Generations: Academic Feminists in Dialogue*, Minneapolis: Minnesota University Press, pp. 13–30

Kavka, M. (2001) 'Introduction', in E. Bronfen & M. Kavka eds. *Feminist Consequences: Theory for the New Century*, New York: Columbia University Press, pp. ix–xxvi

Kerber, L. (2002) "I Was Appalled": The Invisible Antecedents of Second-Wave Feminism', *Journal of Women's History*, 14.2: 90–101

King, K. (1994) *Theory in Its Feminist Travels*, Bloomington: Indiana University Press

Knight, P. (1997) 'Naming the Problem: Feminism and the Figuration of Conspiracy', *Cultural Studies*, 11.1: 40–63

Lamb, B. (1993/2002) 'Betty Friedan: The Fountain of Age', in J. Sherman ed. *Interviews with Betty Friedan*, Jackson: University Press of Mississipi, pp. 130–146

Lawrenson-Woods, L. (2014) '(Literary) "Life" in the Death of a Poet: The Posthumous Celebrification and Biomythography of the Australian Bush Balladist, Barcroft Boake', unpublished Master of Cultural Studies thesis, University of Sydney

Lemann, N. (1992) 'Feminism Turns 30', *GQ*, 62.12: 218–226

Lloyd, J. & Johnson, P. (1999) *Sentenced to Everyday Life: Feminism and the Housewife*, London: Bloomsbury

McDonagh, M. (2013) 'Betty Friedan's *The Feminine Mystique* at 50', *The Spectator*, 9 March, accessed via: https://www.spectator.co.uk/2013/03/housewives-choice/

Millett, K. (1970) *Sexual Politics*, New York: Doubleday

Moran, J. (2000) *Star Authors: Literary Celebrity in America*, London: Pluto

Munford, R. & Waters, M. (2013) *Feminism and Popular Culture: Investigating the Postfeminist Mystique*, New York: I.B. Tauris

Murray, S. (2004) *Mixed Media: Feminist Presses and Publishing Politics*, London: Pluto

Negra, D. (2009) *What a Girl Wants: Fantasizing the Reclamation of Self in Postfeminism*, London: Routledge

Nunn, H. and Biressi, A. (2010) "A trust betrayed": celebrity and the work of emotion, in *Celebrity Studies*, 1:1: 49–64

Orr, C. (1997) 'Charting the Currents of the Third Wave', *Hypatia*, 12.3: 29–45

Pearce, L. (2004) *The Rhetorics of Feminism*, London: Routledge

Pearson, R. (2014) 'Remembering Frank Sinatra: Celebrity Studies Meets Celebrity Studies', in B. Thomas & J. Round eds. *Real Lives, Celebrity Stories*, London: Bloomsbury, pp. 187–209

Redmond, S. (2008) 'Pieces of Me: Celebrity Confessional Carnality', *Social Semiotics*, 18.2: 149–161

Rojek, C. (2001) *Celebrity*, London: Reaktion

Roof, J. (1997) 'Generational Difficulties; or the Fear of a Barren History', in D. Looser & E.A. Kaplan eds. *Generations: Academic Feminists in Dialogue*, Minneapolis: University Minnesota Press, pp. 69–87

Sandoval, C. (2000) *Methodology of the Oppressed*, Minneapolis: University of Minnesota Press

Scanlon, J. (2009a) *Bad Girls Go Everywhere: The Life of Helen Gurley Brown*, Oxford: Oxford University Press

Segal, L. (2009) 'Who Do You Think You Are? Feminist Memoir Writing', *New Formations*, 67: 120–133

Serisier, T. (2013) 'Who Was Andrea? Writing Oneself as a Feminist Icon', *Women: a Cultural Review*, 24.1: 26–44

Sheff, D. (1992/2002) 'Playboy Interview with Betty Friedan', in J. Sherman ed. *Interviews with Betty Friedan*, Jackson: University Press of Mississipi, pp. 88–116

Siegel, D. (1997) 'Reading Between the Waves: Feminist Historiography in "Postfeminist" Moment', in L. Heywood & J. Drake eds. *Third Wave Agenda: Being Feminist, Doing Feminism*, Minneapolis: Minnesota University Press, pp. 55–82

—— (2007) *Sisterhood, Interrupted: From Radical Women to Grrls Gone Wild*, New York: Palgrave Macmillan

Smith, S. & Watson, J. (2010, 2nd ed) *Reading Autobiography: A Guide for Interpreting Life Writing*, Minneapolis: University of Minnesota Press

Steiner, W. (2000) 'Hear Her Roar', *New York Times*, 25 June, p. 10

Sullivan, P. (2006) Voice of Feminism's 'Second Wave', *The Washington Post*, accessed via http://www.washingtonpost.com/wpdyn/content/article/2006/02/04/AR2006020401385.html

Suplee, C. (1983/2002) 'Betty Friedan: Her Brave New World', in J. Sherman ed. *Interviews with Betty Friedan*, Jackson: University Press of Mississipi, pp. 59–63

Sweet, C. (2006) 'Groundbreaking Author of The Feminine Mystique Who Sparked Feminism's Second Wave: Betty Friedan', 7 February, *The Independent*

Taylor, A. (2008) *Mediating Australian Feminism: Rereading the First Stone Media Event*, Oxford: Peter Lang

—— (2009) 'Dear Daughter: Popular Feminism, the Epistolary Form and the Limits of Generational Rhetoric', *Australian Literary Studies*, 24(3–4): 96–107

—— (2016) 'Post-mortem Celebrity Feminism: Collective Memory, 'Legacy', and the Obituaries of Betty Friedan and Helen Gurley Brown', unpublished conference paper presented at the Celebrity Studies Conference, University of Amsterdam, 28th–30th June

Temple Emanu-El Sisterhood flyer' (1963), Betty Friedan Papers, MC 575, Box 2, Folder 79, Schlesinger Library, Radcliffe Institute, Harvard University, accessed via https://schlesingerlibrary.omeka.net/items/show/48

Thompson, B. (2002) 'Multiracial Feminism: Recasting the Chronology of Second Wave Feminism', *Feminist Studies*, 28.2: 336–360

Tomlinson, B. (2005) *Authors on Writing: Metaphors and Intellectual Labour*, Basingstoke: Palgrave Macmillan

Tornabee, L. (1971/2002) 'The Liberation of Betty Friedan' in J. Sherman ed. *Interviews with Betty Friedan*, Jackson: University Press of Mississipi, pp. 25–34

Turner, G. (1996) *Literature, Journalism and the Media*, Rockhampton: James Cook University

——— (2014) *Understanding Celebrity*, London: Sage

Vavrus, M.D. (2007) 'Opting Out Moms in the News: Selling New Tradtionalism in the New Millenium', *Feminist Media Studies*, 7.1: 47–63

Walton, M. (1981/2002) 'One More Time to the Ramparts', in J. Sherman ed. *Interviews with Betty Friedan*, Jackson: University Press of Mississipi, pp. 39–51

Warner, J. (2013) 'What Betty Friedan Saw Coming', 15 February, *Time*, accessed via http://ideas.time.com/2013/02/15/what-betty-friedan-saw-coming/

Weber, B. (2012) *Women and Literary Celebrity in the Nineteenth Century: The Translantic Production of Fame and Gender*, Farnham: Ashgate

Whelehan, I. (2005) *The Feminist Bestseller: From Sex and the Single Girl to Sex and the City*, Basingstoke: Palgrave Macmillan

Wilkes, P. (1970/2002) 'Mother Superior to Women's Lib', in J. Sherman ed. *Interviews with Betty Friedan*, Jackson: University Press of Mississipi, pp. 7–24

Williams, R. (2007) 'From Beyond Control to in Control: Investigating Drew Barrymore's Agency/Authorship', in S. Holmes & S. Redmond eds. *Stardom and Celebrity: A Reader*, London: Sage, pp. 111–125

Wolfe, A. (1999) 'The Mystique of Betty Friedan', September, *The Atlantic*, accessed via http://www.theatlantic.com/past/docs/issues/99sep/9909friedan.htm

Woo, E. (2006) 'Catalyst of Feminist Revolution', 5 February, *LA Times*, accessed via http://articles.latimes.com/2006/feb/05/local/me-friedan5

Ziesler, A. (2013) 'The "Bitch" Was Onto Something: A Re-reading of the Feminine Mystique', 11 February, *Los Angeles Review of Books*, accessed via https://lareviewofbooks.org/review/the-bitch-was-onto-something-a-re-reading-of-the-feminine-mystique

CHAPTER 5

Germaine Greer: 'The Star Feminism Had to Have', Unruliness, and Adaptable Celebrity

INTRODUCTION

There is little doubt that Germaine Greer is one of the West's most well-known feminists.[1] To appropriate Chris Rojek's phrase: 'celebrity = impact on public consciousness' (2001, p. 10), and, in terms of the circulation of feminist discourse, Greer's impact has been immense. The emergence of Greer's celebrity can be traced to the publication of her first feminist blockbuster, *The Female Eunuch*, in 1970. As Ann McGrath remarks, 'its massive publicity meant that everybody had heard of it' (1999, p. 178) and, importantly for my purposes, its author. In this vein, a number of studies have illustrated Greer's pivotal role in helping, through *The Female Eunuch* and her subsequent media performances, to shape how so-called 'ordinary' women have come to understand feminism (Skeggs 1997; McGrath 1999; Dux and Simic 2008). In her Australian empirical study, *Living Feminism*, Chilla Bulbeck (1997, p. 137) found that many women accessed feminism through an engagement with Greer-as-celebrity, even while not themselves consuming her blockbuster text. Although she is the only non-American studied here, much of Greer's early celebrity emerged from her engagements with American media, where she was discursively constructed in opposition to local, less 'desirable', feminists (Sheehan 2016). Most recently, in the UK especially, where she has predominantly lived since the 1970s, Greer has been remarkably successful at adapting her blockbuster celebrity feminism for new audiences and new genres (especially those of a comic nature).[2] In this chapter, I argue that throughout her public career Greer has exemplified—and indeed continues to exemplify—Kathleen Rowe's figuration of the 'unruly woman', across various media platforms. Moreover, despite publicly expressing her ambivalence about celebrity, from the publication of *The Female Eunuch* to the present, Greer has herself put into practice a form of strategic media engagement to ensure feminism's (and of course her own) visibility—to which this 'unruly' persona has been pivotal.

As Rowe emphasizes, drawing upon Mikhail Bakhtin's work on the carnivalesque, 'The unruly woman points to new ways of thinking about visibility as power … through body and speech, the unruly woman violates the unspoken feminine sanction against "making a spectacle of herself"' (1995, p. 11). The unruly woman embraces, and creates, such spaces for the performance of this spectacular self. Such unruly women, she continues, 'help sanction political disobedience for men and women alike by making such disobedience thinkable' (1995, p. 44). Throughout her public career, Greer has encouraged—and herself performed—such disobedience, a disobedience for which she is routinely taken to task.[3] Her celebrity, therefore, is part of her performance of a very specific mode of feminist politics in the mediasphere, of publicly embodying the kind of subjectivity she was advocating for all women—of not keeping quiet, of not being 'polite', of refusing to temper her unruly excess. In this way, Greer is a celebrity feminist both in terms of her blockbuster and her explicit interventions into feminist debates in the mediasphere, as well as in her own celebrity 'performative practice' (Marwick and boyd 2011), where she refuses to adhere to prescriptions around the 'correct' way of doing femininity (Butler 1990). Therefore, in addition to the feminism she espouses in her books, journalistic pieces, and interviews, through her celebrity persona she can be seen to offer 'different ways for women to envision themselves and their positions, alternatives for their own performances of gender' (Reed 1997, p. 126). As Greer ages, her 'unruliness' becomes more visible, more potent, and more transgressive, as I will show here.

Given that Greer's media visibility spans almost five decades, it is impossible here to provide a comprehensive account of her representations or self-presentations, or their role in shaping popular understandings of feminism.[4] Accordingly, this chapter moves from a consideration of *The Female Eunuch* and its cultural reverberations, as well as Greer's public self-reflexivity about her own celebrification, to her attempts to adapt her feminist celebrity to forms other than polemic, focusing instead on her more recent television appearances, where this unruly subjectivity remains evident. While Lilburn et al. argue that 'Greer's celebrity advanced the objectives of the women's liberation movement in the early 1970s by making feminism an issue that had resonance in women's every day lives' (2000, p. 338), what are its effects now? And, indeed, what kinds of feminism does she now publicly embody and what kinds of feminist political interventions does she seek to stage in an environment that is markedly different from when she first came to fame?

***

In addition to her initial blockbuster, Greer, a prolific writer, has produced several popular and academic works, including *The Obstacle Race* (1979), *Sex and Destiny* (1984), *The Change* (1991), *Daddy, We Hardly Knew You* (1993), *Slip-shod Sybils: Recognition, Rejection and the Women Poets* (1995), *The Whole Woman* (1999), *The Boy* (2003), *Shakespeare's Wife* (2007), *On Rage* (2008), and, most recently, *White Beech* (2013).[5] As these titles suggest, she has intervened in debates well beyond feminism or sexual politics. That said, it is her status as an iconic feminist that has endured across her entire writing career; her celebrity capital, that is, remains tied to her blockbuster feminism.[6] Although she did eventually publish the 'sequel' to *The Female Eunuch* she said she would never write, *The Whole Woman* (1999), Greer herself 'became far more note-worthy than any follow-up book could possibly have been' (Dux 2010, p. 16). Even Greer's archive, and the announcement in October 2013 that her alma mater, the University of Melbourne, would be purchasing her personal papers for AU$3 million, was the subject of extensive media coverage, including internationally (Dean 2013; Gough 2013; Simons 2013). That the collection would include the original typescript of *The Female Eunuch* was singled out as especially newsworthy.[7] Moreover, in addition to her writing, she has regularly intervened in the mediasphere, often through proffering controversial opinions on ongoing political debates, ensuring her newsworthiness over many decades.

While Greer repeatedly expresses ambivalence about her celebrification, her own performative practice clearly contradicts this position. Here I illustrate that Greer is clearly what Barker-Plummer would call a 'pragmatic feminist media strategist' (2010, p. 172), as indeed are all blockbuster authors. Throughout her public career, and consistent with the blockbuster itself as a popular form, Greer can be seen to deploy celebrity capital to ensure that her brand of feminism reached as wide an audience as possible. From the publication of *The Female Eunuch* and its associated promotional tours to appearances in comic television programmes like *Absolutely Fabulous*, she has kept feminism itself in the media spotlight. Semiotically, Greer has become a visual signifier of feminism; that is, she has become, in a very real sense, the 'public face of feminism' (Sheridan et al. 2006). More broadly, and as with the other women examined in this work, a certain 'Greer' as well as a certain feminism, become visible in media engagements with her and her work. Greer, of course, is an active agent in the cultivation of this persona and this feminism.

Although Greer may have had a troubled relationship with radical feminists, hers is not the palatable equality feminism embodied by other prominent women associated with the second wave, such as Steinem or Friedan, and her feminist politics have remained in many ways consistent over the many decades of her public visibility. As she remarked at a public forum in 2015, 'I'm a liberation feminist, not an equality feminist. Equality is a profoundly conservative aim and it won't achieve anything' (in Denham 2015); this is the feminism of *The Female Eunuch*, one that Greer has espoused ever since. Now well into her seventies, Greer still publishes both journalistic pieces and non-fiction, and is highly active as a public speaker at various international festivals, as well as on news and current affairs programmes. However, as I will show, her more recent feminist interventions are staged predominantly through lifestyle and entertainment television, especially in Britain.[8] Before delving deeper into the ways in which she has actively worked to adapt her celebrity over many decades, while retaining her very unruliness, it is necessary to consider the text responsible for her celebrification and upon which her ongoing ability to attract publicity relies.

'This Will Be a Sensational Book': *The Female Eunuch* and Its Reception

In October 1970, as feminism's second wave gathered momentum, a young Australian academic living in London published a book that purportedly functioned to alter the lives of many women, and especially that of its author. In soliciting a publisher, Greer assured them that it would be a success: 'This will be a sensational book.'[9] And she invested much energy in ensuring this would be so. When *The Female Eunuch* was published in America in 1971, McGraw-Hill expended $25,000 (USD) on various advertising initiatives—an investment that paid off, with readers purchasing the book 'at a peak rate of 89,000 copies per week' and shoring up its status as a bestselling work of non-fiction (Murray 2004, p. 198). *The Female Eunuch* has apparently never been out of print and has been translated into at least 12 languages (Viner 1998). Despite that, its author often publicly draws attention to its limitations: 'If I feel any disappointment at all it is that *The Female Eunuch* is still in print. A tide of better books should have knocked it off its perch within a few months of its first appearance' (Greer 2010). However, the fact they did not reveals much about the book, its initial reception context, and its engaging author.

As a piece of feminist analysis, though less reliant on personal testimony than Brown's or Friedan's blockbusters (Pearce 2004), *The Female Eunuch* attends to the various ways in which gender is produced and reproduced, taking a largely social constructivist approach. Broken into five sections—Body, Soul, Love, Hate, and Revolution—it is a polemical text, contemptuous of the patriarchal economy that so vigorously positions women subordinately, as fundamentally lacking (as its title signals: 'castrated'). She frames it this way: 'This book represents only another contribution to a continuing dialogue between the wondering woman and the world. No questions have been answered but perhaps some have been in a more proper way than heretofore. If it is not ridiculed or reviled, it will have failed in its intention' (1970/1993, p. 26). Greer's blockbuster, then, was designed to be provocative, and, as with Brown's, sexuality and Greer's efforts to reclaim 'cunt power' were key to her feminism as well as to her enormous popularity and resonance with women readers (Le Masurier 2016). As Carmen Winant (2015) recently noted of Greer's position: 'Divorced from their sexuality, women were not self-empowered, but rather submissive, demeaned, and, in some cases, enslaved. Lacking agency of their own, they had come not only to be hated by men but by themselves.' Here she invokes one of the book's most well-known phrases: 'women have no idea how much men hate them' (Greer 1970, p. 279). For Greer, this hatred, which women were themselves internalizing, needed to be rendered visible to be overcome.

Consistent with Friedan's view of women simply needing to escape the 'prison', both metaphorically in terms of their psyches and of the literal suburban home, Greer argued that 'women must learn how to question the most basic assumptions about feminine normality in order to reopen the possibilities for development which have been successfully locked off by conditioning' (1970, p. 17). Despite this apparent similarity to Friedan, Greer's overall approach offered a more radical vision than Friedan's liberal framework allowed, advocating women's withdrawal from capitalism, rather than their incorporation into it (Genz 2009, p. 42). She conjectured, 'if women are the true proletariat, the truly oppressed majority, the revolution can only be drawn nearer by their withdrawal of support from the capitalist system' (1970, p. 25).

As was common in second wave polemical writing, Greer sought, therefore, to make women readers aware of the complex engendering processes to which they were being subjected, as the first step to challenging them. She aimed to provide women with the tools to reconceptualize themselves, while also professing a desire to not be proscriptive (1970, p. 24). Australian historian Marilyn Lake (2016, p. 16) argues that Greer's blockbuster was responsible for bringing a vocabulary around 'sex roles', 'stereotypes', and 'conditioning' into public discourse, thereby substantially shaping the parameters of debate over feminism for many decades. Moreover, the extensive media coverage of the book ensured that Greer and her insights 'got to many thousands of women who might otherwise never (or at least not as soon) have been confronted with these truths about their lives' (Summers 1999, p. 293).

In this vein, copious letters from readers contained in the recently acquired archive at the University of Melbourne reveal just how much the book resonated with readers (Lake 2016) and helped bring them to feminist consciousness. Indeed, in these letters, like those received by Friedan, readers commonly express gratitude to Greer for articulating what they had been feeling and for textually validating their sense of profound dissatisfaction.[10] Such letters are important, given that celebrity relies upon affective investment from fans for its maintenance; in the case of Greer, as well as Friedan, readers characterize their blockbusters as fundamentally transformative. In fact, Greer regularly credits readers with bringing the book, along with its author, into being; as she remarked in 2010 the book sold out on its first day of issue and 'so began the long story of the making of a book by the women who wanted to read it'. Moreover, written viewer responses to Greer's television appearances following *The Female Eunuch*'s publication, including in America (Sheehan 2016), further illuminate how the various mediated spaces available to Greer ensured that her often caustic critique of the castrated woman reached a wide audience, and deeply shaped understandings of women's liberation.

Greer and *The Female Eunuch* in the Mediasphere

Media fascination with Greer has an extensive history, and she—like all the authors examined here—was central to her blockbuster's marketing and commercial success. An advertisement commissioned by *The Female Eunuch*'s USA publisher, McGraw-Hill, extolled:

Who is Germaine Greer? The most loveable creature to come out of Australia since the koala bear? A feminist leader who admittedly loves men? A brilliant writer, 'extraordinarily entertaining'? Great Britain's Woman of the Year? The author of a perceptive, outrageous, devastating book on women? Germaine is all of the above. (in Spongberg 1993, p. 409)

The centrality of Greer's feminist persona to the book's success is exemplified by this quotation from the USA *Newsweek*: 'it is likely that Germaine Greer will make "The Female Eunuch" a best seller in the U.S., just by being herself' (22 March 1971). Her fame was 'meticulously constructed—with Greer's avid participation—by the machinery of book publicity', such as these advertisements (Murray 2004, p. 179) and authorial profiles. Her blockbuster was dubbed 'The Best Feminist Book So Far' (Lehmann-Haupt 1971) and 'a great pleasure to read' (Kempton 1971) in the *New York Times*. Seen as 'the epitome of the liberated woman' (Murray 2004, p. 198), she was reportedly charismatic, feisty, quick-witted, and, of course, opinionated, and on her local and international promotional tours for *The Female Eunuch* her news-value was assured. And while Greer is said to have had an uneasy relationship with movement activists, especially in the USA (Wallace 1997; Sheehan 2016), she was publicly labelled the 'high priestess of women's liberation' (in Spongberg 1993, p. 407).[11]

When *The Female Eunuch* was first published, in spite of her radical politics, Greer was an enormously popular figure. This is perhaps because, as Laura Miller (1999) notes, she was seen to be a 'sexual liberationist first and a feminist second'. Her verve and magnetism is also said to have positively impacted popular characterizations of feminism. In the early phases of her feminist stardom, Greer was regularly photographed laughing, giving feminism 'a subversive sexiness and joie de vivre it needed and appeared to lack' (Showalter 2001, p. 286). However, for some, her cultivation of an appealing celebrity persona mitigated her status as a socially disruptive figure: 'Her pleasure and pursuit of celebrity further provided solace that her radicalism was not very dangerous' (Bradley 2003, p. 138). The antithesis between celebrity and radical politics invoked by Bradley is common in criticisms that being implicated in celebrity culture would necessarily have a deleterious effect on feminism.

As the savage media treatment of celebrity lesbian feminists such as Kate Millett and, later, Andrea Dworkin suggests, it is difficult to downplay the role of sexuality in the public authorization of some feminists over others. It is often presumed that Greer's overt heterosexuality, as well as her physical attractiveness, like Gloria Steinem's, made her more palatable to both the media and the general public than other women's liberationists (Taylor 1971; Toth 1971). As with other female celebrities, profiles of the author frequently draw attention to her physical appearance; she is variously described as 'restlessly attractive' (Weinraub 1971), as having 'the looks of a successful model' (Hazelton 1971), 'magnetically attractive' (Korengold 1971), and as 'imposingly tall and attractive' (Bonfante 1971). Greer's heterosexual desirability—exemplified by the *Life* cover, 'The Saucy Feminist Even Men Like'[12]—was repeatedly overplayed. Second wave feminists were wary of her on these grounds, a sentiment summed up by Spongberg (1993): 'If she's so great, how come so many pigs dig her?' In the *Life* article, exaggerating her femininity, Greer is quoted: 'I don't go for that whole pants and battledress routine. It just puts men off' (Bonfante 1971, p. 30).[13] This in itself could be seen as a strategic gesture to ensure she was given voice. Conversely, the media treatment of Millett, and the fleeting celebrity she was granted, reminds us how integral overt heterosexuality has been to (prolonged) feminist visibility (Dreifus 1971; Gever 2003; Poirot 2004; Hesford 2013).[14]

Although in these earlier narratives she may have been constituted as the less threatening version of the more radical, and often caricatured, second waver, this did not work to contain her often controversial views, articulated in various forums and formats over the next few decades. As one journalist remarked, Greer is 'radical about almost everything, but especially about women' (Bonfante 1971). Despite Spongberg's (1993, p. 417) conclusion that, through their representation of Greer, the media effectively 'castrated' *her*, the coverage may have worked to humanize and personalize her (Barrett-Meyering 2016)—but, I would argue, it did not neutralize her or mitigate her 'unruliness'. Given that Greer was advocating revolution over reform, that she was given so much media space is in itself remarkable—let alone that much of it was supportive, or at least not dismissive, of her feminism. It also works to further complicate the narrative of media hostility towards second wave feminists discussed in Chap. 2 of this volume.

As the above makes clear, Greer, unlike some other movement activists, strategically cultivated her relationship with the media industries (Spongberg 1993, p. 408; Le Masurier 2016). As Lilburn et al. argue, 'she approached the media as a perfect arena to conduct feminist politics (as well as to advance her desire to be famous). Her strategy was impeccable' (2000, p. 338). It is this strategy, and how it has been adapted over the past decade or so in particular, that most interests me here. Prior to that analysis, it is valuable to draw upon Greer's own explicit commentary on celebrity culture and how it could be deployed for feminist purposes. This self-reflexivity provides a way of interpreting her five-decades-long media engagement as a strategic form of political intervention; it also offers further insight into her performative practice as an unruly feminist.

THE FEMALE EUNUCH AND GREER'S PARADOXICAL CRITIQUE OF CELEBRITY

Throughout her public career, and as is common for feminist blockbuster authors, Greer has maintained that she is at worst deeply resentful, at best ambivalent, about her own celebrification. In this section, I will focus on the media coverage following the publication of her blockbuster in 1970 and associated book tours over the following few years, largely from a sample of USA, UK, and Australian newspapers and magazines, as well as some television. In much of this coverage, Greer's ambivalence about publicity comes to be foregrounded. In terms of how authors publicly make sense of their celebrification, Moran identifies a recurrent theme: that writers commonly invoke a 'moralistic, disdainful attitude towards celebrity itself' in order to attempt to place some distance between themselves and the discourses of celebrity. However, as he notes, such a position actually works to highlight what these authors already know: 'that they are not separate from but wholly implicated in their own fame' (Moran 2000, p. 79). The example of Greer is entirely consistent with this argument, as she commonly uses media interviews and her own newspaper and magazine articles to explicitly critique celebrity while yet conceding its strategic value, especially in making feminism widely accessible. Before examining some of Greer's self-reflexive commentary on her celebrification, it is valuable to turn to her original blockbuster for insight into her position on feminism's broader mediatization.

In *The Female Eunuch*, Greer complains that, when it comes to media coverage of the women's liberation movement, 'the same faces appear every time a feminist issue is discussed. Inevitably they are presented as the leaders of a movement that is essentially leaderless' (1970, p. 16). Despite her at best tangential relationship to the women's movement, in light of Greer's own visibility such comments are nothing if not ironic. Later in *The Female Eunuch*, Greer also makes explicit her own position in relation to the mediatization of feminism.[15] Arguing that women's movements around the world have 'been very much a phenomenon of the media' (1970, p. 346), she criticizes the dominant feminist approach regarding engagement with the mainstream media: 'Women's liberation has adopted a suspiciously uncooperative attitude to the press, a tactic which has in no way improved their public image or protected it from figuring so large in Sunday supplements and glossy magazines. In fact, no publicity is still bad publicity' (1970, p. 348). Therefore, even prior to her own widespread celebrification, Greer exhibits a shrewd awareness of feminism's reliance upon the media (and the media's reliance upon feminism). Rather than simply retreating from newspapers or magazines she endorses feminist incorporation into them: 'It is hoped that more and more women decide to influence the media by writing for them, not being written about' (1970, p. 348); this is something Greer herself, like Brown and Friedan, would do across her lifetime, with regular columns in *The Observer*, *The Guardian*, *The Sunday Times*, and *The Spectator*, as well as commissioned articles for *Esquire* and *Harper's Bazaar*.[16] Here, Greer endorses feminist self-representation as a tactical response to a media environment at times hostile to attempts to destabilize the patriarchal status quo.

As is common for celebrities of any ilk, Greer self-reflexively engaged with her positioning as a celebrity feminist in many interviews throughout 1971–2. Through her appearance on the Australian current affairs programme, *This Day Tonight* (ABC, 22 March 1972), Greer articulated her own disdain for the celebrification on which she contradictorily came to rely; she was to do this at various times over the coming decades (and most recently in the ABC documentary series, *Brilliant Creatures*, where she again stated that she never wished to attain fame; Jacobson 2014). Greer suggests that it is only within Australia that she is reduced to a 'superstar', accusing the local media of being preoccupied with intimate details of her life rather than her texts (an accusation, I would suggest, which is not entirely sustainable). On *This Day Tonight*, she laments: 'they're [the Australian media] much more interested in my going to bed with someone or my having V.D. or my getting a divorce than they are about the actual issues which I'm here to promote'. Here, she invokes an understanding of celebrity as representative of the displacement of interest from an individual's work or public activity to their private life (Turner 2014), a shift she bemoans throughout this interview (and indeed in many others). Greer is also seen to mobilize the kind of critique of celebrity that has been common from within feminism. What is most remarkable about these comments, and her contemptuous disavowal of the networks of celebrity, is that they are completely at odds with her own cultivation of a celebrity persona over the subsequent decades. As Lilburn et al. have mapped, these critiques of fame appeared throughout Australian press coverage of her book tour. For example, in Adelaide's *Advertiser* (1972), Greer is quoted as saying 'Fame is a dead bore' and 'fame is a terrible drag' (cited in Lilburn et al. 2000, p. 336).[17]

Throughout such interviews Greer seeks to author herself as the reluctant, yet strategic, celebrity feminist. In doing so, she seeks to shore up her status as feminist du jour while simultaneously assuaging the fears of those who may disparage her celebrification as something entirely inconsistent with feminism. She herself had been publicly subjected to such critiques, most notably in Claudia Dreifus's piece in *The Nation*, 'The Selling of Feminism' (1971), which denounced her for succumbing to the commodification of her own image (see Sheehan 2016). In these interviews, Greer can be seen to anticipate, and in the same gesture neutralize, criticisms that feminism and self-promotion were antithetical. Moran sees such self-reflectivity as 'a necessary working through of the problems of being a public author' (2000, p. 70). As he suggests:

> Celebrity seems to enforce self-reflexiveness: for those authors who experience it, it becomes a constant preoccupation—they talk and write about it constantly, in both fictional and non-fictional forms, usually describing fame as a negative influence pervading their whole life and work. (Moran 2000, p. 10; see also Rojek 2001; Hammill 2007; York 2013)

Fundamentally ambivalent about celebrification, authors often identify a disconnect between their media representation and their veridical selves (Rojek 2001). As a response, Moran notes, some have removed themselves from the spotlight entirely. While this is certainly not the case with Greer, she eventually did withdraw from print media interviews, citing 'misrepresentation' as grounds for such a retreat, thus suggesting a deliberate attempt to intervene in how she was being publicly constructed.[18]

It was not just the Australian book tour that generated extensive metacommentary in the press around the authorization of Greer over other feminist voices. As Linda Scott (2000, p. 25) remarks, 'Germaine Greer's 1971 American tour was a full-blown marketing event in the tradition of P. T. Barnum.' In press coverage of the tour, one of the key tropes was Greer's reticence about promotional activities; so persistent was this narrative that must we must assume it was a calculated approach by the author.

For example, Greer told Sally Quinn (19 May 1971), of the *Washington Post*: 'I'm a complete media freak ... And the only reason I ever submitted to the commercialization of Germaine Greer is to help women in the home, to raise the self-image of women, to spread the movement on the widest possible base.'[19] Here, as in other discursive sites, Greer characterizes herself as effectively having gallantly sacrificed herself to 'commercialization' in an attempt to facilitate the proliferation of feminist ideas to the broadest audience possible. Similarly, in comments that were echoed throughout the tour, in the *New York Post* (10 April 1971) she remarks:

> As far as I'm concerned, I only go through all these flaming hoops because somewhere out there—beyond the TV cameras and the bright lights and the interviewer's head—there's a woman encased in all those shells and you have to make a big noise to be heard. (in Dudar 1971; see also Goldstein 1971; Hamilton 1971; Pruden 1971; Stein 1971; Zito 1971)[20]

Like Friedan, Greer here is positioning herself as willingly sacrificing her anonymity to the feminist cause, exposing herself to invasive media attention, and undertaking extensive promotional labour, to ensure her feminist arguments gather the most momentum (Le Masurier 2016). Moreover, the idea of 'making a big noise' in order to help raise the consciousness of women aligns with the 'unruliness' that I argue has marked her extended public career, and further illustrates that such disruptiveness is vital to and constitutive of her feminist politics. The above comments provide an insight into Greer's strategy for ensuring that she, and her feminism, have remained in the limelight for over five decades. In her myriad public reflections on, and political justifications of, her own fame, Greer also exhibits an awareness of the gendered judgements that have long been made of women who are seen to be active agents in their own celebrification; judgements that have only intensified as she has aged.

COURTING CONTROVERSY; OR THE FEAR OF AN AGEING WOMAN REFUSING TO KEEP QUIET?

In the twenty-first century, Greer's celebrity capital remains undiminished. Her public voice continues to be, in many ways, a highly controversial one. Her 2003 book, *The Boy*, an artistic appreciation of the teenage male form, saw panicked charges of a kind of paedophilia levelled at her. She made provocative comments following the death of Steve Irwin,[21] as well as in essays like 'White Fella Jump Up' (2003a) and the mini-polemic about violence against women in Australia's Indigenous community, *On Rage* (2008). Most recently, she has been taken to task over what are perceived to be her transphobic views.[22] In the mediasphere, her status as an authorized speaker on feminism, based on the success and cultural prevalence of her initial blockbuster, remains largely uncontested—even if her arguments may at times be. That is, the capital she has accrued over many decades facilitates an access to the mediasphere enjoyed by few other feminists.

It is impossible to offer an analysis of Greer's public persona without attending to deeply gendered claims that she simply courts controversy as a means of maintaining visibility. In the following quotation from *The Guardian*, Greer's fame and her feminism are clearly seen to be antithetical, her celebrification thought to compromise her feminist 'legacy' (which itself is neither uncontentious nor uncomplicated). Nonetheless, this journalist ultimately concedes that her very presence concomitantly ensures the continued visibility of feminism:

> She has penned articles for *The Sun* in favour of Page 3, written a book celebrating the objectification of boys, attacked transsexuals and joined *Celebrity Big Brother*. Is it any wonder that some feminists fear Greer, now 72, is trampling on her own legacy because of a desire for publicity? Yet … the controversy she stirs means that 'she's the only feminist most people have ever heard of'. (Khaleeli 2011)

Similarly, in *The Australian*, conservative commentator Janet Albrechtson (2010) accuses Greer of being 'more interested in fame than revolution', invoking the ostensible 'inauthenticity' of her public persona: 'when the lights are turned on, the cameras focused and the audience awaits, Greer turns on the charm. With a voice made for the stage and a sharp wit, television producers and arts organisers love her. Behind the scenes, Greer is a series of grunts and grumbles.' However, such criticism dismisses outright Greer's active—and often highly successful—attempts to keep not only herself but feminism on the public radar over many decades.

Male academics and public commentators have also felt the need to denounce Greer's agency in the maintenance of her celebrity sign as somehow distasteful. For example, in an article on her auto/biography, *Daddy, We Hardly Knew You*, she is criticized for her 'attention-grabbing', accused of engaging in a 'self-publicizing enterprise' (Porter 2007, p. 15). Likewise, comparing her to his 'demented grandmother', Australian playwright Louis Nowra suggests that 'she will say and do anything to get noticed, even if this means whingeing and moaning her way through shows such as *Grumpy Old Women*' (2010, p. 46). However, such an assertion, patronizing and contemptuous of Greer's contemporary media performances, serves to simplify what are very complicated relations between feminism, media, publicity and branding. Moreover, criticisms like these are deeply gendered and reveal anxieties about the presence of a visibly ageing woman who refuses simply to fade away and instead continues to speak publicly on all manner of subjects. Lorraine York's comments regarding Margaret Atwood's embodied celebrity are apposite to Greer and how her celebrity has been publicly figured: '[Greer] ... at numerous points in her career, has been punished by the media, by literary reviewers and readers, for not adhering to this image of the modestly accomplished domestic woman—for inhabiting her celebrity, for the most part, unapologetically' (2007, p. 167). This 'unapologetic' embodiment of celebrity is problematic for speakers gendered feminine, as York makes clear, especially as they age.

The very fact that an ageing Greer continues to be so visible has been the source of much discomfort, from online hate speech on social media forms like Facebook ('Germaine Greer is a Bitter Old Hag') to Nowra's *Monthly* piece. As Dux remarks:

> Part of the uncomfortable legacy of *The Female Eunuch* is that its author has not only grown old but has refused to go away, keep quiet or even to mellow. She and her book have become icons, and yet Greer the woman has declined suspension in the aspic of collective memory. (2010, p. 11)

Her more recent framing by critics in the media reveals much about discourses around ageing, and especially ageing female bodies. As Jermyn and Holmes (2015, p. 17) note, while ageing women may be more publicly visible than ever before, it remains the case, as Susan Sontag argued, that 'Men are "allowed" to age, without penalty, in several ways that women are not.' But although 'the female body [is] pored over for signs of "abject" ageing as well as evidence of cosmetic surgery', a preoccupation which the blockbuster celebrity feminist, and Greer especially, escapes, the other way in which the regulation of older women celebrities is effected is through 'a damning invisibility' (Jermyn and Holmes 2015, p. 19). Relatedly, Greer herself took up the question of women and ageing, and especially invisibility, in *The Change* (1991), suggesting her own concerted effort to remain in the public eye is in itself a feminist attempt to destabilize this gendered dynamic.[23] In the case of

Greer, who has certainly not been rendered invisible, the concern seems to be whether her behaviour is 'appropriate' for a woman well into her seventies; I will take up the ways in which she gleefully performs this inappropriateness now.

Greer in the Twenty-first Century Mediasphere: Feminism, Comedy, and Television

'Celebrity status', Nunn and Biressi argue, 'is an endless project to achieve, sustain and manage' (2010, p. 50). Greer has been overwhelmingly successful in adapting the celebrity for which *The Female Eunuch* was responsible, especially through various (often comedic) performances on quiz and lifestyle programmes on recent British television. In particular, as noted earlier, she can be seen to exemplify what has been called an 'unruly woman' (Rowe 1995), a transgressive figure who offers alternative ways of performing femininity and, in this instance, of performing celebrity feminism. In terms of her public palatability, Greer has been said to combine 'intellectuality, feminism, [and] humor ...' (Bradley 2003, p. 137). It is her humour, and the ways she deploys it to insert feminist counter-narratives into the mainstream media, and especially the televisual sphere, which both ensures her access to these spaces and helps her to cultivate new forms of feminist celebrity. Greer has adapted, not just as feminism itself has, or as its mediatization has taken on increasingly complex forms, but also as the mediasphere itself—and television especially—has witnessed the proliferation of new formats and programmes. Greer uses these new forms, and the spaces they provide to speak, to utter feminism in new ways, for new audiences. As in previous chapters, here I am concerned with Greer's self-representational tactics and the kinds of feminism she is able to circulate through them.

In particular, more recently she is most active in various forms of what Frances Bonner has described as 'ordinary television' (2003): current affairs, lifestyle, sketch comedy, celebrity game and quiz programmes. As Bonner notes, the 'overwhelmingly dominant purpose of television' is now seen to be entertainment (2003, p. 211), and therefore feminists, in order to remain in the public spotlight, must acknowledge this maxim about the contemporary function of television and amend their behaviours accordingly—as Greer has done so skilfully. Feminism, Greer patently recognizes, in order to resonate with audiences must (like television) be entertaining and engaging. Moreover, from her earliest appearances on *Nice Times* with Kenny Everett in the late 1960s, Greer's penchant and aptitude for televisual comedic performances has been evident (Wallace 1997).

As Marshall (1997, p. 130) makes clear, television is central to 'the process of substantiating the significance of public personalities that have emerged in other domains', including in terms of the celebrity feminist author. With regard to Greer's fame, television has always been important; appearances in documentaries, talk shows, news, and current affairs programmes have made her feminism accessible to the widest possible audiences, who have responded favourably to the critique of patriarchal gendered norms that she offers. As Rebecca Sheehan (2016) shows in her study of Greer's appearance on the *Dick Cavett Show* in the USA, television enabled her to reach viewers who would send over 500, largely appreciative, letters to the network following her 1971 appearance.[24] Television is repeatedly seen to be integral to the 'new' form of feminist celebrity that she would come to embody—the following comment is indicative in this regard; Greer 'became one of the first true feminist stars of the television age' (Dux 2010, p. 9; see also Wallace 1997, p. 207). In the *New York Times*, Judith Weinraub (1971) remarked that after the then British Prime Minister, Edward Heath, 'the person most likely to be seen on television screens here [the UK] these days is Germaine Greer'. However, rather than focus on these historically distant television appearances, as part of attempting to come to terms with how Greer has worked to transform her celebrity for the current political and representational environment I have chosen to attend to her more recent televisual performances in one genre in particular: the comedic. They also enable me to demonstrate how the unruliness that characterized Greer's early persona in the years immediately following her blockbuster's publication remains a key feature of her public performances.

Although she appears relatively regularly as a guest on the ABC's *Q&A* current affairs programme in Australia, it is through television appearances in the UK, including sitcoms, that her public visibility has been most vigorously maintained. For example, she featured on the *Absolutely Fabulous* episode, 'Hospital' (1994), where she appears in a dream sequence as Edina's (played by Jennifer Saunders) mother. She also featured on Ricky Gervais's *Extras* (2006), where she performs herself performing herself on the BBC's *Newsnight Review*, offering a critique of the fictional Andy Millman's *When the Whistle*

Blows, and more recently she had a cameo role Matt Lucas and David Walliams' satirical look at the airline industry, *Come Fly with Me* (2014). The list of television programmes on which she has appeared over the past decade is extensive and varied. She has been a housemate on *Celebrity Big Brother* (2005); a guest on comic quiz shows *Never Mind the Buzzcocks* (2008), *What the Dickens* (2008), *Have I Got News for You* (2000, 2002, 2004, 2005, 2009), and *You Have Been Watching* (2009); a regular contributor to the *Grumpy Old Women* (2005) television series; a guest at Heston Blumenthal's *Feasts* (2009) and on variety programmes such as *The Jonathan Ross Show* (2008). More recently, she featured on Ricky Gervais and Stephen Merchant's mockumentary, *The Moaning of Life* (2010), where she engages with Carl Pilkington about what it means to be an intellectual while baking bread in her Warwickshire kitchen. These diverse public appearances, in addition to written works, help maintain her presence on the (British) cultural landscape. These performances, too, situate feminism as an ongoing project, rather than something to be relegated to the past; that is, Greer is not simply a second wave feminist relic but an active contributor to ongoing debates around the liberation of women. In particular, with her challenge to dominant equality feminist discourses, through her continued celebrification, she may also be crucial to efforts to reanimate more radical forms of feminism in so-called postfeminist, neoliberal times (Eichorn 2015).

As I will show, her involvement with such programmes illustrates her adaptability and also how feminism, through public personas such as Greer, can remain publicly visible. It worth noting, however, that sometimes this adaptability is less successful than others, as demonstrated by Greer's decision to leave *Celebrity Big Brother* (2005) after just four days in the house. In the reality television format, unlike the comic shows upon which I focus here, she was not simply performing as a celebrity entertainer but was required to engage in the vagaries of everyday life, including interactions with other celebrity housemates. That is, she had to perform both an everyday self and a celebrity self (as opposed to in the comic shows, where only the latter is being televized). In such a context, Greer had limited control over how her persona came to be framed, something that obviously unsettled her, and prompted her to exercise the agency she did have to depart the house. Moreover, Greer's repeated claim to deeply dislike fame is somewhat compromised by her decision to take part in *Celebrity Big Brother* (Season 3, 2005) in the first instance. This decision too suggests that, while Greer often does appear to exhibit a canny insight into the media industries, she is not immune from making questionable choices as part of her efforts to ensure her ongoing visibility.[25]

Laughter, Celebrity Feminism, and Greer on Variety Television

The celebrity of the feminist, as the example of Greer makes clear, is not confined to one field or form; multiple, overlapping performances constitute her celebrity sign. This sign, like that of all celebrities, is an intertextual construct, made up of diverse texts and performances (Marshall 1997)—her books, her interviews, her opinion pieces, her appearances on variety programmes all work to make and remake a particular public 'Greer'. As Marshall observes, 'performance is a critical component in any public figure's identity' (1997, p. 39). Not just in terms of their 'primary art form', as he says, but in terms of their extra-textual performances such as interviews and other promotional contexts. In most of the recent examples I consider, Greer does not have a commodity to sell, such as a new polemic; instead, 'she herself is the product' (Dux 2010, p. 16). Celebrities are not simply cultural icons but 'brands' (Turner et al. 2000, p. 13). In this regard, 'the celebrity's ultimate power is to sell the commodity that is themselves' (Turner et al. 2000, p. 12). Given the regularity with which she appears on these television panel shows especially, she seems to be quite a hot commodity who must resonate with twenty-first-century audiences. That said, in addition to herself, what Greer seeks to peddle is feminism, and thereby the political importance of these televisual performances cannot be overstated. Furthermore, many of these programmes have a live audience, enabling her to directly connect with viewers in ways precluded by other media forms.

Greer has been described as a 'diva', a 'glorious, melodramatic, chaos-making performer' (Miller 1999, p. 3), and given, as Joshua Gamson (1994, p. 103) notes, 'celebrities are chosen for their ability to perform themselves amusingly', no wonder Greer continues to be granted media visibility. Furthermore, given that 'the legitimacy of celebrity is always radically provisional' (Turner et al. 2000, p. 13), and thereby requires much cultural labour, both by the publicity machinery surrounding them and by the celebrity themselves, it is not surprising that we are witnessing Greer's attempts to reconstitute, and update, her celebrity in order to ensure her viability as a public persona. In all of these instances, what is most pronounced is Greer's own laughter and deployment of humour. That Greer uses the space afforded her within the celebrity zone in this way reveals much about the contemporary relationship between the mediasphere, feminism, and indeed postfeminism.

Much feminist criticism of the media–feminism nexus has referred to the way the trope of the humourless feminist has been mobilized in media accounts of the women's movement, commonly as a strategy of denigration. However, indicative of its continued cultural currency, it has not simply been in media discourse that this trope has been activated; Chilla Bulbeck (2005) found in her interviews with young women that it continues to be used as a justification for their dissociation from feminism or their refusal to claim a feminist identity (see also Scharff 2011). In *The Promise of Happiness*, Sara Ahmed (2010) too unpacked this figure of the 'feminist killjoy', considering how it has operated ideologically to discredit feminism and to position it as destructive, a wilful enemy to women's happiness; that is, as no fun. In her performances on comedy programmes, Greer works to destabilize this notion and by no means could she be categorized as such a killer of joy. In addition to Ahmed, other critics have shown how much postfeminist discourse seeks to situate itself in opposition to feminism on the grounds of its negative attitude towards some pleasures (romance, marriage, consumption), pleasures that can now apparently be embraced because of feminism's overwhelming success (McRobbie 2009). Greer's televisual performances actively trouble the assumption that feminism represents a gloomy seriousness and that, conversely, postfeminism symbolizes enjoyment and pleasure. However, while the humourless feminist trope may indeed have been inscribed at various historical moments, especially in the mainstream media, Australian historian Susan Magarey has underscored how feminists have always deployed irony, parody and humour as part of a broader subversive, liberatory agenda in the public sphere. Indeed, she cites Irigaray on how humour helps to contest the power that would keep women powerless (Magarey 2003, p. 142). 'Comedy', as Maggie Andrews remarks, 'is always potentially threatening to dominant social orders, processes and power relationships' (1998, p. 51). Greer herself once made this explicit when she said 'laughter can be about power' (in Andrews 1998, p. 51). In light of her own use of comedy, then, Greer does continue to wield power in the mediasphere.

In interviews or when being questioned on television, she responds in ways that often allow her to insert a feminist oppositional discourse into these programmes, often through humour. In particular, comic panel shows are those on which Germaine can be seen to excel. On *Never Mind the Buzzcocks* (2008, BBC Two), comedian James Corden (best known for his role as 'Smithy' in *Gavin & Stacey*), at the urging of the host, reluctantly recounts his favoured pick-up line, directing it at Greer. Telling her that she isn't quite aware of her allure, Greer immediately quips: 'Well, you're quite wrong, I know exactly how lovely I am.' Playing on her historical positioning as the 'saucy feminist even men like', she participates actively and willingly in this gag. A certain 'Greer' is produced in these interactions with other comedic figures. She is confident and playful, again subverting the dominant trope of the humourless feminist, and making feminism accessible, and perhaps desirable, to new audiences. In the contemporary televisual environment, well-known figures such as Amy Poehler, Sarah Silverman, Amy Schumer, and Tina Fey suggest that this mobilization of the comedic—and celebrity—for feminism's own ideological purposes, and to reinvigorate young women's interest in feminism as a political project, is certainly not a strategy unique to the iconic Greer.

Even when the programmes are not explicitly comic, Greer manages to insert feminist critique, alongside humour, into these performances. For example, participating in *Gordon Ramsay's Recipe Challenge* (2009), the celebrity chef interviews her while she offers up her own take on *duck à l'orange*. Ramsay's show, unlike some of the others that are more explicitly branded comedy and/or variety shows, nonetheless enables Greer to perform her unruly feminism, with Ramsay himself acting in crucial ways to facilitate this performance. (Ramsay's status as one of the West's most well-known celebrity chefs is also significant here.) Introducing Greer, Ramsay observes: 'My guest tonight is the most famous feminist in the world, so no mother-in-law jokes ...' Although placing a feminist in the kitchen could arguably work to neutralize her feminism, on the contrary Ramsay enthusiastically probes her about what she thinks about today's young women and what she feels may be the legacy of feminism. She criticizes the persistent focus on the body, using the example of Katie Price (former page 3 model in the UK, aka Jordan), whom she remarks is 'destroying herself' by a failure to eat adequately. In contrast, she argues: 'A healthy girl is a fat-bottomed creature.' Greer has always criticized the regulation of women's bodies, including in both *The Female Eunuch* and *The Whole Woman*, a strategy she clearly deploys here.

Offering her another opportunity to make her feminist position clear, Ramsay suggests that he wouldn't expect her, as a feminist, to have agreed to partake in a cooking show, to which Greer responds that when one cooks because it is enjoyable, not because one has to, then it can be pleasurable for women. Here, Greer manages a feminist critique of domestic politics, all the while engaging in witty repartee and banter with Ramsay—combining entertaining television with a feminist politics. Similarly, after remarking that they have both been criticized for their swearing, Ramsay asks Germaine about her fascination with the 'c' word. Greer then comments upon what a powerful signifier it is, suggesting 'it really makes strong men grow pale'. He draws attention to how she has previously compared vaginas to oysters and caviar, to which she quips: 'And we've got half a country who won't eat oysters: I wonder why that is?' Here, a critique of a broader patriarchal fear of women's sexuality is articulated. Thus, during a cooking segment that runs for around four minutes, Greer manages to insert a critique of body, domestic, cultural, and sexual politics, demonstrating a significant amount of skill in rendering feminism accessible to a broader audience who might not have consumed her initial blockbuster.

Greer similarly deploys humour on Heston Blumenthal's *Heston's Feasts* (2009, Channel 4), to be entertaining but also to shore up her status as a powerful, sexually agentic feminist. After discovering she has eaten bull's testicles she cheekily proclaims: 'Bollocks have never frightened me; I'll eat a bollock any time …' She follows up with an exaggerated appreciation: 'Mmmmm, that is goooorgeous.' Of course, audiences are in on this particular gag; Germaine, indeed, has built an entire public and professional career out of demonstrating how she has never been in the grip of such a 'fear'. In particular, Greer has been known for her 'maverick sexual libertine views' (Tait 2006, p. 71) and this comment invokes, as well as pokes fun at, that history. Greer's televisual feminism is irreverent, entertaining, and self-reflexive. Rewriting this narrative about feminism in the popular imaginary is no mean feat, and can arguably result in feminism reverberating with audiences that may not otherwise have been sympathetic to feminism as a project and a politics.

Greer's very presence, then, even when not explicitly articulating her feminist positions (which she often still manages to do in these shows), is in itself a kind of feminist practice; the unruly woman, as Rowe argues, who is 'too fat, too funny, too noisy, too old, too rebellious—unsettles social hierarchies' (1995, p. 19). As an articulate, opinionated woman, with a defiantly ageing female body, Greer disrupts the dominant, intersecting cultural logics of both celebrity and postfeminism, each of which seeks to manage, and even obscure from public view, such politicized women and especially such unruly, visibly ageing bodies. Here, she both embodies and explicitly articulates her wilfully disruptive feminism (Ahmed 2010).

As briefly mentioned, in postfeminist media culture women's ageing provokes intense anxiety and is seen as something that needs to be 'cured' through transformative body labour (Wearing 2007, p. 287; Negra 2009; Holmes and Jermyn 2015). Attempts to halt the ageing process, so visible in postfeminist media culture more broadly (Negra 2009; Wearing 2007), are reported on with glee, while celebrities who fail to invest financially or affectively in this process are also heaped with scorn. The celebrity feminist is a unique, and indeed transgressive, figure in this regard. In particular, Greer's choice to personally reject, and to explicitly critique, the 'girling' of older women in books like *The Whole Woman* (1999) works to successfully trouble these dominant postfeminist discourses on ageing. As she ages, Greer does not receive the same bodily scrutiny to which other celebrities are subjected; there simply is no media attention to her quotidian existence such as her bodily regimes or dress sense (though, ironically, she herself often issues such gendered judgements including through her comments about the sartorial choices of Australia's first female Prime Minister, Julia Gillard). This focus on corporeality is not integral to her continued visibility, as it is to that of other women celebrities. While in other contexts women's behaviours and bodies are, of course, judged, regulated, and policed via the operations of celebrity, this is not the case for Greer. Indeed, her very presence in the mediasphere, as I suggest above, disrupts this idea about the public prohibition of visibly ageing female bodies.

However, is this heightened visibility, in a media context where the cultural logics of postfeminism prevail and where feminism is being relegated to the past, a product of feminism's historicization? That is, is Greer hyper-visible because she is seen to be the embodied sign of feminism's ageing, and thereby its redundancy? Has her oppositional potential been evacuated? In light of the examples I have cited here, I would suggest not. In these performances, feminism is not being ridiculed as perhaps it may have been in the mediasphere at other periods in its history, but becomes a playful, reflexive identity that itself is adaptable, shifting, and mobile—like its most iconic figure. As the above examples illustrate, she exhibits a clear irreverence, which in itself is nothing new for Greer, and arguably she is conscious that the ability to be entertaining is key to the maintenance of her celebrity, and thus to the feminism she has come to publicly embody.

Her 'sauciness' is something upon which media have remarked throughout her career, and which these newer comic forms appear to facilitate and sanction. In the tradition of the 'unruly woman', Greer is unapologetic about, and indeed appears to relish, this performance of playfulness—and it clearly makes for amusing television which undoubtedly helps to ensure these spaces remain open to her and, by extension, to feminism. Moreover, what I want to suggest here is that there is residual feminism operative in Greer's more recent celebrity performances. She is such an iconic feminist figure, publicly embodying feminism, that even when she is not explicitly engaging in feminist criticism or being interviewed about her feminism, it is nonetheless an absent presence. Given the centrality of 'unruliness' to her performative practice as a celebrity, through it she herself is enacting a feminist mode of being that continues to disrupt normative assumptions about femininity, especially as she ages. That said, when given the opportunity, or even seizing it herself, she does use these spaces to more explicitly articulate feminist positions on various issues, as these examples have shown.

Conclusion

Indicative of the celebrity feminist's active role in the construction of her own public persona emphasized throughout this book, Germaine Greer has worked to adapt her celebrity in ways that suggest an acute consciousness of how mainstream media forms, as well as their audiences, are evolving. Shifting from her use of literary forms to even more accessible, far-reaching media technologies represents an attempt to extend feminism's audience and speaks of a recognition that media culture is *the* primary site for the construction and circulation of various forms of feminism. Television, especially, permits Greer to reach an audience at least as large as that of her initial blockbuster—if not larger. Pre-existing celebrity, and indeed notoriety, initially garnered from the publication and reception of her first blockbuster, have made these spaces open to her but how she uses them enables her to build upon, extend, and repurpose her celebrity self—and in the process her feminism—serves to underscore the importance of this ground for feminism. However, consistent across these texts, across a number of decades, is Greer's performance as an unruly woman.

Such transgressive performances 'always hold the possibility of offering *some women* ways to think about change, different ways to conceptualize reality and their own lives' and 'might inspire those women who are looking for other ways to see' (original emphasis, Reed 1997, p. 126). This unruly subjectivity, as I have argued, emerges from her uncompromising feminism, one that exhorts us to think and do feminism more radically than pervasive contemporary equality discourses permit. In this sense, Greer provides a valuable counterpoint to other contemporary celebrity feminists, like Sheryl Sandberg, who reduce feminism to a quest for gender equality, as she encourages audiences to expand their understandings of what feminism is and indeed, in recognition of celebrity's generative capacity, what it might be. She also reveals that, in terms of their politics, celebrity feminists, and thus the celebrity zone in a broader sense, manifest the diversity that has always marked movements towards women's liberation, including in the current environment. In Part II, I move on to consider some more recent blockbuster authors and how their feminisms, as well as their celebrity, may have shifted as a result of socio-political and technological changes.

Notes

1. In her controversial, unauthorized biography, Christine Wallace remarks that Greer was seen as 'the star feminism had to have' (1997, p. 207).
2. It is remarkable that there is no mention, let alone analysis, of Greer in Mendes' (2011) study of how feminism has been represented in the USA and Britain during the second wave.
3. On Australia's *Q&A* programme, in March 2012, Greer suggested that Prime Minister Gillard wore suit jackets that served merely to accentuate her 'fat arse'. She reiterated and defended her comments, which were the subject of much media coverage, on the programme in August 2012 (Curtis 2012; Sparrow 2012).
4. I have recently co-edited (with Atkins and Dever) a special edition of *Australian Feminist Studies*, focusing on the figure of Greer; for analysis of Greer's early media engagement in particular, see Barret-Meyering (2016), Lake (2016), Le Masurier (2016), and Sheehan (2016).
5. While outside the scope of this chapter, it is noteworthy that Greer has more recently moved into the role of celebrity activist, in the field of environmental politics in particular. Indeed, her latest publication, *White Beech* (2013), maps her own efforts to help rejuvenate the Queensland rainforest she purchased, while she reportedly donated Melbourne University's fee for the recent acquisition of her archives to this cause. In this way, she can be seen to use her celebrity capital for philanthropic efforts. That her focus has seem-

ingly now shifted from gender to the environment (though not of course entirely) is worthy of further critical attention.
6. Although Greer is not famous for her academic work, it is undoubtedly the case that her intellectual capital also works to buttress her authority.
7. While I did visit the Greer archive in the Ballieu Library at the University of Melbourne, it is still in the process of being catalogued. In a future research project, I will be engaging more fully with the archive and how Greer has herself curated a particular life/self through the material she has allowed to be included in the archive (see Buchanan 2016).
8. It is worth further considering why it is in the UK that Greer continues to resonate; perhaps this relates to her status as an expatriate Australian and the British media's apparent fascination with successful intellectuals from the colonies, such as Clive James and Barry Humphries, who they come to claim as their own.
9. Germaine Greer Archive, University of Melbourne. Available online via https://digitised-collections.unimelb.edu.au/handle/11343/42261. See also Lake 2016 for an examination of the book's genesis.
10. For example, Lake cites one fan letter, from American Dina Adler, dated September 1971, which notes: 'I have just finished reading *The Female Eunuch*, and like thousands of other women throughout the country, I am sure, I feel I owe you a debt of gratitude for expressing succinctly and wittily what we have felt inside for a long time' (Lake 2016, p. 24).
11. However, alongside largely sympathetic media attention came inevitable attempts to regulate and manage the 'unruly' Greer, including from the state; for example, on a tour of New Zealand in 1972 she was arrested for using profanities while lecturing on sexuality (Winant 2015).
12. The Bantam paperback of *The Female Eunuch* in the USA even included this quote as part of its paratext, featuring it on its first page, with the follow up: '*Life* puts Germaine Greer on its cover!' (Baumgardner 2001, p. 3).
13. Not insignificantly, this quotation is featured as an inset in the article, bolded and in large font, inevitably drawing the reader's attention to it and the gist of the rest of the article.
14. While not engaging with Millett's celebrity in any detail here (precisely because of its fleeting nature), it is worth briefly considering

her celebrification and its undoing. Published in 1970, Kate Millett's *Sexual Politics*, a feminist analysis of the patriarchal underpinnings of a number of modern canonical literary texts, was, like those produced by the women considered here, a bestselling work of non-fiction. Millett initially provided the mainstream media with something it wanted to help anchor stories about the emergent women's liberation movement: a face, an artistic rendering of which even featured on the cover of the 31 August 1970 edition of *Time* magazine. However, while her book did provide the basis for her stardom it did not endure: 'Although *Sexual Politics* propelled Millett into a media maelstrom, her "15 minutes of fame" was short lived' (Poirot 2004, p. 205). When public rumours regarding Millett's bisexuality came to circulate, media coverage became much less sympathetic (Gever 2003).

15. Significantly, these disavowals have continued throughout her public career, including in her subsequent (if not so successful) 'blockbuster' sequel, *The Whole Woman* (1999, p. 228).
16. Greer's newspaper and magazine columns were published as *The Madwoman's Underclothes* in 1986.
17. Television programmes were also preoccupied with the question of Greer's stardom, and especially her own role in its maintenance, with Mike Willesee explicitly questioning her on Channel Nine on this point: 'Are you a limelighter who jumped on the bandwagon at the right time?' (cited in Lilburn et al. 2000, p. 336).
18. Greer's assistant, Carol Horne, wrote to Susan Mitchell outlining Greer's objection to appearing in *Icons, Saints and Divas*: 'Dr Greer decided some years ago to cease giving print interviews. She was fed up being processed by celebrity interviewers for their own aggrandizement.' She continued that, as a means to 'avoid misrepresentation', this strategy 'has worked so well she has no mind to change the rule' (Mitchell 1997, p. 26). This represents a very clear attempt by Greer to control the meanings of her celebrity sign. In terms of the promotional activities around *The Whole Woman*, in a handwritten note on a fax from a marketing agency contained in the archive, Greer wrote of book signings: 'I would rather not do them. The whole business disgusts me' (fax from Colman Getty Public Relations, 2 March 1999, Germaine Greer Archive, 2014.0038.0134, University of Melbourne). Such correspondence suggests that perhaps Greer's public comments about enduring celebrification for the greater feminist good were actually authentic.

19. All the articles referenced in this section regarding Greer's discomfort with celebrity culture were located in the Greer archives at the University of Melbourne, signalling a further effort on her part to reiterate this position in the present. (Germaine Greer Archive, 2014.0038.0217, 'Press USA, 1971', University of Melbourne)
20. In response to a journalist questioning why she would consent to using vehicles like *Cosmopolitan* and *McCall's*—'which contain much feminists find offensive' (Zack 1971)—to promote the book, Greer candidly remarked: '"I don't care who pays as long as it's my message. They paid me and used my words so why not take it?", Miss Greer said'. It was also reported that Greer objected to having to 'autograph copies of her book to promote it. "People are such suckers for marketing. They even buy books that way. My book was even used as a Mother's Day gift because it was signed …"' (Zack 1971).
21. Australian wildlife presenter, Steve Irwin, died after being stung by a stingray while filming one of his documentaries. Arguing in *The Guardian* (5 September 2006) that Irwin provoked the stingray, Greer contentiously concluded 'The animal world has finally taken its revenge on Irwin …'
22. As I have noted, Greer throughout her public career has been an intensely anxiety-provoking figure. In this vein, as I was completing this book Greer became embroiled in yet another controversy that revolved around her authority to speak publicly about gender and feminism. She was due to present a lecture at Cardiff University (the Hadyn Ellis lecture) on women and power in the twentieth century on 18 November 2015, but students started a petition to block—or 'no platform'—her, due to what they argued to be her long-standing transphobia. Despite the furore, the event went ahead. Much media commentary sought to defend Greer, questioning these attempts to silence her (see Lewis 2015; Lyons 2015; Tartellin 2015).
23. She recently received media coverage for comments that feminism itself was ageist and that women need to be allowed to 'grow up' (Denham 2015).
24. These letters are part of the Greer archive at the University of Melbourne (2014.0038.218, 'Audience Response to GG').
25. On her exit, Greer did concede that she made a mistake agreeing to partake in a reality television programme and that when a mistake is made one must seek to rectify it—which she believes she did by asking to be removed from the house: https://youtu.be/mfsQWrycQbg.

References

Absolutely Fabulous (1994) Television series. Season 2, Episode 1, BBC One: UK

Ahmed, S. (2010) *The Promise of Happiness*, Durham: Duke University Press

Albrechtson, J. (2010) 'Celebrity Feminist Is an Intellectual Paris Hilton', March 10, *The Australian*, accessed via http://www.theaustralian.com.au/opinion/columnists/greer-is-an-intellectual-paris-hilton/story-e6frg7bo-1225838986055

Andrews, M. (1998) 'Butterflies and Caustic Asides: Housewives, Comedy and the Feminist Movement', in S. Wagg ed. *Because I Tell a Joke or Two: Comedy, Politics and Social Difference*, London: Routledge, pp. 50–64

Barrett-Meyering, I. (2016) 'Germaine Greer's 'Arch Enemy': Arianna Stassinopoulos' 1974 Australian Tour', *Australian Feminist Studies*, 31.87: 43–61

Baumgardner, J. (2001) 'Introduction', in G. Greer, *The Female Eunuch*, New York: Farrer & Strauss, pp. 1–7

Bonner, F. (2003) *Ordinary Television: Analyzing Popular Television*, London: Sage

Bonfante, J. (1971) 'Saucy Feminist Even Men Like', 7 May, *Life*, pp. 30–32

Bradley, P. (2003) *Mass Media and the Shaping of American Feminism, 1963–1975*, Jackson: University of Mississippi Press

Bulbeck, C. (1997) *Living Feminism: The Impact of the Women's Movement on Three Generations of Australian Women*, Cambridge: Cambridge University Press

———. (2005) 'Women Are Exploited Way Too Often: Feminist Rhetorics at the End of Equality', *Australian Feminist Studies*, 20.46: 65–76

Buchanan, R. (2016) 'The Record Keeper', *Australian Feminist Studies*, 31.88: 22–27

Butler, J. (1990) *Gender Trouble*, New York: Routledge

Celebrity Big Brother (2005) Television series. Season 3, ITV: UK. 'Celebrity Big Brother 3 – Germaine Walks', accessed via https://www.youtube.com/watch?v=mfsQWrycQbg

Come Fly with Me (2014) Television series. Season 1, Episode 5. UK: BBC One

Curtis, K. (2012) 'Greer Defends 'Fat Arse' PM Comment', 27 August, *The Daily Telegraph*, accessed via http://www.dailytelegraph.com.au/greer-defends-fat-arse-pm-comment/story-e6freuz0-1226459413409?sv=5292064df264586d38a4ad1c3a64728a

Dean. K. (2013) 'Why Greer's Life in Letters Is One for the Archives', 1 November, *The Conversation*, accessed via https://theconversation.com/why-germaine-greers-life-in-letters-is-one-for-the-archives-19625

Denham, J. (2015) 'International Women's Day 2015: Germaine Greer Brands Feminism 'Ageist' and Demands Right to 'Grow Up'', 8 March, *The Independent*, accessed via http://www.independent.co.uk/news/people/international-womens-day-2015-germaine-greer-brands-feminism-ageist-and-demands-the-right-to-grow-up-10094000.html

Dreifus, C. (1971) 'The Selling of Germaine Greer', *The Nation*, Germaine Greer Archive, 2014.0038, Box 217, 'Press USA, 1971', University of Melbourne

Dudar, H. (1971) 'Female, but Not Feminine', *New York Post*, April 10, Germaine Greer Archive, 2014.0038, Box 217, 'Press USA, 1971', University of Melbourne

Dux, M. (2010) 'Temple of *The Female Eunuch*: Germaine Greer Forty Years On', *Kill Your Darlings*, Issue 2: 9–17

Dux, M. & Simic, Z. (2008) *The Great Feminist Denial*, Melbourne: Melbourne University Press

Eichorn, K. (2015) 'Feminism's There: On Post-ness and Nostalgia', *Feminist Theory*, 16.3: 251–264

Extras (2006) Television series. Season 2, Episode 5, BBC: UK

Gamson, J. (1994) *Claims to Fame: Celebrity in Contemporary America*, Berkeley: University of California Press

Genz, S. (2009) *Postfemininities in Popular Culture*, Basingstoke: Palgrave Macmillan

'Germaine Greer Discusses Feminism and Duck a l'Orange – Gordon Ramsay' (2009), 4 November, accessed via https://www.youtube.com/watch?v=mrnnUfag2T0

Gever, M. (2003) *Entertaining Lesbians: Celebrity, Sexuality, and Self-Invention*, New York: Routledge

Goldstein, M. (1971) 'Fem-lib's Hottest New Act', 21 May, *Newsday*, Germaine Greer Archive, 2014.0038, Box 217, 'Press USA, 1971', University of Melbourne

Gordon Ramsay's Recipe Challenge, Channel 4, London, accessed via https://youtu.be/mrnnUfag2T0

Gough, D. (2013) 'Germaine Greer Sells Archive to Melbourne University', 28 October, *The Age*, accessed via http://www.theage.com.au/victoria/germaine-greer-sells-archive-to-melbourne-university-20131028-2wbho.html

Greer, G. (1970/1993 ed) *The Female Eunuch*, London: Flamigo

———. (1979) *The Obstacle Race: The Fortunes of Women Painters and Their Work*, Melbourne: Secker and Warburg

———. (1984) *Sex and Destiny: The Politics of Human Fertility*, Melbourne: Seeker and Warburg

———. (1986) *The Madwoman's Underclothes: Essay and Occasional Writings, 1968–1985*, London: Picador

———. (1991) *The Change: Women, Ageing and the Menopause*, London: Hamish Hamilton

———. (1993) *Daddy, We Hardly Knew You*, London: Hamish Hamilton

———. (1995) *Slip-Shod Sybils: Recognition, Rejection and the Woman Poet*, London: Viking

———. (1999) *The Whole Woman*, London: Transworld

———. (2003) *The Boy*, London: Rizzoli

———. (2003a) 'Whitefella Jump Up', *Quarterly Essay*, Issue 11

———. (2006) 'That Sort of Self-Delusion Is What It Takes to Be a Real Aussie Larrikin', 5 September, *The Guardian*, accessed via https://www.theguardian.com/world/2006/sep/05/australia

———. (2007) *Shakespeare's Wife*, London: Harper Perennial

———. (2008) *On Rage*, Melbourne: Melbourne University Press

———. (2010) 'Change Is a Feminist Issue', 8 March, *The Age*, accessed via http://www.theage.com.au/it-pro/change-is-a-feminist-issue-20100307-pqs8.html

———. (2013) *White Beech*, London: Bloomsbury

Grumpy Old Women (2005) Television Series. Season 2, Episodes 1–4, BBC Two: UK

Hamilton, M. (1971) 'The Enraged Feminist', 13 May, *San Francisco Examiner*, Germaine Greer Archive, 2014.0038. 217, 'Press USA, 1971', University of Melbourne

Hammill, F. (2007) *Women's Literary Celebrity Between the Wars*, Austin: University of Texas Press

Have I Got News For You (2000, 2002, 2004, 2005, 2009) Television Series. BBC: UK

Hazelton, N. (1971) 'Germaine Greer Talks', 24 November, *Australian Women's Weekly*, pp. 24–25

Hesford, V. (2013) *Feeling Women's Liberation*, Durham: Duke University Press

Heston's Feasts (2009) Television series. 'Fruity Bulls Balls', 11 March, Channel 4: UK, accessed via: https://www.youtube.com/watch?v=PoPA3R9cAZ0

Jacobson, H. (dir) (2014) *Brilliant Creatures*, Australian Broadcasting Corporation

Jermyn, D. & Holmes, S. (2015) 'Introduction: A Timely Intervention — Unravelling the Gender/Age/Celebrity Matrix', in D. Jermyn & S. Holmes eds. *Women, Celebrity and Cultures of Ageing*, Basingstoke: Palgrave Macmillan, pp. 1–10

Jonathan Ross Show (2008) Television series. ITV: UK, 'Germaine Greer talks about "The Female of the Species"', accessed via https://www.youtube.com/watch?v=L4Xp-8OMTnk

Kempton, S. (1971) 'Little Patience with Much and Much Advice for Her Own Victimised Class', 25 April, *The New York Times*, accessed via http://www.nytimes.com/books/99/05/09/specials/greer-eunuch.html

Khaleeli, H. (2011) 'Germaine Greer: Academic and Feminist Commentator Who Bulldozed Her Way into Women's Minds', 8 March, accessed via http://www.guardian.co.uk/books/2011/mar/08/germaine-greer-100-women

Korengold, R.J. (1971) 'Suddenly the world love Germaine Greer...', 19 May, *Sunday Telegraph*, Germaine Greer Archive, 2014.0038.217, 'Press USA, 1971', University of Melbourne

Lake, M. (2016) '"Revolution for the Hell of It": The Transatlantic Genesis and Serial Provocations of *The Female Eunuch*', *Australian Feminist Studies*, 31.87: 7–21

Le Masurier, M. (2016) 'Ressurrecting Germaine's Theory of Cuntpower', *Australian Feminist Studies*, 31.87: 43–61

Lehman-Haupt, C. (1971) 'The Best Feminist Book So Far', 20 April, *New York Times*, Germaine Greer Archive, 2014.0038.217, 'Press USA, 1971', University of Melbourne

Lewis, H. (2015) 'What the Row over Banning Germaine Greer Is Really About', 27 October, *New Statesman*, accessed via http://www.newstatesman.com/politics/feminism/2015/10/what-row-over-banning-germaine-greer-really-about

Lilburn, S., Magarey, S. & Sheridan, S. (2000) 'Celebrity Feminism as Synthesis: Germaine Greer, *The Female Eunuch* and the Australian Print Media', *Continuum*, 14.3: 335–348

Lyons, K. (2015) 'I Think Greer Is Wrong on Trans, but Banning Her Is Not the Answer' 28 October, *The Guardian*, accessed via https://www.theguardian.com/commentisfree/2015/oct/27/germaine-greer-transphobia-cardiff-feminism-inclusive

Magarey, S. (2003) '"The Color of Your Moustache" or Have Feminists Always Been Humourless?', *Journal of the Association for the Study of Australian Literature*, 2: 141–156

Marwick, A. & boyd, d. (2011) 'To See and Be Seen: Celebrity Practice on Twitter', *Convergence*, 17.2: 139–158

McGrath, A. (1999) '*The Female Eunuch* in the Suburbs: Reflections on Adolescence, Autobiography and History Writing', *Journal of Popular Culture*, 33.1: 177–190

McRobbie, A. (2009) *The Aftermath of Feminism*, London: Sage

Marshall, P.D. (1997) *Celebrity and Power*, Minneapolis: University of Minnesota Press

Mendes, K. (2011) *Feminism in the News: Representations of the Women's Movement Since 1960*, Basingstoke: Palgrave Macmillan

Miller, L. (1999) 'Germaine Greer', 22 June, *Salon*, accessed via http://www.salon.com/1999/06/22/greer/

Millett, K. (1970) *Sexual Politics*, New York: Doubleday

Mitchell, S. (1997) *Icons, Saints and Divas: Intimate Conversations with Women Who Changed the World*, Sydney: Harper Collins

Moran, J. (2000) *Star Authors: Literary Celebrity in America*, London: Pluto

Murray, S. (2004) *Mixed Media: Feminist Presses and Publishing Politics*, London: Pluto

Negra, D. (2009) *What a Girl Wants: Fantasizing the Reclamation of Self in Postfeminism*, London: Routledge

Never Mind the Buzzcocks (2008) Television series. Series 22, Episode 5, UK: BBC2

Nowra, L. (2010) 'The Better Self: Germaine Greer and *The Female Eunuch*', February, *The Monthly*, accessed via https://www.themonthly.com.au/issue/2010/february/1329283585/louis-nowra/better-self

Nunn, H. & Biressi, A. (2010) '"A Trust Betrayed": Celebrity and the Work of Emotion', *Celebrity Studies*, 1:1: 49–64

Pearce, L. (2004) *The Rhetorics of Feminism*, London: Routledge

Poirot, K. (2004) 'Mediating a Movement, Authorizing Discourse: Kate Millett, Sexual Politics, and Feminism's Second Wave', *Women's Studies in Communication*, 27.2: 204–235

Porter, R.J. (2007) '*Love Is No Detective*': Germaine Greer and the Enigma Code', *Life Writing*, 3: 3–16

Pruden, W. (1971) 'Here's a Style of Women's Lib That, Well, Somewhat Different', 10 April, *The National Observer*, Germaine Greer Archive, 2014.0038.217, 'Press USA, 1971', University of Melbourne

Q&A (2008–present) Television series, Australian Broadcasting Corporation, Australia

Quinn, S. (1971) 'The Greering of the Press', 19 May, *The Washington Post*, Germaine Greer Archive 2014.0038, Box 217, 'Press USA, 1971', University of Melbourne

Reed, J. (1997) 'Roseanne: A "Killer Bitch" for Generation X', in L. Heywood & J. Drake eds. *Third Wave Agenda*, Minneapolis: University of Minnesota Press, pp. 122–133

Rojek, C. (2001) *Celebrity*, London: Reaktion

Rowe, K. (1995) *The Unruly Woman: Gender and the Genres of Laughter*, Austin: University of Texas Press

Scharff, C. (2011) *Repudiating Feminism: Young Women in a Neoliberal World*, Farham: Ashgate

Scott, L. (2000) 'Market Feminism: The Case for a Paradigm Shift', in M. Catteral, P. MacLaran, & L. Stevens eds. *Marketing and Feminism: Current Issues and Research*, London: Routledge, pp. 16–38

Sheehan, R. (2016) '"If we had more like her we would no longer be the unheard majority": Germaine Greer's Reception in the United States', *Australian Feminist Studies*, 31.87: 62–77

Sheridan, S., Magarey, S. & Lilburn, S. (2006) 'Feminism in the News', in J. Hollows & R. Moseley eds. *Feminism in Popular Culture*, Oxford: Berg, pp. 25–40

Showalter, E. (2001) *Inventing Herself: Claiming a Feminist Intellectual Tradition*, London: Picador.

Simons, M. (2013) 'Germaine Greer Sells Archive to University of Melbourne', 28 October, *The Guardian*, accessed via http://www.theguardian.com/books/2013

Skeggs, B. (1997) *Becoming Respectable: Formations of Class and Gender*, London: Sage

Sparrow, R. (2012) 'Germaine? You lost me at "big arse" ...', 20 March, *Mamamia*, accessed via http://www.mamamia.com.au/germaine-gree-you-lost-me-at-big-arse/

Spongberg, M. (1993) '"If She's So Great, How Come So Many Pigs Dig Her?": Germaine Greer and the Malestream Press', *Women's History Review*, 2.3: 407–419

Stein, R. (1971) Germaine Greer Archive, 2014.0038.217, 'Press USA, 1971', University of Melbourne

Summers, A. (1999) *Ducks on the Pond: An Autobiography*, Sydney: Penguin

Tait, P. (2006) 'Greer, Bad Language and Performative Emotions in Protests', *Journal of Australian Studies*, 86: 65–78

Tartellin, A. (2015) 'When You Tell Germaine Greer to Sit Down and Shut Up Because of Her Views on Transgender Women, You Become a Misogynist Too', 28 February, *The Independent*, accessed via http://www.independent.co.uk/voices/when-you-tell-germaine-greer-to-sit-down-and-shut-up-because-of-her-views-on-transgender-women-you-a6710821.html

Taylor, B. (1971) 'Woman's Deforming Bondage to Man', 29 September, *The Evening Star*, Germaine Greer Archive, 2014.0038.217, 'Press USA, 1971', University of Melbourne

The Moaning of Life (2010) Television series, Sky: UK. 'Karl Pilkington – Satisfied Fool (Part 1 of 3)', accessd via: https://www.youtube.com/watch?v=mNlSOTf6XHI

This Day Tonight (1972) Television series. 22 March. 'Germaine Greer and women's liberation 1972', Australian Broadcasting Corporation, Australia, accessed via http://splash.abc.net.au/home#!/media/1245334/germaine-greer-and-women-s-liberation-1970

Toth, S. (1971) 'Have All Women Been 'Castrated?', 23 May, *The Minneapolis Tribute*, Germaine Greer Archive, 2014.0038.217, 'Press USA, 1971', University of Melbourne

Turner, G. (2014) *Understanding Celebrity*, London: Sage

Turner, G., Marshall, P.D. & Bonner, F. (2000) *Fame Games: The Production of Celebrity in Australia*, Cambridge: Cambridge University Press

Viner, K. (1998) 'Look Forward in Anger', 26 February, *The Guardian*, accessed via http://mg.co.za/article/1998-04-17-look-forward-in-anger

Wallace, C. (1997) *Greer: Untamed Shrew*, Sydney: Pan Macmillan

Wearing, S. (2007) 'Subjects of Rejuvenation: Aging in Postfeminist Culture', in D. Negra & Y. Tasker eds. *Interrogating Postfeminism*, Durham: Duke University Press, pp. 277–310

Weinraub, J. (1971) 'Germaine Greer – Opinions That May Shock the Faithful', 22 March, *New York Times*, Germaine Greer Archive, 2014.0038.217, 'Press USA, 1971', University of Melbourne

What the Dickens (2008) Television Series. Season 2, Episode 7. Sky: UK

Winant, C. (2015) 'The Meaningful Disappearance of Germaine Greer', *Cabinet*, Issue 57, Spring, accessed via http://www.cabinetmagazine.org/issues/57/winant.php

York, L. (2007) *Literary Celebrity in Canada*, Toronto: University of Toronto Press

———. (2013) *Margaret Atwood and the Labour of Literary Celebrity*, Toronto: University of Toronto Press

You have been watching (2009) Television Series. Season 1, Episode 6, Channel 4: UK

Zack, M. (1971) 'Feminist Allows Use of Message to Those Who Pay', 12 May, *Minneapolis Tribune*, Germaine Greer Archive, 2014.0038.217, 'Press USA, 1971', University of Melbourne

Zito, T. (1971) *Washington Post*, 22 April, Germaine Greer archives, 2014.0038.217, 'Press USA, 1971', University of Melbourne

PART II

The New Bestsellers, Online Media, and Branding Feminism in the Twenty-first Century

In the second part of this book, I turn my attention to celebrity feminists and blockbusters primarily from the twenty-first century as a means to ascertain whether the blockbuster's salience, vis-à-vis feminism's public meanings, is being maintained. In addition, I will consider how the blockbuster has transformed, as well as how its authors' ways of intervening in the construction of their public selves have changed in the wake of new technologies. The fact that feminists are no longer 'fresh meat' for the media (Millett in Wallace 1997), in the way Brown, Friedan, and Greer may have been in the 1960s and 1970s, has fundamentally altered the ways in which feminist renown is now secured, negotiated, and maintained, as well as how feminist books have been received. Perhaps books published in the twenty-first century do not culturally reverberate in the same way as their predecessors not simply because feminism is no longer novel but that 'today's young women face such a spectrum of obstacles that one single book can no longer address them' (Scott 2013).

Nonetheless, popular feminist works of non-fiction continue to make the bestseller lists, and precipitate intense debate. They have not been displaced, contra arguments around technology leading to the 'death of the book', but they have been augmented—not least by new media platforms, which have become central promotional and presentational tools for the contemporary blockbuster author. Feminism is, of course, 'an ongoing project, a process' and is 'constantly being reinvented' (Douglas 1994, p. 273); it is, then, no surprise that contemporary blockbusters and the women who author them are in many ways different from those featured in Part I. But there are, too, some important continuities, including in the texts and in the processes of their authors' celebrification, self-representational tactics, and, in some cases, in terms of their feminisms.

The celebrities in Parts I and II are united, not least because they use different forms to achieve the same ends: to attempt to exert some form of control over their celebrity signs and thereby their feminisms. Perhaps unsurprisingly, yet not insignificantly, none of the three women in the earlier part of this study—although they maintained their iconic status until their deaths (2006 and 2012 for Friedan and Brown respectively) and in, the case of Greer, into the present—availed themselves of the opportunities provided by new technologies to help shape their public personas. This may be because they had each, during their long engagement with the mediasphere, developed their own strategic forms of persona management, or it may suggest—less convincingly, I think—something about generation and where they were situated along the life course in the 2000s. Whatever the reasons, it is clear that the success of blockbusters published now—and the celebrity of their authors—is deeply indebted to new, and especially social, media.

Social media forms, then, are now central to maintaining visibility, not just for the celebrity feminist but increasingly for all, especially girls and young women (Banet-Weiser 2012, pp. 55–6, original emphasis): 'Postfeminism and interactivity create what I would call a neoliberal *moral* framework, where each of us has a duty to ourselves to cultivate a self-brand.' According to such logic, the labour that these authors undertake works to ensure the kind of visibility we are all exhorted to seek, though of course they have actual commodities, as well as themselves, to sell. Given the centrality of new media in this self-branding process, women like Wolf, Sandberg, Gay, Poehler, and Dunham can be seen as significant case studies into 'the formation and utility of a convergent star text' (Ellcessor 2012, p. 47). That said, it is also important to note that the authors examined in the remainder of this book utilize new media to different degrees, and often for different purposes. Indeed, one of them (Lena Dunham) even very publicly announced her retreat from Twitter due to the intense misogyny she experienced on this platform, turning instead to the e-newsletter format. As I explore here, Sandberg, Poehler, Dunham, and, to a lesser extent, Gay, all use their celebrity capital for activist purposes beyond the discursive politics of their books, with initiatives reliant upon various forms of digital media. The first blockbuster celebrity examined in this section, Naomi Wolf, demonstrates how social media can be incorporated into celebrity feminist practice, including to shore up authority being contested elsewhere.

REFERENCES

Banet-Weiser, S. (2012) *Autheticity, TM*, New York: New York University Press
Banet-Weiser, S. & Mukherjee, R. (2012) 'Introduction: Commodity Activism in Neoliberal Times', in S. Banet-Weiser & R. Mukherjee eds. *Commodity Activism: Cultural Resistance in Neoliberal Times*, New York: New York University Press, pp. 1–17
Douglas, S. (1994) *Where the Girls Are: Growing Up Female with the Mass Media*, London: Penguin
Ellcessor, E. (2012) 'Tweeting@feliciaday: Online Social Media, Convergence, and Subcultural Stardom', *Cinema Journal*, 51.2: 46–66
Scott, C. (2013) '50th Anniversary of *The Feminine Mystique*: Is This Groundbreaking Book Still Relevant Today?', 1 March, *The Telegraph*, accessed via: http://www.telegraph.co.uk/culture/books/9900886/50th-anniversary-of-The-Feminine-Mystique-is-this-groundbreaking-book-still-relevant-today.html
Wallace, C. (1997) *Greer: Untamed Shrew*, Sydney: Pan Macmillan

CHAPTER 6

Naomi Wolf: Twitter and the Transformation of a 'Third wave' Celebrity

INTRODUCTION

Since the publication of her first book, *The Beauty Myth* (1990), Naomi Wolf has been one of the most visible celebrity feminists in the Anglo-American mediasphere. While this polemical text—which is often identified as one of the 'origin' texts of the 'third wave' (including by its author)—sought to attack the beauty industrial complex and to 'free' women from the bonds of such an industry, for which it has received much feminist criticism, later work embraced a seemingly more diluted, liberal form of feminism. In this vein, *Fire with Fire* (1993), less critical of heteropatriarchy and careful to position women as agents not dupes, adopted a more reformist position, and mobilized the victim/power dichotomy that dominated much 1990s popular feminist writing. In many ways, then, the author appears to reinvent herself with each iteration of the feminist blockbuster she offers.

For Wicke, such ideological and rhetorical shifts are inseparable from Wolf's celebrification. In this vein, she argues that with her second blockbuster Wolf 'makes a 180-degree turn, retaining only her celebrity orientation'. She continues: 'Where *The Beauty Myth* was meant to grab the brass ring of celebrity feminism, *Fire with Fire* is feminism as espoused by the celebrity' (1994, p. 764). More recently, media attention to Wolf's controversial, and reductionist, thesis about the neurobiological vagina–brain connection and its link to female creativity in her latest blockbuster, *Vagina*, suggests that she retains her attention capital.[1] That said, her feminism and authority to speak are indeed now contested, suggesting that, like any form of celebrity, renown associated with the blockbuster is never entirely secured but is a 'recursive process', requiring ongoing labour and investment—not least by the celebrity herself (Galow 2010). Even then, the cultural legitimation of the blockbuster author is by no means guaranteed. As one reviewer remarked of *Vagina*'s reception process, 'Is this the fall of the onetime angel in the house of feminism … ?' (Sandler 2012).

In this chapter, underscoring these processes of (self-)reinvention and what might be driving them, I will concentrate on only three of her texts: *The Beauty Myth* and *Fire with Fire*, with the majority of the analysis to be centred on her celebrity performances following the publication of *Vagina*.[2] The latter provides important insights into the ways in which both Wolf's feminism and her celebrity practice have mutated over the past few decades. And given that *Vagina*'s appearance corresponds with technological transformations that have further displaced the responsibility for the production and maintenance of a viable celebrity self onto the author, through this chapter I am also able to explore what such shifting dynamics reveal about the ways in which blockbuster celebrity feminism is now managed and practised, something I take up even further in the final three chapters. In particular, the second part of this chapter is preoccupied with how Wolf has thoroughly incorporated Twitter into her celebrity feminist practice, largely as a response to her waning legitimacy. Before moving on to consider Wolf and her celebrity feminism in more detail, it is necessary to place it in the context of its initial development.

THE BLOCKBUSTER IN THE 1990S

In the previous chapters, my focus has been on women whose initial feminist blockbuster was produced in the years immediately preceding or during the modern Anglo-American women's liberation movement. In such a socio-political context, the ideas contained in their bestsellers were, as we have seen, somewhat novel, working as they did to destabilize gendered certainties and challenge patriarchal social relations. Although popular feminist books did appear in the 1980s (such as Gloria Steinem's *Outrageous Acts and Everyday Rebellions*, Friedan's *The Second Stage*, and Greer's *Sex and Destiny*), none held the same appeal or bestseller status as the books discussed in the previous chapters—not least because feminism was permeating public discourse, from the academy to media and popular culture (Dow 1996). Conversely, the early 1990s saw a number of commercially successful books published that attempted, for better or worse, to frame how feminism was being widely understood.

Murray (2004, p. 182) proffers an explanation for the 20-year gap between Greer's blockbuster and the next bestselling work of feminist non-fiction, Wolf's *The Beauty Myth*: that feminist thought had 'retreated into the academy' and the prose style favoured by academic feminist authors was 'so opaque and terminologically dense as to be unintelligible to the majority of women'. While I would not necessarily agree with this assessment—a more compelling reason may be, to take up thesis posited in Susan Faludi's *Backlash* (1991), that the gap resulted from a wider hostility towards feminism that made non-fiction in this period seem less than lucrative—the blockbuster does appear to have languished until the 1990s. Acknowledging this hiatus, Murray (2004, p. 182) argues that through *The Beauty Myth*, a book that 'harks back to a more activist age of feminist consciousness', Wolf effectively 'reviv[ed] the concept of the mass selling feminist polemic'.

In the 1990s, in addition to Faludi's bestseller, a number of feminist non-fiction publications emerged that precipitated intense debate about what feminism had become: Camille Paglia's *Sexual Personae* (1990), Rene Denfeld's *The New Victorians* (1995), Katie Roiphe's *The Morning After* (1993), and Christina Hoff Sommers' *Who Stole Feminism* (1994). They, along with Wolf, have been aptly described as 'the frenemies of feminism' (Wright 2012, p. 160). These women have also been dubbed 'impersonator feminists', who, with the support of a sympathetic media culture, are argued to have 'resurrected the spectacle of the catfight in an attempt to trash and discredit the contemporary women's movement' (Hammer 2000, p. 209; see also Douglas 1994). Much has been written on these so-called third wave 'dissidents', especially in critiques of the wave metaphor and its accompanying constraining generationalist logic, but given that none of them retained their celebrity capital in the way that Wolf did I will only briefly attend to them here.

In the early to mid-1990s, as Rebecca Stringer tells us, the 'ur narrative' of popular feminist books presumed that feminism had become wrongly preoccupied with positioning women as passive victims. In this story, modern feminism is organized 'into a dichotomy between a bad feminism that persists with a false and obsolete theory of women as passive victims, and a good feminism that is cognizant of Western women's present agency' (2014, p. 21). Although adopting slightly different rhetorical strategies and lines of augmentation to Roiphe and other critics of victim feminism (like Christina Hoff Sommers), Wolf's *Fire with Fire* is one of the key texts in this pervasive narrative of a feminism gone decidedly wrong (Stringer 2014, p. 26).[3] It is also the book that was most clearly reliant upon her adoption of a wayward daughter subjectivity, seeking—as is common in popular feminist rhetoric—to define herself in opposition to the limited feminism of literal and symbolic mothers, performing a kind of discursive 'matricide' (Rich 1976; Henry 2004; Taylor 2008).

In the 1990s, such a positioning became crucial to her authority to publicly speak on behalf of the ill-defined 'third wave'. After producing their own less successful 'blockbuster', *Manifesta* (2000), Baumgardner and Richards argued that the media found it difficult to represent the third wave because it was predicated on ideas about feminism's 'multiplicity', thereby precluding the designation of a singular 'third wave super leader' (2003, p. 159). They remarked: 'The fact that there is no one third wave leader tapped by the media is progress ...' (Baumgardner and Richards 2003, p. 166). That said, the prominence of the writers of these feminist—and not so feminist—blockbusters in the 1990s somewhat troubles their claim that third wave stars were not constructed by the media. And in 1990, when *The Beauty Myth* first appeared, it was Wolf who emerged as the third wave's most visible representative.

The Beauty Myth and the Revival of the Blockbuster

As Murray argues, 'the marketing of the feminist blockbuster reaches its apotheosis in the persona of American author and iconic figure of third wave feminism: Naomi Wolf' (2004, pp. 201–2). When *The Beauty Myth* was first published its author was young, highly educated (enrolled in an Oxford doctoral programme at the time), and conventionally attractive. Of course, given the subject matter of her first feminist work of nonfiction, the role of her physical appearance in its marketing and widespread circulation is nothing if not ironic. Nonetheless, while her beauty may have functioned to create the sense that she was a less threatening version of the historically much maligned feminist, like Gloria Steinem before her, her initial blockbuster was by no means politically cautious.

Much as early promoters of *The Feminine Mystique* had done vis-à-vis the second wave, the biography section on Wolf's website (a platform now integral to feminist celebrification) frames *The Beauty Myth* as *the* key text of the 'third wave': 'Wolf's landmark international bestseller, *The Beauty Myth*, challenged the cosmetics industry and the marketing of unrealistic standards of beauty, launching a new wave of feminism in the early 1990s.' Similarly, in terms of the book's paratext, the first edition back cover featured a testimonial from Greer: 'The most important feminist publication since *The Female Eunuch*.' Such an affirmative if self-serving comment, of course, works to authorize the book in important ways, placing it in a longer tradition of ground-breaking, polemical feminist work. As Andrew Wernick has argued of book publishing, 'the biggest names' (in which we could certainly include Greer), 'become free-floating signifiers, in which capacity they serve to publicize not just their own books, but those of others ...' (1991, pp. 175–6). Here, Greer's signature is used both to lend value to Wolf's text and to further ensure the visibility of her own. Moreover, the book's various reprints evidence its continuing reverberations. Like Brown's, Friedan's, and Greer's blockbusters, *The Beauty Myth* is a 'long seller' (Feather and Woodbridge 2007).

Accordingly, in 2002, HarperCollins published a ten-year anniversary commemorative edition, with an updated introduction mapping the public response to the book—including reader reluctance to question ideal beauty standards. The new edition of the book featured an endorsement from Gloria Steinem; again, as with Greer's earlier praise, such support locates Wolf in a privileged field of authorized feminist voices, signalling and buttressing her capital as a celebrity feminist (despite its flagging nature in 2013). Further illustrative of its ongoing commercial viability, in 2015 it was re-released as a 'Vintage Feminism Short Edition'. In its introduction, Wolf reflects on the book's publication, and confidently proclaims that she was one of the first women to coin the term 'third wave' feminism:

> The initial edition of *The Beauty Myth* benefited from a lot of good fortune. It was an argument that hit at just the moment in which a generation of young women did indeed want to embrace a new version of feminism—did indeed want to analyse the unique conditions around them and take their own oppression seriously—and did indeed want to reinvigorate the discourse of feminism to take action once again, collectively as well as individually. The book was a bestseller in fourteen countries, but even more important, it was part of a new awakening of discussion and debate about many feminist topics in many new feminist voices—an awakening that writer

> Rebecca Walker and I, working independently, both happened to identify with a freshly coined term, The Third Wave. (Wolf 2015)

Here, like Friedan before her, Wolf seeks to position herself as integral to a resurgence of feminist thought and activism, a process in which her blockbuster—and by extension the author herself—was argued to be central.

In *The Beauty Myth*, Wolf argues that, as feminist gains have expanded the kinds of subjectivities available to modern women, attempts to control them through the beauty industrial complex have considerably intensified. As she puts it in the book's introduction:

> The more legal and material hindrances women have broken through, the more strictly and heavily and cruelly images of female beauty have come to weigh upon us ... More women have more money and power and scope and legal recognition than we have ever had before; but in terms of how we feel about ourselves physically, we may actually be worse off than our unliberated grandmothers. (1990, p. 10)

In this way, her argument, regarding the rolling back of feminist gains, echoes Friedan's. Using the trope of the 'iron maiden' to signal the constraints upon women, Wolf argues that women are being exhorted to ameliorate men's fears regarding their increasing public sphere presence through an intensified bodily self-surveillance and regulation: 'I contend that this obsession with beauty in the Western world—which has intensified in my lifetime—is, in fact, the last way men can defend themselves against women claiming power.' Accordingly, she argues that women must (re)mobilize, and subsequently maps out the beginnings of a new feminist wave.

In the book's conclusion, Wolf outlines her vision of 'a feminist third-wave', drawing upon familial tropes while critiquing the postfeminist rhetoric that was coming to circulate in the early 1990s:

> While transmitting the previous heritage of feminism intact, it would need to be, as all feminist waves are, peer-driven: No matter how wise a mother's advice is, we listen to our peers ... it can all begin by rejecting the pernicious fib that is crippling young women, who face many of the same old problems, once again blame themselves—since it's all been fixed, right? (1990, p. 281)

While not perfoming the discursive matricide common in third wave texts, here Wolf nonetheless asserts the necessity of some generational differentiation. The above is also indicative of maternal tropes that dominate in popular feminist writing, especially in the 1990s, where there seem to be only two available subject positions: mother or daughter (Henry 2004). In fact, the use of the familial metaphor had even become so common during this time, in both popular and academic writing, that one critic even coined the term 'matrophor' (Quinn 1997, p. 179) to mark this figurative tendency. Of course, one of the biggest limitations of the generational, and even the 'wave', model is that it obscures from view intragenerational differences and intergenerational commonalities (Roof 1997, p. 92). Additionally, the generational frame 'fails to account for women who may come to feminism later in life or indeed how individual women's relationship to feminism may shift over time' (Taylor 2008, p. 195). It also works to homogenize often radically divergent political positions as well as diverse groups of women, positioning feminism as a singular, monolithic body of thought specific to one's generational location rather than a shifting, mobile, plural set of practices, concepts, and discourses (Taylor 2008). Moreover, within such a framework, political differences come to be misconstrued as generational ones (Hogeland 2001, p. 107). Nonetheless, for Wolf, such differentiation was key to positioning herself as representative of a new 'brand' of feminism. That said, *The Beauty Myth* seems much less reliant upon generational logic than Wolf's subsequent blockbuster, as we will see.

Like all blockbusters, the book was widely covered in the mainstream media, including national and state-based newspapers. Wolf was accused of offering readers a 'dogmatic puritanism' (Rapping 1991) that was being taken up, mistakenly, as representative of feminism. The machinery of book publicity and celebrity was both product and producer of such an assumption. As is common with the blockbuster author, coverage included a consideration of the authority granted Wolf over other feminists. As Rapping's review suggests:

> *The Beauty Myth* has already made an explosion in the media; Naomi Wolf has been on more than a handful of talk shows that I've seen and her book has had plenty of publicity. She is perceived as speaking for feminism and, in the vacuum left by the rest of us, she has a right to that title. I think we need to think about that some. (Rapping 1991, p. 4)

Here, Wolf is seen to fill a gap in public discourse around feminism, a situation that Rapping argues requires further interrogation.

In the *New York Times* (1991), Caryn James deemed the book 'slick and provocative' and 'a sloppily researched polemic'. Despite these criticisms, James also notes: 'But Ms. Wolf's theory—that the pressure on women to look thin, young and gorgeous is the last bastion of male power, a reactionary way to undermine the feminist gains of the last 25 years—is valuable nonetheless.' A review in the *Washington Post* was much less critical, observing: 'What makes this book persuasive is not its already familiar subject, but its accumulated evidence that the beauty mandate has gotten worse' (Yalom 1991). Like *The Feminine Mystique*, Wolf's book deploys the figuration of conspiracy (Knight 1997), as advertising and beauty/fashion industries work together in an orchestrated attempt to undermine the small degree of power available to some women. Accordingly, in *People* magazine, it was described as 'a manifesto of sorts, an indictment of the cosmetics, diet, pornography and plastic-surgery industries, and a call for a new wave of feminism to free women from enslavement to beauty's dictates' (Hubbard 1991). It is in this assumption, of 'enslavement', that Wolf's book has been most troublesome for feminists. For Murray (2004, p. 202), Wolf—like Friedan and Greer before her—was caught in a paradox: *The Beauty Myth* was, at its heart, a critique of the media and culture industries, yet her own involvement in the marketing of the book 'fundamentally compromised' this position. While there may be some contradictions in Wolf's thorough implication in the system against which her book appeared to rally, I would disagree that her celebrification effectively undermines her argument.

However, despite attempts to position the text as offering something new in terms of popular feminism, critics have underscored that there was nothing distinctive about the kind of feminism espoused in *The Beauty Myth*. As Catherine Lumby notes, despite being heralded as the origin text of the third wave, Wolf's first bestselling book was 'in no sense a departure from critiques routinely mounted by second wave feminists of the way women were valued for their appearance and sexual availability to men' (2014, p. 601). Nonetheless, 'the author herself, who became an international celebrity on its publication, was hailed as the harbinger of the bold new generation' (Lumby 2014, p. 601). Moreover, it is remarkable that Wolf became conflated with critics of feminism like Rene Denfeld and Katie Roiphe in the USA and Kathy Bail (*DIY Feminism*) in Australia and Natasha Walter (*The New Feminism*) in the UK, given her text's clear indebtedness to second wave thinking. That said, in *Fire with Fire* (1993) she did thoroughly adopt the disillusioned daughter subject position, thereby facilitating these assertions of generational, transnational cohesion.

Fire with Fire: Celebrifying the Third Wave

In the mid-1990s, Wolf often found herself located in a trio of other so-called young 'high-profile feminist dissenters' (Orr 1997, p. 36). Along with Rene Denfeld and Katie Roiphe, the terms of her authority shifted and it was the wayward 'feminist daughter' positioning that helped ensure her public presence. Such writers, mobilizing a troublesome 'rhetoric of repossession' (Siegel 1997, p. 59), construct an opposition between their generation's 'good feminism' against the 'bad' of their censorious mother (Henry 2004; Taylor 2008). With Wolf's celebrity capital assured by the success of her first book, she was guaranteed a platform on which to speak with some authority about feminism's deficiencies. While Wolf has been dubbed a 'victim feminist' by celebrity anti-feminists Christina Hoff Sommers and Katie Roiphe, because of her presumptions regarding women's passivity in *The Beauty Myth*, in *Fire with Fire* Wolf adds her own voice to this critique of victim feminism (Stringer 2014, p. 24).

Fire with Fire's constitutive binary is that of power/victim feminism, used as an explicit framing device. Accordingly, Wolf proffers a definition of these two terms early in the text; the former 'sees women as human beings—sexual, individual, no better or worse than their male counterparts—and lays claim to equality simply because women are entitled it' (1993, p. xvii). Victim feminism, by contrast, purportedly 'casts women as sexually pure and mystically nurturing, and stresses the evil done to these "good" women as a way to petition for their rights' (1993, p. xvii). Though she stresses that her own position differs markedly from those of Paglia and Roiphe, noting that she will be challenging the 'destructive, categorical hype' (1993, p. xvii) about victim feminism, such a caveat comes undone as she devotes a large proportion of the book to her own critique of feminism's apparent penchant for emotive rhetoric steeped in victimhood. Later, in a section where she discursively constructs the opposition she claims to be merely cataloguing—'Part Three: Victim Feminism Versus Power Feminism'—Wolf further expands upon the limits of victimology and its apparent stymying of feminist 'progress':

> Victim feminism is when a woman seeks power through an identity of powerlessness ... This feminism has slowed women's progress, impeded their self-knowledge, and been responsible for most of the inconsistent, negative, even chauvinistic spots of regressive thinking that are alienating many women and men. (1993, p. 147)

Despite her own efforts to distinguish herself from other anti-victim authors, it is unsurprising that her position became conflated with theirs. However, Wolf's previous blockbuster meant that she received the kind of widespread, ongoing media support that eluded these other figures.

Following the publication of *Fire with Fire*, Wolf featured on the front over of the *New York Times* weekend magazine; with the headline 'Feminists Didn't Used to Look Like This', the article pronounces: 'Time was when you couldn't describe a feminist as gorgeous. Naomi Wolf is this and much more: successful, clever and articulate—and fed up with the sisterhood's dead-end political correctness and victim-speak' (6 November 1993). As Hinds and Stacey put it, as part of generational differentiation, 'So-called "new feminism" is thus billed as the glamorous make-over of the old-fashioned, drab and over-serious "women's liberationists" of the past' (2001, p. 153). In academic scholarship, it has also been common to suggest that Wolf's desirability rendered her, regrettably, somewhat of a media darling; for example, despite the book's limitations, 'Wolf's supermodel looks and media-friendly philosophies continue to make her good copy in the mainstream media' (Orr 1997, p. 35). Such assumptions, however, serve to simplify a much more complicated representational environment, one that continues to rely upon the personification of specific figures to render feminism legible in the popular imaginary (Hesford 2013).

As during the second wave, discursive constructions of the third wave were refracted through Wolf, along with other anti-victim authors, as a media personality. Many scholars, problematically, pit these often provocative authors in opposition to 'real' feminist activists: 'At the same time that Roiphe, Wolf, and Denfeld are travelling the country on publicity tours attempting to "reclaim" feminism for the majority, young feminist activists … are coming of political age and are beginning to organize' (Bailey 1997, p. 47). Such an opposition is common in critical reflections on feminist blockbuster authors—that, while fame is being relentlessly pursued by them (as it is perceived to be), 'real' feminist work is being done elsewhere. Granted, Roiphe and Denfeld especially offer deeply problematic manifestos, built upon a discursive construction of feminism as oppressive, monolithic, and fundamentally unnecessary, that render them figures of feminist concern. That said, we need not entirely dismiss the realm of celebrity—and in particular blockbuster celebrity feminism—in its entirety, based on these few 'anti-victim' tracts.

The book's ideological and conceptual limitations aside, as Wicke observed of *Fire with Fire* and its author's celebrity feminist performances, 'However problematic, some form of feminist discourse is occurring within the Wolfian celebrity space' (1994, p. 765). As Wicke (1994, p. 765) further notes, in a comment applicable to all blockbusters with political limitations, 'My tart criticisms are meant for the insufficiencies of her book and her politics, not for celebrityhood itself ...'. Moreover, it is my contention that, through the intense public debates precipitated by books like Wolf's, Roiphe's, and Denfeld's, even such problematic blockbusters can produce unpredictable discursive effects and possibilities, opening up a space for dialogue about what feminism is and can be, and who might speak in its name.[4] If Wolf's most recent blockbuster is any indication, though, her feminism – like her celebrity – continues to be a source of controversy.

VAGINA: TRANSFORMING THE FEMINIST BLOCKBUSTER

Wolf's eighth work of non-fiction was published towards the end of 2012. The celebrity that *The Beauty Myth*, and subsequently *Fire with Fire*, garnered for Wolf ensured it—and its author—a high media profile. Just fourteen months after it was first published, in December 2013 Harper Collins released *Vagina: Revised and Updated*, with its front cover boasting its *New York Times* bestseller status. The blurb of the revised and updated edition of *Vagina* (2013) proclaims:

> A brilliant and nuanced synthesis of physiology, history, and cultural criticism, *Vagina* explores the physical, political, and spiritual implications for women—and for society as a whole—in this startling series of new scientific breakthroughs from a writer whose conviction and keen intelligence have propelled her works to the tops of bestseller lists, and firmly into the realm of modern classics.

Despite this marketing effort to position it as offering radical new insights into the 'vagina–brain connection', reviews of the book in the mainstream media were overwhelmingly derisive. The book's argument was scrutinized and in some cases ridiculed: 'I doubt the most brilliant novelist in the world could have created a more skewering satire of Naomi Wolf's career than her latest book' (Roiphe 2012). Another reviewer sardonically remarked: 'It's lucky vaginas can't read, or mine would be cringing in embarrassment' (Pollitt 2012). Such comments reveal much about the way the book came to be received, as I will further explore.

Like a number of Wolf's popular books, her latest offering is part memoir, part self-help book, part cultural history, and part polemic. As she notes: 'Due to a medical crisis, I had a thought-provoking, revelatory experience that suggested a possible crucial relationship of the vagina to female consciousness itself. The more I learned, the more I understood the ways in which the vagina is part of female creativity, confidence, and even character' (Wolf 2013, p. 3). The book, therefore, functions as a form of life writing as much as the cultural history she claims it to be; this in itself need not render it problematic, given that the personal voice has always been crucial to the blockbuster and arguably its success. The book is divided into four parts in which Wolf seeks initially to 'explore the ways in which the vagina has been misunderstood' (2012, p. 5); to provide a historical assessment of how the vagina has been 'socially controlled'; to explore the effect of pornography on the vagina, which throughout is bizarrely personified; and, finally, to 'reclaim the Goddess', to radically transform women's relationships with their vaginas. For Wolf, a woman's creativity and indeed sense of self is inseparable from this part of her anatomy; no wonder feminist response was often scathing. However, Wolf herself clearly sought to position her latest publication as consistent with her earlier attempts to make feminist critique widely accessible, noting in an interview with trade publication, *Publishers Weekly*: 'Today, a huge amount of the energy of younger feminists still has to do with the trivializing and demeaning of their sexuality. Over and over again we have to fight the same fight. The culture is just not letting women have a positive relationship to their sexuality, to their vaginas' (in Potter 2012). Wolf implies that, through her book, she seeks to have this relationship publicly revalued.

In 2012, the imminent release of *Vagina* prompted pre-publicity newspaper profiles of the author, many of which explicitly interrogated the celebrity that has ensured the audibility of her voice in the public sphere in the decades since *The Beauty Myth*'s publication. Reviews of *Vagina* in the mainstream press were overwhelmingly negative and came from a number of other celebrity feminists, including Greer and Roiphe. In the *Sydney Morning Herald* (15 September 2012) Greer astutely observes, '*Vagina: A New Biography* is largely a biography of Naomi Wolf herself.' As she makes explicit, Wolf is at the centre of the book which maps a health crisis that prevented her from experiencing orgasms, and her attempts, through various medical and spiritual intermediaries, including a male tantric 'guru', to regain that capacity. She uses this self-discovery to track the devalued 'power' of the vagina over centuries; to argue for a link between orgasmic activity and creativity; and to place its reaffirmation at the centre of contemporary feminism. As she notes in an interview: '"The sexual revolution is not working for women, many women, or not working well enough," Ms. Wolf said, her voice rising. "To me that's a feminist issue that we're not reaching our potential"' (Sandler 2012). However, Greer expressed concerns about Wolf's placement of the vagina at the centre of women's subjectivity: 'The ultimate misunderstanding would be to conclude that a woman is her vagina, and Wolf comes perilously close, apparently unconcerned that some such notion is the central tenet of misogyny' (Greer 2012). While Greer had enthusiastically supported *The Beauty Myth*, she saw Wolf's latest work as bordering on the anti-feminist.

It was not only Greer who called into question Wolf's credentials to speak with any authority about feminism. In the *Los Angeles Times*, Meghan Daum (2012) laments that, given the myriad issues yet facing women, 'we could all benefit from some smart, substantive thinking from one of America's foremost feminist thinkers. If Naomi Wolf ever really qualified—and that is debatable—she appears to have excused herself from the table.' The book was also largely seen as an attempt by Wolf to buttress her diminishing celebrity capital; by doing so she was judged harshly, as women, and especially feminists, seeking popularity always are. Although herself a contentious figure in terms of popular feminism, Katie Roiphe (2012) notes:

> The very public story of how Naomi Wolf went from a bright, promising Rhodes Scholar to this inventive variety of navel-gazer tells us some uncomfortable things about the culture and more specifically, the media. There is a way in which bookers on television shows, consumers of magazines, publicists, television viewers, blockbuster book buyers, and Amazon reviewers are implicated in what Naomi Wolf has become.

For Roiphe, whose review must be seen in the context of her own status as erstwhile celebrity feminist, it is the celebrity industry in its broadest sense that has worked to construct a particular 'Wolf'; an especially undesirable one at that. But it was not just Roiphe who used her review to negatively remark upon Wolf's celebrification. In *The Guardian* (2012), Jenny Turner was somewhat more sympathetic, remarking upon the difficulties that must face the feminist who has historically enjoyed high media visibility:

> I watched her at a distance, observing how tough the job of celebrity feminist can be: you have to keep publishing and opining, no matter whether

you have much you really want to say. You have to present your ideas to public scrutiny even if they're still half-baked. A single wobble, and the media will leap …

Compared to Turner, others were more acerbic, and associated Wolf's latest pronouncements about women and sexuality with a hunger for publicity they disdained.

For example, Katha Pollitt (2012) remarks: 'Perhaps opinion-mongering, black-and-white thinking and relentless TMI are the price of remaining a world-class celebrity feminist.' Here we can identify the presumption that I have critiqued throughout: that celebrity feminism is necessarily or a priori a form of *bad* feminism. In the *New York Times Sunday Book Review*, Toni Bentley (2012) sees Wolf as having effectively misused her public platform, as she is accused of doing over a number of years, rendering her 'less than reliable' as an authorized feminist speaker. For others, Wolf is seen to use her existing celebrity capital in ways that are fundamentally at odds with feminism. Laurie Penny (2012),[5] for example, writing for the *New Statesman*, argues that through her vocal defence of Julian Assange in the wake of rape allegations: 'Naomi Wolf has done great damage by using her platform as one of the world's most famous feminists to dismiss these women's allegations.' And like Pollitt, Penny positions writers like Wolf as effectively distracting attention from 'the real and pressing problems facing three billion women and girls across the world because of their gender'. This is a common critique of mass-mediated forms of feminism, especially its celebrity variants. As she continues, she locates the blame squarely at the feet of celebrity culture: 'The point of a kind of celebrity faux-feminism seems to be, if you'll permit me to bastardise the late lamented Douglas Adams, not to challenge patriarchy, but to distract attention away from it.' This is a familiar refrain; Penny presumes that celebrity feminism comes at the cost of 'real' feminist activism. Given the extent of these critical reviews, and their challenge to the author's celebrity, for the remainder of this chapter I examine how Wolf adapted her social media usage to effectively rewrite the reception of *Vagina* and to reassert her own diminishing authority.

TWITTER AND BRANDING THE CELEBRITY FEMINIST SELF

Celebrity feminism, as Wicke reminds us, is 'a complicated social practice' (1994, p. 757); this is even more the case in the context of the technologies that have developed in the intervening years. Social media, and Twitter especially, are said to have shifted both the actual terrain of celebrity as well as how it is practised and consumed, including for celebrity feminists (Marwick and boyd 2011, p. 139). In terms of the range of techniques to maintain public visibility currently deployed by contemporary blockbuster feminists, Twitter is a site that cannot be ignored, either in terms of 'achieved celebrity' (Rojek 2001) or micro-celebrity (Senft 2008).[6]

As Marwick and boyd (2011, p. 140) observe, and as I argue throughout, celebrity is not something one *has* but something one *does*; it is:

> an organic and ever-changing performative practice rather than a set of intrinsic personal characteristics or external labels. This practice involves ongoing maintenance of a fan base, performed intimacy, authenticity and access, and construction of a consumable persona.

So what kind of a 'consumable persona' do figures like Wolf construct and what might this reveal about the operations and logics of feminism, celebrity, and their interrelatedness? What, and how, in terms of their discursive practices, do these blockbuster celebrity feminists use their 140 characters to say? And how do they engage with their followers in ways that suggest something about their active attempts to shape their feminist celebrity personas? How might Twitter, and the responses of others, create ruptures in this celebrity self-performance? Does celebrity feminist practice, including online, differ from other forms? These are some of the questions with which I engage both here and in the remaining chapters.

As I have noted, in addition to selling products such as books, celebrities can themselves be seen as commodities; in the contemporary context, central to the process of ensuring their commercial viability are new media. In terms of Twitter especially, 'online personas have become an indispensable part of self-branding' (van Dijick 2013, p. 202). Marshall (2010) argues that new media, and especially social media, have effected a displacement from a 'representational media system' to what he dubs 'presentational culture'. As he remarks, 'given that major celebrities have often had teams managing their media and public relations, it is no surprise to see that celebrities are in fact at the forefront of the expansion and use of social media and networks for reputation management' (2010, p. 500; see also Turner 2014). This presumption that stars use social media to 'take back' their image, and mould it into something they find more desirable or more marketable, is often seen to offer a new way for public figures to exercise agency over their celebrity signs. As previous chapters have made clear, though, such strategies of self-branding and active persona management have long been evident, including in terms of the celebrity feminist. However, as well as perhaps offering more opportunities for such celebrity intervention, social media platforms render these attempts visible in ways they previously were not (Thomas 2014, p. 242). Next, I provide an overview of how Wolf uses Twitter before offering a more in-depth analysis of tweets relating to her latest work of non-fiction.

Social Media and Blockbuster Celebrity Feminism: Wolf's Twitter Practice

Wolf is a prolific Tweeter; she has over 52,600 followers and follows 33,600 (as at March 2015), itself not a massive number in terms of celebrity accounts—something that should be remembered with regard to the potential efficacy of Wolf's attempts to regain some control over how her book was being made to mean offline. While Marshall notes that it is common for celebrities to follow far fewer people than follow them (2010, p. 43), Wolf follows more than half as many, suggesting perhaps that this is an attempt to foster a sense of reciprocity and mutuality. When I signed up for this project she, or perhaps one of her publicists, followed me immediately. For Henry Jenkins (2009), Twitter is either 'here it is' (links to news, blogs, clips, and so on) or 'here I am' (celebrities revealing something intimate about themselves). Wolf's Twitter relates much more to the former, constituted by a series of explicitly and implicitly promotional gestures. For example: 'Please join me for a discussion & book signing tomorrow night at Yale University bookstore. Please share!' (10 February 2014).[7] Such events offer the promise of unmediated intimacy, a chance for readers to connect with the author 'in the flesh' (Gunter 2014); through such tweets, Wolf invites her audience to be co-present, albeit in the overtly commercial space of the bookshop.[8]

Twitter, as well as other forms of social media, is seen to be vital for contemporary authors (Robinson 2013; Murray 2015). For some fans, lack of blatant self-promotion creates the sense of a more 'authentic', genuine connection and sense of interactivity, feeling as if they 'really know' the celebrity in question with whom they are in direct communication rather than being positioned solely as consumers (Marwick and boyd 2011, p. 140; see also Click et al. 2013). However, when used in service of literary marketing there is a risk that tweeting will seem purely promotional (York 2013, pp. 146–7), indeed as Wolf's often does. Nevertheless, alongside this is the 'lure of making contact—even of an electronic sort—with that author' (York 2013, p. 147). As we will see, Wolf's fans appear to relish these new communicative opportunities.

Through her Twitter feed, Wolf attempts to shift the terms of debate around *Vagina*, from critics to 'ordinary' readers, with whom she actively engages on various levels. The relationship between readers and authors, as well as celebrities in a more general sense, is seen as having been reconfigured by social networking (Robinson 2013). Now involved in a rather less parasocial interaction, readers and writers can participate in dialogic exchange with their favourite celebrities, and in some senses work to collaboratively constitute their celebrity personas (Marwick and boyd 2011). As Murray notes: 'Now, the author is engaged in one-to-many or even one-to-one real-time relationships with readers ... the digital-era author now aims for consistency and "stickiness" (in web parlance) in reader–writer relationships' (2015, p. 323). Twitter is a site of such potential 'stickiness', including for blockbuster celebrity feminists. That said, although social media, and Twitter especially, may act as a space for fan–celebrity interaction hitherto not so readily available, thereby complicating previous assumptions regarding parasociality, a number of critics have underscored that:

> there are clear hierarchies of power within the "Twittersphere" with celebrities, journalists and "official" accounts from organisations playing a very visible role in (re)circulating information and influencing debate, which must be recognised when we consider the claim for it being a democratic space where all can participate. (Deller 2011, p. 237)

Therefore, while perhaps opening a channel of communication between celebrity and fans, Twitter does not serve to equalize participants or destabilize existing 'power differentials' but makes clear how they can be leveraged for the celebrity's own purposes (Marwick and boyd 2011, pp. 155–6).

Another question often raised in relation to celebrity and Twitter accounts is that of authenticity; in these terms, readers might ask: how do we know it is Wolf who is using this account, given that celebrities commonly employ 'ghost twitters' (Ellcessor 2012)? Emphasizing that Twitter should not be seen as 'an unmediated form of authentic self-presentation' (Thomas 2014, p. 6), I would follow Keller's argument here: because 'social media is commonly understood as inherently authentic within the public imagination, it may not matter if it is actually [Wolf] behind the computer, as we are meant to read her online presence as authentic' (2012, p. 7). Indeed, it has been argued that it is the inability to tell that affords fans immense pleasure (Marwick and boyd 2011, p. 153), effectively adding 'interest to the game of interpreting the performance of celebrity in play' (Turner 2014, p. 74). Moreover, much like television personalities—as Bennett (2011) has argued—feminist celebrities, and blockbuster authors especially, first and foremost are seen to perform themselves, notwithstanding of course that this in itself is a construction. In the case of Wolf, and indeed other feminist authors, her Twitter 'voice' is presumed to be identical to the narrative voice of her non-fictional texts, and popular feminist writing—as Pearce (2004) has convincingly argued and I have noted in Chap. 2—is reliant upon this conflation of narrator and author, a lack of distinction that is clearly reinforced by/through Twitter. Further, authors—like their narrators—need to continually establish and re-establish their authority through these rapidly expanding kinds of public performances (Carter 1997, p. xii). This is certainly the case for blockbuster feminist celebrities, whose authority to speak is often contested from both within and without feminism, and therefore these extra-textual performances, including within the field of social media, are crucial.

As I argue throughout, there are a number of ways in which blockbuster celebrity feminists can be seen to exceed some of the dominant ways of theorizing celebrity, including in terms of Twitter usage. Many have suggested that Twitter's appeal for celebrities is that it permits some control over gossip regarding their personal lives circulating elsewhere; this is not the function of Twitter for the blockbuster celebrity feminist, whose private life is not generally publicly consumed, or indeed sought after, in the same way as other forms of female celebrity. That is, in the case of Wolf, 'the veridical self is [not] a site of public evacuation' (Rojek 2001, p. 19) and she does not use social media for 'strategically managed self-disclosure' (Marwick and boyd 2011). This is perhaps because she has already done so in her deeply confessional book. Nonetheless, through Twitter Wolf clearly does seek to exercise control over the way her text, as well as her persona, is being made to mean publicly, and she does clearly work to create a sense of authenticity for, and intimacy with, her followers. Such a process, of course, relies upon much labour. As Alice Marwick notes (2013, p. 196), online self-branding 'necessitates the careful construction of an edited yet authentic self, which demands ongoing self-monitoring … and an ongoing awareness and evaluation of the audience'. While there are some crucial differences between celebrity feminists and other forms of stardom, as I discuss throughout, Marwick's argument here applies as much to feminist authors as to those involved in other industries.

Remarkably, given that she is a celebrity feminist, there is little explicitly feminist content on Wolf's Twitter feed, revealing that in this instance it is being used more to supplement her feminist performances in other realms rather than to become a primary site for its articulation. That is, it is an addendum to the blockbuster not its substitute/replacement; in this respect, it can be seen to operate as a form of 'public authorial epitext' (Genette 1997) which seeks to circumscribe the meanings of the primary work, a form of authorial intervention, materially separate from the book itself, but which is designed to help shape its reception, much as a preface or afterword does. It is, in particular, central to her attempts to frame her book as a meaningful feminist text, including through publicly broadcasting how it has affected readers.

#LIFECHANGINGREAD AND BUILDING THE WOLF BRAND

There are four key ways that *Vagina*, and thus Wolf's reinvented feminism, remains visible in and through her Twitter account. First, in explicitly promotional (i.e. 'broadcast') tweets such as signings at book-stores (as above) as well as those from her publishers regarding the book, especially at the time of its 2013 re-release; second, in links to glowing reviews or interviews she has done in other forms of media; third, other less overtly promotional tweets, such as support from other celebrities; and, finally, tweets of readerly gratitude (i.e. #lifechangingread). Tweets are, of course, 'written with different publics in mind' (Deller 2011), and for Wolf, in many instances, her addressees appear to be actual or potential consumers of *Vagina*. Further, in this instance, Wolf's imagined publics seem to be, not necessarily explicitly feminist, but those open to ideas about women's sexual entitlement, individual empowerment, and agency—those perhaps more appropriately figured as postfeminist.

In terms of *Vagina*, reviews, as outlined, have been overwhelmingly negative, so it is not surprising Wolf uses Twitter to effectively rewrite the book's critical history. Whether she is successful in this endeavour is another question. As Turner has argued, 'some celebrities clearly see Twitter as offering their own dedicated media channel, through which they can shape what the rest of the media say about them …' (2014, p. 74). And this can certainly be seen to be the case with Wolf, especially through her retweeting of sympathetic reviews. The circulation of links to other forms of media is a feature of Twitter, as much as opinion or revelation sharing, ensuring that it 'functions as a "hub" between other media forms and texts as well as between users' (Deller 2011). Wolf's strategic emphasis on these affirmative texts is an important gesture, and one that seeks to secure future readers, thereby helping to ensure the book's commercial viability and status as valuable feminist writing.

It is commonly emphasized that contemporary celebrities use social media to create 'a heightened sense of intimacy' with their followers, 'and thus fans now expect celebrities to interact with them and maintain ongoing affiliations with them' (Click et al. 2013, p. 366). That is, the management of celebrity has shifted from a highly regulated and controlled model to 'one in which performers and personalities actively address and interact with fans' (Marwick and boyd 2011, p. 140). There are a number of ways in which celebrities work to foster intimacy and connection with their fans via Twitter, including direct @replies or through retweeting their comments. In this instance, retweeting is a central part of Wolf's celebrity practice, and is a strategy that can create the sense of a supportive public, which contrasts markedly to the hostile responses she was receiving via other media platforms. As Deller (2011) remarks, 'the process of retweeting helps messages or links circulate quickly and provides affirmation and recognition for the original sender, as well as giving them and their tweets a level of status'. Motivations for retweeting, as boyd et al. (2010, p. 6) emphasize, are diverse, although some factors they identify clearly apply to Wolf's retweeting practice: ensuring that tweets spread to wider audiences; publicly demonstrating agreement with someone; and validating the opinions or thoughts of others. For example: 'Thank you! RT @kyokochurch: Just pages 40 in to #Vagina by @naomiwolf and I'm already blown away! #enlightening' (19 May 2013).[9] This type of retweet commonly appears in Wolf's feed. boyd et al. refer to these as 'ego retweets', which are 'when people retweet messages that refer to them. Some see this as "narcissistic" or "self-serving," while others see it as a way of giving credit to and appreciating the person talking about them' (boyd et al. 2010, p. 9). Whatever the motivation, retweeting followers who appear deeply invested in her book and its argument is clearly central to Wolf's online celebrity practice.

Given the way *Vagina* has been at times quite savagely attacked in the mainstream media, these retweets help circulate discourses around the text that run counter to these readings. That is, these readerly affirmations are used as evidence of the book's resonance, in spite of negative responses elsewhere. Retweeting, especially with additional comments, as Ruth Page argues, 'acknowledges the value of the audience as satisfied customers' of a celebrity's product—in this case, a book—'and so builds the reputation of the retweeter by reproducing the audience's endorsement of the consumer goods and their producer' (2012, p. 198). In particular, and consistent with Page's assessment about value, Wolf draws upon the transformative discourses being mobilized by so-called 'ordinary' readers, with the implication that reviewers (and the vocal feminist critics like Greer) are 'out of touch' with the audience. In this vein, she retweets one reader who simply chants: 'Vagina vagina vagina! #LifeChangingRead' (@RaeboRenee, 15 January 2014). Tweets commonly suggest that all women need to read Wolf's 'life-changing' book, with one reader identifying *Vagina* as her 'new bible' (@moniqueruffin, 21 November 2013). Changing women's lives, raising their consciousness, was an explicit goal of second wave feminism, and of the blockbuster itself; arguably, this remains its key aim. In this respect, and if Wolf's Twitter followers are any indication, her attempt, through *Vagina*, to refigure how women conceptualize their sexuality can be deemed to have been successful.

In terms of the direct fan engagement made possible by social media, Wolf at times thanks followers for their praise but often she simply retweets it as a gesture of appreciation, and, of course, promotion. When she does engage directly it is primarily in response to the most effusive tweets about the book's transformative effect. In response to another tweet about the book's impact, Wolf writes: 'wow! thank you RT @BasementBeauty: @naomirwolf Not even finished and already feel this book is changing my life #Vagina' (1 September 2013). Engaging with readers who make their affective investments in the book explicit, Wolf at times replies with expressions of gratitude and kisses.[10] Such public acts of appreciation work to position Wolf as generous, humble, and grateful that her readers are implicitly feeling sexually empowered following their consumption of *Vagina*—her feminist work is thereby done (#thankyou). In January 2014, she offers a blanket thank you to the book's consumers, creating the sense of a global community of like-minded fans: 'Thank you to my readers around the world!' (6 January 2014). For Wolf, maintaining this fan network is central to her attempts at shoring up her reputation as a viable feminist speaker.

These readerly expressions of gratitude can be seen as the contemporary equivalent of the fan letters received by figures like Friedan and Greer; in the case of the former, often it could take up to six months for a reply,[11] while through social media, by contrast, Wolf is able to almost instantaneously, and publicly, express her own appreciation of these effusive readers either individually or collectively (as above). While seemingly fostering intimacy, such interactions, and especially apparent validation in the form of retweeting, must be recognized as calculated marketing exercises, part of the ongoing process of celebrity promotional labour. As Hearn and Schoenhoff argue (2016, p. 205), 'a canny celebrity on social media rarely has to promote their own product because fans will do it for them; all they have to do is retweet a fan's praise and the chorus of promotion grows'. Along these lines, Wolf retweets @RachelMeeker, who enthuses: '"Vagina: A New Biography" by @naomi wolf is life changing. I'm not exaggerating either. Everyone must read it and be enlightened' (2 January 2014), for which she receives an expression of gratitude from the author. Similarly, to a reader who posted a glowing review on Amazon.com, Wolf tweets: 'Thank you! xx RT @CrazyIdealist @naomi wolf Thank you for writing a life-changing book. Here's my review' (11 February 2014). Such followers then are, in many senses, recruited to help shape the Wolf brand—*as a feminist who changes lives*; other blockbuster celebrity feminists have relied upon such a trope, as the chapter on Friedan in particular demonstrated. Further validating the author, readers also use tweets to praise Wolf for her apparent bravery as an outspoken feminist, which she retweets without comment: 'I am so grateful for your courage and perseverance @naomi wolf. I am loving Vagina: A New Biography. It's helping me understand so much!' (@tabbybiddle, 28 December 2013). Similarly, another reader credits Wolf with 'breaking down barriers of shame in discussion "Beyond the Vagina"', which she found to be 'inspiring' and which Wolf of course retweeted (@VerseEverday, 14 January 2014). However, impassioned defences of the book came not just from 'ordinary' readers but from other figures of renown, working to bolster Wolf's own celebrity.

Celebrity–Celebrity Interaction: Boosting Capital

Followers with whom celebrity feminists interact themselves seek, and perhaps gain, a particular form of capital from these very publicly performed engagements. Receiving an @reply or being retweeted by a celebrity feminist has particular cachet, perhaps in turn celebrifying the follower, if temporarily and if only within their own networks (Marwick and boyd 2011, p. 145). Moreover, it is not only 'ordinary readers' who are retweeted by Wolf—celebrity-to-celebrity interaction also features prominently, producing its own effects and affects. For example, former Hole singer and widow of Nirvana's Kurt Cobain, Courtney Love, tweets Wolf in praise of the book and her followers take up her call about this purportedly life-changing book, while actress and founder of online 'lifestyle' website, Goop, Gynweth Paltrow is cited in a tweet from @Virago Press: 'If you have a vagina you must read this book. It's astonishingly good' (7 March 2014). Wolf's Twitter followers, like Love, engage in a dialogue with each other, as well as the author, about their own responses to the controversial book. As Turner has noted, readers are effectively eavesdropping on this celebrity-to-celebrity conversation (2014, p. 73), again creating the sense of being privy to an intimate exchange, thus adding another layer to the 'authenticity' of this medium: 'Celebrity practitioners also interact with other famous people on Twitter, creating revealing performances of what appear to be intimate interactions' and giving 'the impression of candid, uncensored looks at the people behind the personas' (Marwick and boyd 2011, p. 151). Wolf thereby provides this sense of authenticity while performing what is essentially a promotional function.

Wolf's response to Love extends beyond the usual 'thank you' or simple tweet: 'How delightful that Courtney Love is tweeting support for Vagina: A New Biography ... Thank you so much @Courtney ... questions? Let me know!' (16 September 2012). Such a response emphasizes that not all followers are engaged with equally, thereby undermining claims regarding the democratization of this sphere (Marwick and boyd 2011), something I take up further in the final chapter of this book. Echoing the intimate tone, Love replies: 'yes yes yes. We should talk soon xc' (16 September 2012). These tweets, effectively celebrity endorsements, such as those we may find on a bookcover blurb, work to buttress Wolf's own standing as a credible speaker on feminism. Moreover, through making such connections to other celebrities visible, in this case via the gesture of retweeting, Wolf's own fame is boosted (Ellcessor 2012, p. 63).

To conclude, then, Wolf's Twitter appears less concerned with personal revelations or even with articulating explicitly feminist tweets, and more with maintaining her authority to speak—which, especially in the case of this book, is being called into question in other media platforms. While Wolf may no longer be 'the media-appointed spokeswoman-in-chief' she was in the 1990s (Murray 2004, p. 202), she seeks to use social media to secure support for her current feminist political positions and, in turn, to buttress her attenuated celebrity. Like all celebrities examined thus far, this analysis of Wolf has highlighted the labour that underpins celebrity feminism and its maintenance, while also showing how readers/tweeters are integral to this process. In the case of *Vagina*, Twitter represents a space in which Wolf attempts, as celebrity authors in the public sphere always have done, to delimit the interpretive possibilities of her text, and to widely circulate readerly affective investments as a means to demonstrate the cultural reverberations of her controversial book. In regard to her efforts to rewrite the book's critical history, her Twitter feed does not have the same audience as a *New York Times* book review; that is, questions of scale and reach must always be in play when making claims about the capacity of social networking sites to shape public debate or even to bring publics into being (Turner 2016).

As this analysis has shown, the purpose and effects, as well as affects, of Twitter as a site of celebrity practice for feminists requires further investigation, and once again demonstrates that, while there are points of overlap, it is often difficult to map existing work on celebrity onto what is happening around feminism in the mediasphere. In subsequent chapters I will build upon this analysis, shifting the focus from how social media are central to the maintenance of celebrity feminism to their role in helping in its initial creation. In the next chapter, I turn to two very different manifestations of the feminist blockbuster, clearly establishing that neither the contemporary non-fiction feminist bestseller nor the 'brand' of feminism embodied by its authors can be considered homogeneous.

Notes

1. For a critique of the dangers of what she calls 'neurosexism', see Cordelia Fine's *Delusions of Gender* (2010).
2. Although she has written on subjects other than feminism, which have arguably worked to shift the tenor of her feminism—for example *The End of America: A Letter of Warning to a Young Patriot* (2007) and its sequel, *Give Me Liberty: A Handbook for American Revolutionaries* (2008)—I am concerned here only with her popular feminist writing.
3. While in the USA this story was figured as the daughter performing symbolic 'matricide' on her feminist mother, in Australia it manifested as the mother lamenting what feminism had become in the hands of her daughters. In this regard, Helen Garner published a work of creative non-fiction, *The First Stone* (1995), which took two young women students to task for taking action against their college Master for sexual assault. The book precipitated intense discursive contestation over the meanings of Australian feminism, and a 'media event'—with the celebrity author at the centre—was

staged throughout 1995 and well into 1996. For a detailed analysis of this event, including how celebrity feminism was constructed and framed therein, see my *Mediating Australian Feminism* (2008).
4. Since *Fire with Fire*, Wolf has not reiterated her critique of victimhood (Stringer 2014, p. 26). In 2004 Wolf published an article titled 'The Silent Treatment', in which she accuses veteran literary critic, Harold Bloom, of sexual harassment. In media responses to the allegations, despite her own critique of gendered victimisation, Wolf was once more herself coded as a 'victim feminist' (Stringer 2014, p. 26).
5. Penny herself has written a number of popular feminist books but does not enjoy the kind of celebrity that the women examined here do.
6. Micro celebrity is defined as 'new style of online performance that involves people in "amping up" their popularity over the Web using technologies like video, blogs, and social networking sites' (Senft 2008, p. 25).
7. Likewise with this tweet: 'I'm at Columbia book store for a talk about my book "Vagina: Revised and Updated"—starts at 6pm! Come say hi!' (6 February 2014).
8. Other promotional tweets relate to measures of the book's success, such as '"Vagina Revised and Expanded" has now hit the Amazon Hot New Releases top sellers in four categories' (6 January 2014).
9. Given the ethical issues posed by material drawn from the Twittersphere, it is important to note that all the tweets discussed here 'were publicly available and discoverable at the time of writing and research, and thus, as published material, need no permission from authors to analyse them' (Tsaliki 2016, p. 244).
10. For example, she retweets Lucy Dancer: 'I'm only 3 chapters into the book and already "Vagina" is already giving me a-ha moments— will u be speaking in London anytime soon?' (25 January 2014), to which Wolf directly responds: '@Lucymdancer Thank you! Should be, will announce dates when confirmed' and she signs off with two kisses (25 January 2014).
11. Like Greer, Friedan received myriad letters from readers outlining how the book had resonated with them. It was not uncommon for replies to be sent up to six months following; replies commonly repeated this phrase (following an apology at the delay in responding due to the book's immense success and the demands it placed

on her time): '...it continues to sustain me that my efforts in writing The Feminine Mystique made a difference in other women's lives besides my own' (23 October 1965, to a reader in Westover, West Virginia) (Betty Friedan Papers (MC 698.57), Schlesinger Library, Radcliffe Institute, Harvard University).

References

Bail, K. ed. (1996) *DIY Feminism*, St Leonards: Allen & Unwin

Bailey, C. (1997) 'Making Waves and Drawing Lines: The Politics of Defining the Vicissitudes of Feminism', *Hypatia*, 12.3: 17–28.

Baumgardner, J. & Richards, A. (2000) *Manifesta: Young Women, Feminism, and the Future*, New York: Farrar, Straus and Giroux

———. (2003) 'Who's the New Gloria: The Quest for The Third Wave Super Leader', in R. Dicker & A. Piepmeir eds. *Catching a Wave: Reclaiming Feminism for the Twenty-First Century*, Boston: Northeastern University Press, pp. 159–170

Bennett, J. (2011) *Television Personalities: Stardom and the Small Screen*, London: Routledge

Bentley, T. (2012) 'Upstairs, Downstairs', 12 September, Sunday Book Review, *New York Times*, http://www.nytimes.com/2012/09/16/books/review/vagina-a-new-biography-by-naomi-wolf.html?_r=0

Betty Friedan Papers (1933–2007), Schlesinger Library, Radcliffe Institute, Harvard University

Biddle, T (@tabbiebiddle). 'I am so grateful for your courage and perseverance @ naomi wolf. I am loving Vagina: A New Biography. It's helping me understand so much!' 28 December 2013. Tweet.

Boyd, D., Golder, S. & Lotan, G. (2010) 'Tweet, Tweet, Retweet: Conversational Aspects of Retweeting on Twitter', *System Sciences*, accessed via: DOI: 10.1109/HICSS.2010.412

Carter, D. (1997) *Judah Waten: A Career in Writing*, Toowoomba: ASAL

Click, M.A., Lee, H. & Willson Holladay, H. (2013) 'Making Monsters: Lady Gaga, Fan Identification, and Social Media', *Popular Music and Society*, 36.3: 360–379

Cobain C.L. (@courtney) 'yes yes yes we should talk soon xo', 16 September 2012. Tweet.

Dancer, L. (@Lucymdancer) 'I'm only 3 chapters into the book and already 'Vagina' is already giving me a-ha moments – will u be speaking in London anytime soon?' 25 January 2014. Tweet.

Daum, M. (2012) 'Naomi Wolf's vaginal sideshow', 13 September, *Los Angeles Times*, accessed via http://articles.latimes.com/2012/sep/13/opinion/la-oe-daum-naomi-wolf-vagina-20120913

Deller, R. (2011) 'Twittering On: Audience Research and Participation Using Twitter', *Participations: Journal of Audience and Reception Studies*, 8.1, accessed via http://www.participations.org/Volume%208/Issue%201/deller.htm

Denfeld, R. (1995) *The New Victorians: A Young Woman's Challenge to the Old Feminist Order*, New York: Grand Central Publishing

Douglas, S. (1994) *Where the Girls: Growing Up Female with the Mass Media*, London: Penguin

Dow, B. (1996) *Prime Time Feminism: Television, Media Culture and the Women's Movement Since 1970s*, Philadelphia: University of Pennsylvania Press

Ellcessor, E. (2012) 'Tweeting@feliciaday: Online Social Media, Convergence, and Subcultural Stardom', *Cinema Journal*, 51.2: 46–66

Faludi, S. (1991) *Backlash: The Undeclared War Against American Women*, London: Vintage

Feather, J. & Woodbridge, H. (2007) 'Bestsellers in the British Publishing Industry, 1998–2005', *Publishing Research Quarterly*, 23.3: 210–223

Fine, C. (2010) *Delusions of Gender: How Our Minds, Society, and Neurosexism Create Difference*, New York: W.W. Norton

Friedan, B. (1981) *The Second Stage*, New York: Summit Books

Galow, T. (2010) 'Literary Modernism in the Age of Celebrity', *Modernism/Modernity*, 17.2: 313–329

Genette, G. (1997) *Paratexts: Thresholds of Interpretation*, Cambridge: Cambridge University Press

Greer, G. (1984) *Sex and Destiny: The Politics of Human Fertility*, Melbourne: Seeker and Warburg

Greer, G. (2012) 'Her Knickers in a Twist', 15 September, *Sydney Morning Herald*, accessed via: http://www.smh.com.au/entertainment/books/her-twist-in-the-knickers-20120914-25wyh.html

Gunter, B. (2014) *Celebrity Capital*, London: Bloomsbury Academic

Hammer, R. (2000) 'Antifeminists as Media Celebrities', *Review of Education, Pedagogy, and Cultural Studies*, 22.3: 207–222

Hearn, A. & Schoenhoff, S. (2016) 'From Celebrity to Influencer: Tracing the Diffusion of Celebrity Value Across the Data Stream', in P.D. Marshall & S. Redmond eds. *A Companion to Celebrity*, London: Wiley Blackwell, pp. 194–211

Henry, A. (2004) *Not My Mother's Sister*, Bloomington: University of Indiana Press

Hesford, V. (2013) *Feeling Women's Liberation*, Durham: Duke University Press

Hinds, H. & Stacey, J. (2001) 'Imaging Feminism, Imaging Femininity: The Bra-Burner, Diana, and the Woman Who Kills', *Feminist Media Studies*, 1:2, 153–177

Hogeland, L.M. (2001) 'Against Generationalist Thinking, or, Some Things That "Third Wave" Feminism Isn't', *Women's Studies in Communication*, 24.1: 107–121

Hubbard, K. (1991) 'The Tyranny of Beauty', 24 June, *People Magazine*, accessed via http://www.people.com/people/archive/article/0,,20115393,00.html

James, C. (1991) 'Critics Notebook: Feminine Beauty as a Masculine Plot', 7 May, *New York Times*, accessed via http://www.nytimes.com/1991/05/07/books/critic-s-notebook-feminine-beauty-as-a-masculine-plot.html

Jenkins, H. (2009) 'The Message of Twitter: "Here It Is" and "Here I Am"', 23 August, *Confessions of an Aca-Fan*, accessed via http://henryjenkins.org/2009/08/the_message_of_twitter.html

Keller, J. (2012) 'Virtual Feminisms: Girls' Blogging Communities, Feminist Activism and Participatory Politics', *Information, Technology and Society*, 15.3: 429–447

Knight, P. (1997) 'Naming the Problem: Feminism and the Figuration of Conspiracy', *Cultural Studies*, 11.1: 40–63

Lumby, C. (2014) 'Post Postfeminism', in C. Carter, L. Steiner & L. Maclaughlin eds. *The Routledge Companion to Media and Gender*, London: Routledge, pp. 600–609

Marshall, P.D. (2010) 'The Specular Economy', *Soc*, 47: 498–502

Marwick, A.E. (2013) *Status Update: Celebrity, Publicity, and Branding in the Social Media Age*, New Haven: Yale University Press

Marwick, A. & boyd, d. (2011) 'To See and Be Seen: Celebrity Practice on Twitter', *Convergence*, 17.2: 139–158

Murray, S. (2004) *Mixed Media: Feminist Presses and Publishing Politics*, London: Pluto

—— (2015) 'Charting the Digital Literary Sphere', *Contemporary Literature*, 56.2: 311–339

Orr, C. (1997) 'Charting the Currents of the Third Wave', *Hypatia*, 12.3: 29–45

Page, R. (2012) 'The Linguistics of Self-Branding and Micro-Celebrity in Twitter: The Role of Hashtags', *Discourse and Communication*, 6.2: 181–201

Paglia, C. (1990) *Sexual Personae: Art and Decadence From Nefertiti to Emily Dickinson*, New Haven: Yale University Press

Pearce, L. (2004) *The Rhetorics of Feminism*, London: Routledge

Penny, L. (2012) 'Laurie Penny on the problem with Naomi Wolf's vagina', 10 September, *New Statesman*, accessed via: http://www.newstatesman.com/laurie-penny/2012/09/problem-naomi-wolfs-vagina

Pollitt, K. (2012) 'Naomi Wolf's "Vagina": No Carnations, Please, We're Goddesses', 1 October, *The Nation*, accessed via https://www.thenation.com/article/naomi-wolfs-vagina-no-carnations-please-were-goddesses/

Potter, B. (2012) 'Reclaiming the Vagina: PW Talks with Naomi Wolf', 20 July, *Publisher's Weekly*, accessed via http://publishersweekly.com/pw/by-topic/

authors/interviews/article/53078-reclaiming-the-vagina-pw-talks-with-naomi-wolf.html

Quinn, R.D. (1997) 'An Open Letter to My Institutional Mothers', in D. Looser & E.A. Kaplan eds. *Generations: Academic Feminists in Dialogue*, Minneapolis: University Minnesota Press, pp. 174–182

Rae (RachelMeeker) '"Vagina: A New Biography" by @naomi wolf is life changing. I'm not exaggerating either. Everyone must read it and be enlightened', 2 January 2014. Tweet.

Rapping, E. (1991) '*The Beauty Myth: How Images of Beauty Are Used Against Women* by Naomi Wolf', *The Women's Review of Books*, 9.1

Renee, R. (@RaeboRenee) 'Vagina vagina vagina! #LifeChangingRead', 15 January 2014. Tweet.

Rich, A. (1976) *Of Woman Born: Motherhood As Experience and Institution*, London: Virago

Robinson, D. (2013) 'Novel Forms and Brand New Relations: Exploring Convergence Culture and Australian Literary Celebrity', *Limina*, pp. 1–12, accessed via http://www.limina.arts.uwa.edu.au

Roiphe, K. (1993) *The Morning After: Sex, Fear and Feminism*, New York: Bayback Books

———. (2012) 'Naomi Wolf's New Book About Her Vagina', 10 September, *Slate*, http://www.slate.com/articles/double_x/roiphe/2012/09/naomi_wolf_s_new_book_about_her_vagina_is_ludicrous_.html

Rojek, C. (2001) *Celebrity*, London: Reaktion

Roof, J. (1997) 'Generational Difficulties; or the Fear of a Barren History', in D. Looser & E.A. Kaplan eds. *Generations: Academic Feminists in Dialogue*, Minneapolis: University Minnesota Press, pp. 69–87

Sandler, L. (2012) 'Naomi Wolf Sparks Another Debate (About Sex of Course)', *New York Times*, accessed via http://www.nytimes.com/2012/09/20/fashion/naomi-wolf-on-her-new-book-vagina.html

Senft, T. (2008) *Camgirls: Celebrity and Community in the Age of Social Networks*, New York: Lang

Siegel, D. (1997) 'Reading Between the Waves: Feminist Historiography in "Postfeminist" Moment', in L. Heywood & J. Drake eds. *Third Wave Agenda: Being Feminist, Doing Feminism*, Minneapolis: Minnesota University Press, pp. 55–82

Sommers, C. Hoff (1994) *Who Stole Feminism? How Women Have Betrayed Women*, New York: Simon and Schuster

Steinem, G. (1983) *Outrageous Acts and Everyday Rebellions*, New York: Holt, Rinehart, and Winston

Stringer, R. (2014) *Knowing Victims: Feminism and Victim Politics in Neoliberal Times*, New York: Routledge

Taylor, A. (2008) *Mediating Australian Feminism: Rereading the First Stone Media Event*, Oxford: Peter Lang

Thomas, S. (2014) 'Celebrity in the "Twitterverse": History, Authenticity and the Multiplicity of Stardom', *Celebrity Studies*, 5.3: 242–255.

Tsaliki, L. (2016) '"Tweeting the Good Causes": Social Networking and Celebrity Activism', in P.D. Marshall & S. Redmond eds. *A Companion to Celebrity*, London: Wiley Blackwell, pp. 235–257

Turner, J. (2012) 'Vagina: A New Biography by Naomi Wolf', 7 September, *The Guardian*, accessed via http://www.theguardian.com/books/2012/sep/07/vagina-new-biography-naomi-wolf-review

Turner, G. (2014) *Understanding Celebrity*, London: Sage

——— (2016) 'Celebrity, Participation, and the Public', in P.D. Marshall & S. Redmond eds. *A Companion to Celebrity*, London: Wiley Blackwell, pp. 83–97

van Dijick, J. (2013) *The Culture of Connectivity: A Critical History of Social Media*, Oxford: Oxford University Press

Virago Press (@ViragoBooks) 'Gwyneth Paltrow on Vagina: A New Biography by @naomirwolf: If you have a vagina you must read this book: It's astonishingly good', 7 March. Tweet

Walter, N. (1998) *The New Feminism*, London: Virago

Wernick, A. (1991) *Promotional Culture: Advertising, Ideology and Symbolic Expression*, London: Sage

Wicke, J. (1994) 'Celebrity Material: Materialist Feminism and the Culture of Celebrity', *South Atlantic Quarterly*, 93.4: 751–778

Wolf, N. (1990) *The Beauty Myth*, London: Virago

———. (1993) *Fire with Fire: The New Female Power and How It Will Change the 21st Century*, London: Chatto and Windus

———. (2004) 'The Silent Treatment', 1 March, *New York Magazine*, accessed via http://nymag.com/nymetro/news/features/n_9932/

———. (2007) *The End of America: A Letter of Warning to a Young American Patriot*, New York: Chelsea Green Publishing

———. (2008) *Give Me Liberty: A Handbook for Young American Revolutionaries*,

———. (2012) *Vagina: A New Biography*, London: Virago

———. (2013) *Vagina: Revised and Updated*, New York: Ecco

———. (2015) *The Beauty Myth: Vintage Feminism Short Edition*, London: Penguin

Wolf, N. (@naomirwolf) 'How delightful that Courtney Love is tweeting support for Vagina: A New Biography...Thank you so much! @Courtney...questions? Let me know!' 16 September 2012. Tweet

——— (@naomirwolf) 'xoxo RT @moniqueruffin, @naomirwolf my new bible just arrived!' 21 November 2012. Tweet

——— (@naomirwolf) 'Thank you! RT @kyokochurch: Just pages 40 in to #Vagina by @naomiwolf and I'm already blown away! #enlightening', 19 May 2013. Tweet

―――― (@naomirwolf) 'wow thank you RT @BasementBeauty @naomirwolf Not even finished & already I feel this book changing my life', 1 September 2013, 3.40am. Tweet

―――― (@naomirwolf) 'Thank you to my readers around the world!', 6 January 2014. Tweet

―――― (@naomirwolf) 'Vagina Revised and Expanded" has now hit the Amazon Hot New Releases top sellers in four categories', 6 January 2014. Tweet

―――― (@naomirwolf) 'Thank you! Should be, will announce dates when confirmed. You can keep an eye out on bitly/1hxVzne in the meantime. xx' 25 January 2014. Tweet

―――― (@naomirwolf) 'Join me for a discussion & book signing tomorrow at Yale University bookstore', 10 February 2014. Tweet

―――― (@naomirwolf) 'Thank you! xx RT @CrazyIdealist @naomi wolf Thank you for writing a life-changing book. Here's my review'. 11 February 2014. Tweet

Wright, J.L. (2012) 'Who's afraid of Naomi Wolf? Feminism in Post-feminist Culture', in S. Crasnow & J. Waugh eds. *Philosophical Feminism and Popular Culture*, New York: Rowman & Littlefield, pp. 151–172

Yalom, M. (1991) 'Feminism's Latest Makeover', 16 June, *Washington Post*

York, L. (2013) *Margaret Atwood and the Labour of Literary Celebrity*, Toronto: University of Toronto Press

CHAPTER 7

Sheryl Sandberg and Roxane Gay: The Limits and Possibilities of Contemporary Blockbuster Feminism

INTRODUCTION

As my preceding analysis of Naomi Wolf's most recent book has demonstrated, contemporary 'feminist' blockbusters as well as their celebrity authors look and feel (for their affective pull is also crucial) in some ways quite different from the books I have previously considered. However, the next two chapters make clear that, despite rhetorical and political differences, blockbusters remain key vehicles in the process of feminist celebrification, and for ensuring that some feminisms come to receive cultural legitimacy over others. Here, I engage with two very different manifestations of the feminist blockbuster: one whose rhetoric aligns more closely with the postfeminist neoliberalism that characterizes the twenty-first century (Gill 2007; Vavrus 2007; Taylor 2012), and another whose feminist politics are less ambivalent as it works to challenge the normative whiteness that has been at the heart of celebrity feminism: Sheryl Sandberg's *Lean In* (2013) and Roxane Gay's *Bad Feminist* (2014) respectively.

This chapter illustrates, perhaps more so than any others, Wicke's description of the 'celebrity zone' as a site where 'good things happen, and bad things happen' (1994, p. 758). Continuing Part II's emphasis on how new media work to augment blockbuster celebrity feminism, here I focus on practices of self-branding and how these two authors strategically position themselves within the online attention economy, with the effect of extending the reach of their particular feminism. To do so, this chapter engages with Sandberg's use of online media to develop and extend her 'lean in' strategy, including—consistent with wider celebrity involvement in various causes—to young girls, and then explores the role of the digital sphere in the establishment and maintenance of Gay's blockbuster celebrity feminism. Here I demonstrate how, just as the blockbusters themselves differ, so does the kind of celebrity feminism embodied and practised by their authors. Although the authors occupy the same generational location (Sandberg and Gay were born in 1969 and 1974 respectively), they represent a challenge to the presumption of generational unity upon which popular feminism often relies (Henry 2004). That is, 'their substantial differences signal a little conceded diversity in the way feminism is conceptualized and represented in mainstream discourse' (Taylor 2008, p. 231). Moreover, neither of them chose to identify themselves or their feminism according to the wave metaphor, further complicating the dominant way of figuring feminism, thus urging us to concede popular feminism's complexity, multiplicity, and potentiality.

This chapter considers, too, how Sandberg's professional positioning in the corporate world, and Gay's in the academy, work to mediate their celebrity in important, and at times troublesome, ways. These case studies show that, in terms of both politics and practice, celebrity feminism is necessarily a heterogeneous phenomenon, and in this respect reveals both its constraints and possibilities. These publications, their reception, and their authors' different forms of celebrity also provide an insight into the racial politics of celebrity feminism. For Sandberg, race goes totally unacknowledged in her 'lean in' strategy, and for Gay it is central to the way she problematizes the whiteness of mainstream feminism, exposing the interlocking oppressions that constitute many women's everyday realities. This necessarily impacts the way they publicly perform their feminism, as well as the ways in which it is able to circulate and be consumed; Sandberg's neoliberal, 'post-race' vision is much less disruptive or threatening, a kind of 'feel-good' feminism for the status quo, while Gay's is uncomfortable, in her words 'messy', and seeks to destabilize commonsensical understandings of feminism, race, gender and their intersections. Nonetheless, their two books became feminist blockbusters within a year of one another, suggesting that popular feminism—including its blockbuster variants—remains complicated, uneven terrain.

Lean In: A New Model of Feminist Blockbuster – and Celebrity?

In March 2013, Sheryl Sandberg, the Chief Operating Officer (COO) of global social networking corporation Facebook, published *Lean In: Women, Work and the Will to Lead*,[1] which became an immediate bestseller. Indicative of the transnational nature of the contemporary blockbuster, *Lean In* was published in 24 languages (Rowley 2013). Under the 'Lean In' banner there has been an empowerment campaign for girls (#banbossy); conferences; campus tours where devotees extol the virtues of 'leaning in' to undergraduates; an updated edition of the book, *Lean In for Graduates* (2014); and a spin-off campaign aimed at men (#leanintogether), all with associated merchandise. *Lean In* is, therefore, 'less a book than a phenomenon' (Dowse 2013).

In regard to the book's generic location, Sandberg attempts, with some difficulty, to frame it in terms of what it is *not*: 'a memoir, although I have included stories about my life. It is not a self-help book, although I truly hope it helps. It is not a book on career management, although I offer advice in that area. It is not a feminist manifesto—okay, it is sort of a feminist manifesto …' (2013a, pp. 9–10). Given the context in which the book was produced, the 'feminism' of this new type of blockbuster is entirely consistent with neoliberalism,[2] and Sandberg can be seen to 'espouse an ever-expanding program of self-discipline rather than structural reform' (Negra 2014, p. 284). The individualism underpinning the book is succinctly indicated by the first chapter's title: 'Internalizing the Revolution'. Although Sandberg undoubtedly does adopt a feminist voice and frames her interventions in the rhetoric of social movements, it is the individual, not the socio-political context in which she operates, that is seen to be in need of recalibration: 'We can reignite the revolution by internalizing the revolution. The shift to a more equal world will happen person by person. We move closer to the larger goal of true equality with each woman who leans in' (2013a, p. 11). The book features a number of anecdotes about how she has personally performed the tactic advocated therein, with considerable success, and its cover offers a portrait of a contented, even beaming Sandberg, implicitly reaping the rewards of 'leaning in'. Not surprisingly, the book's emphasis on 'what women could do for themselves' (Greenhouse 2015) has been widely criticized, while its neoliberal tenor has been the subject of much recent feminist scholarship (McRobbie 2013; Negra 2014; Rottenberg 2014a; Banet-Weiser 2015b).

As feminist social theorists like Nancy Fraser (2013) have made clear, feminism has become 'entangled in a dangerous liaison with neoliberal efforts to build a free market society', resulting in the reframing of a formerly radical 'worldview' in 'individualist terms'; as evidence of this, she cites Sandberg's 'lean in' philosophy.

The book's governing trope—that of 'leaning in'—evokes women's apparent tendency to 'lean out' in professional contexts, or to fail to assert themselves. In this way, Sandberg offers 'her own brand of motivational and aspirational corporate feminism' (Banet-Weiser 2015a). In keeping with the neoliberal logic in which her argument is framed, women are positioned at the centre of the 'problem' of under-representation in senior leadership roles; for example, the trope of women 'holding themselves back' (2013a, pp. 9, 150) is a recurrent one. As Rottenberg notes (2014b, p. 154), rather than advocating societal transformation, 'Sandberg focuses on changing women's attitudes about work and self.' That women themselves are responsible for managing the ongoing gender inequities shaping our lives, and thus it is women who need to be recalibrated, is by no means a new sentiment. However, what is distinctive is the way feminism is being recruited in service of such arguments. In such accounts feminism, rather than merely being disavowed as per the logics of postfeminism, is given 'new life through an articulation with a specific range of value pertaining to the project of contemporary neoliberalism' (McRobbie 2015, p. 120; see also Faludi 2013; Rottenberg 2014a). Furthermore, Sandberg illustrates, perhaps more than any other woman examined in this book, the mutually sustaining privileges that often still govern who gets to speak (and be heard) in and through modern media systems, and in this case who is granted the authority to shape popular understandings of feminism. Hers is a form of 'do-it-yourself' feminism (Bail 1996), eliding the multiple factors that make her vision both unimaginable and undesirable for many women.

In this vein, Sandberg's work, and indeed her celebrity and its viability, cannot be extricated from the post-race and postfeminist discursive context from which it emerges; her book is also exceedingly heteronormative (Gay 2014a). In assertions that race-based discrimination has been firmly relegated to the past, 'it is popularly assumed that the civil rights movement effectively eradicated racism to the extent that not only does racism no longer exist, but race itself no longer matters' (Joseph 2009, p. 240). This presumption implicitly underpins Sandberg's personalized 'equality' strategy. As bell hooks (2013) remarks, 'the "lean in" woman is never given a racial identity …' Therefore, 'the corporate infusion of gender equality she [Sandberg] evokes is a "whites only" proposition'. While Sandberg may appear to challenge postfeminist claims about the redundancy of feminism, her vision is thoroughly indebted to the assumption that, in millennial America, race simply does not matter. In this way, her feminism is indicative of 'liberal [and indeed neoliberal] feminism's key weakness', as Stringer notes, 'a call for equality without including racial analysis' (2007, p. 251). Indeed, that feminism itself is reduced to a call for 'equality' is deeply problematic, something that dates back at least to Friedan's blockbuster; that is, the dominant way of 'telling feminist stories' (Hemmings 2011) in the mainstream media has been overwhelmingly through a liberal lens (Farrell 1998; Henderson 2006). This becomes even more important, given the wide reach of Sandberg's ideas, including before the book itself came into being.

The 'TED' Phenomenon and Celebrity Feminism

As is often the case with the blockbuster, Sandberg's promotion of the book was a multi-media event, including television interviews, a website with links to various forms of social media, promotional videos, print newspaper and magazine profiles, and celebrity endorsements. For Negra (2014, p. 279), the success of books like *Lean In* 'depend[s] heavily on the persona creation of their authors and operate[s] as just one element in a convergent set of interrelated promotional activities', including the TED talk. The latter represents a platform, unavailable to the women examined in the first part of this book, via which the blockbuster celebrity feminist now works to secure her renown and expand the reach of her book. A not-for-profit organization whose mission is to make 'great ideas' freely accessible via its website (ted.com/talks), TED has become an important communicative vehicle in feminist terms.

Indeed, Sandberg's initial TED talk, in 2010, pre-dates the publication of her blockbuster but it has been positioned (including by the author) as central to the book's genesis.[3] As Anne Marie Slaughter (2013)[4] remarks, 'Sandberg's career as a feminist champion began with her 2010 TED talk', which went viral. Paratextually, her TED talk is even invoked on the book's back-cover blurb, where it is described as 'electrifying'. As at December 2015, the October 2010 talk—'Why We Have Too Few Women Leaders'—has been viewed nearly 6 million times and is available in 45 subtitled languages. Such consumption figures reveal just how crucial such a medium has become in the promotion of public figures across a wide range of fields. In December 2013 Sandberg returned to the TED stage for an interview, noting:

> After I did the TED Talk, what happened was—you know, I never really expected to write a book, I'm not an author, I'm not a writer, and it was viewed a lot, and it really started impacting people's lives ... And I realized that other women and men could find their voice through it, which is why I went from the talk to the book.[5]

Sandberg's comments here are reminiscent of those made by Friedan in particular, who, as a marker of her text's value, regularly invoked the large numbers of women readers who spoke of its transformative role. Here she positions the book as a natural progression from the talk, though of course this performance served to effectively pre-fabricate an audience for her subsequent corporate manifesto.[6]

It is possible to suggest that while it was certainly not what Genette (1997) envisaged when he spoke of the 'publisher's epitext', the TED talk has become a key vehicle for generating the 'hype' upon which so-called 'big books' rely (Thompson 2010). When performed following the publication of a work of feminist non-fiction, as was the case with Gay (2015c), it can be seen as analogous to the book readings undertaken by early literary celebrities such as Charles Dickens and Mark Twain, who 'performed authorship publicly' and developed the 'close interactive relationships with readers that became standard practice in the next century' (Glass 2016, p. 43). Such public performances are, as Gardiner (2000, p. 65) observes, central to the process of the modern author not simply being required to write the text but also to publicly speak it, increasingly through videos posted online (either on the author's website or on specific YouTube channels). That is, blockbuster celebrity—like other forms—relies upon the author's accessibility, something facilitated by digital media.

As Murray (2015, p. 328) observes, 'authorial embodiment and performativity have come to be key—and controversial—criteria in the marketing, reception, and evaluation of literary fiction [and indeed, as I show here, non-fiction]'. However, TED presentations extend beyond the co-present audience to the virtual publics who are able to subsequently view them online; arguably this adds a transnational dimension to this kind of celebrity feminism, which can be accessed from various parts of the globe (notwithstanding issues around the persistent digital divide). Although the platform may be new, the strategies of public performance and self-presentation have altered little (Thomas 2014). While social media have made being 'seen' central to our ways of being in the twenty-first century (Banet-Weiser 2012), the TED forum also permits a wider dissemination of the ideas informing these new-style feminist blockbusters, and therefore represents the extension of their reach and potential consumers. In terms of Sandberg, though, we also cannot ignore the role of Facebook in the book's success or in her celebrification.

Although not strictly a 'business celebrity' (Littler 2007; van Krieken 2012), Sandberg's 'attention capital' is clearly reliant upon her professional location in one of most commercially successful and culturally penetrative technology firms. As Negra (2014, p. 282) notes, 'we should ask how the Facebook brand benefits from being seen as interested in and supportive of feminism'. It is undoubtedly the case that Facebook, as a brand, provided the platform through which Sandberg could secure public visibility and whose own corporate identity would arguably be strengthened by its COO's expanding public profile and representation of the company as sympathetic to her (neo)liberal feminist agenda: 'while *Lean In* is technically separate from Facebook, it is supported by Facebook in ways ranging from Zuckerberg's book jacket endorsement to the fact that Facebook provided Sandberg with time to write and complete an intense publicity tour for the book while serving as COO' (Losse 2013). That is, Facebook is a condition of *Lean In*'s possibility, as well as its author's celebrity. Morally and ethically, Facebook is held up as the model employer, both throughout the narrative of *Lean In* and also in its author's myriad public appearances; this, of course, can do nothing to harm its brand as the millennial technology company par excellence, especially given feminism's apparent newfound cultural currency. Media coverage, as well as online engagement with the book, however, reveals that Sandberg's authority as a celebrity feminist has been subject to contestation.

Debating *Lean In*, Debating Celebrity Feminism

In the tradition of the feminist blockbuster, *Lean In* certainly did precipitate intense public debate, both on- and offline, about the kinds of privileged 'solutions' it proffered to a very specific audience (Faludi 2013; Garcia 2013; Grant 2013), thereby opening up a space for consideration of feminism as an ongoing political project (as opposed to something relegated to the past). As blockbuster celebrity feminists often are, Sandberg has largely been a polarizing figure, with the book's copious reviews 'more or less divided between those who praise the book and those who disagree with its premise or castigate the author for being who she is' (Dowse 2013). Moreover, its author was seen to successfully embody the strategy she advocated, and thereby her status as a highly successful, corporate 'working mother' was central to legitimizing her feminism. Even prior to the book's publication she was being positioned as successfully enacting the 'work–life balance in an unthreatening way', exemplified in particular by an Annie Leibowitz photograph for a 2012 cover of *Vanity Fair*, an intimate portrait with her children which embodies 'affluent celebrity maternalism' (Negra 2014, p. 282). Such portrayals, as is always the case with the blockbuster, are an integral part of the book's paratext, helping to inform responses to the book and its author's feminism. Furthermore, as Woods notes (2015, p. 38), all forms of cultural production, including bestselling feminist non-fiction, are 'produced and made complex through discussion and active consumption'. Therefore, rather than meaning being immanent, the book as well as 'Sandberg'—the exemplary 'lean in' subject, as she was clearly positioned in *Time*'s profile following *Lean In*'s publication (Luscombe 2014)—are brought into being in and through public talk around them.

Despite much public debate about her relationship to feminism, Sandberg does publicly identify with it; this, I would argue, is a necessary gesture for all authors of blockbusters deemed feminist. In the book she describes herself as the 'pom-pom girl for feminism' (2013, p. 159), despite earlier hostility towards the term. Similarly, in an interview she suggests that she eventually chose to accept feminism on these patently liberal grounds: 'I embrace it now because what feminism is, it is a belief that the world should be equal, that men and women should have equal opportunity' (in Meltzer 2013). Throughout her text and its public career, Sandberg deploys an equal rights rhetoric consistent with that of other celebrity feminists like Gloria Steinem, Hillary Clinton, and even Friedan. In fact, her text was repeatedly compared to Friedan's, and seen as having similarly sparked a new phase of feminism (Yadegaren 2013; see also Hirshman 2013; Kantor 2013; Maslin 2013); Maureen Dowd (2013) even dubbed Sandberg 'Betty Friedan for the digital age', while the *New York Times* review was, rather ambitiously, entitled 'In Sandberg, Echoes of De Beauvoir' (Freeland 2013). Placing Sandberg in such a long lineage of feminist 'blockbuster' authors works as an authorizing gesture, despite the not-inconsiderable political differences of these texts (see Rottenberg 2014a, p. 423).

Many commentators used Sandberg's obvious investment in celebrity to discredit her feminism—not a unique strategy when it comes to blockbuster authors. As argued in Chap. 2, feminists who actively court celebrity are commonly believed to have 'sold out feminism's progressive agenda for media attention and personal wealth and fame' (Hammer 2000, p. 218). Seeking or benefiting from celebrity, with its privileging of the individual, then, is decried as a selfish, narcissistic practice (Taylor 2008), and such women are seen in opposition to altruistic feminists who are 'more preoccupied with this issues' (hooks 1994, pp. 92–3).[7] This common refrain in feminist critiques of celebrity resurfaced in reviews of *Lean In*.

Consistent with the surveillance experienced by female celebrities more broadly, public feminists can be subject to intense judgement and regulation (on which the conclusion will elaborate). In Sandberg's case, such judgement is predicated on a critique not of her appearance or corporeality as it often is with other women stars, nor primarily of her politics, but of her techniques of self-branding which were seen, mostly by other women, to be fundamentally at odds with feminism. For example, in the *Washington Post* Grant (25 February 2013) expressed concerns about the 'branding' of its author: 'The "movement" Sandberg seeks to lead with *Lean In* resembles a social movement only so far as it supports the growth of her brand as leader' (see also Roberts 2013). Likewise, in a *Vogue* article entitled 'Why Sheryl Sandberg's Brand of Feminism Isn't for Me', Patricia Garcia (13 March 2014) asked: 'why is it starting to feel like the image being best served by this campaign is Sandberg's?' However, as I conclude, it is Sandberg's politics, rather than her strategies of (self-)branding or celebrity, that should be the subject of critique. Nonetheless, indicative of the meta-commentary in which blockbusters commonly become enmeshed, its author did receive significant support, including from feminists, who critiqued the response to the book and its author. Along with many others (Filipovic 2013; Walsh 2013), Jessica Valenti, founder of website Feministing[8]—who herself is a micro-celebrity, if not a blockbuster celebrity feminist or even celebrity feminist journalist[9]—defended Sandberg in the *Washington Post* (1 March 2013), questioning the public adjudication of her feminism:

> When was the last time you heard someone with a platform as big as hers argue that women should insist that their partners do an equal share of domestic work and child care? ... Here's a nationally known woman calling herself a feminist, writing what will be a wildly popular book with feminist ideas, encouraging other women to be feminists. And we're worried she has too much influence?

These comments reveal that, despite the political limitations of the book, it did result in an ongoing dialogue about different forms of feminism and their efficacy, as well as the question of feminist authority itself. For critics, Sandberg's discursive power is to be lamented, while for sympathetic commentators, her use of her attention capital in the service of broadly feminist goals should be commended. Such diverse responses—to the book as well as its heavily celebrified author—also suggest that feminist debate is not simply confined to or being relegated to the digital sphere but has in many ways been entirely normalized in the mainstream media, not least because of blockbuster celebrities. The political limitations of the book aside, such public conversations over feminism are in themselves generative: 'Public debate has always been essential to the health of feminism as to any movement for equitable, empowering social change' (Minnich 1998, p. 174). Blockbuster celebrity feminists, including Sandberg and the others examined here, are the figures through which such, often highly charged, debate is refracted. The book, however, was only one part of the 'lean in' strategy, thereby taking the blockbuster, and its author, into new political territory.

The 'Lean In' Brand: Activism, Celebrity, and Commodification

The development of the various cross-platform 'Lean In' initiatives demonstrates how, although Sandberg's celebrity capital is certainly the product of her blockbuster's success, it does not end there. While this in itself is not remarkable—Betty Friedan's involvement with NOW is an obvious counterpoint in that regard—what is apparently different is how the 'Lean In' mantra has been effectively created as a 'brand' that spans services, resources, campaigns, as well as products, such as the book itself and associated merchandise. Sandberg, of course, is pivotal to this brand and its extension. Although there are a number of commodities associated with it, LeanIn.org itself is a not-for-profit organization launched by Sandberg, as per its Twitter banner, 'to empower all women to achieve their ambitions'. As part of the 'Lean In' brand, there is a series of initiatives that appear to borrow many of the activist strategies commonly deployed during feminism's second wave, not the least of which is consciousness-raising (CR; McRobbie 2015). At the book's conclusion, Sandberg urges readers to take up the issues she has raised further, including through active participation in what she dubs 'lean in circles'. Reminiscent of the second wave, such 'CR' groups are 'predicated in part on the conviction that women's lives can be transformed through talking with other women' and seek to mobilize 'the power of women telling stories' (Young 1997, p. 13).

This indebtedness to such second wave strategies, although not explicitly acknowledged, is patent in the website's description of the circles: 'Lean In Circles are small groups who meet regularly to learn and grow together. Circles are as unique as the individuals who start them, but they all share a common bond: the power of peer support.' To facilitate a successful 'circle', a series of resources are provided, including videos by 'experts'; 'a system for connecting with other circles'; meeting guides and 'activities'; and materials to help promote the circle, 'including a logo!' (leanincircles.org) This latter point is important as it makes clear the role of branding in the 'Lean In' franchise. In addition to the 'lean in circles', Sandberg launched an 'empowerment' initiative targeted specifically at young girls; before considering this, it is necessary to place this activism in wider debates about the shifting relations of politics, celebrity, philanthropy, gender, and feminism.

Politics, especially in terms of movements seeking social change such as women's liberation, is widely recognized to have dramatically shifted over the past fifty years or so (Banet-Weiser and Mukherjee 2012, p. 2). Celebrity culture has been crucial to such a radically transformed sociopolitical environment: 'Social action in the neoliberal era is, thus, characterized by the increasing presence of Hollywood celebrities, pop icons, and corporate moguls who have stepped in where the state used to be, proliferating privatized forms of welfare and redistribution' (Banet-Weiser and Mukherjee 2012, p. 93). Much has been written recently on how celebrities deploy their attention capital for philanthropic and/or activist purposes, and they have been variously described as 'celanthropists' (Rojek 2011) or 'celebvocates' (Tsaliki 2016). As Sarah Casey (2015, p. 15; see also Littler 2008) argues: 'Visibility through connection to a "cause" is now almost synonymous with celebrity as both an expectation and a method to sponsor leverage for individual celebrity "brand(s)".[10] This is not least the case for contemporary celebrity feminists, like Sandberg, who uses the 'Lean In' political initiatives to position herself sympathetically, both with audiences and with corporate champions. Although there has been considerable debate about the efficacy of celanthropy, and its role in stars' self-branding, celebrity support for charities or campaigns can ensure additional media coverage; attract new audiences; and encourage sponsorship and raise public awareness (Hassid and Jeffreys 2015). However, as Alison Trope contends, although it is not possible to 'dismiss the crossover between star and philanthropy completely, it is clearly a model we cannot naively embrace and celebrate' (2012, p. 155). Here, therefore, it is necessary to address the ideological underpinnings of such initiatives, especially in relation to Sandberg's attempts to repurpose her book's corporate feminist discourse, ostensibly for the empowerment of young girls.

Launched in 2014 to mark the book's first anniversary, the 'Ban Bossy' campaign, a joint initiative of the Lean In Foundation and the Girl Scouts of USA, questions the gendered assumptions around young girls' assertiveness. In this regard, seeking to cultivate girls' desire for future leadership, the banner on the website reads:

> When a little boy asserts himself, he's called a 'leader.' Yet when a little girl does the same, she risks being branded 'bossy.' Words like bossy send a message: don't raise your hand or speak up. By middle school, girls are less interested in leading than boys—a trend that continues into adulthood. Together we can encourage girls to lead. (banbossy.com)

It seems, therefore, that 'Ban Bossy' locates the roots of women's failure—for it is indeed positioned as theirs—to effectively 'lean in' in their later professional lives in childhood. The girl invoked in this material is clearly 'at risk' (Harris 2004), in need of early intervention to put her on the path to full neoliberal postfeminist citizenship, thus negating the need for an orchestrated strategy of 'leaning in' in adulthood. Seeking to normalize leadership for young girls, Ban Bossy is consistent with Sandberg's overarching 'Lean In' brand. Moreover, it further elucidates how celebrity involvement in not-for-profit organizations participates in an 'economy of hyperindividualised solutions to broader social and cultural problems' (Littler 2008, p. 245). Given this, Sandberg's campaign is entirely consistent with the approach taken in her book, thereby representing a multimedia extension of her political agenda. In addition to using the resources and guides proffered on the website, girls themselves are encouraged to take the pledge, 'I will #ban bossy', on various social networking sites. Further, as its website makes clear, 'Ban Bossy' has a number of corporate 'partners', which is not unusual for community or non-government projects based on mobilizing the potential of girls (Harris 2004, p. 19) and shores up the corporate basis of Sandberg's feminism. It also deploys the celebrity capital of Condoleezza Rice and Beyoncé—both of whom appear on the campaign video, the latter confidently pronouncing 'I'm not bossy. I'm the boss'—to garner support for the campaign, which had been critized for its inherent whiteness.

At the present juncture, Ban Bossy is not unique as a celebrity initiative, nor are projects that take young girls as the figures most in need of recalibration. In this sense, it is consistent with the increased trend towards 'empowerment feminism'. These rapidly proliferating 'girl empowerment organisations', as Banet-Weiser tells us, are on the rise in the USA; she conjectures that this is both because girls are seen to be a group 'in crisis' and because 'they are seen as an incredibly lucrative consumer market' (2015b, p. 60); these are 'mutually sustaining' ways of positioning girls (2015b, p. 61; see also Harris 2004). These organizations have emerged at the same time as the girl is being foregrounded in international development discourses. Texts, ranging from policy documents to international advertising campaigns, commonly invoke assumptions about the 'extraordinary capacity and potency of adolescent girls' (Koffman and Gill 2015, p. 89). It is clear that Ban Bossy, like other girl empowerment strategies, presumes a universally experienced girlhood. Although the girls it invokes are the middle-class, implicitly white, 'ideal subjects of neo-liberalism', entrepreneurial actors capable of confidently writing their own 'choice biographies', they are also coded as 'vulnerable' (Koffman and Gill 2015, p. 87). While organizations focusing on increasing girls' self-esteem, leadership, and confidence have laudable goals, it is their emphasis on individual subjectivities at the expense of broader social critique that renders them especially problematic (Banet-Weiser 2015b, pp. 61–2). Consistent with the neoliberal brand economy, girls' lack of confidence is being mined in ways that function to privilege the individual as the site of change. In this sense, Sandberg's use of her attention capital for such an initiative represents one of the more limited forms of celebrity feminist engagement.

However, as with *Lean In* itself, the response to Ban Bossy was ambivalent, with many critics unconvinced that the 'banning' of this particular adjective was a productive or workable political strategy. One commentator notes that, despite the star power of the woman behind it, she will not be adhering to the banning tactic: 'I don't intend to stop using it, even if the feminist super-team tells me to. They're not the boss of me' (Waldman 2014). Another expresses concerns about the impact this strategy would have on the public perception of feminism, remarking 'it makes feminists look like thought police rather than the expansive forward-thinkers we really are' (Friedman 2014). There was also criticism that the Facebook COO was (mis)using her celebrity capital:

> If Sheryl Sandberg wants to use her corporate connections to help more working women—if she knows better and better the societal barriers holding them back—why not create a hashtag in the service of an increased minimum wage? #BanPoverty, maybe? (Greenhouse 2014; see also Friedan 2014; Roy 2014)

The reception of Ban Bossy further suggests that the authority of celebrity feminists by no means goes uncontested—even when sponsored by a multi-billion dollar, globally successful corporation.

While we may scrutinize Sandberg's multi-media feminist brand, however, it is not an adequate critical response to completely dismiss it as 'faux feminism' (hooks 2013), a common gesture that precludes any consideration of why this form, and its personification through this author, may be resonating with contemporary audiences. If this is a feminism that engages consumers, we need to think through why this might be so and what its effects might be—something to which I return in the conclusion. As the next author examined here suggests of Sandberg, although not all women will be able, or want, to adopt her 'lean in' strategy, 'that doesn't mean that Sandberg has nothing to offer, or that *Lean In* should be summarily dismissed' (Gay 2014a, p. 312). Moreover, my criticism in relation to Sandberg is not about blockbuster celebrity feminism per se but about some of the limits of tethering it to a neoliberal corporate agenda for ostensibly feminist purposes.[11] Here I have shown how Sandberg's bestseller is augmented with other online texts, initiatives, and practices that work to broadly circulate her 'lean in' feminism, though there has been much debate about her politics as well as her celebrity itself. Accordingly, although given a heightened platform, blockbuster celebrity feminists do not necessarily silence other voices or other ways of publicly figuring feminism, and the discursive space they open for public debate over feminism—including questions regarding who is authorized to speak on its behalf—is in itself productive (Lilburn et al. 2000; Whelehan 2000; Taylor 2008). Moreover, as the next section makes clear, celebrity feminism itself is by no means a homogeneous field, even among bestselling authors.

Roxane Gay and the 'Bad Feminist' Subjectivity

Roxane Gay's *Bad Feminist* (2014) appeared within a year of Sandberg's text, but clearly moved away from its troublesome individualistic ethos. Both were *New York Times* bestsellers, yet the type of feminism they articulate—one steeped in neoliberalism and post-racialism, the other preoccupied with intersectionality and social justice—could not be more different. What are we to make of the fact that such starkly contrasting works of feminist non-fiction resonated in such a way as to constitute them both blockbusters at virtually the same cultural moment? How did contemporary celebrity culture facilitate the foregrounding of such disparate voices?

Through *Bad Feminist*, and her celebrity feminist persona, Gay works to destabilize the dominant discourses of both postfeminism and post-racialism. If celebrity results in certain 'faces of feminism' coming to shape popular understandings of feminism (Sheridan et al. 2006), then Gay's very public visibility challenges the normative whiteness at the heart of much popular feminism. In this respect, she reveals the importance of, and the ability to, tell feminist stories *differently* (Hemmings 2011). As in Chap. 6, here I attend to the role that online media play in the construction and maintenance of Gay's 'bad feminist' persona. In addition, given her academic role, I consider how Gay's micro-celebrity can be read as part of the self-branding labour and reputation management that is an imperative of the contemporary neoliberal university.

Consisting of a number of memoir-style essays, popular culture critiques, and celebrations, *Bad Feminist* has been described as 'a clarion call to bad feminists everywhere—for pluralism, collective effort and mutual respect—and the most persuasive feminist recruitment drive in recent memory' (Cochrane 2014). As is often common in the blockbuster, the essays are grouped into five themed sections: 'Me', 'Gender and Sexuality', 'Race and Entertainment', 'Politics, Gender, and Race', and 'Back to Me'. Cultural politics is a key focus of the book, with Gay adeptly covering various forms of cultural production such as teen fiction (*Sweet Valley High* and *The Hunger Games*), fictional and reality television (*90210*, *Private Practice*, *CSI* and *Girls*, and *Flavor of Love* and *Rock of Love*), contemporary cinema (*Django Unchained* and *The Help*), and popular music. Her focus on popular culture, and figurations of race in particular, is important, given that 'seemingly harmless cultural representations of black women are incorporated into institutional enactments of discrimination' (Stringer 2007, p. 250). Through drawing attention to the constitution of racial difference in films such as *The Help*, Gay works to contest 'post-racial' discourses that 'obfuscate institutional racism and blame continuing racial inequalities on individuals making poor choices for themselves or their families' (Squires 2014, p. 6). It is predominantly through discursive activism, in her book and through online media, that Gay publicly stages her intersectional feminist interventions.

Like Nancy K. Miller (1991), and indeed many other feminist critics, Gay uses these essays to 'get personal' and most of them do have an autobiographical bent, or at the very least make clear the author's affective investments in the texts, cultural practices, or issues she canvasses. Again, this foregrounding of an autobiographical 'I' has long been a staple of the feminist blockbuster, but it takes on another dimension with regard to Gay's racial location. The confessional mode characterizes many of the pieces, including her own experiences of sexual assault, and embodiment as an American African woman of Haitian descent. For Gay, being the text's eponymous 'bad feminist' signals an opposition to the subject on whose behalf Western feminism has commonly spoken: white, middle-class, heterosexual, cis gendered. This focus on cultural politics could easily align her with the so-called third wave (Heywood and Drake 1997; Henry 2004), as could the book's emphasis on interlocking oppression (Crenshaw 1991), which—defined in opposition to the second wave—recognizes that the differences among women are as substantial as the differences between women and men. That is, 'third wavers' argue that 'the category of "woman" is no longer the only identity worth examining' (Dicker and Piepmeir 2003, pp. 9–10). However, given the pervasiveness of generationalism in popular feminism, it is significant, and productive, that Gay does not choose to locate her feminism according to the logic of the restrictive wave paradigm (nor does Sandberg).

Despite her institutional location (i.e. within the academy), Gay's audience, like the implied readers of all blockbusters, is not predominantly other feminist scholars; it is women whose relation to feminist ideas is ambivalent at best, and at worst hostile. In the introduction I emphasized that celebrity feminism needs to become a more inclusive mode of feminist subjectivity, and *Bad Feminist* is certainly indicative of the ongoing political possibilities of the feminist blockbuster. That said, the blockbuster has, unsurprisingly and appropriately, been critiqued on the grounds of privileging certain voices, and certain feminisms, over others. hooks, for example, draws attention to the whiteness of feminist blockbusters and the ways in which they overwhelmingly elide racial difference: 'as more and more books by privileged individual feminist thinkers (most white, materially privileged) are marketed to a mass public and become the "texts" that teach these audiences what feminism is or is not, there is danger that any critical interrogation of the category "woman" will be erased' (1994, p. 102).[12] hooks' concerns are indeed valid, and are more applicable to some texts than others, such as Sandberg's.

In contrast to hooks' fears that popular feminism, especially through the mainstream publishing industry, will reinscribe the privileging of white voices, experiences, and political concerns, *Bad Feminist*'s most significant achievement is arguably in bringing an intersectional approach to popular consciousness. As Gay (2014a, p. iv) notes, 'feminism has, historically, been far more invested in improving the lives of heterosexual white women to the detriment of all others.' In many ways, then, her feminism is clearly indebted to critical thinkers like hooks, Adrienne Rich, and Audre Lorde who sought to underscore that gender and sexuality cannot be readily separated, or foregrounded over, other modalities of difference—though she does not make explicit this debt, something that has been the source of criticism (Rapp 2014). That is, Gay effectively elides the substantial challenges mounted by black and Latina women during the second wave and since, regarding the inextricability of racial and gender politics, a common rhetorical move in popular, and at times academic, historicizations of these earlier feminisms (Thompson 2002). Nonetheless, as a blockbuster feminist author, Gay does suggest the heterogeneity of celebrity feminism as well as illustrating that whiteness need not be one of its constitutive elements.

Given the complexities of racial politics in the USA, which co-exist with the 'post-race' discourses examined in the previous section, the fact that Gay's blockbuster achieved such an expansive reach and that she continues to be authorized to speak about racial tensions, especially as they intersect with gender, itself works to disrupt or destabilize the 'whitewash' (Gabriel 1998) that has long characterized American media and popular culture. No other popular non-fictional author has worked to underscore the systems of interlocking oppression that mediate how race and gender are embodied in the way Gay has done.[13] This is not to suggest Gay's position has gone unchallenged; the trope of the 'angry black woman'

(Stringer 2007) has been mobilized in representations of her, especially online, underscoring that media visibility does not always equate with power (Banet-Weiser 2015b). In particular, she has been vilified for her appearance, most notably her weight, an issue she takes up further in her forthcoming memoir, *Hunger*, and which cannot be disentangled from her racialized embodiment.

Like other celebrity feminists, Gay uses her polemic to question the authorization of some voices over others when it comes to popular feminism. In her introduction, she mounts her own critique of feminism's implication in the circuits of celebrity—despite her own obvious complicity with it:

> The problem with movements is that, all too often, they are associated only with the most visible figures, the people with the biggest platforms and the loudest, most provocative voices. But feminism is not whatever philosophy is being spouted by the popular media feminist flavor of the week … Feminism, as of late, has suffered from a certain guilt by association because we conflate feminism with women who advocate feminism as part of their personal brand … We forget the difference between feminism and Professional Feminists. (2014a, p. x)

This seems somewhat disingenuous, as Gay was to become one of the 'Professional Feminists' she here decries; in so doing, she echoes Greer's critique of the celebrification of feminist authors while subsequently embracing the cultural visibility it proffers.

The trope uniting the diverse essays in the collection—that of the 'bad feminist'—requires some unpacking here, especially as it has been central to her public persona. As a form of subjectivity, 'bad feminist' signifies the contradictions, ambivalence, and tensions in modern feminism. In terms of this subject position, one reviewer notes: '"Bad feminist" is a way for her to claim the title of feminist while distancing herself from the essentialism that she feels has never represented her, that has at times even rejected her' (McKeon 2014). In order to celebrate, or at least become reconciled to, her own 'badness', Gay must invoke a feminism that judges its proponents: 'I am failing as a woman. I am failing as a feminist. To freely accept the feminist label would not be fair to good feminists. If I am, indeed, a feminist, I am a rather bad one. I am a mess of contradictions' (2014a, p. 314). Her badness, as she tells us, manifests through her propensity for all things pink; that she 'very much likes men'; and her lack of knowledge about cars (2014a, pp. 315–16); she is presuming an external feminist gaze judging her performances of gender and feminism. In discursively positioning her new, 'bad' feminist subjectivity against an 'Essential feminism', rather than performing its disavowal as she claims to do (2014a, p. xiii), Gay effectively reinscribes assumptions about a dominant, personally oppressive, feminist orthodoxy that many scholars have worked to contest. That is, 'bad' feminism can only be defined in opposition to its 'good' counterpart.

The implication, therefore, that she may be judged 'bad' invokes a 'good' feminist, who polices the borders of what constitutes appropriate feminism; it also is framed by a narrative of feminism's homogeneity, against which Gay defines her messy, complicated, intersectional 'brand'. Although Gay does not explicitly deploy generationalist discourse, her rhetorical manoeuvres are consistent with those who do: 'Within contemporary feminist writing, certain feminisms are depicted as old or outdated in order to posit the new generation's progress and improvement' (Henry 2004, p. 6). This has been a common discursive strategy in popular feminist writing, especially from the 'third wave' (Bailey 1997; Orr 1997; Siegel 1997). However, in her *Bad Feminist* TED talk (28 May 2015), she makes explicit that what she is speaking against is not the feminism of an earlier generation but a 'mainstream' feminism that excludes women of colour, queer women, and transgender women; her feminism is 'bad' because it is not what she perceives as hegemonic feminism. Despite its limitations, she is ultimately unambiguous about her own identification with feminism: 'I am a bad feminist. I would rather be a bad feminist than no feminist at all' (2014a, p. 318).

Reviews of *Bad Feminist* in the mainstream media were overwhelmingly supportive, with most seeking to emphasize the apparent 'newness' of Gay's brand of feminism: 'In a personal and political way, the book tracks one woman's journey to avoid categorization in any form, all the while knowing this is impossible. Gay expands our definition of what being a feminist might be someday…' (Rapp 2014). In the tradition of the best 'consciousness-raising' texts, it is positioned as having the capacity to shift readerly understandings of feminism and race. In the *Washington Post*, Dvorak (5 September 2014) notes: 'there is no doubt something in this collection will make them [readers] view race or feminism—or even *The Hunger Games*—a little bit differently'. In particular, Gay is roundly seen to be productively intervening in an ongoing cultural conversation over what it means to identify as a feminist in a context where the signifier is often demonized or seen as irrelevant (McKeon 2014) but remains necessary (Schickel 2014). Many reviews seek to address the book's marketability, foregrounding especially the role that the trope of 'bad feminist' may have in this regard (Rosenberg 2014). In the *New York Times*, for example, Alice Gregory (10 October 2014) questions Gay's adoption of, and motivation for, the 'bad feminist' persona: 'The eager pride she takes in being different—"I am an acquired taste"—can read more like personal branding than political conviction.' That feminist investment in the construction of a public persona is suspect has dogged all the women examined in this book, and Gay is no exception.

Micro-celebrity and The Genesis of the New Blockbuster

Given that, as I have argued throughout, celebrity is not something possessed by an individual, but an ongoing performative practice, it is unsurprising that new media are becoming increasingly central in the authorization of feminist voices, including those of writers. Prior to the widespread adoption of social media by celebrities, including authors, Hugh Look argued that 'the Internet provides a means for star authors to reach their public without the intermediation of their publisher, but it is not yet a medium in which stars are born' (1999, p. 12). However, the example of Gay suggests that this is no longer necessarily the case. In terms of social media usage, she is a prolific Tweeter as well as regular contributor to various websites and online opinion and news platforms. It would not be an overstatement to suggest that her blockbuster would not have come into being had it not been for her immense online presence. This represents a noteworthy shift in the production of the feminist blockbuster; here, Gay's pre-existing audience would have signalled to her publisher, Harper, her viability as a profit-making author, thereby minimizing the risks that investment in a first-time non-fiction author might otherwise entail. Moreover, many of the pieces in *Bad Feminist* were originally published via online magazines such as *Salon*, *BuzzFeed*, and *Jezebel*. That is, as somewhat of a 'micro-celebrity' online (Senft 2008), Gay had already established herself as a feminist voice that spoke in new and interesting ways to an audience keen to reconsider the meaning of contemporary feminism.

Nonetheless, collation of these pieces and publication in book form ensured that Gay moved from the more niche spaces in which she had first come to prominence and into a more mainstream imaginary. That is, in Foucault's (1969) terms, through publication of her work in material form, Gay effectively morphed from writer to 'author', and thereby the author-function around her came into being with the appearance of her offline published texts. However, the book fails to acknowledge the role of various internet sites in its genesis, a significant omission that works to privilege its status as a print publication. As Menzies-Pike suggests (2014, p. 187), 'What a list of acknowledgements would reveal is the way the internet has shaped Gay's career. It would signal the importance of online publications and journals beyond the mainstream media as incubators of new voices.' It is also important that, far from simply migrating from the online sphere to that of mainstream publishing, since *Bad Feminist* appeared Gay has continued to publish intersectional feminist commentary online.[14] However, none of this writing has had the public profile or same reach as *Bad Feminist*. Furthermore, the publication of her first work of non-fiction, in the same year as her fictional debut, *An Untamed State* (2014e), certainly can be seen to have given her access to myriad mainstream news sites, thereby considerably extending and boosting the visibility she may have enjoyed in online spaces. In this regard, as a marker of her success and resonance, the USA's *Time* magazine even dubbed 2014 'the year of Roxane Gay' (Feeney 2014). Through the publication of her blockbuster Gay, like Sandberg, despite their texts' ideological and rhetorical differences, was seen to have initiated 'the most persuasive feminist recruitment drive in recent memory' (Cochrane 2014). Both are seen to be reimagining feminism for audiences desirous of such a reconfiguration.

In some respects, the example of Gay also reveals a shift in how celebrity capital, as a feminist, is now accrued. In terms of the possibilities of coming to public visibility in the contemporary environment, it is often remarked that the opportunities to achieve fame—without reliance upon managers or publicity agents—are greater than at any other time in history (Rojek 2011, p. 33; see also Gamson 2011; Marshall 2010a). Nevertheless, 'while it is possible for a celebrity to be produced and circulated in alternative media forms, it remains much more usual for such individuals to be rapidly subsumed within the mainstream media' (Drake and Miah 2010, p. 55), such as being taken up by a multinational publisher. Therefore, while perhaps Gay may have once been a 'micro-celebrity', her status as *New York Times* bestselling author shifts this celebrity into altogether different terrain—though the self-presentational practices remain largely the same (Marwick 2016). Prior to considering this further, it is necessary to engage with the role that technology now plays in the creation of blockbusters and their authors.

BEING A 'BAD FEMINIST' IN CYBERSPACE

It seems mandatory for authors in the twenty-first century to have a significant web and social media presence, and the author of the contemporary feminist blockbuster is no exception. On roxanegay.com, readers are given information about the author's various public appearances, links to news coverage and testimonials and reviews of her publications, and to her active Tumblr account. There is also a Twitter and Facebook icon that leads directly to her sites on these platforms. Of authors' websites, Robinson remarks that the author's goal must now be 'to maintain a sustainable presence in an audience-centric environment'; with social media being central in the process of becoming a 'mediagenic author' (2013, pp. 3–4). Similarly, Marshall suggests that 'official celebrity sites' are effectively 'changing the relationships and mediations between user and public personality' (2007, p. 635). Given such sites are fundamentally marketing tools, there are, of course, links to online bookstores where readers can purchase either *An Untamed State* or *Bad Feminist*. Though such a site is important, perhaps Gay's most pronounced online presence comes via her Twitter account.

With almost a million followers (as at December 2015), Gay's Twitter feed is instructive in terms of the processes of persona-building that I have been mapping here throughout. With an account dating back to June 2007, Gay is a prolific Tweeter, generally offering a dozen or more posts per day. Much has been made of the ways in which forms of social media, and Twitter especially, now permit celebrities to craft themselves and enable fans to experience a new form of intimacy with their idols. While I explored some of these issues in my analysis of Naomi Wolf's Twitter practices, I found that she uses it less to offer readers access to an authentic 'Wolf' than as a broadcasting medium, posting dates of tours and/or appearances, as well as retweeting affirmative posts regarding her much maligned book. What Gay offers differs considerably from Wolf, revealing the diversity of celebrity social media practice, including when it comes to blockbuster authors.

As I have mentioned, it is important not to overplay the 'newness' of the kinds of self-representational practices facilitated by new media. Though tweets can differ considerably, from those gesturing more towards interactivity to those following the 'broadcast' model, they all 'share characteristics with the earliest paradigms of stardom in the way they seek to manage (online) identity, image and "reality"' (Thomas 2014, p. 242). That is, Twitter does not create these practices but exposes them, and 'there remain important continuities and contexts between "old" and "new" celebrity behaviours and media forms' (Thomas 2014, p. 242). In previous chapters I have explored various ways in which celebrity feminists have intervened to shape their public personas; Twitter usage, therefore, merely continues and makes this process further visible (Thomas 2014). What it also brings into sharp relief is a persistent anxiety around the authority granted women speakers.

As Banet-Weiser and Miltner (2016, p. 171) note: 'We are in a new era of the gender wars, an era that is marked by alarming amounts of vitriol and violence directed toward women in online spaces. These forms of violence are not only about gender, but are also often racist, with women of color as particular targets.' In line with this observation, Gay regularly receives anti-feminist and racist tweets, and has publicly reflected on attempts to silence her; she recently expressed her frustration in this regard: 'So fucking tired of the harassment on Twitter. Just goddamn' (3 February 2016).[15] Rather than remove herself from this forum, Gay (2015b) refuses to be silenced: 'I allow myself to believe my life experiences have relevance. I allow myself to believe my voice matters in a world where as a woman, as a black woman, as a Haitian American woman, as a bisexual woman, I am told to remain silent in so many harmful ways.' Despite celebratory rhetoric about 'hashtag feminism' as a space for 'multiplicity' and 'coalition building' across difference (Clark 2014, p. 1109), such trolling must temper claims regarding the feminist potentialities of online media (Mantilla 2013). But while departing Twitter was seen as an option for Dunham (see Chap. 8 in this volume), who has so many other spaces in which to be heard, Gay's continued use of this space is an important political gesture to combat marginalization and invisibility.

Given that 'interacting with fans is considered a necessary part of acquiring and maintaining followers' (Marwick 2013, p. 119), Gay is exemplary in this regard. As Melissa Maerz (2016) recently observed, on the eve of the publication of Gay's new work of non-fiction, *Hunger: A Memoir of (My) Body*, 'On Twitter and her popular Tumblr, Gay creates an intimate relationship with readers by using details from her own life to explore the anxieties we share as a culture.' In terms of Twitter content, Gay's 'performed intimacy' (Marwick and boyd 2011) manifests on a number of levels; the personal as political is clearly operative and, in *Bad Feminist*, she sees Twitter as just another literary way to do her 'bad feminism' (2014a, p. 318). She discusses her own cultural consumption, such as the television she is currently watching (sometimes the culturally denigrated forms that a 'good' feminist would denounce); familial dynamics and conversations she has had with her parents; her teaching; feelings of self-doubt (especially around her body); when she is fatigued, upset ('Crying in my office like a boss', 27 January 2016), or lonely ('I am so tired. Bummed that the other side of my bed is empty', 12 January 2016). She intervenes in ongoing debates, especially about gender and racial inequality; often her tweets morph into opinion pieces (to which she links), as when she lamented the media focus on the slaughter of a lion in Zimbabwe, and extended her tweet about the lack of value placed on black lives ('I'm personally going to start wearing a lion costume when I leave my house so if I get shot, people will care', 29 July 2015) into a *New York Times* opinion piece (Gay 2015a). Her Twitter usage, through either explicitly feminist or anti-racist tweets, or through fostering a sense of active engagement, dialogue, and intimacy with followers, can be seen to be a crucial part of Gay's celebrity practice. It is also impossible to extricate her persona construction and management from her academic labour. That is, as a (then) pre-tenured academic, these social media performances, and the construction of her 'bad feminist' public persona more broadly, necessarily have broader ramifications.

ACADEMICS AND SOCIAL MEDIA 'BRANDING': CELEBRITY AND THE NEOLIBERAL UNIVERSITY

Although various 'cultural intermediaries' are active in the manufacture and maintenance of celebrity, including of feminists, so too is the author herself—especially in the context of increased self-branding practices. As Marwick (2013, p. 161) notes, 'blatant self-promotion is now stock in trade for not only for up and coming rap stars and actresses, but also for software developers, journalists, and academics. Creating a public presence has become a required part of securing and maintaining a job.' For Gay, a professor of English at Purdue University in the USA, the production of a public persona via platforms such as Twitter is indicative of an increasingly normalized form of labour in which the contemporary academic in the neoliberal university is expected to engage: 'Institutions, publics, and some media elites are encouraging academics to be more visible in the public sphere. From the institutional perspective, it makes sense to encourage your academic superstars to represent a university's brand in widely read publications' (Cottim 2015). Here, then, it is not simply Gay's personal 'bad feminist' brand being produced in these public acts of persona-building but also her employer's.

As Moran argues, the hierarchical nature of the academy is seen to lend itself to celebrification, wherein a star system has clearly developed (2000, p. 158). Although it is difficult to maintain a strict bifurcation between the public sphere more broadly and the university, or indeed between a public persona and an institutional one, it is clear that Gay's renown does not stem from her institutional affiliation as a literary studies scholar. While she is not strictly an 'academostar' (O'Dair 2001), given her stardom is not a product of her scholarship, like Jacques Derrida's or Judith Butler's, it cannot be entirely detached from it and her institution would certainly benefit from her visibility. Although neither her Twitter account nor her publications mention her institutional affiliation in the author biography, in authorial profiles and interviews, as well as her opinion pieces in sites like the *New York Times*, it commonly appears and thereby is being invoked as a marker of authority. Moreover, her status as a bestselling author features on Purdue University's website, suggesting that this success is important in terms of her employer's own branding.

This example, however, elucidates more about a shifting academic environment and management expectations around public visibility. In a context where academics are under increasing pressure to produce work that is marketable, Gay's 'bad feminist' public persona, as well as the book itself, arguably represents much more than an effort to popularize a particular form of feminism. It is, perhaps, a much more strategic response to academic precarity; as Wernick notes, 'the adoption of a promotional mode has become indispensable to academic survival' (1991, p. 177). Similarly, in light of the changing nature of labour and the academy, Barbour and Marshall (2012) argue that we need to consider 'the creation of authentic, intentional, constructed personas that extend the boundaries of an academic's individual influence beyond institutional boundaries, and allows them to work more effectively in the radically changed worldwide academic environment'. These comments reveal, therefore, that while Gay's celebrity does not appear to be a direct product of her academic labour, her public persona management necessarily cannot be easily detached from this institutional context.

Academics can, and indeed increasingly must, deploy the tools of social media to 'develop a personal brand, to leverage attention to generate income or job prospects, and to distill media and public attention of social movements' (Cottim 2015; see also Gill 2014). Arguably, Gay's Twitter account has been used in the service of all of these goals. Significantly, when Gay published *Bad Feminist* she was not tenured (she refers to herself therein as having a 'tenure track' job), and appeared to remain so until very recently.[16] In fact, she even used the Twitter platform to announce her bid: 'Ya girl is going up for tenure this year!!!!' (28 September, 2015), for which she received multiple expressions of support and validation.[17] Here, she makes visible the precarity of the academic environment in which she operates, publicly sharing its instabilities and contingencies. In a context in which 'reputation becomes a key commodity', the labour of updating profiles, tweeting, and blogging is normalized as a part of securing and maintaining one's viability in the academic marketplace (Gill 2014, p. 16). Related to this, is the unpaid feminist labour in which women like Gay are engaged (Banet-Weiser and Juhasz 2011), something that requires further critical attention. In addition to this digital reputation management, yet consistent with the market insistence on new modes of public visibility, might it now be the case that the blockbuster itself and the widespread exposure it guarantees, rather than being perceived as suspect by the academy or as extraneous to 'real' scholarly work, is becoming a phenomenon that, in part, will help secure the academic's position within an ever more precarious employment environment? The knotty intersections of academic and blockbuster celebrity feminism, too, are worthy of deeper critical engagement.

However, despite these myriad performances of her 'public private self' via social media (Marshall 2010a, b), when asked about what her career would look like without it, Gay noted: 'I think my career would look similar without social media. I've been writing for a long time, publishing for a long time. Social media has also helped immeasurably but I think cream rises to the top one way or another' (in Puvanenthiran 2015). Here, she obscures the extensive labour she puts into maintaining a public persona via forms like Twitter. That said, with the publication of *Bad Feminist* Gay has firmly crossed into mainstream media, regularly writing for newspapers and magazines with high-level distribution such as the *New York Times*, and appearing on various national and international television current affairs programmes. Rather than being confined to her Twitter audience, her celebrity practice involves remaining visible in mainstream media sites, ensuring that her political stances on a vast array of issues around race and gender receive widespread circulation. In this way, her celebrity feminist strategies are multi-pronged, with online, particularly social, media representing only one aspect of this public performance. Importantly, Gay, like Sandberg, is illustrative of the multi-modal nature of celebrity construction and maintenance, including when it comes to the blockbuster celebrity feminist (Negra 2014). As an intersectional feminist with uncompromising politics, she is also indicative of the political potential of the feminist blockbuster, and of celebrity feminism itself.

Conclusion

As this analysis has shown, Sandberg's and Gay's texts, as well as the feminism they each publicly come to embody, are markedly different. While one offers a form of individualistic feminism that could only be available to the most privileged women (Sandberg), the other articulates an intersectional brand that works to publicly critique exclusions of dominant ways of figuring feminism (Gay). Moreover, in Sandberg's 'lean in' feminism and its extra-textual campaigns, race goes completely unacknowledged, while for Gay such an elision is completely unimaginable. Their practices, as well as their politics, reveal that blockbuster feminism is by no means static or unified, and that they deploy different strategies for branding the self and maintaining their attention capital, for contrasting purposes and effects.

As in Chap. 6, this analysis has focused on how the success of feminist blockbusters relies on other sites and discursive realms, sometimes even prior to publication. Here, I have shown how Sandberg has leveraged her institutional affiliation with Facebook to build a multi-platform brand based on her 'Lean In' mantra. The often hostile response to the book, and the various associated political initiatives, has demonstrated that, even when their politics may be dubious, the blockbuster celebrity feminist remains a lightning rod for discursive contestations around the meanings of feminism, and in this sense cannot merely be dismissed as unproductive. In this vein, Gay's intersectional feminism illustrates the potentialities of the blockbuster form, and the resultant celebrification, while also underscoring some of the limitations of the impetus to self-brand in the contemporary neoliberal academy and beyond. As this discussion has shown, the feminist blockbuster—as both a genre and a cultural phenomenon—is alive and well. However, it—and the labour involved in creating and sustaining the author's celebrity feminism—has changed since the blockbusters analyzed in Part I. The next chapter further underscores how convergence culture has become integral to celebrity feminist activism, and examines the overlap between blockbuster feminism and wider celebrity culture.

Notes

1. The Lean In website also features a 'Discussion Guide—For All Audiences', proffering chapter-by-chapter questions for readers to further consider, seeking to guide readers towards particular interpretations of the text and its key arguments.
2. As Wendy Brown argues, 'neo-liberalism normatively constructs and interpellates individuals as entrepreneurial actors in every sphere of life. It figures individuals as rational, calculating creatures whose moral autonomy is measured by their capacity for "self-care".' According to Brown, therefore, neoliberalism 'carries responsibility for the self to new heights' (2003, p. 3).
3. In contrast to Sandberg, Gay's TED talk, titled 'Confessions of a Bad Feminist' (2015c), appeared following her blockbuster's publication.
4. Slaughter herself is well known for her 2012 *Atlantic* article, 'Why We Can't Have It All', which has recently been expanded and published as *Unfinished Business: Women, Men, Work, Family* (2015). It has not, however, earned blockbuster status.
5. See: http://www.ted.com/talks/sheryl_sandberg_so_we_leaned_in_now_what/transcript?language=en.
6. Faludi (2013) cites a number of effusive comments from those who had viewed the talk.
7. This is problematic as 'reactionary arguments about "feminist narcissism"' have been 'central to the vilification of feminist politics' (Tyler 2005, p. 26).
8. For an analysis of feminist blogging, see Frances Shaw (2013) and J.M. Keller (2015).
9. Valenti published a popular feminist book in 2007, *Full Frontal Feminism*, and has translated the capital generated online into mainstream media visibility, with regular *Guardian* columns.
10. See Casey (2015) for an examination of the activist possibilities of celebrity feminism.

11. As we saw in Chapter 6, Wicke (1994) makes a similar comment in relation to Naomi Wolf.
12. Similarly, Aileen Moreton-Robinson (2000) has argued that the subject at the centre of Australian feminist discourse is largely unmarked, and her whiteness in particular invisibilized.
13. Although hooks has made similar arguments, her books have not been bestsellers in the way Gay's has and her media presence has not been as extensive.
14. For example, from October 2014 she acted as Editor of The Butter, a 'vertical' of online site, The Toast.
15. That said, in a response to a recent Tweet asking why she won't lose weight, Gay replies: 'You created an account just to ask that? Fuck you, you fucking coward' (26 January 2016), or she responds with humour: 'By all means, continue to treat me with blatant rudeness and disrespect. Please. It brightens my day' (16 January 2016).
16. She announced that her tenure bid was successful on Twitter (29 February 2016). Her tweet—'Tenure. Shrug'—suggests some ambivalence about the achievement.
17. This was not the first time Gay referred to seeking tenure on her Twitter. For example, on 21 February 2015 she remarked: 'Filling out tenure documents really makes you rethink your life choices.'

References

Bail, K. ed. (1996) *DIY Feminism*, St Leonards: Allen & Unwin

Bailey, C. (1997) 'Making Waves and Drawing Lines: The Politics of Defining the Vicissitudes of Feminism', *Hypatia*, 12.3: 17–28

Banet-Weiser, S. (2012) *Autheticity, TM*, New York: New York University Press

—— (2015a) 'Popular Misogyny: A Ziegiest', 15 January, accessed via http://culturedigitally.org/2015/01/popular-misogyny-a-zeitgeist/

—— (2015b) 'Keynote Address: Media, Markets, Gender: Economies of Visibility in a Neoliberal Moment', *The Communication Review*, 18:1, 53–70

Banet-Weiser, S. & Juhasz, A. (2011) 'Feminist Labor in Media Studies/Communication: Is Self-Branding Feminist Practice?', *International Journal of Communication*, 5: 1768–1775

Banet-Weiser, S. & Mukherjee, R. (2012) 'Introduction: Commodity Activism in Neoliberal Times', in S. Banet-Weiser & R. Mukherjee eds. *Commodity Activism: Cultural Resistance in Neoliberal Times*, New York: New York University Press, pp. 1–17

Banet-Weiser, S. & Miltner, K.M. (2016) '#MasculinitySoFragile: culture, structure, and networked misogyny', *Feminist Media Studies*, 16.1: 171–174

Barbour, K. & Marshall, D. (2012) 'The Academic Online: Constructing Persona Through the World Wide Web', *First Monday*, 17.9, accessed via http://ojs-prod-lib.cc.uic.edu/ojs/index.php/fm/rt/printerFriendly/3969/3292

Brown, W. (2003) 'Neo-liberalism and the End of Liberal Democracy', *Theory and Event*, 7.1, accessed via https://muse.jhu.edu/article/48659

Casey, S. (2015) *Australian Feminist Approaches to Mass Awareness Campaigns: Celanthropy, Celebrity Feminism and Online Activism*, unpublished doctoral thesis, Griffith University, Australia

Clarke, R. (2014) '#NotBuyingIt: Hashtag Feminists Expand the Commercial Media Conversation', *Feminist Media Studies*, 14.6: 1108–1110

Cochrane, K. (2014) 'Roxane Gay: Meet the Bad Feminist', 2 August, *The Guardian*, accessed via http://www.theguardian.com/world/2014/aug/02/roxane-gay-bad-feminist-sisterhood-fake-orgasm

Cottim, T.M. (2015) '"Who Do You Think You Are?": When Marginality Meets Academic Microcelebrity', *Ada: A Journal of Gender, New Media and Technology*, 7, accessed via http://adanewmedia.org/2015/04/issue7-mcmillancottom/

Crenshaw, K. (1991) 'Mapping the Margins: Intersectionality, Identity Politics, and Violence against Women of Color', *Stanford Law Review*, 43.6: 1241–1299

Dicker, R. & Piepmier, A. (2003) 'Introduction', in R. Dicker & A. Piepmeir eds. *Catching a Wave: Reclaiming Feminism for the Twenty-First Century*, Boston: Northeastern University Press, pp. 3–30

Dowd, M. (2013) 'Pompom Girl for Feminism', 23 February, *The New York Times*, accessed via www.nytimes.com/2013/02/24/opinion/sunday/dowd-pompom-girl-for-feminism.html?_r=0

Dowse, S. (2013) 'Feminism at the Top Table', 3 April, *Inside Story*, accessed via http://insidestory.org.au/feminism-at-the-top-table/

Drake, P. & Miah, A. (2010) 'The Cultural Politics of Celebrity', *Cultural Politics*, 6.1: 49–64

Dvorak, K. (2014) 'Bad Feminist', 5 September, *Washington Independent Review of Books*, accessed via http://www.washingtonindependentreviewofbooks.com/bookreview/bad-feminist

Faludi, S. (2013) 'Facebook Feminism, Like It or Not', *The Baffler*, No. 23, accessed via http://thebaffler.com/salvos/facebook-feminism-like-it-or-not

Farrell, A.E. (1998) *Yours in Sisterhood: Ms Magazine and the Promise of Popular Feminism*, Chapel Hill: University of North Carolina Press

Feeney, N. (2014) 'Roxane Gay's Riveting Debut Novel 7 May, *An Untamed State*, *Time*, accessed via http://time.com/90402/roxane-gay-an-untamed-state-review

Filipovic, J. (2013) 'Sheryl Sandberg Is More of a Feminist Crusader than People Give Her Credit For', 1 March, *The Guardian*, accessed via http://www.theguardian.com/commentisfree/2013/mar/01/sheryl-sandberg-lean-in-has-feminist-ideals

Foucault, M. (1969/1984 ed) 'The Author Function', in P. Rainbow ed. *The Foucault Reader*, London: Penguin, pp. 101–120

Fraser, N. (2013) 'How Feminism Became Capitalism's Handmaiden', 14 October, *The Guardian*, accessed via http://www.theguardian.com/commentisfree/2013/oct/14/feminism-capitalist-handmaiden-neoliberal

Freeland, C. (2013) 'In Sandberg, Echoes of De Beauvoir', 14 March, *The New York Times*, accessed via http://www.nytimes.com/2013/03/15/us/15iht-letter15.html

Friedan, A. (2014) 'The Problem with Sheryl Sandberg's 'Ban Bossy' Campaign', 13 March, *NY Magazine*, accessed via ymag.com/thecut/2014/03/problem-with-the-ban-bossy-campaign.html#

Gabriel, J. (1998) *Whitewash: Racialized Politics and the Media*, London: Routledge

Garcia, V. (2013) 'Why I Won't Lean in', 20 July, *Huffington Post*, accessed via http://www.huffingtonpost.com/vanessa-garcia/why-i-wont-lean-in_b_3586527.html?ir=Australia

Garcia, P. (2014) 'Why Sheryl Sandberg's Brand of Feminism Isn't For Me', 13 March, *Vogue*, accessed via http://www.vogue.com/872584/why-sheryl-sandbergs-brand-of-feminism-isnt-for-me/

Gardiner, J. (2001) '"What Is an Author?": Contemporary Publishing Discourse and the Author Figure', *Publishing Research Quarterly*, Spring: 63–76

Gamson, J. (2011) 'The Unwatched Life Is Not Worth Living: The Elevation of the Ordinary in Celebrity Culture', *PMLA*, 126.4: 1061–1069

Gay, R. (2014a) *Bad Feminist: Essays*, New York: Harper

———. (2014b) 'Lena Dunham, a Generation's Gutsy Ambitious Voice', 24 September, *Time*, accessed via http://time.com/3425759/lena-dunham-a-generations-gutsy-ambitious-voice/

———. (2014c) 'Emma Watson? Jennifer Lawrence? These Aren't the Feminists You Are Looking For', 10 October, *The Guardian*, accessed via http://www.theguardian.com/commentisfree/2014/oct/10/-sp-jennifer-lawrence-emma-watson-feminists-celebrity

———. (2014d) 'Roxane Gay Talks to Lena Dunham About Her New Book, Feminism, and the Benefits of Being Criticized Online', 2 October, *Vulture*, accessed via http://www.vulture.com/2014/10/roxane-gay-interview-lena-dunham-bad-feminist-not-that-kind-of-girl-books.html

———. (2014e) *An Untamed State*, New York: Grove/Atlantic

——— (2015a) 'Of Lions and Men: Mourning Samuel DuBose and Cecil the Lion', 31 July, *New York Times*, accessed via http://www.nytimes.com/2015/08/01/opinion/of-lions-and-men-mourning-samuel-dubose-and-cecil-the-lion.html

―――― (2015b) 'My PEN USA Freedom to Write Acceptance Speech', 16 November, accessed via http://roxanegay.tumblr.com/post/133381735475/my-pen-usa-freedom-to-write-acceptance-speech

―――― (2015c) 'Confessions of a Bad Feminist', May, TED Talk, accessed via https://www.ted.com/talks/roxane_gay_confessions_of_a_bad_feminist?language=en

Gay, R. (@rgay) 'Filling out tenure documents really makes you rethink your life choices', 21 February 2015, 7.06pm. Tweet

――――. (@rgay) 'Ya girl is going up for tenure this year!!!!' 28 September 2015, 12.55pm. Tweet

――――. (@rgay) 'I am so tired. Bummed that the other side of my bed is empty', 12 January 2016, 8.12pm. Tweet

――――. (@rgay) 'You created an account just to ask that? Fuck you, you fucking coward', 26 January 2016, 9.47pm. Tweet

――――. (@rgay) 'Crying in my office like a BOSS', 27 Jan 2016, 12:41pm. Tweet

――――. (@rgay) 'Tenure. Shrug', 29 February 2016, 2.01pm. Tweet

Genette, G. (1997) *Paratexts: Thresholds of Interpretation*, Cambridge: Cambridge University Press

Gill, R. (2007) 'Postfeminist Media Culture: Elements of A Sensibility', *European Journal of Cultural Studies*, 10.2: 147–166

――――. (2014) 'Academics, Cultural Workers, and Critical Labour Studies', *Journal of Cultural Economy*, 7.1: 12–30

Glass, L. (2016) 'Brand Names: A Brief History of Literary Celebrity', in P.D. Marshall & S. Redmond eds. *A Companion to Celebrity*, London: Wiley Blackwell, pp. 39–57

Grant, M.G. (2013) 'Sheryl Sandberg's 'Lean In' Campaign Holds Little for Most Women', 25 February, *Washington Post*, accessed via https://www.washingtonpost.com/opinions/sheryl-sandbergs-lean-in-campaign-holds-little-for-most-women/2013/02/25/c584c9d2-7f51-11e2-a350-49866afab584_story.html

Greenhouse, E. (2014) 'Lean In's Business Friendly Message', 10 April, *The New Yorker*, accessed via http://www.newyorker.com/business/currency/lean-ins-business-friendly-message

――――. (2015) 'How Sheryl Sandberg Is Turning Feminism into a Tech Brand', 5 March, *Bloomberg*, accessed via http://www.bloomberg.com/politics/articles/2015-03-05/how-sheryl-sandberg-is-turning-feminism-into-a-tech-brand

Gregory, A. (2014) 'Daphne Merkin's "The Fame Lunches" and Roxane Gay's "Bad Feminist"', 10 October, *New York Times*, accessed via http://www.nytimes.com/2014/10/12/books/review/daphne-merkins-the-fame-lunches-and-roxane-gays-bad-feminist.html?_r=1

Hammer, R. (2000) 'Antifeminists as media celebrities', *Review of Education, Pedagogy, and Cultural Studies*, 22.3: 207–222

Harris, A. (2004) *Future Girl: Young Women in the 21st Century*, London: Routledge

Hassid, J. & Jeffreys, E. (2015) 'Doing Good or Doing Nothing? Celebrity, Media and Philanthropy in China', *Third World Quarterly*, 36.1

Hemmings, C. (2011) *Why Stories Matter: The Political Grammar of Feminist Theory*, Durham: Duke University Press

Henderson, M. (2006) *Marking Feminist Times: Remembering the Longest Revolution in Australia*, Bern: Peter Lang

Henry, A. (2004) *Not My Mother's Sister: Generational Conflict and Third Wave Feminism*, Bloomington: University of Indiana Press

Heywood, L. & Drake, J. 'Introduction', in L. Heywood & J. Drake eds. *Third Wave Agenda: Being Feminist, Doing Feminism*, Minneapolis: Minnesota University Press, pp. 1–24

Hirshman, S. (2013) 'Ten Things Sheryl Sandberg Gets Exactly Right in "Lean In"', 4 March, *Forbes Magazine*, accessed via http://www.forbes.com/sites/susanadams/2013/03/04/10-things-sheryl-sandberg-gets-exactly-right-in-lean-in/#2c1f19ee466f

hooks, b. (1994) *Outlaw Culture*, New York: Routledge

———. (2013) 'Dig Deep: Beyond Lean In', 28 October, *The Feminist Wire*, accessed via http://www.thefeministwire.com/2013/10/17973/

Joseph, R.L. (2009) '"Tyra Banks Is Fat": Reading (*Post*-)Racism and (*Post*-) Feminism in the New Millennium', *Critical Studies in Media Communication*, 26.3: 237–254

Kantor, J. (2013) 'A Titan on How to Break the Glass Ceiling', 21 February, *New York Times*, accessed via https://www.washingtonpost.com/opinions/sheryl-sandbergs-lean-in-campaign-holds-little-for-most-women/2013/02/25/c584c9d2-7f51-11e2-a350-49866afab584_story.html

Keller, J. (2015) 'Girl Power's Last Chance? Tavi Gevinson, Feminism and Popular Media Culture', *Continuum*, 29.2: 274–285

Koffman, O. & Gill, R. (2015) "The revolution will be led by a 12-year-old girl': girl power and global biopolitics', *Feminist Review*, 105: 83–102

Lilburn, S., Magarey, S. & Sheridan, S. (2000) 'Celebrity Feminism as Synthesis: Germaine Greer, *The Female Eunuch* and the Australian Print Media', *Continuum*, 14.3: 335–348

Littler, J. (2007) 'Celebrity CEOs and the Cultural Economy of Tabloid Intimacy', in S. Redmond & S. Holmes eds. *Stardom and Celebrity: A Reader*, London: Sage, pp. 230–243

——— (2008) '"I Feel Your Pain": Cosmopolitan Charity and the Public Fashioning of the Celebrity Soul', *Celebrity Studies*, 18.2: 237–251

Look, H. (1999) 'The Author as Star', *Publishing Research Quarterly*, Fall: 12–29

Losse, K. (2013) 'Feminism's Tipping Point: Who Wins from Leaning In?' *Dissent*, 26 March, accessed via https://www.dissentmagazine.org/online_articles/feminisms-tipping-point-who-wins-from-leaning-in

Luscombe, B. (2014) 'Confidence Woman', 7 March, *Time Magazine*, accessed via http://ideas.time.com/2013/03/07/confidence-woman/

Maerz, M. (2016) 'Roxane Gay Previews Forthcoming Memoir, Hunger: This Is Not a Book About Triumph', 4 January, *Entertainment Weekly*, accessed via http://www.ew.com/article/2016/01/04/roxane-gay-memoir-hunger

Mantilla, K. (2013) 'Gendertrolling: Misogyny Adapts to New Media', *Feminist Studies*, 39.2: 563–570

Marshall, P.D. (2007) 'Intimately intertwined in the most public way: Celebrity and Journalism', in P.D. Marshall ed. *The Celebrity Culture Reader*, London: Routledge, pp. 315–323

———. (2010a) 'The Promotion and Presentation of the Self: Celebrity as Marker of Presentational Media', *Celebrity Studies*, 1.1: 35–48

———. (2010b) 'The Specular Economy', *Soc*, 47: 498–502

Marwick, A.E. (2013) *Status Update: Celebrity, Publicity, and Branding in the Social Media Age*, New Haven: Yale University Press

———. (2016) 'You May Know Me from YouTube (Micro-)Celebrity in Social Media', in P.D. Marshall & S. Redmond eds. *A Companion to Celebrity*, London: Wiley Blackwell, pp. 333–350

Marwick, A. & boyd, d. (2011) 'To See and Be Seen: Celebrity Practice on Twitter', *Convergence*, 17.2: 139–158

Maslin, J. (2013) 'Lessons from the Stratosphere, and How to Get There: Sheryl Sandberg's 'Lean In' Offers Lessons', 6 March, *New York Times*, accessed via http://www.nytimes.com/2013/03/07/books/sheryl-sandbergs-lean-in.html

McKeon, L. (2014) 'Let's Be Real: Two New Books by Roxane Gay', 28 August, *Boston Review*, accessed via http://bostonreview.net/books-ideas/lucy-mckeon-roxane-gay-bad-feminist-untamed-state

McRobbie, A. (2013) 'Feminism, the Family and the New Mediated Maternalism', *New Formations*, 80–81: 119–137

———. (2015) 'Notes on the Perfect: Competitive Femininity in Neoliberal Times', *Australian Feminist Studies*, 30.83: 3–20

Meltzer, M. (2013) 'Who Is a Feminist Now?', 21 May, *New York Times*, accessed via www.nytimes.com/2014/05/22/fashion/who-is-a-feminist-now.html

Menzies-Pike, C. (2014) 'How Should a Feminist Critic Be?: On Roxane Gay's Bad Feminist', *Kill Your Darlings*, 20, accessed via https://killyourdarlings.com.au/article/how-should-a-feminist-critic-be-on-roxane-gays-bad-feminist/

Miller, N.K. (1991) *Getting Personal: Feminist Occasions and Other Autobiographical Acts*, London: Routledge

Minnich, E. (1998) 'Feminist Attacks on Feminisms: Patriarchy's Prodigal Daughters', *Feminist Studies*, 24.1: 159–175

Moran, J. (2000) *Star Authors: Literary Celebrity in America*, London: Pluto

Moreton-Robinson, A. (2000) *Talkin' Up to the White Woman: Indigenous Women and Australian Feminism*, St Lucia: University of Queensland Press

Murray, S. (2015) 'Charting the Digital Literary Sphere', *Contemporary Literature*, 56.2: 311–339

Negra, D. (2014) 'Claiming Feminism: Commentary, Autobiography and Advice Literature for Women in the Recession', *Journal of Gender Studies*, 23.3: 275–286

O'Dair, S. (2001) 'Academostars Are the Symptom: What's the Disease?', *Minnesota Review*, 52–54: 159–174

Orr, C. (1997) 'Charting the Currents of the Third Wave', *Hypatia*, 12.3: 29–45

Puvanenthiran, B. (2015) '"Bad Feminist" Author Roxane Gay on Germaine Greer, Domestic Violence and the Real Housewives of Melbourne', 6 March, *Sydney Morning Herald*, accessed via http://www.smh.com.au/entertainment/books/bad-feminist-author-roxane-gay-on-germaine-greer-domestic-violence-and-the-real-housewives-of-melbourne-20150306-13x3sc.html#ixzz3oznYVN9M

Rapp, E. (2014) 'Roxane Gay's Bad Feminist', 9 August, *Boston Globe*, accessed via http://www.bostonglobe.com/arts/books/2014/08/09/review-bad-feminist-roxane-gay/XpXAd6GWNqF9lIROZ7UXPI/story.html

Roberts, Y. (2013) 'Is Facebook's Sheryl Sandberg Really the New Face of Feminism?', 17 March, *The Observer*, accessed via http://www.theguardian.com/books/2013/mar/17/facebook-sheryl-sandberg-lean-book

Robinson, D. (2013) 'Novel Forms and Brand New Relations: Exploring Convergence Culture and Australian Literary Celebrity', *Limina*, pp. 1–12, accessed via http://www.limina.arts.uwa.edu.au

Rojek, C. (2011) *Fame Attack*, London: Bloomsbury

Rosenberg, A. (2014) '"Bad Feminist" and the Subversive Thinking of Roxane Gay', 7 August, *Washington Post*, accessed via http://www.washingtonpost.com/news/act-four/wp/2014/08/07/bad-feminist-and-the-subversive-thinking-of-roxane-gay/

Rottenberg, C. (2014a) 'The Rise of Neoliberal Feminism', *Cultural Studies*, 28.3: 418–437

———. (2014b) 'Happiness and the Liberal Imagination: How Superwoman Became Balanced', *Feminist Studies*, 40.1: 144–168

Rowley, E. (2013) 'Do Women Wreck Their Own Careers? Sheryl Sandberg Urges "Lean In"', 2 February, *The Telegraph*, accessed via http://www.telegraph.co.uk/women/womens-business/9839883/Facebooks-Sheryl-Sandberg-urges-lean-in-a-new-book-sparking-the-question-Are-women-wrecking-their-own-careers.html

Roy, J (2014) 'I Don't Give a $*%& If You Call Me Bossy', 12 March, *Time*, accessed via http://time.com/21498/i-dont-give-a-if-you-call-me-bossy/

Sandberg, S. (2010) 'Why We Have Too Few Women Leaders', December, TED Talk, accessed via https://www.ted.com/talk/sheryl_sandberg_why_we_have_too_few_women_leaders?language=en

———. (2013a) *Lean In: Women, Work, and the Will to Lead*, London: WH Allen

———. (2013b) 'So We Leaned In...Now What?', December, TED Talk, accessed via https://www.ted.com/talks/sheryl_sandberg_so_we_leaned_in_now_what?language=en
———. (2014) *Lean In for Graduates*, New York: Alfred A. Knopf
Schickel, E. (2014) 'American Hates Women', 3 August, *Los Angeles Review of Books*, accessed via http://lareviewofbooks.org/review/america-hates-women
Senft, T. (2008) *Camgirls: Celebrity and Community in the Age of Social Networks*, New York: Lang
Shaw, F. (2013) 'Blogging and the Women's Movement', in S. Maddison & M. Sawer eds. *The Women's Movement in Protest, Institutions and the Internet: Australia in Transnational Perspective*, Oxford: Routledge, pp. 118–131
Sheridan, S., Magarey, S. & Lilburn, S. (2006) 'Feminism in the News', in J. Hollows & R. Moseley eds. *Feminism in Popular Culture*, Oxford: Berg, pp. 25–40
Siegel, D. (1997) 'Reading Between the Waves: Feminist Historiography in "Postfeminist" Moment', in L. Heywood & J. Drake eds. *Third Wave Agenda: Being Feminist, Doing Feminism*, Minneapolis: Minnesota University Press, pp. 55–82
Slaughter, A. (2012) 'Why Women Still Can't Have It All', July/August, *The Altantic*, accessed via http://www.theatlantic.com/magazine/archive/2012/07/why-women-still-cant-have-it-all/309020/
———. (2013) 'Yes, You Can: Sheryl Sandberg's Lean In', 7 March, *New York Times*, accessed via http://www.nytimes.com/2013/03/10/books/review/sheryl-sandbergs-lean-in.html
———. (2015) *Unfinished Business, Women, Work, Men and Family*, New York: Random House
Squires, C. (2014) *The Post-Racial Mystique: Media and Race in the Twenty-First Century*, New York: New York University Press
Stringer, K. (2007) 'Divas, Evil Black Bitches and Bitter Black Women: African American Women in Postfeminist and Post Civil Rights Popular Culture', in Y. Tasker & D. Negra eds. *Interrogating Postfeminism: Gender and the Politics of Popular Culture*, Durham: Duke University Press, pp. 249–276
Taylor, A. (2008) *Mediating Australian Feminism: Rereading the First Stone Media Event*, Oxford: Peter Lang
———. (2012) *Single Women in Popular Culture: The Limits of Postfeminism*, Basingstoke: Palgrave Macmillan
Thomas, S. (2014) 'Celebrity in the "Twitterverse": History, Authenticity and the Multiplicity of Stardom', *Celebrity Studies*, 5.3: 242–255
Thompson, B. (2002) 'Multiracial Feminism: Recasting the Chronology of Second Wave Feminism', *Feminist Studies*, 28.2: 336–360
Thompson, J.B. (2010) *Merchants of Culture: The Publishing Business in the Twenty First Century*, London: Polity

Trope, A. (2012) 'Mother Angelina: Hollywood Philanthropy Personified', in R. Mukherjee & S. Banet-Weiser eds. *Commodity Activism*, New York: New York University Press, pp. 154–173

Tsaliki, L. (2016) '"Tweeting the Good Causes": Social Networking and Celebrity Activism', in P.D. Marshall & S. Redmond eds. *A Companion to Celebrity*, London: Wiley Blackwell, pp. 235–257

Tyler, I. (2005) 'Who Put the "Me" in Feminism?: The Sexual Politics of Narcissism', *Feminist Theory*, 6: 25–4

Valenti, J. (2007) *Full Frontal Feminism: A Young Woman's Guide to Why Feminism Matters*, New York: Seal Press

———. (2013) 'Sheryl Sandberg Isn't the Perfect Feminist. So What?', 1 March, *Washington Post*, accessed via https://www.washingtonpost.com/opinions/dear-fellow-feminists-ripping-apart-sheryl-sandbergs-book-is-counterproductive/2013/03/01/fc71b984-81c0-11e2-a350-49866afab584_story.html

Van Krieken, R. (2012) *Celebrity Society*, New York: Routledge

Vavrus, M.D. (2007) 'Opting Out Moms in the News: Selling New Tradtionalism in the New Millenium', *Feminist Media Studies*, 7.1: 47–63

Waldman, K. (2014) '*Bossy* Doesn't Have to Be a Bad Word', 10 March, *Slate*, accessed via http://www.slate.com/blogs/xx_factor/2014/03/10/ban_bossy_sheryl_sandberg_and_the_girl_scouts_team_up_with_beyonc_but_miss.html

Walsh, J. (2013) 'Trashing Sheryl Sandberg', 3 March, *Salon*, accessed via http://www.salon.com/2013/03/02/trashing_sheryl_sandberg/

Wernick, A. (1991) *Promotional Culture: Advertising, Ideology and Symbolic Expression*, London: Sage

Whelehan, I. (2000) *Overloaded: Popular Culture and The Future of Feminism*, London: The Women's Press

Wicke, J. (1994) 'Celebrity Material: Materialist Feminism and the Culture of Celebrity', *South Atlantic Quarterly*, 93.4: 751–778

Woods, F. (2015) 'Girls Talk: Authorship and Authenticity in the Reception of Lena Dunham's Girls', *Critical Studies in Television*, 10.2: 37–54

Young, S. (1997) *Changing the Wor(l)d: Discourse, Politics and the Feminist Movement*, London: Routledge

CHAPTER 8

Amy Poehler and Lena Dunham: Celebrity Memoirs, Comedy, and Digital Activism

INTRODUCTION

This chapter engages with two blockbusters, Amy Poehler's *Yes Please* and Lena Dunham's *Not That Kind of Girl*, by authors whose initial celebrification was not reliant upon their articulation of a feminist identity; that is, their fame stems largely from their work as television writers, comedians, actors, and directors. Nevertheless, in late 2014, their non-fictional bestsellers came to be important vehicles in the maintenance of their celebrity feminism. In the twenty-first century, the ways in which the celebrity feminist is constituted and reaffirmed has, in many senses, altered, as have the kinds of women who are being celebrified. However, as in the previous chapter, here I want to argue that what has remained a core part of this celebrification and its maintenance is the bestselling work of non-fiction, the 'blockbuster'. That is, such blockbusters are, if not its originating feature in the case of these two women, yet central to the 'performative practice' (Marwick and boyd 2011) of celebrity feminism. As has always been the case with feminist blockbuster authors, there has been significant public debate, in online media and in more traditional forms, about their books, and especially their feminism.

Rather than their feminism being initially responsible for the public visibility of the authors in question, in these examples it now appears *after* some degree of recognition has already been achieved, making it a vehicle for buttressing rather than establishing renown; that said, the elevation to bestselling author transforms and secures their feminist celebrity. In the current environment, celebrity feminism has also become more obviously part of an intermedial network (Negra 2014), though as earlier chapters have shown, multiple forms of media have always been integral to ensuring that the blockbuster continues to culturally reverberate. In terms of doing the work of publicly constructing feminism in certain ways, I argue, the blockbuster remains pivotal.

The women examined in this chapter—Poehler and Dunham—are themselves cultural producers, writing, directing, and often starring in works they have created. These are not simply celebrities who later pronounce some affiliation with feminism, a category I further discuss in the final chapter. Instead, feminism is in many ways central to the many creative projects in which they have been involved, thus suggesting that the blockbuster alone is not the only way in which these women seek to construct feminism. In this sense, these figures represent a complex amalgam of those whose fame is a direct product of their feminism (celebrity *feminists*) and the female stars who proclaim a feminist identity during some stage of their careers (*celebrity* feminists). Despite their fame preceding their blockbusters, I demonstrate how, like all other authors here, they deploy it to ensure that their brand of feminism reaches as many women as possible. The blockbusters they have produced are forms of memoir, coupled with elements of the advice manual. Though there does appear to have been a proliferation of celebrity feminist autobiographical narratives over the past few years, I argue that there has been a much longer tradition of foregrounding the self in popular feminist non-fiction, which is also consistent with celebrity culture's desire to access the interiority of the figures upon which it relies.

In addition to their blockbusters, and in line with my approach throughout, I consider the series of online texts and initiatives in which these women have been engaged and which are also crucial to the overall performance of their celebrity feminism. In particular, I am concerned with how these celebrities intervene in public conversations around female subjectivity through deploying participatory media forms for patently feminist purposes, something that has been largely overlooked in efforts to overstate convergence culture's empowerment of 'ordinary people' (Turner 2010). In doing so, I consider the assumptions they make about audiences, especially the young women they largely target, and about feminism and its continuing viability and necessity. As I will show, like all blockbuster authors examined here, Poehler and Dunham are heavily involved in feminist 'discursive politics' (Young 1997), through their memoirs but also via various online platforms and public campaigns.

Comedy, Celebrity Memoirs, and Feminism

Poehler and Dunham are both central to remarkably successful, female-centred comedies, in *Parks and Recreation* and *Girls* respectively, as well as being involved in the production of films (*Mean Girls*, *Baby Mama*, and *Sisters* in the case of Poehler, and *Tiny Furniture* for Dunham). As Amanda Lotz argues: 'Scholars generally concur that feminist discourse is predominantly found in the comedy genre because of narrative and generic qualities that both introduce and then contain potentially subversive content' (2001, p. 111). Similarly, Linda Mizejewski notes that 'women's comedy has become a primary site in mainstream pop culture where feminism speaks, talks back, and is contested' (2014, p. 6), a point substantiated by figures such as Amy Schumer, Sarah Silverman, and Mindy Kaling. Poehler and Dunham, in particular, have secured stardom through a creative practice located in the intersection of feminism and comedy, and their blockbusters are no exception.

In the twenty-first century, in some ways a radically different time from that in which Brown, Friedan, and Greer wrote their initial bestsellers, the feminist blockbuster is often a much less polemical piece of writing, and one that focuses more on the individual's gendered experiences as a way of engaging with feminist concerns. Such books are, by and large, less about offering grand narratives or pronouncements about the need for wider structural change or social upheaval (as in other iterations of the blockbuster), than in showing how a feminist life, including its attendant tensions, may be lived in the twenty-first century. They offer no prescriptions, just personalized, humorous narratives about their own experiences of navigating and negotiating the ongoing difficulties of being gendered feminine in a context where such subjectivity continues to be devalued and even pathologized. For some, this makes them deeply problematic, as I will show.

The celebrity 'autobiography', although commonly ghost written (Yellin 2015), is becoming increasingly popular as a genre. While this may be seen as a corollary of foregrounding the self in neoliberal discourses, such forms have long been important in feminist terms. Feminism has always had a 'strong interest in the autobiographical, beginning with the attempt to connect the "personal" with the "political", and the concomitant emphasis on women's experience as a vital resource in the creation of women's knowledge' (Cosslett 2000, p. 2; see also Smith and Watson 2010). As noted in the Friedan chapter, memoirs represent significant textual vehicles in the construction of a particular public self, one that often contradicts and/or purports to access an 'authentic' self-hitherto obscured by celebrification. Viewing them as the non-fiction equivalent to 'chick lit', Suzanne Ferriss (2014) has dubbed celebrity autobiographical texts like Tina Fey's *Bossypants* (2011) 'chick non-fic', a classification also applicable to Poehler's *Yes Please* and Dunham's *Not That Kind of Girl*. Ferriss argues that, despite claims to reality, such texts deploy remarkably similar tropes and techniques to 'chick lit' fiction to write certain feminine selves into being. As she notes, however: 'These are not the voices of fictional protagonists of chick lit but of actual thirty- or forty-somethings publically navigating the shoals of personal relationships, family life, and professional challenges, the stock conflicts of chick lit' (Ferriss 2014, p. 206). It is also a sub-genre now apparently favoured by female celebrities.

These memoirs are being used to give some texture to lives only otherwise accessed in snippets through news and magazine coverage, or interviews on entertainment networks, with the autobiographical form necessarily providing the sense of intimacy upon which fandom relies. In particular, it is said to be through representations of their fallibility that they seek to secure readerly identification (Ferriss 2014, p. 209); that is, while they are indeed crafting a particular persona, the inclusion of comically portrayed moments of failure or despair from various stages of their lives seemingly renders the sense of closeness or intimate bond even more authentic. In commercial terms, they pose reasonably low risks to publishers, bringing with them as they do a more or less guaranteed audience: 'The authors of chick non-fic who write about their own experiences are also public personalities speaking in the voice of their celebrity selves. Owing to their carefully crafted public personas, they have attracted loyal fans, the likely target audiences for their books' (Ferriss 2014, pp. 206–7). Their celebrity also helps to ensure that the book's publication is itself newsworthy, and media commentary on Poehler's and Dunham's bestsellers was extensive. In the next section, I engage with Poehler's *Yes Please*, before moving on to consider the various online activist ventures through which she also publicly performs and negotiates her feminism.

Amy Poehler's Blockbuster and Online Feminist Activism

Amy Poehler is most well-known for her seven-season appearance on *Parks and Recreation* (2009–15, NBC), a mockumentary featuring Lesley Knope, the earnest city council worker who eventually becomes mayor of fictional town, Pawnee. The character's feminism has been roundly praised, including in the *Huffington Post*, where Rachel Khona (2015), bidding farewell to the 'fictional feminist icon', noted that she 'boldly brought feminism to the small screen showing us that women can be career-focused, smart, bossy, feminists and at the same time love men, love life and really love waffles ... She shows us how awesome feminism is simply by being herself.' Such comments are also applicable to Poehler herself, who is renowned for her *Saturday Night Live* feminist comic skits with Tina Fey, especially those featuring impersonations of Hillary Clinton and Sarah Palin. Her comedy does have a distinctly feminist tenor, and publicly she routinely claims a feminist identity. Unlike the celebrities who later make very vocal pronouncements about their sudden feminist awakening, Poehler's position is more like that articulated by Baumgardner and Richards: 'The presence of feminism in our lives is taken for granted. For our generation, feminism is like fluoride. We scarcely notice we have it—it's simply in the water' (2000, p. 71). For example, asked by *Time Out* magazine about how feminism informs her work, Poehler said: 'It's always just been in my nature—it's just kind of my everyday. Sometimes I access it in a conscious way, but it wasn't always the headline of stuff that I was doing' (in Pitt 2013). The danger of such a position, of course, is that feminism becomes, in the logic of postfeminism, taken for granted (McRobbie 2009) rather than an ongoing political project. Nevertheless, both Poehler and her celebrity feminist sidekick, Tina Fey,[1] have garnered media coverage centring on their feminist identification,[2] suggesting that celebrities—even if not initially famous for their feminism—occupy an important role in terms of the negotiation of the public meanings granted feminism, including through social media practices.

Although Poehler rejects Twitter because of its focus on 'self-disclosure and self-promotion' (in Combe 2014), she is involved in new media in other ways, such as websites, YouTube, and online television series: 'So, although the fame game is being recalibrated across an expanding range of media sources, including Twitter, it seems that celebrity political performance varies considerably' (Tsaliki 2016, p. 253). This comment is relevant to blockbuster celebrity feminism, as well as celebrity feminism more broadly. Prior to considering some of her online activism, I want to address the publication of Poehler's 'memoir' as one crucial aspect of her celebrity feminist performance.

Saying Yes to Feminism: Amy Poehler's *Yes Please*

Yes Please reached the number one spot on the *New York Times* bestseller list (16 November 2014) and remains in the top ten as at November 2015. Covering Poehler's professional and personal lives in equal measure, *Yes Please* is not a chronological memoir. As Zach Dione (2014) remarks in *Rolling Stone*: '*Yes Please* is a 329-page nonlinear hopscotch across Poehler's life and career, from Chicago's Second City and the creation of the Upright Citizens Brigade to the glory days of *SNL* and *Parks and Rec*'. Nor is it solely a memoir; it appears, in many places, as Poehler concedes, like 'an open scrapbook' (2014, p. xvii). In the Preface, 'Writing is Hard', she remarks:

> In this book there is a little bit of talk about the past. There is some light emotional sharing. I guess that is the 'memoir' part. There is some 'advice', which varies in its levels of seriousness. Lastly, there are just 'essays', which are stories that usually have a beginning and an end, but nothing is guaranteed. Sometimes these three things are mixed together, like a thick stew. I hope it is full of flavor, but don't ask me to list all the ingredients. (2014a, p. xviii)

In her characteristic comic voice, Poehler advises readers to not necessarily expect a clear narrative thread. Given its positioning as a form of memoir, discourses of authenticity are central: 'I tried to tell the truth and be funny. What else do you want from me, you filthy animals?' (2014a, p. xvi). Her book, therefore, seeks to both inform and amuse.

Yes Please features many photographs, lists, copies of hand-written notes, and double pages featuring platitudes; that is, it contains 'a lot of filler' (Garner 2014). Like *Bossypants*, much of it is centred on Poehler's professional identity, including her interactions with various celebrities. The narrator also displays much affection and respect for the women in her life, with an entire chapter devoted to Poehler's relationship with Fey. That said, her personal life too features heavily and, as Dwight Garner (2014) remarks in the *New York Times*, 'There's a lot about childbirth and raising sons in "Yes Please."' The book also outlines her charity work, with a chapter on her work in Haiti working with the Worldwide Orphans Foundation (WOF), a move that some reader-reviewers saw cynically.[3]

Her memoir does not have a singular key feminist 'message' like some of those examined earlier, and is definitely not a manifesto or polemic; its feminism is largely subtle and integrated in Poehler's observations about gendered experiences, and especially those about working as a female comedian (much as in Fey's *Bossypants*). Statements like this are indicative of the book's quiet feminism: 'It takes years as a woman to unlearn what you have been taught to be sorry for. It takes years to find your voice and your real estate' (2014a, p. 65). As Rodriguez (2014) notes of the book, 'Feminism isn't a topic of conversation, but it *informs* every conversation' (original emphasis). Nonetheless, the book's structure reflects the liberal, or perhaps neoliberal, brand of feminism that underpins the loosely united pieces. Broken into three parts, 'Say whatever you want', 'Do whatever you want', and 'Be whoever you want', the book's feminism revolves mostly around the idea of respecting other women's life choices, a gesture which of course obscures the conditions of possibility governing such choices (Rodrigues 2014). 'Good you, not for me' (2014a, p. 149), as she puts it, seems to encompass her philosophy about judging (or rather not judging) other women and their choices, and it is a phrase that caused contention in the feminist blogosphere.

Yes Please, like many of the other blockbusters examined here, has been critiqued on the grounds of its author's privileged feminism; the following title is indicative in this regard: '"Yes Please" is White Liberal Feminism in Full Force' (Rodrigues 2014). In contrast, feminist web magazine *Bustle* applauds Poehler, featuring a piece entitled: '3 Times Amy Poehler said Yes to Feminism in Her Memoir, and We're On Board, Naturally' (Rodriguez 2014). In it, referring to Poehler's approach to career, motherhood, and relationships, Maddie Rodriguez (2014) praises the accessibility of her feminism:

> The world—especially women teetering on the edge of feminism, the "I'm not a feminist, but" women—also need representations of feminism like Poehler's. A feminism that doesn't take centre stage 100 percent of the time, but is always present. Feminism that is inherent and integrated into one's sense of self ... Feminism that just *is*. (original emphasis)

On the *Ms.* magazine blog, Audrey Bilger (2014) concurs: 'It's not clear why the words "feminism" and "feminist" don't actually appear *in* the book; however, there's no doubt that her memoir earns the F-word seal of approval' (original emphasis). While of course we could see this lack of explicit invocation of the signifier 'feminism' as consistent with approaches that render feminism the unspeakable 'f-word', these online commentators conversely interpret this implicit engagement as representing feminism's thorough acceptance and indeed normalization.

Nevertheless, on 30 January 2014, Poehler appeared on the front cover of USA's *Elle* magazine, reaffirming the crucial role of women's magazines in popular and especially celebrity feminism. In the accompanying interview, challenging celebrity refusal to identify as feminist, Poehler comically remarked:

> I don't get it. That's like someone being like, 'I don't really believe in cars, but I drive one every day and I love that it gets me places and makes life so much easier and faster and I don't know what I would do without it.' But that's everyone else's trip, not mine. (in Combe 2014)

Such public adoption of an overtly political subjectivity not only ensures feminism's visibility in a context where postfeminist discourses have become hegemonic but may, concomitantly, encourage other young women to (re)consider their own relationship with feminism (Keller 2015, p. 278). In keeping with this identification with, and commitment to, feminism, in 2012 Poehler developed an online initiative aimed at young girls, suggesting that feminism had already become fully incorporated into her celebrity 'brand'.

Amy's Smart Girls: Doing Celebrity Feminist Activism Online

As we saw with Sandberg, an integral part of Poehler's celebrity feminist practice has been the establishment of an online feminist initiative aimed at young girls, *Amy Poehler's Smart Girls*. Given all the media ventures—film and television production, publishing, and various online initiatives—in which she is now involved, *Elle* magazine even described her as a 'media mogul' (Combe 2014) but *Amy Poehler's Smart Girls* is perhaps the most prominent. It spans all key forms of social media: Twitter, Instagram, Facebook (with over 1.2 million 'likes' as at January 2016), Pintrest, and YouTube. The fact that Poehler's name features in the initiative clearly shows how integral her celebrity capital is to its branding and ultimately its success. In addition to being indicative of the way celebrities now routinely deploy their attention capital for charitable or philanthropic purposes, *Smart Girls* is consistent with the growth in GEOs, 'girls' empowerment organisations' (Banet-Weiser 2015), as discussed in Chap. 7. Perhaps in response to Sandberg's campaign, which she had previously satirized by quipping that her follow up to *Yes Please* would be titled 'Lean Out' (Poehler 2014a, p. 238), the *Smart Girls* website features a graphic with the following quotation, in upper case to accentuate the sentiment, from Poehler: 'I LIKE BOSSY GIRLS. I ALWAYS HAVE. PEOPLE FILLED WITH LIFE.' Poehler's branded empowerment, then, looks a little different to Sandberg's, though they both work, in neoliberal fashion, to varying degrees, to 'market' empowerment to what are perceived to be vulnerable young women (Banet-Weiser 2015).

The *Smart Girls* website features regular articles giving advice to young readers, while the Facebook page provides links to interviews with inspirational women from various backgrounds/industries, as well as relevant current affairs material. The initiative also spawned a number of online series, including *Smart Girls at the Party, Book Report, Girls of the World, She Said*, and *Ask Amy*.[4] Poehler outlines the premise underpinning *Smart Girls at the Party*, co-created with friends Meredith Walker and Amy Miles: 'We wanted to build a brand that attempted to combat the shit young people see every day online … Our hope is for people who can't stand to look at another awful website highlighting some fame obsessed garbage person' (2014a, pp. 325–6). Here, as is common, the initiative is set up in opposition to a vacuous celebrity culture; in doing so, Poehler obscures how fandom and audience investment in her is integral to its success.

With the upbeat motto 'change the world by being yourself', *Smart Girls* articulates a message of self-acceptance for young girls, and provides advice on how to negotiate the tensions of adolescence and conflicting expectations of how to be a good female citizen; it is also consistent with the approach taken in Poehler's blockbuster book, including its use of humour. In its 'About Us' section, the *Smart Girls* website is framed in this way:

> Amy Poehler's Smart Girls organization is dedicated to helping young people cultivate their authentic selves. We emphasize intelligence and imagination over 'fitting in.' We celebrate curiosity over gossip. We are a place where people can truly be their weird and wonderful selves. We are funny first, and informative second, hosting the party you want to attend. (amysmartgirls.com)

This goal of cultivating an 'authentic self' is entirely consistent with ideas of an entrepreneurial self whose 'authenticity' will serve as a bulwark against social inequality and discrimination, which, as young girls, they will invariably come to face. In terms of addressees, these are postfeminism's 'can do' girls (Harris 2004, p. 10), those who are positioned as responsible for their own life trajectories, urged to deploy individualized tactics of resilience and self-confidence to guarantee their success.

Smart Girls has also made its feminist politics explicit through an intervention into celebrity culture itself. At the 2015 Emmy Awards, Poehler spearheaded the #SmartGirlsAsk campaign on Twitter, where questions from users were posed to stars on the red carpet as they entered the ceremony. The campaign was launched in an effort to combat the banal, and often sexist, questions to which actors are commonly subjected at awards ceremonies, the most obvious being 'Who are you wearing?', a question largely if not solely directed towards women. Alternative questions included: 'How do you think the film industry could better portray the lives, struggles and joys of real women?' and 'What prominent female entertainment figure would make a great late night host of a talk show and why?' (Fisher 2015). Celebrities such as Britney Spears, Hillary Clinton, and Shonda Rhimes also intervened, posting questions via their Twitter accounts using the hashtag (Fisher 2015).

Through this initiative, Poehler used her celebrity capital to attempt to redirect the media's representational practices; that numerous celebrities participated is itself a reflection of Poehler's extensive celebrity network, as well as indicating the extent of the Smart Girl community. In such instances, 'Twitter's digitally networked action would capitalize on the personalized social networking between celebvocates and their followers and among followers themselves to spread the word for the "good causes"' (Tsaliki 2016, p. 238). Clearly a political gesture, this intervention into deeply gendered ways of figuring celebrities represents one of the more productive uses of 'attention capital', necessitating a way of thinking through such interventions that moves beyond figuring them as cynical and ineffectual modes of political practice. Such initiatives necessarily raise questions about fandom and 'how social media can be used as a tool to promote specific causes and to secure an active response from fan networks' (Bennett 2014, p. 138). As Lucy Bennett (2014, p. 139) argues:

> Although traditional celebrity involvement in philanthropy and activism has often relied on appeals to fan bases, social media now allows celebrities the possibility to instantly secure mobilisation and direct action from an audience without the filters of news media.

The success of the 'Smart Girls Ask' hashtag is undoubtedly bound up in such a process, in which Poehler's celebrity (feminism) is central.

As Couldry (2016, p. 110) argues: 'celebrities, or would-be celebrities, and their promoters, need to be ever more active in securing or sustaining their celebrity status, and digital media platforms fortunately provide ever more channels for doing so'. In this vein, *Amy Poehler's Smart Girls* has its own dedicated YouTube channel. As van Dijck argues: 'A far cry from its original design, YouTube is no longer an alternative to television, but a full-fledged player in the media entertainment industry' (2013, p. 127). Given this, it is not surprising celebrities are taking it up in varied ways, to maintain their visibility as well as to become involved in various causes. As Littler (2008, p. 239) argues, public involvement in causes represents 'a way for celebrities to appear to raise their profile above the zone of the crudely commercial into the sanctified, quasi-religious realm of altruism and charity, whilst revealing or constructing an added dimension of personality: of compassion and caring'. In this way, Poehler is seen to be selflessly sacrificing her time, and her apparent expertise, for the betterment of young, implicitly needy, girls, thereby clearly coding her as a celebrity with a feminist agenda, helping to brand her as a celebrity who cares. Although it would be easy to dismiss this project entirely as a cynical branding exercise, such a presumption would simplify a complex ideological, representational and moral project.

YouTube has been overwhelmingly framed as 'everyday people [seizing] the means of cultural production and distribution' (Burgess et al. 2013, p. 109; see also Jenkins 2006; Bruns 2008); but increasingly—as Poehler demonstrates—it is just not 'ordinary people' making use of this platform. While there has been scholarly focus on YouTube's enabling of micro-celebrities (Marwick 2016), much less attention has been paid to how celebrities in the more traditional sense are using this platform, not to mention how they are using it for distinctly feminist purposes. As Turner remarks: 'the techniques of micro-celebrity ... have been "borrowed back" by the "real" celebrities—those who operate within mainstream commercial media structures—in order to increase *their* control over their own celebritisation' (2014, p. 73, original emphasis). Relatedly, van Dijick has mapped the shift from 'active user agency to passive consumer behavior' and indicates that the claim that the majority of YouTube content comes from 'amateurs' has come under significant strain (2013, p. 116), a claim also destabilized by increased celebrity usage of the platform to engage directly with audiences.

A YouTube video series, *Ask Amy* (Poehler 2014b), responds to questions largely from teenage girls. As at January 2016, there are 28 uploaded videos, which cover intimate topics such as friendship; jealously; stress; courage; parents; power; letting go; anxiety; empowerment; and love. In taking young girls as subjects in need of advice to manage their very girlhood, the *Ask Amy* videos are consistent with figurations of young girls as simultaneously empowered individuals and as in crisis (Banet-Weiser 2015). As addressees, and as those who seek Amy's advice, girls as consuming figures are targeted as most in need of assistance to become efficient entrepreneurial girl subjects. Contemporary girlhood is no longer necessarily predicated on a 'ritualistic denunciation' of feminism (McRobbie 2009, p. 18), but, interestingly, *Ask Amy*, like *Yes Please*, appears rather covert in its embrace of feminism.

Ask Amy can be seen as part of a wider trend towards 'crowd sourcing' celebrity interviews, where the professional interviewer is effectively removed and audiences are invited to pose questions to their idol. As Bethany Usher (2015, p. 306) argues, celebrities 'encourage their followers to participate in this performance through the reward of direct interaction', which they use 'to extend promotion and build celebrity brands'. Often this is directly linked to the promotion of a new product (Usher 2015), as in the case of Dunham's *Ask Lena* YouTube series, attached to the publication of *Not That Kind of Girl*. However, in both these instances, it is not necessarily unimpeded insight into the celebrity's private life that fans seek (though this is part of what they receive), but advice about how to negotiate the tensions of being gendered feminine. The end result for the celebrity, however, is the same: a particular persona is constructed via these audience interactions, one that is empathic, open, compassionate, and patently feminist.

While the realm of celebrity is often seen as 'a mediatized public sphere where entertainment is privileged over information, affect over meaning' (Lewis 2010, p. 234), Poehler's YouTube activity challenges such an assumption as it seeks to reposition her from comic entertainer to authoritative voice on everyday issues relevant to teenage girls. Each response, offered by Amy herself, often in personal spaces, like her kitchen or car, and at times with little or no make-up, provides personal insights into the specific problem that followers have asked about; this arguably represents a refigured form of celebrity intimacy. Given that celebrity personas are constructed in large part 'through [online] public interaction with fans' (Marwick and boyd 2011, p. 155), videos such as these, responding directly to fans' questions, are important both for the producer and the consumer. Almost all responses serve to universalize the 'problem' for which the viewer seeks advice, 'everybody experiences that' is a refrain common to nearly all videos, thus helping create the sense of a supportive online community being facilitated by Poehler, while self-help rhetoric is also a key characteristic of the responses. These videos substantiate the claim that 'advice-giving represents a key discursive formation defining feminist media production across second and third [and now fourth] wave feminist practices of communication' (Rentschler 2014, p. 77). Moreover, such 'emotion work' and expressions of support and empathy can themselves be seen as important forms of political activity (Rentschler 2014, p. 77).

In terms of production, *Ask Amy* YouTube videos are constructed to appear like those of the amateur 'produser' (Bruns 2008) simply talking into their webcam, once again seeking to shore up the sense of 'ordinariness' and further situating Poehler as just 'one of the girls'. The confessional voice with which her blockbuster readers would be familiar, and which is integral to celebrification (Redmond 2008), is also evident here. As Lewis (2010, p. 583) argues, media celebrity 'involves being presented as a kind of exemplar of "ordinariness"', something these videos clearly overplay in an effort to establish authenticity and genuineness. While television has been seen as central in these processes of 'ordinarization' (Bonner 2003; Lewis 2010), this example suggests that YouTube is now being recruited in the service of such orchestrated familiarization. In a move away from the alienation and distanciation traditionally associated with spectacle and stardom, 'celebrity lifestyle experts present us with images and modes of advice embedded in, rather than abstracted from, everyday life' (Lewis 2010, p. 586). Through these videos, Poehler is clearly positioned as a kind of celebrity 'lifestyle expert', such as those found on reality television, and whose increasing presence is seen as indicative of the privatization of citizenship (Lewis 2010). Accordingly, she could be seen merely as the model citizen of neoliberalism. But there is no doubt that this initiative is informed by feminism.

Amy Poehler's Smart Girls, and especially *Ask Amy*, are clearly representative of a new way of popularly figuring feminism. As Banet-Weiser and Miltner argue: 'While popular feminisms have varied goals and different means of expression, there is a predominant theme: what women need is self-confidence ... in their inner selves, they simply need to be more confident and sure of themselves to overcome the often structural and societal problems that are keeping them down' (2016, p. 172). Through the videos, Poehler seeks to provide young women with the tools to become these confident, self-actualizing subjects. Deploying the rhetoric of choice and agency throughout, she is also positioned as a kind of sisterly figure, helping girls navigate universalized difficulties of feminine adolescence. As is common in girl empowerment rhetoric, difference is flattened out and a common girlhood is evoked (Koffman and Gill 2015). However, importantly, Poehler lacks the scrutinizing and judgemental gaze that Alison Winch (2012) sees as marking the contemporary postfeminist 'girlfriend culture' exemplified by makeover reality programmes; she is a much more empathic figure whose advice is clearly underpinned by a feminist ethic of care towards those seeking her counsel. However, it is worth noting that in October 2014, Legendary Entertainment purchased *Smart Girls at the Party*; this corporate investment, as the coming section on *Lenny*'s Hearst buyout illustrates, is indicative of what is increasingly perceived to be the current commercial viability of feminism itself.[5]

Through a combination of her comedy, her book, and her online empowerment initiatives, Amy Poehler is one of Hollywood's most visible feminists. The feminism she embodies, based as it is in 'respecting' other women's choices and in fostering improved self-esteem and confidence, bears the marks of its neoliberal postfeminist time and thereby cannot simply be uncritically celebrated but nor should its flaws render it entirely ineffectual. Here, I have located the blockbuster within a series of other mutually reinforcing, cross-platform, celebrity feminist practices, where the different 'Poehlers' are presumed indistinguishable, authentic, and most of all, accessible. Like Poehler, Lena Dunham's blockbuster is but one aspect of a wider intertextual network through which her celebrity feminism is performed and publicly negotiated.

Lena Dunham, Not That Kind of Girl, *and Celebrity Digital Media*

Lena Dunham, creator of the hit HBO television show, *Girls* (2012–), is routinely positioned as the voice of her purportedly 'postfeminist' generation. Much debate has been staged around the extent of the show's (and indeed its creator's) 'brand' of feminism; and in this regard her memoir is no exception. In *Not That Kind of Girl: A Young Woman Tells You What She Has 'Learned'* (2014), the narrator frames the text as significant in feminist terms: 'There is nothing gutsier to me than a person announcing that their story is one that deserves to be told, especially if that person is a woman' (2014, p. xvi). In addition to looking at her memoir, this section will explore how digital media have become a central part of the book promotion apparatus as well as maintaining a viable celebrity self. With regard to her attempts to shore up her feminist credentials, it examines how Dunham deploys her celebrity capital to create her own form of feminist media and online feminist community through her *Lenny* e-newsletter.

Importantly, Dunham is not simply a celebrity who has recently decided to incorporate feminism into her celebrity brand, in the way some other politicized stars (such as Emma Watson) have done. On the contrary, her work, preoccupied as it has been with gendered subjectivities, sexuality, and gendered intimacies, has always displayed a heightened form of 'feminist literacy' (Hogeland 1998). And, unlike some other celebrities, Dunham has never steered away from public feminist identification. When asked by fellow celebrity feminist Roxane Gay (2014d) about how feminism influences her work, Dunham replied: 'I just think feminism *is* my work. Everything I do, I do because I was told that as a woman, my voice deserves to heard, my rights are to be respected, and my job was to make that possible for others' (original emphasis). Here, Dunham identifies how critical feminism is, not just to her own life but to her politics and, relatedly, her creative practice.

Girls, the *Auteur*, and Feminism

Lena Dunham's *Girls* has been airing on HBO in the USA since April 2012; in February 2016 it will enter its fifth season. As its website brands it: 'the show is a comic look at the assorted humiliations and rare triumphs of a group of girls in their mid-20s'. Often figured (not without debate or controversy) as the current generation's *Sex and the City*, it similarly tracks the lives of a group of female friends living in Brooklyn (as opposed to Manhattan). The central protagonist, Hannah Hovath, is a struggling writer, whose failures, professionally and personally, are at the centre of the narrative arc. Her fellow millennials, likewise, embody angst and entitlement, as they negotiate the tensions and contradictions of being gendered feminine. Critically the programme is often seen to represent a new form of 'quality' television (Fuller and Driscoll 2014), frequently associated with HBO, while Dunham's celebrity has, at least partially, been predicated on her *auteur* status (Nelson 2014).

In feminist terms, the series is in many ways contradictory, but its 'explicit address to feminism and its evasion of a range of contemporary feminist expectations are equally crucial to how this series compels continuing conversations about feminism' (Fuller and Driscoll 2014, p. 253).

Rather than representing a reinscription of postfeminist cultural logics, *Girls* has been seen to engage with such discourses only in an effort to scrutinize them (Bell 2013, p. 363). Feminist criticism has, however, been largely preoccupied with why *Girls* 'failed to manifest the Perfect Feminist TV series' (Fuller and Driscoll 2014, p. 255). As Fuller and Driscoll argue, this expectation is one commonly levelled at series with female creators/directors but rarely at those authored by men. Likewise, female celebrities are expected to be the embodiment of the 'Perfect Feminist', an expectation from which male celebrity 'feminists' are immune (see Cobb 2015). In particular, Dunham has been heavily criticized for her privilege and the 'stark whiteness' underpinning *Girls*' diegetic world (Gay 2014a; see also Freeman 2014).[6] While a textual analysis of *Girls* is beyond the scope of this book, it is clear that these assumptions about the TV series' ambivalent feminism have also dogged Dunham's status as a celebrity feminist. However, like those of all celebrities, her feminist star text is established across multiple media platforms, including her recently published bestselling memoir.

LESSONS FROM LENA: *NOT THAT KIND OF GIRL*

Not That Kind of Girl entered the *New York Times* bestseller list on 19 October 2014 at number 2. Random House reportedly paid Dunham a $3.7 million advance for the work (Freeman 2014). Like Poehler's, Dunham's is not an autobiography in the traditional sense, though it clearly adopts a confessional mode, covering her personal experiences of various health conditions, such as endometriosis, anxiety, and obsessive compulsive disorder, as well as sexual assault and issues around consent. Generically, the book was largely positioned as life writing, with the blurb describing it as 'a candid collection of personal essays'. Celebrities, as Redmond argues, 'rely on the confessional to authenticate, validate, humanize, resurrect, extend and enrich their star and celebrity identities' (2008, pp. 109–10). As a common 'revelatory mode of self-enunciation', the confessional mode, as the chapter on Friedan has shown, 'has become one of the dominant ways in which fame is circulated and consumed' (Redmond 2008, p. 110). Rather than simply using her memoir to create a sense of intimacy with fans, Dunham announces that she is sharing her stories in the hope of helping other young women, with the book's didactic goal made explicit in the subtitle: *A Young Woman Tells You What She's 'Learned'*. Positing gender as something to be 'learned', Dunham implicitly conceptualizes it as a doing rather than a being (Butler 1990) and, throughout the book, maps her own negotiation of this complicated, ongoing process. She does not privilege one specific way of 'doing' femininity but offers a confessional insight into this process, as she seeks to mine her 'missteps' (2014, p. xvii) ostensibly for the benefit of other women; in this respect, it appears to be a bildungsroman for millennials.

In *Not That Kind of Girl*, Dunham suggests that Helen Gurley Brown's *Having It All* (1982) provided the inspiration for her text, a gesture that seeks to place her in a long lineage of outspoken feminist authors/celebrities (although it also aligns her with postfeminism, wherein the trope of 'having it all' for women marks the ongoing tensions between the public and private spheres). Making clear her debt to Brown, she notes: 'I am a girl with a keen interest in having it all, and what follows are hopeful dispatches from the front line' (2014, p. xvii). It is this location on the 'front line' that Dunham claims to be the basis of her authority; she is, she wishes readers to believe, despite her immense public profile, commercial success, and resonance, an 'ordinary girl'. Therefore, as is often the case with blockbusters, her claims to authority are personal, although placing the word 'learned' in scare quotes functions to call into question the value of the coming advice. The book is broken into five sections—'Love and Sex', 'Body', 'Friendship', 'Work', and 'Big Picture'—each made up of short autobiographical essays, interspersed with lists such as '15 things I've learned from my mother' and '13 things I've learned are not ok to say to friends'. In the *New York Times*, Michiko Kakutani (2014) describes the book as 'a kind of memoir disguised as an advice book, or a how-to book (as in how to navigate the perilous waters of girlhood) in the guise of a series of personal essays'. Indicative of the feedback loop in which celebrity feminism is implicated, Roxane Gay (2014c) reviewed the book for *Time* magazine, concluding: 'Dunham is not only a voice who deserves to be heard but also one who will inspire other important voices to tell their stories too.' By contrast, in *The New Republic* James Wolcott (2014) described the book as 'callow, grating and glib'. Like other blockbuster celebrity feminists, therefore, Dunham appears to be a polarizing figure.

Unsurprisingly, given its marketing as a memoir, the book became enmeshed in discourses of 'authenticity', as *Girls* itself has (see Woods 2015).[7] With it, and its 'remorseless self-exposure' (Freeman 2014), Dunham is considered to be giving readers/fans access to an unmediated self, however impossible such a project might be: 'With "Not That Kind of Girl," Ms. Dunham brings a similar candor to the story of her own life, getting as naked in print as her alter ego Hannah often does in the flesh' (Kakutani 2014; see also Freeman 2014; Jones 2014). However, while not in itself an innovative literary trope, Dunham herself cautions against assumptions of simple verisimilitude that came to be inscribed in most reviews: 'I'm an unreliable narrator' (2014, p. 51). Positioning Dunham as the ultimate celebrity oversharer, one commentator remarks: 'The question is, after all this can there really be anything left for Lena to share?' (Jones 2014). This question presumes that Dunham's self-exposure, both physically and in terms of the intimate details she shares about herself, is excessive, and needs to be regulated or curtailed; this approach to women's voices, of course, is nothing new. Contrastingly, another reviewer views this self-disclosure as the book's greatest virtue: 'this very inviting voice has spilled intimacies on every page' (Dry 2014; see also Baum 2014). Regardless, it is clear all reviewers, consistent with the 'autobiographical pact' (Lejeune 1989), presume the veracity of Dunham's truth-claims.

As noted earlier, celebrity autobiography is an ever-expanding subgenre of life writing. As Lee argues, we use 'the autobiographies of the famous to understand not just the individual, her cultural products, and her experiences of celebrity, but also her strategies of brand management' (2014, p. 87). Dunham's book is just one text in the vast intertextual network that constitutes her celebrity (feminist) sign; that is, like those of all celebrities, 'her memoir cannot be read as a discrete, self-contained text' (Yellin 2015, p. 13) but instead needs to be seen as having been 'supplemented by a repository of stories and impressions that circulate around her star image'. Across such texts, Dunham's cross-platform voice merges and is conflated, especially with that of Hannah (McRobbie 2015; Woods 2015). That is, *Girls* and her other media interventions are seen to act as a kind of unified feminist 'performance', which some have dismissed as 'quasi-feminism' (McRobbie 2015, p. 15). I am not, however, interested here in whether Dunham—or indeed any of the authors examined here—is feminist 'enough' or the 'right' kind of feminist but in the political conversations she has precipitated, including around the meanings of feminism. As Dunham herself once tweeted: 'The debate about good and bad feminism makes me want to take a nap for a year' (in Fuller and Driscoll 2015, p. 253).

Due to new media technologies 'the process of maintaining a stable star persona isn't what it used to be' (Muntean and Petersen 2009), nor are the processes of book promotion and marketing (Murray 2015). Promotional material for *Not That Kind of Girl* even included the creation of a dedicated YouTube channel shortly before the book's publication, featuring short *Ask Lena* (Dunham 2014b) videos, where Dunham responds to questions posted by fans. Topics, if not responses, are often explicitly feminist in nature and those covered include: Dunham's own feminism; 'bad sex'; OCD (from which the author confesses she suffers); bullies; death; friendships and romantic relationships; and being 'plus size'. As in Poehler's *Ask Amy* videos, Dunham's common refrain is the empathic 'I know exactly how you feel', and she gives practical advice on how women can take care of themselves, physically and psychically. As the use of such promotional videos elucidates, more traditional types of celebrity are increasingly utilizing the same tactics of self-presentation upon which the so-called micro-celebrity so heavily relies (Turner 2014). Dunham is often self-deprecating about the value of her advice, and these videos are framed as an extension of her memoir's narrative voice 'telling us what she's learned'. These kinds of initiatives are more than likely becoming a publishing house staple, extending the idea that the visible author is more effective than paid advertising (Moran 2000). Such epitextual performances are also central to the creation and maintenance of an 'authentic' (feminist) self in which readers can affectively invest, and public engagement with fans has itself been seen as central to the process of persona construction (Marwick and boyd 2011, p. 155). As I have noted, Dunham's persona is presumed to be consistent across myriad texts, but this sense of consistency is, of course, the product of much labour.

However, it was not only through online activities that the book, and its author's feminism, were being publicized; Dunham formally linked her promotional activities to her feminist politics, by teaming up with Planned Parenthood during her 2014 USA book tour (Nash and Grant 2015). In a press release about the partnership, she remarks:

> I'm thrilled that Planned Parenthood is my guest on my book tour ... Planned Parenthood will have a presence on my tour so that people can learn about Planned Parenthood health services and the invaluable information that Planned Parenthood educators provide, and become involved as advocates and volunteers. ('Planned Parenthood Joins Lena Dunham Book Tour in Nine Cities 2014')

On behalf of the reproductive rights organisation, Dunham marketed a fundraising pink t-shirt, pronouncing—in the same font as the book's cover—'Lena loves Planned Parenthood'. Here, she quite literally wears her feminist politics on her sleeve. Described by Dunham on Twitter as 'the official shirt of my book tour' (Stampler 2014), thus making it a form of authorial epitext which shores up her literary text's feminist credentials, it was sported by various celebrities, including Poehler, on Instagram, reaffirming their own (and Dunham's) feminist identities as well as increasing the visibility of Planned Parenthood.[8] In this way, and like fellow blockbuster authors, Dunham uses the promotional mechanisms surrounding her book not just to foreground the book as a commodity but a particular form of feminism, one that has reproductive rights at its core. In a context where women's reproductive freedom is being called into question, and although the efficacy of celebrity activism has been the subject of much debate (see Chap. 7 here), such explicitly feminist celanthropic interventions are symbolically and politically important. They also reveal that Dunham's feminist politics are integral to her public persona, and shape her social media practice in ways that have irked some consumers.

Dunham's Twitter Retreat

As many feminist scholars have demonstrated, integral to contemporary celebrity culture, and indeed to postfeminist media culture more broadly, is the extreme shaming of women's bodies (Wearing 2007; Holmes and Negra 2011; Winch 2012). Celebrity gossip magazines gleefully provide photographic 'evidence' of cellulite-ridden thighs and other weight-related bodily transgressions. Attempts to resist or contest this evaluative gaze are not given much traction, with Dunham being one notable exception. It is not simply in the context of *Girls* that this occurs; Dunham regularly posts photographs to Instagram and formerly Twitter, consistent with her body pride politics, confidently displaying herself in various states of undress.[9] However, unfortunately, despite her persistent attempts to destabilize assumptions around the 'appropriate' or legitimate female celebrity body, Dunham has been subject to intense vitriol and what has been variously labelled misogynistic 'e-bile' (Jane 2014a, b) or 'networked misogyny' (Banet-Weiser and Miltner 2016) following her uploading of many of these images. Rather than acting as a utopian space in which all voices can be equally heard, the internet has proved to be a haven for, often anonymously delivered, anti-feminist sentiments.

After experiencing first hand how 'gendered vitriol is proliferating in the cybersphere' (Jane 2014b, p. 558), in September 2015 Dunham took a very public stand against Twitter and the hostile discursive environment it fosters. She stated: 'I don't look at Twitter anymore. I tweet, but I do it through someone else. I don't even know my Twitter password, which may make me seem like I'm no longer a genuine community user.' Given that 'authenticity' in social media practice is a quality highly prized by fans (Muntean and Petersen 2009), this frank admission is perhaps remarkable and potentially alienating. However, Dunham noted that she sees the maintenance of a Twitter account with which she is only marginally involved as a better alternative to being emotionally 'unsafe' (in Ward 2015), thereby shining a spotlight on the potentially 'toxic' nature of online environments for feminists (Thelandersson 2014):

> I think even if you think you can separate yourself from the kind of verbal violence that's being directed at you, that it creates some really kind of cancerous stuff inside you, even if you think, 'Oh I can read like 10 mentions that say I should be stoned to death.' That's verbal abuse. Those aren't words you'd accept in an interpersonal relationship. […] For me, personally, it was safer to stop. (in Ledbetter 2015)

Celebrities have long expressed concerns about the effects of celebrification, which mainly relate to lack of privacy or loss of control over their image (Moran 2000; Rojek 2001; York 2007), and social media have undoubtedly intensified this pressure, especially through the kinds of abuse Dunham outlines here. Choosing to remain on Instagram, which she identifies as a 'more positive community' (in Dodge 2015) and which she has used in support of political campaigns like Planned Parenthood's 'Women are Watching', she does not reject online media outright, but rather differentiates between platforms that facilitate productive public building and those that can be seen to foster hate speech. This withdrawal is, in itself, a significant feminist intervention by a celebrity with the capital to publicly foreground, and critique, digital misogyny.

That her decision garnered such intense media attention also suggests the way in which engagement with various social media platforms has been completely normalized as a celebrity performative practice, including for feminists. But, most importantly, her retreat draws public attention to one of the greatest limitations of new media and especially women's participation in social networking—surveillance, judgment, regulation, and, worst of all, intense misogyny. If social media are now vital to the maintenance of celebrity feminism, then such misogyny, as well as the kind of overt racism experienced by authors such as Gay, could come to seriously threaten its viability. However, while forms like Twitter *may* act as important vehicles for/of celebrification, they are not the *only* means to secure or sustain renown, or to establish a sense of intimacy with readers, including for blockbuster feminist authors. Showing how other online forms can be more productively used than social networking platforms, Dunham launched her feminist e-newsletter, *Lenny*, in September 2015.

LENNY: A CELEBRITY FEMINIST'S E-NEWSLETTER

Despite Dunham's public detachment from Twitter, she has certainly not removed herself from all forms of online media; in 2015 she spearheaded a number of new media initiatives, such as *Lenny*, branded a feminist e-newsletter, and a podcast series, *Women of the Hour* (produced by Buzzfeed). In terms of the former, she even explicitly framed the venture, initially founded and funded by herself and *Girls* co-producer Jennifer Konner (Lenny is a portmanteau of their names), as a way of creating a more productive online space: 'the Internet has the power to take you into quiet places—something we don't usually use it for' (in Petersen 2015). Such media interventions work as important ways in which Dunham can, despite contests over how feminist, postfeminist, or unfeminist her series is, work to establish her identity as a celebrity feminist as well as to create online feminist communities.

The inaugural issue of *Lenny*, a newsletter that subscribers receive twice a week, was released on 29 September 2015. In contrast to Poehler, whose initiative uses empowerment rhetoric without being framed as an explicitly feminist site, Dunham's *Lenny* is overt about its ideological positioning. Talking about *Lenny*, the launch of which received extensive media coverage, underscoring the role of her celebrity capital in its visibility (and indeed viability) she told *Entertainment Weekly*: 'We want to be a useful place for women to go to think about feminism, to promote equality *and* to, you know, learn about tube tops! We're so excited that people have responded as hungrily as they have …' (in Li 2015, original emphasis). In this statement, seeking to reconcile feminism with formerly trivialized preoccupations (here signalled by an interest in women's fashion), *Lenny* appears to reinscribe third wave rhetoric and its celebration of devalued, feminized cultural practices (Baumgardner and Richards 2000). However, while there may appear to be points of discursive overlap, a notable difference is that Dunham and Konner seem much less interested in positioning themselves according to the restrictive wave model or differentiating themselves from their feminist 'mothers'; as many feminists critiquing wave metaphors and generational logics have shown, 'matricide' (Rich 1976; see also Henry 2004; Taylor 2008) is a common symbolic gesture in attempts to revitalize feminism but its absence here, as in the previous chapter, is noteworthy.

On the contrary, through showcasing interviews with prominent second wave celebrity feminist Gloria Steinem, as well as well-known supporter of women's rights and 2016 USA Democratic Presidential candidate, Hillary Clinton, *Lenny* (and thereby Dunham) is refusing to perform the disavowal of anterior forms of feminism upon which both so-called third wave and postfeminism are largely predicated. Instead, it works to stage cross-generational conversations, thereby underscoring intergenerational commonalities rather than differences. Therefore, the cultural amnesia that is often said to characterize young women's engagement with feminism (Taylor 2009) seems to be absent from this initiative, again demonstrating how much celebrity feminism can be seen to destabilize (or at least not reinscribe) the deeply flawed wave model.

With *Lenny*, it is clear that Dunham leverages her celebrity capital to draw upon likeminded celebrities to attract readers to the newsletter—and indeed to a particular form of feminism itself. In addition to interviews with Clinton and Steinem mentioned above, she has published thus far articles by actors who have publicly identified as feminist (something I discuss further in the concluding chapter of this book). For example, *Hunger Games*' star Jennifer Lawrence (2015) wrote a piece critiquing the gender pay gap and associated expectations around women's passivity in Hollywood ('Why Do I Make Less Than My Male Co-stars' (14 October)). Moreover, as *Lenny* has developed, the kinds of voices it privileges and the experiences it renders visible, in interviews, articles, or advice pieces, appear to have diversified, perhaps in response to critiques of the whiteness of Dunham's own feminism as manifest in other textual spaces.

Of the audience they were seeking to attract and the approach to feminism that the newsletter would be taking, Dunham noted: 'We'll be allowed to show the ugly and complicated thought processes that go into forming your own brand of feminism, and your own identity, because it's not all clean back here' (in Peterson 2015). This rhetoric around the 'messiness' of feminism, and the necessity of negotiating one's own form of feminism, is something we can also see underpinning Gay's 'bad feminist' subjectivity, and an emphasis that feminism is not incompatible with other popular cultural activities/texts is also a key feature of both authors' rhetoric. When users subscribe to the e-newsletter, opting in to this feminist community, they receive an email from Dunham and Konner thanking them for their subscription; it also outlines the patently feminist philosophy of *Lenny* and its creators. The welcome email, though not explicitly invoking the signifier 'feminism', reads:

> Our subscribers are everything to us, because we want to entertain and inform you, but we also want to make the world better for women and the people who love them. That means keeping abortion safe and legal, keeping birth control in your pocket and getting the right people elected, all the while wearing extremely fierce jumpsuits. (in Bonner 2015)

As many scholars have argued, new media now work in a significant way to facilitate forms of intimacy and sociality between celebrities and 'ordinary' people (Rojek 2011; Click et al. 2013), and this personalized message is evidence of that. Moreover, here, they are attempting to bring into being a community of like-minded women; they seek to hail such women, whom they encourage to effectively spread the word of *Lenny*'s arrival and its governing philosophy. In particular, the feminist issue Dunham and Konner most clearly foreground is reproductive rights, around which they seek to mobilize women.

As this example, and indeed those in the previous chapters, reveals, celebrity feminism—even for authors of bestselling works of non-fiction—is heavily reliant upon multiple media platforms. In this instance, as part of her wider project of feminist discursive activism, Dunham appeared to be effectively creating a media channel to bypass major media corporations. However, *Lenny* was not to remain the entirely independent feminist publishing initiative it was first framed as being. Although initially funded by Dunham and Konner, its website now brands it 'A Part of Hearst Digital Media'—the company responsible for *Cosmopolitan* (linking Dunham again with Brown), *Elle*, and *Marie Claire*.[10] As part of the recent deal, Hearst's magazines will publish material from *Lenny* the day after it reaches subscribers, alongside regular magazine advertising, while Hearst will also own the media rights to the newsletter (Peterson 2015). Rather than being an online form that anyone could have produced, the site has huge commercial and technological support and serves to illustrate the inextricability of online platforms from the multinational corporations who power them (Peterson 2015). The *Lenny* buy-out thus substantiates the following claims regarding the limits placed on how we might make productive use of the internet: 'the online world is increasingly governed and delimited by private interests who own and control the platforms and affordances in and through which we express ourselves, and, as a result, is shot through with promotion and marketing' (Hearn and Schoenhoff 2016, p. 203). Moreover, the Hearst buy-out example underscores the need for consideration of corporate engagement and cross-platform interactions rather than artificially separating new media from what have been problematically dubbed 'heritage' or 'legacy' forms of media (Turner 2016a) like magazines. That is, it is not possible to conceptualize new media as existing in a utopian space outside or beyond the commercial networks that constitute other forms of media.

This initiative represents, in a very real sense, the inseparability of new media from other platforms and institutions. In this way, it is useful to shift the discourse from 'social' to 'connective media' (Lovink 2013), a term signalling not just the potential connectivity across citizens and borders but also commercial enterprises. Feminists, like those from other politically progressive movements, must recognize, and develop new strategies for dealing with, such an environment. Through this deal, as with Brown's 'Woman Alone' column and Friedan's 'Notebook', *Lenny*'s audience moves far beyond those who have identified with its mission to readers of women's magazines who may not have consciously elected to receive the newsletter but who come to access its content within the frame of *Cosmo* or *Vanity Fair*. Perhaps, then, we should commend Dunham and Konner for their recognition that the circulation of what might broadly be constituted feminist material is reliant upon these new kinds of commercial, and technological, arrangements.

With an emphasis on commercial viability, Dunham and Konner explained the buy-out to *Lenny* readers: 'Why are we doing this? Because we want Lenny to be a self-sustaining, kick-ass, women-run business for a long, long time. We want to … get our content to as many people as we possibly can' (in Ingram 2015). Here, they retain the feminist principle of a woman-only enterprise, but acknowledge that this is contingent upon corporate support, while the point about making their overtly feminist material accessible to a broad audience itself echoes the impetus of the feminist blockbuster. Moreover, just as the blockbuster requires the support of a commercially successful publisher, with widespread resources and promotional strategies, so too these new media initiatives require substantial investment from those with the capital to help sustain them. The initiative underscores 'that much participatory and activist culture is rarely positioned completely outside of commercialization' (Shaw 2014, p. 276;

see also Wicke 1994; Banet-Weiser and Mukherjee 2012). *Lenny*, and especially the Hearst deal, offers further evidence of the unsustainability of such a politically pure 'outside', and highlights the importance of such connections for feminism in the twenty-first century.

Aside from its feminist work, *Lenny* is indicative of a wider tendency among celebrities to seek out 'alternative means of publicity' in an attempt to exercise some control over their representation (Marwick and boyd 2011, p. 155), and, like other forms of digital media, it is undoubtedly an important vehicle for Dunham to communicate with, and expand her network of, feminist fans. Furthermore, while celebrities transforming themselves into media producers is not necessarily innovative, and nor is the use of the newsletter form for feminist purposes, the online media environment provides the opportunity for famous women like Dunham and Poehler not just to contribute to the construction of their public personas but to help actively mediate public conversations around feminism itself (something that Dunham also does through her television series). Though *Lenny* can be seen as analogous to feminist zines,[11] especially in its collaborative approach, it is significantly different—not just because of the way in which it has now been subsumed into the mainstream media, through the Hearst deal, but also because of its co-creator's extant celebrity. There is no doubt that with this initiative the controversial author/*auteur* is using her attention capital to secure support for this venture as well as buttressing that capital. Nonetheless, though in its infancy, as a representational space created by and for women, *Lenny* is important in feminist terms; an explicitly political intervention into the digital media landscape, it seeks to host productive conversations around femininity, sexuality, race, creativity, fashion, art, and feminism, especially reproductive rights, illustrating the generative capacity of celebrity feminism.

Conclusion

In this chapter I have shown that what constitutes a 'feminist blockbuster' has necessarily altered and with it the blockbuster celebrity feminism identified in the first part of this book. The women featured here, I have argued, act as a kind of bridge between those considered earlier and those celebrities who, having achieved fame in their chosen fields, later publicly claim a feminist identity—to whom I briefly turn in the concluding chapter. That is, in the case of Poehler and Dunham, feminism is not the initial source of their renown, but nor is it something with which they chose to associate themselves once established. Rather, it has always been an important part of their public identities and, indeed, has contributed greatly to their success as writers, directors, and performers. As authors, these women have suggested generic changes in the feminist blockbuster form itself. While the confessional voice, to varying degrees, has always been central to polemical feminist writing, the memoirs of these funny feminists suggest that it is predominantly through life writing, and coming to feminist consciousness style narratives, that their literary feminism manifests. In addition, these examples have revealed that humour is central to keeping feminism in the public imagination, something demonstrated earlier in the section on Greer's comedic television performances.

These women, too, have been shown to use their celebrity capital for various feminist media and political projects, prompting the questions: Is this now the core ground for celebrity feminist activism? If so, what might we make of this presumption of girls and young women, in particular, as needing feminist care from their idols? Given that such campaigns and online media aimed at young girls who are purportedly 'in crisis' proliferate, it is incumbent upon us to think through the politics of the subjects they seek to bring it into being, and to/for what ends. Of these kinds of interventions, Lewis (2015) argues: 'Our celebrity feminists laureate [in which he includes Tina Fey as well as Dunham] are not actually feminists, then, but lobbyists for specific causes that fall under the umbrella of feminism.' While for Lewis such a situation is lamentable, is the kind of feminist celebrity activism in which Poehler and Dunham are involved necessarily problematic, merely evidence of celebrities seeking to be publicly seen to be 'doing good' (Tsaliki 2016, p. 235)? My analysis of their respective projects would suggest not, and certainly we should not dismiss them in favour of a 'real' or more 'authentic' feminist activism occurring outside the zone of celebrity (Wicke 1994). Finally, as their blockbusters have been produced after their celebrification, these women represent a different mode of blockbuster celebrity feminism—but, nonetheless, these non-fictional bestsellers, along with their authors' online activism, have proven integral to their celebrity feminist practice. Building upon this work on Poehler and Dunham, in the concluding chapter I move the focus towards some of the other ways in which celebrity and feminism can be seen to intersect, and also consider what the role of the blockbuster and its feminist authors might be in the future.

Notes

1. Fey and Poehler are routinely positioned as offering not just similar comedic work but as having similar relationships to feminism. Like Poehler, Fey produced a bestselling memoir, *Bossypants*, in 2011. Fey and Poehler's celebrity feminism cannot easily be extricated from their other forms of performance, which involve often caustic critique of gender norms and double standards. They have co-hosted the Golden Globe awards three times; most recently, they opened the ceremony with a monologue publicly celebrated for its feminism (Freeman 2015). Significantly, although Fey has been the subject of a number of academic journal articles and book chapters (Lauzen 2014; Mizejewski 2014; Patterson 2012), which all take up the question of her publicly performed feminism, Poehler has not yet been the subject of any scholarship. This is remarkable, given that Poehler's feminism is much less ambivalent than Fey's.
2. In an article in *Salon*, 'Tina Fey and Amy Poehler: Hollywood's Imperfect Feminists', Daniel D'Addario (2014) criticized them for what he saw as their limited form of feminism.
3. See reader reviews on: http://www.amazon.com/Yes-Please-Amy-Poehler/product-reviews
4. In what is a contemporary form of 'sisterhood', Poehler has also worked to increase opportunities for other female writers and directors through online media channels like YouTube. For example, *Broad City*, a web series that was eventually produced by Poehler, and subsequently taken up by Comedy Central.
5. 'Through the acquisition, the female-targeting brand will have access to Legendary's fully supported platform—which provides advertising, marketing, audience development and production infrastructure—for which it will develop branded premium content' (Sandberg 2014).
6. See also Bell (2013) for an analysis of this issue.
7. The book became enveloped in controversy when Dunham's narrativization of sexual experiences in the same room as her sister came to figure in the mainstream media as a form of child abuse (see Flood 2014; Tolentino 2014).
8. I am indebted to my Honours student, Samantha Elass, for bringing these celebrity endorsements of Dunham's planned parenthood shirt on Instagram to my attention.

9. For an analysis of the role of Dunham's body in *Girls*' reception, see Marghitu and Ng (2013).
10. As its website suggests, 'Hearst Magazines is one of the world's largest publishers of monthly magazines, with 21 U.S. titles and close to 300 international editions. Hearst Magazines also publishes 19 magazines in the United Kingdom through its wholly owned subsidiary, Hearst Magazines UK' (https://www.hearst.com/magazines).
11. See Piepmeier (2009) for an extended analysis of feminist zines.

REFERENCES

Amy Poehler's Smart Girls, http://amysmartgirls.com/
Banet-Weiser, S. (2015) 'Keynote Address: Media, Markets, Gender: Economies of Visibility in a Neoliberal Moment', *The Communication Review*, 18:1, 53–70
Banet-Weiser, S. & Mukherjee, R. (2012) 'Introduction: Commodity Activism in Neoliberal Times', in S. Banet-Weiser & R. Mukherjee eds. *Commodity Activism: Cultural Resistance in Neoliberal Times*, New York: New York University Press, pp. 1–17
Banet-Weiser, S. & Miltner, K.M. (2016) '#MasculinitySoFragile: Culture, Structure, and Networked Misogyny', *Feminist Media Studies*, 16.1: 171–174
Baum, M. (2014) 'Lena Dunham Is Not Done Confessing', 14 September, *New York Times Magazine*, accessed via http://www.nytimes.com/2014/09/14/magazine/lena-dunham.html?_r=0
Baumgardner, J. & Richards, A. (2000) *Manifesta: Young Women, Feminism, and the Future*, New York: Farrar, Straus and Giroux
Bell, C. (2013) 'Obvie, We're the Ladies! Postfeminism, Privilege and HBO's Newest Girls', *Feminist Media Studies*, 13.2: 363–366
Bennett, L. (2014) "If We Stick Together We Can Do Anything': Lady Gaga Fandom, Philanthropy and Activism Through Social Media', *Celebrity Studies*, 5.1–2: 138–152
Bilger, A. (2014) 'For Amy Poehler, Writing Is Hard, Feminism Comes Naturally', 2 December, *Ms* magazine blog, accessed via http://msmagazine.com/blog/2014/12/02/for-amy-poehler-writing-is-hard-feminism-comes-naturally/
Bonner, F. (2003) *Ordinary Television: Analyzing Popular Television*, London: Sage
Bonner, M. (2015) 'Lean Dunham Is Leading a Game-Changing Feminist Newsletter', 15 July, *Marie Claire*, accessed via http://www.marieclaire.com/celebrity/news/a15101/lena-dunham-lenny-newsletter/

Brown, H.G. (1982) *Having It All: Love, Success, Sex, Money – Even If You're Starting with Nothing*, New York: Simon and Schuster

Bruns, A. (2008) *Blogs, Wikipedia, Second Life, and Beyond: From Production to Produsage*, New York: Peter Lang

Butler, J. (1990) *Gender Trouble*, New York: Routledge

Burgess, J., Green, J. & Jenkins, H. (2013) *You Tube*, New York: Wiley Blackwell

Click, M.A., Lee, H. & Willson Holladay, H. (2013) 'Making Monsters: Lady Gaga, Fan Identification, and Social Media', *Popular Music and Society*, 36.3: 360–379

Cobb, S. (2015) 'Is This What a Feminist Looks Like? Male Celebrity Feminists and the Postfeminist Politics of "Equality"', *Celebrity Studies*, 6.1: 136–139

Combe, R. (2014) 'Amy Poehler Talks Feminism, Friendship, and Staying Away from Selfies', 30 January, *Elle*, accessed via http://www.elle.com/culture/celebrities/a6/amy-poehler-women-in-tv-2014-interview/?src=rss

Cosslett, T. (2000) 'Matrilinieal Narratives Revisited', in T. Cosslett, C. Lurie & P. Summerfield eds. *Feminism and Autobiography: Texts, Theories, Methods*, London: Routledge, pp. 141–153

Couldry, N. (2016) 'Celebrity, Convergence, and the Fate of Media Institutions', in P.D. Marshall & S. Redmond eds. *A Companion to Celebrity*, London: Wiley Blackwell, pp. 98–113

D'Addario, D. (2014) 'Tina Fey and Amy Poehler: Hollywood's Imperfect Feminists', 13 January, *Salon*, accessed via http://www.salon.com/2014/01/12/tina_fey_and_amy_poehler_hollywoods_imperfect_feminists/

Dione, Z. (2014) '9 Things We Learned from Amy Poehler's Yes Please', 30 October, *Rolling Stone*, accessed via: http://www.rollingstone.com/tv/features/9-things-we-learned-from-amy-poehlers-yes-please-20141030#ixzz3w879lGvr

Dodge, S. (2015) '"It's Verbal Violence!" Lena Dunham Says She Stopped Managing Her Twitter Account Due to Body-Shaming Comments After She Posted Underwear Selfie', 29 September, *Daily Mail*, accessed via http://www.dailymail.co.uk/tvshowbiz/article-3253042/Lena-Dunham-says-stopped-managing-Twitter-account-body-shaming-comments-posted-underwear-selfie.html#ixzz3pHW2HCau

Dry, R. (2014) 'Review: Not That Kind of Girl', 24 September, *The Washington Post*, accessed via https://www.washingtonpost.com/entertainment/books/review-not-that-kind-of-girl-by-lena-dunham/2014/09/24/4e482c04-42c0-11e4-b437-1a7368204804_story.html

Dunham, L. (2014) *Not That Kind of Girl*, New York: Random House

———— (2014b) 'Ask Lena', *Not That Kind of Girl* (YouTube Channel), accessed via https://www.youtube.com/channel/UCETNuDGcBVT5hAao-bSkW0Q

Ferriss, S. (2014) 'Chick Non-Fic: The Comedic Memoir', *Feminist Media Studies* 14(2): 206–221.

Fey, T. (2011) *Bossypants*, New York: Little, Brown and Company

Fisher, L.A. (2015) '#SmartGirlsAsk aims to change tonight's Emmy's red carpet conversation', 20 September, *Harper's Bazaar*, accessed via http://www.harpersbazaar.com/celebrity/red-carpet-dresses/news/a12249/smart-girls-ask-emmys-2015/

Flood, A. (2014) 'Lena Dunham apologises after critics accuse her of sexually molesting sister', 6 November, *The Guardian*, accessed via https://www.theguardian.com/books/2014/nov/05/lena-dunham-statement-abuse-claims

Freeman, H. (2014) 'Not That Kind of Girl, Review: Lena Dunham Exposes It All, Again', 1 October, *The Guardian*, accessed via http://www.theguardian.com/books/2014/sep/30/not-that-kind-of-girl-lena-dunham-review-memoir

────── (2015) 'How Amy Poehler and Tina Fey Made the Golden Globes the First Feminist Film Awards Ceremony', 13 January, *The Guardian*, accessed via http://www.theguardian.com/film/filmblog/2015/jan/12/amy-poehler-tina-fey-golden-globes

Fuller, S. & Driscoll, C. (2015) 'HBO's Girls: Gender, Generation, and Quality Television', *Continuum*, 29.2: 253–262

Garner. D. (2014) "S.N.L.' Memories and Getting-Some-Rest Dreams', 4 November, *New York Times*, accessed via http://www.nytimes.com/2014/11/05/books/book-review-amy-poehlers-yes-please.html

Gay, R. (2014a) *Bad Feminist: Essays*, New York: Harper

────── (2014b) 'Lena Dunham, a Generation's Gutsy Ambitious Voice', 24 September, *Time*, accessed via http://time.com/3425759/lena-dunham-a-generations-gutsy-ambitious-voice/

────── (2014c) 'Emma Watson? Jennifer Lawrence? These Aren't the Feminists You Are Looking For', 10 October, *The Guardian*, http://www.theguardian.com/commentisfree/2014/oct/10/-sp-jennifer-lawrence-emma-watson-feminists-celebrity

────── (2014d) 'Roxane Gay Talks to Lena Dunham About Her New Book, Feminism, and the Benefits of Being Criticized Online', 2 October, *Vulture*, accessed via http://www.vulture.com/2014/10/roxane-gay-interview-lena-dunham-bad-feminist-not-that-kind-of-girl-books.html

Girls (2012-) Television Series, HBO: USA, accessed via http://www.hbo.com/girls/about/index.html

Harris, A. (2004) *Future Girl: Young Women in the 21st Century*, London: Routledge

Hearn, A. & Schoenhoff, S. (2016) 'From Celebrity to Influencer: Tracing the Diffusion of Celebrity Value Across the Data Stream', in P.D. Marshall & S. Redmond eds. *A Companion to Celebrity*, London: Wiley Blackwell, pp. 194–211

Henry, A. (2004) *Not My Mother's Sister: Generational Conflict and Third Wave Feminism*, Bloomington: University of Indiana Press

Hogeland, L.M. (1998) *Feminism and Its Fictions: The Consciousness Raising Novel and the Women's Liberation Movement*, Philadelphia: University of Pennsylvania Press

Holmes, S. & Negra, D. eds (2011) *In the Limelight and Under the Microscope: Forms and Functions of Female Celebrity*, London: Continuum

Ingram, M. (2015) 'Lena Dunham: Actor Turned Media Mogul Signs Deal with Hearst', 27 October, *Fortune*, accessed via http://fortune.com/2015/10/27/lena-dunham-hearst/

Jane, E. (2014a) '"You're a Ugly, Whorish, Slut": Understanding E-bile', *Feminist Media Studies*, 14.4: 531–546

——— (2014b) 'Back to the Kitchen, Cunt': Speaking the Unspeakable About Online Misogyny, *Continuum*, 28.4: 558–570

Jenkins, H. (2006) *Convergence Culture: Where Old and New Media Collide*, New York: New York University Press

Jones, A. (2014) 'Lena Dunham, Not That Kind of Girl, Review: Roller-Coaster Memoir from the 'Voice of a Generation'', 22 September, *The Independent*, accessed via http://www.independent.co.uk/arts-entertainment/tv/features/lena-dunham-not-that-kind-of-girl-a-roller-coaster-tale-from-the-voice-of-a-generation-9747013.html

Kakutani, M. (2014) 'Hannah's Self-Aware Alter Ego Lena Dunham's Memoir-ish 'Not That Kind of Girl', 23 September, *New York Times*, accessed via http://www.nytimes.com/2014/09/24/books/lena-dunhams-memoir-ish-not-that-kind-of-girl.html?_r=0

Keller, J. (2015) 'Girl Power's Last Chance? Tavi Gevinson, Feminism and Popular Media Culture', *Continuum*, 29.2: 274–285

Khona, R. (2015) 'Leslie Knope's Most Feminist Moments', 21 April, *Huffington Post*, accessed via http://www.huffingtonpost.com/rachel-khona/leslie-knopes-most-feminist-moments_b_6709052.html

Koffman, O. & Gill, R. (2015) "The revolution will be led by a 12-year-old girl': girl power and global biopolitics', *Feminist Review*, 105: 83–102

Lauzen, M. (2014) 'The Funny Business of Being Tina Fey: Constructing a (Feminist) Comedy Icon', *Feminist Media Studies*, 14.1: 106–117

Lawrence, J. (2015) 'Why Do I Make Less Than My Male Co-stars', 14 October, *Lenny*, accessed via http://www.lennyletter.com/work/a147/jennifer-lawrence-why-do-i-make-less-than-my-male-costars/

Ledbetter, C. (2015) 'Lena Dunham Says "Twitter Really Wasn't a Safe Space for Me"', 29 September, *Huffington Post*, accessed via http://www.huffingtonpost.com.au/entry/lena-dunham-twitter-recode-interview_us_5609b3afe4b0af3706dd7df3?section=australia

Lee, K. (2014) 'Reading Celebrity Autobiographies', *Celebrity Studies*, 5.1–2: 87–89

Lejeune, P. (1989) *On Autobiography*, Minnesota: University of Minneapolis Press
Lewis, C. (2015) 'Sisterhood to Lena Dunham, Tina Fey & Co.: Shut up!', 10 August, *Macleans*, accessed via http://www.macleans.ca/culture/sisterhood-to-lena-dunham-tina-fey-co-shut-up/
Lewis, T. (2010) 'Branding, Celebritization and the Lifestyle Expert', *Cultural Studies*, 24.4: 580–598
Li, S. (2015) 'Lena Dunham Praises Jennifer Lawrence for Wage Gap Essay', 28 October, *Entertainment Weekly*, accessed via http://www.ew.com/article/2015/10/28/lena-dunham-jennifer-lawrence-hollywood-wage-gap-lenny
Littler, J. (2008) '"I Feel Your Pain": Cosmopolitan Charity and the Public Fashioning of the Celebrity Soul', *Celebrity Studies*, 18.2: 237–251
Lotz, A. (2001) 'Postfeminist Television Criticism: Rehabilitating Critical Terms and Identifying Postfeminist Attributes', *Feminist Media Studies*, 1.1: 105–121
Lovink, G. (2013) 'A World Beyond Facebook: Alternatives in Social Meda. The Research Agenda of the Unlike Us Network', *Mediascapes Journal*, 1: 58–64
McRobbie, A. (2009) *The Aftermath of Feminism*, London: Sage
—— (2015) 'Notes on the Perfect: Competitive Femininity in Neoliberal Times', *Australian Feminist Studies*, 30.83: 3–20
Marghitu, S. & Ng, C. (2013) 'Body Talk: Reconsidering the Post-feminist Discourse and Critical Reception of Lena Dunham's Girls', *Gender Forum*, 45
Marwick, A.E. (2016) 'You May Know Me from YouTube (Micro-)Celebrity in Social Media', in P.D. Marshall & S. Redmond eds. *A Companion to Celebrity*, London: Wiley Blackwell, pp. 333–350
Marwick, A. & boyd, d. (2011) 'To See and Be Seen: Celebrity Practice on Twitter', *Convergence*, 17.2: 139–158
Mizejewski, L. (2014) *Pretty/Funny: Women Comedians and Body Politics*, Austin: University of Texas Press
Moran, J. (2000) *Star Authors: Literary Celebrity in America*, London: Pluto
Muntean, N. & Petersen, A.H. (2009) 'Celebrity Twitter: Strategies of Intrusion and Disclosure in the Age of Technoculture', *M/C Journal*, 12.5, accessed via http://journal.media-culture.org.au/index.php/mcjournal/article/view/194
Murray, S. (2015) 'Charting the Digital Literary Sphere', *Contemporary Literature*, 56.2: 311–339
Nash, M. & Grant, R. (2015) 'Twenty-Something Girls v. Thirty-Something Sex And The City Women', *Feminist Media Studies*, 15.6: 976–991
Negra, D. (2014) 'Claiming Feminism: Commentary, Autobiography and Advice Literature for Women in the Recession', *Journal of Gender Studies*, 23.3: 275–286
Nelson, E.M. (2014) 'Embracing the Awkwardness of Auteurship in Girls', in B. Kaklamanidou & M. Tally eds. *HBO's Girls: Questions of Gender, Politics, and Millenial Angst*, Newcastle Upon Tyne: Cambridge Scholars Press, pp. 91–107

Parks and Recreation (2009–2015) Television Series. NBC: USA
Patterson, E. (2012) 'Fracturing Tina Fey: A Critical Analysis of Postfeminist Television Comedy Stardom', *The Communication Review*, 15.3: 232–251
Petersen, A. (2015) 'Lena Dunham Is Launching a Newsletter for Young Women', 14 July, *Buzzfeed*, accessed via http://www.buzzfeed.com/annehelen-petersen/lena-dunham-lenny?bftw&utm_term=.ggdG7bMgv#.uxLrvyNQD
Peterson, T. (2015) 'Lena Dunham's Newsletter Lenny Gets a Site, Ads from Hearst', 27 October, *AdAge*, accessed via http://adage.com/article/media/lena-dunham-s-newsletter-lenny-a-site-ads-hearst/301081/
Piepmeier, A. (2009) *Girl Zines: Making Media, Doing Feminism*, New York: New York University Press
Pitt, A. (2013) 'Parks and Recreation's Amy Poehler on NYC, her costars and more', 9 July, *Time Out*, accessed via https://www.timeout.com/newyork/things-to-do/parks-and-recreations-amy-poehler-on-nyc-her-costars-and-more
'Planned Parenthood Joins Lena Dunham Book Tour in Nine Cities' (2014) press release, accessed via https://www.plannedparenthood.org/about-us/newsroom/press-releases/planned-parenthood-joins-lena-dunham-book-tour-in-nine-cities#sthash.3ww6smj2.dpuf
Poehler, A. (2014a) *Yes Please*, London: Picador
—— (2014b) *Ask Amy* (YouTube Channel), accessed via https://www.youtube.com/playlist?list=PL0F5894A2EBEA8BA0
Redmond, S. (2008) 'Pieces of Me: Celebrity Confessional Carnality', *Social Semiotics*, 18.2: 149–161
Rentschler, C.A. (2014) 'Rape Culture and the Feminist Politics of Social Media', *Girlhood Studies*, 7.1: 65–82
Rich, A. (1976) *Of Woman Born: Motherhood As Experience and Institution*, London: Virago
Rodrigues, S. (2014) "Yes Please' Is White Liberal Feminism in Full Force', *PopMatters*, 9 December, accessed via http://www.popmatters.com/column/188928-yes-please-is-white-liberal-feminism-in-full-force/
Rodriguez, M. (2014) "3 Times Amy Poehler Said Yes to Feminism in Her Memoir, and We're on Board, Naturally', 7 November, *Bustle*, accessed via http://www.bustle.com/articles/47745-3-times-amy-poehler-said-yes-please-to-feminism-in-her-memoir-and-were-on-board
Rojek, C. (2001) *Celebrity*, London: Reaktion
—— (2011) *Fame Attack*, London: Bloomsbury
Sandberg, B.E. (2014) 'Legendary Acquires Amy Poehler's Smart Girls Online Community', 13 October, *Hollywood Reporter, accessed via* .http://www.hollywoodreporter.com/news/legendary-acquires-amy-poehlers-smart-740426
Shaw, A. (2014) 'The Internet Is Full of Jerks, Because the World Is Full of Jerks: What Feminist Theory Teaches Us About the Internet', *Communication and Critical/Cultural Studies*, 11.3: 273–277

Smith, S. & Watson, J. (2010, 2nd ed) *Reading Autobiography: A Guide for Interpreting Life Writing*, Minneapolis: University of Minnesota Press

Stampler, L. (2014) 'Lena Dunham Is Posting Pictures of Celebrities in Her Planned Parenthood Shirt', 30 October, *Time Magazine*, accessed via http://time.com/3548041/lena-dunham-planned-parenthood/

Taylor, A. (2008) *Mediating Australian Feminism: Rereading the First Stone Media Event*, Oxford: Peter Lang

—————— (2009) 'Dear Daughter: Popular Feminism, the Epistolary Form and the Limits of Generational Rhetoric', *Australian Literary Studies*, 24(3–4): 96–107

Thelandersson, F. (2014) 'A Less Toxic Feminism: Can the Internet Solve the Age Old Question of How to Put Intersectional Theory into Practice?', *Feminist Media Studies*, 14.3: 527–530

Tolentino, J. (2014) 'The Right to a Sexual Narrative: On the Lena Dunham Abuse Claims', 11 April, *Jezebel*, accessed via http://jezebel.com/the-right-to-a-sexual-narrative-on-the-lena-dunham-abu-1654187731

Tsaliki, L. (2016) '"Tweeting the Good Causes": Social Networking and Celebrity Activism', in P.D. Marshall & S. Redmond eds. *A Companion to Celebrity*, London: Wiley Blackwell, pp. 235–257

Turner, G. (2010) *Ordinary People in the Media: The Demotic Turn*, London: Sage

—————— (2014) *Understanding Celebrity*, London: Wiley Blackwell, pp. 235–257

—————— (2016a) *Re-inventing the Media*, London: Routledge

—————— (2016b) 'Celebrity, Participation, and the Public', in P.D. Marshall & S. Redmond eds. *A Companion to Celebrity*, London: Wiley Blackwell, pp. 83–97

Usher, B. (2015) 'Twitter and the Celebrity Interview', *Celebrity Studies*, 6.3: 306–321

van Dijick (2013) *The Culture of Connectivity: A Critical History of Social Media*, Oxford: Oxford University Press

Ward, M. (2015) 'Lena Dunham Says She Quit Twitter Following "Verbal Abuse"', 30 September, *Sydney Morning Herald*, accessed via http://www.smh.com.au/lifestyle/celebrity/lena-dunham-says-she-quit-twitter-following-verbal-abuse-20150929-gjxput.html#ixzz3pHWYXCb6

Wearing, S. (2007) 'Subjects of Rejuvenation: Aging in Postfeminist Culture', in Y. Tasker & D. Negra eds. *Interrogating Postfeminism*, Durham: Duke University Press, pp. 277–310

Wicke, J. (1994) 'Celebrity Material: Materialist Feminism and the Culture of Celebrity', *South Atlantic Quarterly*, 93.4: 751–778

Winch, A. (2012) *Girlfriends and Postfeminist Sisterhood*, Basingstoke: Palgrave Macmillan

Wolcott, J. (2014) 'Callow, Grating, and Glib: The First-Person Fodder of Lena Dunham Inc.', *New Republic*, accessed via https://newrepublic.com/article/120027/not-kind-girl-review-lena-dunhams-callow-grating-memoir

Women of the Hour, accessed via https://www.buzzfeed.com/womenofthehour

Woods, F. (2015) 'Girls Talk: Authorship and Authenticity in the Reception of Lena Dunham's Girls', *Critical Studies in Television*, 10.2: 37–54

Yellin, H. (2015) "A Literary Phenomenon of the Non-literate': Classed Cultural Value, Agency and Techniques of Self-Representation in the Ghostwritten Reality TV Star Memoir', *Celebrity Studies*, DOI: 10.1080/19392397.2015.1117392

York, L. (2007) *Literary Celebrity in Canada*, Toronto: University of Toronto Press

Young, S. (1997) *Changing the Wor(l)d: Discourse, Politics and the Feminist Movement*, London: Routledge

CHAPTER 9

Conclusion: The Future of Celebrity Feminism—Contemporary Celebrity Culture, the Blockbuster, and Feminist Star Studies

INTRODUCTION

In the contemporary context, Wicke's (1994, p. 758) comments—that 'the energies of the celebrity imaginary are fueling feminist discourse and political activity as never before'—are even more salient than when they were initially made. Here, therefore, I am going to engage with some other ways in which feminists are now being celebrified, and especially ask whether these new ways of authorizing feminists work to ameliorate some of the limitations identified in the previous chapters, or whether—as I suspect—they raise a series of other concerns that need to be addressed. To do so, here I home in on two significant recent shifts impacting how feminism comes to publicly mean: the increased prevalence of celebrities publicly adopting a feminist identity; and the development of internet, participatory, or convergence culture and the so-called democratization of celebrity. Both phenomena reveal shifts in terms of representation and public self-representation that have specific ramifications for feminism, however we may figure it in the twenty-first century.

Following previous work undertaken with Hannah Hamad (2015), here I consider feminism and celebrity culture more broadly, focusing on 2014 and 2015 in particular, when many celebrities very publicly claimed a feminist identity, prompting debate about what constitutes feminism and who gets to speak on its behalf—questions that celebrity feminism, and indeed feminism more broadly, has always provoked. Though superstars such as Beyoncé, unlike blockbuster celebrity feminists, have not achieved celebrity on the grounds of their feminism, they—representing as they do new ways of publicly embodying feminism (Weidhause 2015)—provide an opportunity to broaden our understanding of the complicated relationship between celebrity and feminism. However, questions provoked by such identifications include: Are figures like Emma Watson, through publicly staged associations with feminism, the new voices working to shape the identity of modern feminism, in the way I argue blockbuster authors have always done? And if so, what does feminism come to mean in and through them? Here I will also be further exploring how new media may impact upon the type of women we may see being authorized to speak for/about feminism (themselves by no means the same thing). Finally, after addressing whether the historically central role of the blockbuster, in terms of producing and sustaining celebrity feminism, will continue into the future, I conclude by considering how empirical research into the uses of celebrity feminism may work to extend the kinds of analysis I have offered here. To begin, I discuss the boom in celebrity identification with feminism in a representational landscape often characterized as 'postfeminist'.

***

As Hannah Hamad and I (2015, p. 124) recently observed in a special *Celebrity Studies* Forum section on 'Feminism and Celebrity Culture':

> Media culture in 2014 was littered with touchstone moments that saw some of the highest profile female celebrities, as well as many male celebrities, openly identify as feminist. This could be seen in declarations that ranged from those carefully orchestrated to garner high-profile publicity, to others that were more responsive to unforeseen events or reactive to what was fast becoming a celebrity zeitgeist.

In this vein, on 19 December 2014, the *Ms.* Foundation, in conjunction with *Cosmopolitan*, announced their list of the 'top ten feminist celebrities of 2014'. Emma Watson (known for her portrayal of proto-feminist school girl, Hermione Granger, in the *Harry Potter* film franchise and, more recently, as the UN Women Goodwill Ambassador) topped the list, which featured other prominent defenders of women's rights, including Tina Fey, Meryl Streep, Beyoncé, and Laverne Cox. These are all women who have used their celebrity capital, the platform they have from which to speak authoritatively, to raise awareness about ongoing gendered inequalities. The list was reportedly initiated to 'highlight the resurgence of support for the word "feminist"'. The press release featured the following quotation from the Foundation's President and CEO, Teresa Younger: 'We celebrate all feminists every day, but today we're giving a hat tip to celebrities who are helping to promote women's equality. Every celebrity on the list has either embraced the term "feminist," spoken out for women's equal rights or battled against sexist oppression' (in Aran 2014). It is significant that feminism, once again, becomes conflated with the quest for 'equality'.

Rather than the contempt for celebrity culture articulated by some second wave activists, this list and the following justification of it reveals a fundamental shift in the way in which the feminism–renown nexus is being figured in the twenty-first century: 'Celebrities who embrace feminism or speak out for women's equality are helping to spread the word and build support for women's rights. With this survey, we're expanding the conversation about women's empowerment to even more people' (Younger in Aran 2014). Younger's comments here invoke the consciousness-raising potentialities of celebrities who publicly and unashamedly take up a feminist subject position. In a representational landscape where feminism is often disavowed, being conceptualized as victim of its own success (Gill 2007; McRobbie 2009; Negra 2009; Taylor 2012), alongside the 'I'm not a feminist but' propensity among young women in the 1990s and 2000s (Scharff 2011), such explicit identifications arguably have great political and symbolic import. Moreover, they can help shape how audiences respond to feminism itself, and transform understandings of what remains a heavily loaded term in the popular imaginary. However, the hierarchical nature of such a list, which deems Emma Watson the number one celebrity feminist, was seen to render it less than unproductive, shifting the focus as it necessarily does from other kinds of feminisms, including in the celebrity sphere (Aran 2014).

As Drake and Miah argue (2010, p. 56), 'The prominence of celebrity in media representations raises questions of the symbolic power of celebrity culture in defining our sense of cultural identities—what we think of as glamorous, for instance, or fashionable, or cool, or sexy.' This seems to be with the case with feminism, which appears to be both 'fashionable' and 'cool' among stars (male and female alike), with celebrities more often than not expected to defend their disidentification, as if association with feminism has been totally normalized. These performative utterances, where such celebrities effectively bring themselves into being as feminist by publicly naming themselves so (Butler 1990), have been occurring relatively regularly over the past year or so in the Western mediasphere. Perhaps the most well-known example is Beyoncé's proclamation, during the 2014

Video Music Awards (VMAs), where the word 'feminist' appeared quite literally in neon lights, during her performance of the song 'Flawless' (see Valenti 2014a; Weidhause 2015). In the context of celebrity identifications, as in others, 'what feminism actually means varies, literally, from one self-declared feminist to the next' (McRobbie 2009, p. 2). As McRobbie continues, such indeterminacy or variability in terms of feminist principles and practices 'does not reduce its field of potential influence, quite the opposite'. However, such potential is managed and contained in ever more complicated ways, as McRobbie's work makes clear.

There has been intense public debate about these self-identifications and, conversely, disavowals, by celebrities. In terms of those who came to publicly associate themselves with feminism throughout 2014, media response to them 'reveal[ed] little or no consensus on feminism among celebrities (what it is, what it should be, what is at stake for celebrities in self-identifying as feminists or not), and some reveal standpoints on feminism more reminiscent of the individualist, apolitical or backlash discourses of millennial postfeminism' (Hamad and Taylor 2015, p. 125). That is, these public endorsements are rarely left to stand uncontested and 'opinions on the feminist political efficacy of these celebrity self-outings have—unsurprisingly—been divided' (Hamad and Taylor 2015, p. 125), further illustrating that it is within the mediasphere, including online, that discursive struggles over the meanings of contemporary feminism are predominantly being conducted. Critique of the celebrity articulation of feminist positions has been extensive, further revealing that it was not only during the peak of the women's movement that celebrity and feminism were seen to be uneasy associates.

Those who choose to intervene politically in debates around what a feminist subjectivity might now look and *feel* like often have to endure intense scrutiny, especially from within the feminist blogosphere: 'Nearly every time it happens, a fierce debate ensues among the online commentariat over whether or not the celebrity lives up to feminist ideals and politics' (Cobb 2015, p. 136). These judgements, as Cobb persuasively argues, are deeply gendered, given that male celebrity self-identification is routinely celebrated while women's is questioned.[1] Nevertheless, while this focus on whether celebrities identify with feminism is limited (see Banet-Weiser 2015), it is worth attempting to come to terms with what might be driving these escalating public endorsements, and how they might be working to shape popular debates about feminism and its efficacy.

The growth of celebrity culture more broadly, as well as the affordances of new media, have been seen as central to this intensification of celebrity intervention into public debate around feminism: 'media interest in celebrities, and celebrities' interest in utilizing the extensive digital media platforms afforded by their fame, ensures that celebrities take a high profile in setting the public agenda of feminist debate' (Brady 2016, p. 6). However, while otherwise astute, such a comment downplays the way in which celebrity feminists have always 'set the agenda', in terms of mediating how feminism comes to mean in the popular imaginary. Nonetheless, celebrities whose fame comes from something other than their feminism (as opposed to the celebrity feminists I focus on) are undoubtedly active in these public conversations in ways they have not been historically, and certainly not in such numbers.

These public proclamations of feminist identity are most remarkable in that they emerge from a context that some have dubbed 'post-identity' (McNay 2010), where the instability and indeterminacy of identity calls into question a stable, unified political subject of social movements like feminism. Others, such as Wendy Brown (1995), have questioned the 'wounded attachments' and *ressentiment* upon which identity politics are built. Despite such critiques, what I call feminist border policing (see also Simic 2010) is now most evident around the figure of the celebrity who publicly pronounces an affiliation with feminism. These women, like their blockbuster counterparts, appear to be intensely anxiety-provoking figures, revealing both a discomfort with opinionated women in the public sphere and concerns about the 'discursive power' (Marshall 1997) embodied by these female celebrity figures. Accordingly, to mitigate such power, they are subject to attempts to manage and regulate them, including from other women (and even other feminists).

These kinds of popular feminist articulations have been routinely dismissed on the grounds of their subject's privilege; the following is indicative of such a position: 'pop star feminist celebrities like Beyoncé and Swift may do more harm than good ...' (Hopkins 2016). However, as I have argued of blockbuster feminism, we need a more nuanced approach to these increasingly common gestures of feminist affiliation than reproach. In this regard, I concur with Anita Brady, who has recently argued that:

> the value of celebrity feminism might be precisely in the inability of feminists to agree on which celebrity feminists are hurting or hindering "feminism". It is the demonstration and production of this permanent contingency with

regard to who gets to count as a legitimate feminist that I would argue is the substance, and the *work*, of celebrity feminism. (2016, p. 10, original emphasis)

In Brady's reading, it is this contingency that renders celebrity feminism most generative. Given, then, that the 'imposition of definitional closure', in terms of feminism, can itself be seen as 'an inevitably reductionist and exclusionary act' (Taylor 2008, p. 172), as can the presumption of a singular, privileged form of feminist identity, celebrity feminism may allow us to view such boundaries as productively porous rather than as fixed, constraining certainties. Moreover, given that celebrity culture can now be seen as an 'essential component of public debate about the issues that require public resolution', including those around women's position in Western culture, it is impossible to simply dismiss celebrities as 'external to the world of public issues' (Couldry and Markham 2007, p. 404). That is, we should not be surprised about this intensified celebrity involvement in what we can broadly designate the field of feminist politics, and arguably we can expect it to escalate even further. So, what kinds of feminism are these celebrities investing in and working to promote?

As I have argued, much scholarly work on the ways in which feminism is represented in and through mainstream media culture has underscored that liberal feminism (Douglas 1994; Dow 1996; Henderson 2006)—as the least disruptive to the status quo—is the form most commonly endorsed (or at least not as derided as its more radical counterparts). In this way, these celebrity testimonials regarding feminism's continuing validity/necessity are entirely consistent with the dominant way of figuring feminism in the mainstream mediasphere, and they—most problematically—reinscribe its elisions. Emma Watson's comments (below) exemplify the tendency in media engagements with feminism, dating back at least to Friedan and *The Feminine Mystique*, whereby it comes to be reduced to the search for reformist policies that will help effect gender 'equality'. She tells those who are unclear: 'For the record, feminism by definition is: "The belief that men and women should have equal rights and opportunities. It is the theory of the political, economic and social equality of the sexes"' (Watson 2014). Given that, popularly, she has been embraced as—in *Elle*'s terms—the 'fresh face of feminism' (Keller and Ringrose 2015), Watson's speech and the extensive public response that followed are worth some brief consideration here.

Hermione Does Feminism

Harry Potter star Emma Watson was appointed UN Women Goodwill Ambassador in July 2014. The HeforShe campaign, dubbed 'a solidarity movement for gender equality', was spearheaded by Watson and launched during her speech at the UN headquarters in New York on 20 September 2014. The speech, which went viral and was described by *Vanity Fair* (among others) as 'game-changing' (George 2014), received extensive media coverage, as well as endorsement from other celebrities via social media platforms such as Twitter. In particular, its message—which was by no means innovative or original: feminism is not a dirty word, and men need to get on board—precipitated public debate, to a large extent online, about the role of celebrity in feminist politics, and especially about privilege. As Michelle Smith (2014) notes:

> the ability of a white, privileged celebrity to act as a spokesperson for women's rights on a global scale is immensely fraught … The voices of women who lack the privilege of a wealthy, white woman like Watson—those who suffer most at the hands of gender inequality—have not been given the same platform or the same global attention. (see also Mackenzie 2015)

Such critiques have been common, and Watson herself is self-reflexive on this point about feminist authority:

> You might be thinking who is this Harry Potter girl? And what is she doing up on stage at the UN? It's a good question and trust me, I have been asking myself the same thing. I don't know if I am qualified to be here. All I know is that I care about this problem. And I want to make it better. (Watson 2014)

Here, Watson positions herself as an 'ameliorative actor', moved to act compassionately in light of the state's failure to do so and, in line with neoliberal imperatives, further shift the redemptive focus from government policy and legislative solutions to individuals and corporations (Berlant 2004; Furqua 2011). Although it has been her seeming lack of awareness about her own privilege that appears most irksome to feminists, Watson has also expressed some anxiety over her authority to speak in other spaces, including Twitter where she responded to a question, through #AskEmma, about the whiteness of her feminism: 'I want as many people as possible to feel seen, heard and included in this movement' (9 October 2015).[2]

However, despite this professed desire for inclusiveness, ongoing criticism of Watson, especially online, reveals that celebrity feminism continues to be dismissed, as emphasized here throughout, in favour of some form of 'authentic' feminism beyond its boundaries (Wicke 1994; Brunsdon 1997).[3] Whatever we may think of her politics, her adoption of a feminist identity may encourage other young women (and audiences more widely) to rethink their perceptions of what feminism is or, perhaps more importantly, to negotiate with her way of embodying feminism and creatively develop their own in response (Ringrose and Kellner 2015). That said, the exclusions of Watson's brand of feminism are indeed troublesome in terms of race, class, gender, and sexuality, so perhaps we should not be surprised—or even be buoyed up by the fact—that its elisions have prompted intense debate about the ongoing exclusions of dominant ways of figuring feminism.[4] Another recent incident that, in both the mainstream media and the feminist blogosphere, many framed as indicative of the inevitable limitations of the collision of celebrity and feminism was Patricia Arquette's 2015 Oscars speech.

THE 'WRONG' KIND OF FEMINIST?

Patricia Arquette's speech at the 2015 Oscars, after she won the Best Supporting Actress Academy Award for her role in *Boyhood*, generated intense debate about what feminism is and could be in the twenty-first century. In her acceptance speech, she sought to draw attention to persistent gendered inequalities, expressing gratitude 'to every woman who gave birth, to every tax payer and citizen of this nation we have fought for everybody else's equal rights, it's our time, to have wage equality once and for all, and equal rights for women in the United States of America' (Arquette 2015).[5] Many viewed the comment as offensive, especially in terms of its assumption that white women have been left behind in social movements seeking equality; debate on social media especially was intense, with celebrity feminists like Roxane Gay tweeting: 'The idea that queers & POC have had their time in the struggle spotlight long enough. Eek. Ma'am. Congrats on yr Oscar tho. You are talented' (22 February 2015). Feminist online sites, as well as mainstream newspapers, were preoccupied with what Arquette's comments revealed about the limits of celebrity feminism.

Commentators viewed the incident as evidence of the kind of 'oversimplified feminist messages' that come to circulate 'when we'—implicitly those charged with policing feminism's borders – '*allow* celebrities to become spokespeople for feminism' (Kilpatrick 2015, emphasis added). In 'The Trouble with Celebrity Feminism' (2015), Aya de Leon, writing for feminist site *bitch*, questioned the class and racial privilege of the women publicly speaking on feminism's behalf, and used the incident to mount a wider critique of celebrity feminism itself: 'Our celebrity culture highlights and celebrates pop stars when they dare to talk about feminism, sometimes to the detriment to activists who have actually committed their lives to building feminist movements.' Although de Leon makes a number of important points, she reinscribes the opposition between 'real', activist feminism versus a popular or celebrity version, which has long been deployed (including in the case of blockbuster authors) to discredit the latter, arguing that celebrities fail to offer 'fleshed-out political platforms', or undergo 'movement or leadership training or education' in the way movement leaders supposedly do. Here, there is the presumption that celebrity feminists do not have the cultural competence or authority to speak on feminism's behalf, lacking the appropriate background, politics, or skills to make adequate political interventions. For this commentator, there is a correct way of publicly 'doing' feminism, at which celebrities invariably fail; such sentiments are common (McDonald 2015), including from blockbuster celebrity feminists.

In 'Emma Watson? Jennifer Lawrence? These Aren't the Feminists You Are Looking For', published in *The Guardian*, Roxane Gay (2014c) also took feminist celebrities to task, similarly invoking an opposition between 'real' feminist work and the superficial pro-equality utterings of a handful of (predominantly) Hollywood stars: 'There is nothing wrong with celebrities (or men) claiming feminism and talking about feminism … We run into trouble, though, when we celebrate celebrity feminism while avoiding the actual work of feminism.' Here, reminiscent of the contempt for celebrity feminism articulated by hooks (1994), for Gay 'celebrity feminism' is necessarily the derided second term in the recalcitrant authentic/celebrity feminism binary. Given her own thorough implication in the circuits of fame (though, as a feminist who has been celebrified, her celebrity is of a different tenor to that of the women she criticizes), such comments are somewhat disingenuous and represent the kind of border policing she purports to decry through her own 'bad feminist' subjectivity. She concludes by figuring celebrity feminism a mere distraction: 'So long as we continue to stare into the glittery light of the latest celebrity feminist, we avoid looking at the very real inequities that women throughout the world continue to face.' As Marwick and boyd argue, 'for something to be deemed authentic, something else must be inauthentic' (2011, p. 124); in Gay's critique of celebrity feminism, she implicitly embodies the former. This is especially significant, as in *Bad Feminist* she actually takes issue with the idea that 'there are right and wrong ways to be a feminist' and remarks that some women unfairly endure 'consequences for doing feminism wrong' (Gay 2014a, p. 304).

These public disagreements over what it means to be a feminist, as if there were a singular, privileged 'model', and more overtly staged, spectacularized battles between celebrities such as Annie Lennox and Beyoncé (Weidhause 2015) or Sinead O'Connor and Miley Cyrus, are indicative of the persistent idea that celebrity feminism 'is at odds with the aims and strategies of the feminist movement' (Brady 2016, p. 2). Such a notion is problematic, not least because it presumes that feminists are unified and that feminism has 'a clear agenda and boundaries' (Keller 2012, p. 433). For the critics considered above, as well as some feminist scholars, celebrity association with feminism is the ultimate manifestation of 'faux feminism' (McRobbie 2009), which merely packages it in a neat, commodified form. These critiques, too, tend to homogenize celebrities who identify with feminism, collapsing often diverse political positions and obscuring the work of women like star of *Orange is the New Black* and trans activist Laverne Cox (Romano 2014), as well as singer-songwriter Beyoncé, in challenging the privileged, often white and cis-gendered feminism that dominates mainstream media (Weidhause 2015). Given the variety of feminism offered by stars, as by women in general (Keller 2016; Schraff 2011), it is more apt to speak of celebrity *feminisms* (while some, of course, become more visible than others). To return to Gay's assessment, though, feminism being espoused by those under 'glittery lights' in itself is not the issue, the problem is the limited, often liberal, version embodied by such figures. That is, as with blockbuster celebrity feminism, we can identify the limitations of their politics without seeing these limitations as an unavoidable consequence of the celebritization of feminism (Wicke 1994). As Wicke suggests, feminism does not stand 'on an exalted moral or political, or even theoretical, plane', in a 'privileged autonomous space' exempt from celebrity culture: 'stigmatizing it or prematurely moralizing over it ignores its reality and its political potential' (1994, p. 754). Adding another layer of complexity to these debates, co-existing with celebrities who do identify with feminism are those who refuse to associate themselves with it in any form.

CELEBRITY DISSIDENTS: FEMINIST DISIDENTIFICATION IN THE MEDIASPHERE

As Jessica Valenti (2014b) observed in *The Guardian*: 'Feminists are everywhere these days. Beyoncé performed in front of the f-word in towering lights, feminism is being celebrated on magazine covers the world over, and every young female celebrity gets put through the "are you or aren't you" feminist bona fides test.'[6] In such an environment, feminism is often dismissed as having done its work, as having been thoroughly incorporated into public culture; while this is commonly seen to constitute our contemporary postfeminist representational environment, Jo Reger (2012, p. 4) dubs this 'nowhere-everywhere feminism': 'Just as contemporary feminists exist in a time when they are told that feminism is nowhere [as she suggests, most evident in proclamations that it is "dead"], they also live in a time where feminism is everywhere.' And celebrity culture is by no means immune from this duality; for some, self-identification is confidently proclaimed to be unnecessary due to the diffusion of feminist ways of comprehending social relations throughout all forms of public discourse and relevant institutional spaces.

Binary oppositions have always been mobilized in media coverage of feminism, with different groups of women pitted against each other, usually through the ubiquitous trope of the 'cat fight' (Douglas 1994): mothers versus daughters, liberals versus radicals, anti-sex versus pro-sex, activists versus academics, and so on. The opposition between celebrities who do and do not explicitly identify with feminism is the latest manifestation of this prolonged discursive trend. For some, the 'f-word' is still a signifier that may damage a celebrity's brand. However, as Shelley Budgeon notes, 'Non-identification may display a refusal to be fixed into place as a feminist, but may also be a sign of the inability to position oneself as feminist because of confusing and contradictory messages about what feminism really is' (2001, p. 23). It is, nevertheless, significant that female celebrities are being expected to justify their lack of identification with feminism, and that this in itself is newsworthy. For example, in addition to regular news stories on individual celebrity hostility towards feminism, in December 2013 the *Huffington Post* featured an article titled '10 Celebrities Who Say They Aren't Feminists' (17 December), including Katy Perry, Lady Gaga, Madonna, and Kelly Clarkson, while Shailene Woodley, Geri Halliwell, and Kaley Cucuo all received extensive media coverage in 2014 for their refusal to identify as feminist.

It is common for such women to 'conflate feminism with misandry' (Hamad and Taylor 2015, p. 125) or, as is the case with *Big Bang Theory* star Cucuo, to reject it on the grounds that it supposedly exists in opposition to femininity, and the traditional gendered position she chooses to adopt in her marriage, from which she professes to receive so much pleasure (Saad 2015). Even in such disavowals, then, these celebrities are working to circulate certain understandings of feminism—whether audiences take them up is another question. These celebrity disavowals substantiate the claim that, when it comes to feminism, the postfeminist context is peppered with 'utterances of forceful non-identity' (McRobbie 2004, p. 257) but—as argued earlier—such denunciations exist simultaneously alongside, and are arguably outnumbered by, passionate expressions about feminism's continuing efficacy and viability as an identity. It appears that feminism has become a key addition to the celebrity brand, and that those who fail to make such an addition are regularly judged harshly—though so are its proponents. As the above discussion makes clear, the intersections of celebrity culture and feminism are now 'myriad, complicated and contradictory' (Hamad and Taylor 2015, p. 125). In addition to the charged celebrity identifications and dismissals by women discussed above, there are other developments that may require us to rethink the celebrity–feminism relationship as a key site through which feminism is accessed: the appearance of so-called micro-celebrities and the participation of 'ordinary people' (Turner 2010) in the blogosphere and various forms of connective media.

'Fourth wave' Feminism: Online Activism and Celebrity Democratized?

Social media, as the chapters in Part II have suggested, have come to represent a site where diverse feminist voices can contribute to public debates and contests over the meanings of feminism (in its past, present, and future imaginings). Feminism, as Valenti (2015) argues, is now more accessible than ever. She suggests that, rather than having to seek out a feminist organization or enrolling in a women's studies class—or indeed consuming a blockbuster—'Now women stumble across feminism while they're on Tumblr or Facebook, reading about everything from politics to pop culture, and have the ability to learn more in just a few clicks.' Valenti's comments neatly encapsulate the role of digital media in making feminism accessible in ways it may not have been previously (although she elides the e-misogyny of which I have previously spoken).

Increased internet activism, and social media-based campaigns commonly, following Twitter, labelled 'hashtag feminism', are often seen to mark a resurgence of feminism that has, not unproblematically, been dubbed the 'fourth wave'. On *Bustle*, Kristin Sollee (2015) identifies six constitutive elements of fourth wave feminism: it is queer; sex-positive; trans inclusive; anti-misandrist; body positive; and, finally, it is digitally driven. Significantly, however, contra these designations of a new 'wave', Keller found that the feminist girl bloggers she interviewed understood their 'feminist identities in more fluid ways' and did not seek to effect a pronounced break from their predecessors (2016, p. 115), and the women I have discussed, such as Lena Dunham or Roxane Gay, similarly do not invoke the wave model to describe their discursive activism. So while I remain deeply sceptical of the deployment of the wave metaphor and its attendant generational metaphors to temporally differentiate online activism from earlier forms, the past few years do seem to have witnessed a shift in public contestations around the meanings of feminism, not least due to social media and the popularity of the blogosphere for the articulation and public performance of progressive politics. As Banet-Weiser (2015) describes, in recent years:

> feminist manifestos have crowded most media platforms, making a particular feminist subjectivity and its parent political commitments both hypervisible and normative within popular media. Instagram and Twitter hashtags like #girlboss, #nomakeupselfie, #maletears, misandry-oriented ironic tumblrs and blogs, and fashion sites like The Man Repeller have exploded within digital media.

As these comments make clear, different forms of feminism are pervasive in various online spaces.[7] Such activism, of course, is remarkable in a Western context otherwise deemed 'postfeminist', and much scholarship has focused on the feminist possibilities of digital media (Keller 2012, 2016; Shaw 2013; Casey 2015). There is no doubt that the capacity for feminists to speak, both to feminist publics and to wider audiences, and themselves engage in feminist media practices and creative labour, has increased due to new media technologies (Baer 2015, p. 2). However, as I have suggested, this is not a situation that can be uncritically celebrated, especially given that online participation is inevitably constrained by 'hierarchies of power that interweave offline and online contexts' (Page 2012, p. 192), including in terms of gender.

As the list with which I started this chapter suggests, feminism now appears to have a certain cachet—though so does a rebranded misogyny (Banet-Weiser 2015), especially online—something that must always act as a counterpoint to celebrations of feminism's more pronounced public presence. That is, this visibility should not imply that feminism is now allowed to stand uncontested or that it has simply become a commonsensical discourse immune to challenge. On the contrary, as shown here in my sections on Lena Dunham and Roxane Gay, feminists also experience vitriolic and misogynist attempts to silence them on social media (Jane 2014a, b), reaffirming that arguments about democratization must always be nuanced—not least when it comes to feminism. Nevertheless, feminists are using the same tools to speak back to online misogyny. In Australia, for example, in November 2015 a public campaign was launched to show solidarity for one of the country's most outspoken feminist advocates, journalist Clementine Ford. The #EndViolenceAgainstWomen campaign, launched by Australian journalist Kerry Sackville, sought to target the authors of misogynistic taunts received online by Ford. As Sackville told *Daily Life*, 'The campaign was born of reading through the messages on Clem's social media posts and I was horrified. There are men threatening to rape, maim and murder her ... I want these men to know that if you attack one of us, you attack all of us' (in Moran 2015). Such experiences are not uncommon for publicly visible feminists, especially for micro-celebrities like Ford, and Sackville's campaign sought to offer public support to Ford as well as to 'call out' such deeply troubling, misogynistic behaviour.

As Joshua Gamson (2011, p. 1067) notes, in an environment of increased participatory media, 'Alternative visions of celebrity are thriving, many of them more egalitarian than their predecessors.' Although at times their localized fame is translated into forms more reminiscent of traditional celebrity (Turner 2014), feminist micro-celebrities generally speak to a small, often self-contained audience, so, in addition to attempts to silence them outlined above, their capacity to inform or extend the meanings of feminism for a large audience in the way bestsellers and their authors patently still do is hampered in ways we cannot ignore. For some, the opportunities provided by new media enable us to sidestep an inequitable distribution of newspaper column or televisual space, allowing myriad voices to insert themselves into previously tightly controlled discursive spaces. And in many ways this is the case. Conversely, a number of media and cultural studies scholars (Hindman 2009; Turner 2010) have problematized the idea that increased access to and participation in various forms of media necessarily results in democratization. Turner (2006), for example, argues that the greater involvement of 'ordinary people' in the media should not be figured in terms of democratization but as a 'demotic turn'. In his rendering, the demotic turn does not necessarily result in the empowerment forecast by some critics.

Concurring with Turner's (2010, pp. 128–9) approach, and its challenge to the 'myth of digital optimism', I would argue that just because (some) feminists can access Twitter accounts or produce blogs, does not mean that all women are heard equally or even have unfettered access to high-speed broadband (Taylor 2011). And though, of course, the act of speaking publicly as a feminist (indeed as a woman) is significant in and of itself, one presumes that it is this potentiality for *being heard* that attracts politicized women to participate in various forms of social media—something that, despite more celebratory accounts, remains unevenly distributed (Turner 2010). Important political questions that need to be asked of new media include: 'Who gets to participate and on what terms? What are the implications of this participation? And what forms of privilege are necessary to be viewed as capable of participating at all?' (Hasinhoff 2014, p. 270). Moreover, within the Twitterverse, as in media more broadly, there is a star system operating and some voices always appear more 'equal' than others, as evidenced by measurements as basic as the number of followers one may accumulate on Twitter, how many times one may be 'retweeted', and whether online celebrity plays out in other contexts.

Has the celebrity zone, when it comes to feminism, thereby been democratized, as many 'digital optimists' would have it? Perhaps, in some respects; however the celebrity field remains fundamentally hierarchical (Rein et al. 1997), in this sub-category as much as in any other. As Sean Redmond reminds us, 'Celebrity culture is centrally involved in producing the illusion of greater democratization but in fact masks the truth that power remains in the hands of the select few' (2016, p. 80; see also Turner 2006). This is no less true in the zone of celebrity feminism, including in its 'micro' manifestations. That is, the more celebratory claims about new media's feminist potential can be seen—to appropriate Sara Ahmed's words—as 'a fantasy of inclusion that conceals its own exclusions' (2000, p. 4). Hence we must be mindful not to overstate claims about democratization, including when it comes to feminism. Nonetheless, given that commentators in other fields are also helping to craft the meanings of feminism in the current environment, for the remainder of this chapter I consider the future of the blockbuster and its potential for feminist celebrification, as well as possible research directions for feminist star studies.

BLOCKBUSTER CELEBRITY FEMINISM, NOW AND INTO THE FUTURE

What of the feminist blockbuster in the context of online feminisms, and in a representational environment in which the adoption of a feminist identity by celebrities has been entirely normalized? Is it still viable, as a form of feminist discourse and cultural product? Is feminist fame garnered from the publication of a bestselling work of non-fiction now possible in the same way it was pre- and during the women's liberation movement? Despite arguments about the 'death of the book' (and indeed the 'death of feminism') prevalent in the 1990s especially, the examples considered in the second part of this work suggest that demand for accessible feminist non-fiction remains strong. Indeed, the past decade or so has witnessed increased publisher, and reader, investment in popular feminist books. For example, other high-profile feminist non-fictional books published in the UK, the USA, and Australia in the past year include Rachel Hills' *The Sex Myth* (2015), Laurie Penny's *Unspeakable Things* (2015), Anne Marie Slaughter's *Unfinished Business* (2015), and Polly Vernon's *Hot Feminist* (2015). But is this still where women predominantly access feminism—through such popular literary texts—or is it through online newspaper columns, blogs, tweets, or Facebook pages, or indeed an amalgam of these?

Given that there are more examples of the blockbuster, and that feminism itself is not 'original' or 'novel' in the ways it may have been in the 1960s and 1970s, the potential for 'big books' purporting to represent modern feminism may have somewhat diminished (not to mention that there are now even more feminisms). Although at this point it is difficult to know for sure, arguably today's 'blockbuster' authors will not maintain decades-long visibility in the way that Brown, Friedan, and Greer have done—something which reveals much about feminism in its past, present, and future variants. That is, the cultural and affective power of the contemporary blockbuster cannot be considered commensurate with that of its antecedents. The reasons for this are over-determined, but it is worth sketching out a few key (at times overlapping) factors here that may impact the ability of contemporary feminist non-fiction to resonate in the same way as earlier books: the diffusion of feminism throughout Western media and popular culture as well as the recognition/articulation of many different feminisms; changes in the publishing industry as well as audiences' cultural tastes and preferences; a postfeminist representational environment wherein feminism has been perceived to have done its work; the expansion, including the so-called 'democratization', of celebrity culture; and, relatedly, the development of convergence culture.

These shifts notwithstanding, and in relation to the new media environment in particular, I would argue that it is not that bestselling works of feminist non-fiction have been superseded by online commentary or other new media discursive interventions, but that they are one nodal point in a much larger communicative network that includes (but is not limited to) forms such as social media. That is, celebrity feminism is a cross-media phenomenon (Negra 2014), of which the blockbuster is just one aspect, and it can both pre-date and follow the creation of an author's specific form of feminist 'brand' (as my chapter on Poehler and Dunham has suggested). Rather than supplanting blockbusters, then, new media, including online activism, work to augment blockbuster celebrity feminism in significant ways, including through their affordances in terms of self-branding.

The feminist blockbuster itself, therefore, continues to be commercially viable and to precipitate intense discursive contestations over the meanings of feminism, suggesting little diminution of its cultural and political significance. As I hope to have shown here, moreover, it is still possible to make the bestseller list on the back of a patently feminist work of non-fiction, a condition that speaks both to the commercial viability and perceived necessity of this form of cultural production. In addition, a public persona secured primarily on an author's feminist enunciative practice, via the blockbuster, continues to be possible (though of course some voices continue to be privileged over others). It is not just the contemporary blockbuster that is evidence of the persistence of this cultural form, however; all the books discussed in Part I remain in print and continue to culturally reverberate, as do their authors, not least because of the extensive labour they each put into their own persona-building (despite claims that this is a recent phenomenon in regard to feminists). Friedan and Brown retain the status of celebrity feminists, even post-mortem, while Greer remains a key feminist player in the mediasphere, though not without controversy. Furthermore, these blockbusters and their authors, along with those examined in Part II, reveal that (despite the 'wave' model) there has never been a singular feminism, nor a singular mode of performing celebrity feminism; instead, multiple, at times contradictory, feminisms have existed in and through them, revealing that this field is complicated and contested, and will undoubtedly continue to be into the future.

Generically, as is inevitable, the feminist blockbuster has not remained static. As the chapters in Part II of this book have made clear, the autobiographical 'I', and especially the confessional mode, have become even more pronounced than in the earlier forms I have studied. Though of course Brown, Friedan, and Greer, to varying extents, used personal 'authenticating anecdotes' (Pearce 2004) to help buttress their often polemical claims, their books are less easily generically categorized as 'memoirs' than those of Poehler, Dunham, Gay, and even Sandberg. Indeed, while I was writing this conclusion, Gloria Steinem's memoir, *My Life on the Road* (2015), was published, suggesting that narratives about the feminist past, as articulated through its most famous figures, continue to be highly marketable. Given that through celebrity culture we to seek to gain access to the authentic self that ostensibly lies beneath its public performances (however impossible this goal may be), does the blockbuster's narrative voice satisfy the intimacy and authenticity desired by audiences, or—when it comes to feminism—does telling personal tales, politicizing the personal, simply have the most potential to resonate? I could myself proffer a response to some of these questions, based on my own uses of feminist non-fiction books and the authors who signed them, but perhaps we need to look elsewhere to gain a better sense of why readers have invested, and indeed continue to invest, literally and affectively, in these books and these authors.

Throughout I have made claims about the cultural reverberations of these figures and their blockbusters. Future studies could engage in empirical work around how these voices have worked to shape 'real' women's perceptions of, and affective responses to, feminism; indeed, such work would respond to Turner's (2014) exhortation for celebrity studies to move beyond critical approaches predominantly concerned with the celebrity-as-text to more fully come to terms with the 'social function' of celebrity and the kinds of interventions it might make into the social (Bratich 2007). As Turner argues, 'while there is general agreement that celebrity contributes to the construction of cultural identities [including feminist ones], there is no agreement on exactly how that occurs, or to what effect' (2016a, p. 110). Given that the 'audience is central in sustaining the power of any celebrity sign' (Marshall 1997, p. 65), feminist star studies (in the dual sense I noted at the beginning) could also benefit from an engagement with audiences about the celebrities they believe to be noteworthy, or who help to shape their understandings of feminism.

Doing so, would necessarily impact the kinds of women chosen for analysis as well as the analysis itself.

In this regard, as Heather Mendick et al. (2015, p. 375) argue, 'taking everyday uses of celebrity as our starting point impacts which celebrities we study ... [and] can disrupt our settled ideas about what makes a public figure significant and to whom'.[8] Are blockbuster authors most resonant with audiences, or are celebrities such as Watson and Beyoncé the ones now helping to shape understandings of feminism? What types of feminist politics might celebrities facilitate, or conversely impede? How might women's own feminist media practices work to challenge the authority of these privileged voices? Along these lines, Jessica Ringrose and Jessalyn Keller (2015, p. 132) examined how girls respond to celebrities who identify as feminists, with their interviews pointing to the 'nuanced and complex ways in which young people are problematizing celebrity feminism'. They found that rather than simply uncritically adopting the kinds of feminism made possible by such figures, 'girls are intent on shaping their own debates, producing their own media, and negotiating the contradictions presented by celebrity feminism with a great deal of wit and sensitivity' (Ringrose and Keller 2015, p. 135). Given that, perhaps in addition to new media forums, young women now access feminism predominantly through these celebrity figures, we cannot simply dismiss the realm of celebrity outright as 'liberal feminism's vessel of choice' (Griffin 2015, p. 165). More such work, then, would add some texture to arguments, such as the one made here, about the ideological and cultural work being done by celebrity feminists—and indeed who they might be, from the audience perspective.

Similarly, while this study has not focused on reader and/or fan responses to these 'blockbusters' and their celebrity authors,[9] which can take the form of personal letters, letters to the editor, or more recently, Amazon or goodreads.com reviews, and other forms of online media such as blogs, there is potential for work that seeks to further tease out the affective investments that readers have made/are making in such texts and their authors, and the public responses they are driven to circulate as a result. For example, the Friedan and Greer archives both contain hundreds of letters from appreciative, largely women, readers; such letters, illuminating as they do just how deeply the books resonated with contemporary readers, are themselves worthy of extensive critical engagement. In terms of blogs and other forms of participatory media, what are so-called 'citizen critics' (Eberly 2000) making of these texts and their authors, and how are they publicly interacting with these feminisms? I have briefly provided some insight into these processes, especially in Chap. 6, where I discussed fan Twitter responses to Wolf's latest book as integral to her attempts to challenge her diminishing celebrity feminist capital, but a study that focused solely on reader engagement with these and other texts positioned as representative of modern feminism would also help to augment the kinds of claims I am making here about the reverberative power of these particular women. Who is consuming these blockbusters, and otherwise engaging with their authors and their feminisms? Are some readers eschewing the blockbuster altogether in favour of the seemingly more democratized, less privileged voices circulating via new media? It would also be valuable to explore the kinds of feminist publics, and indeed networked counter-publics (boyd 2013; Keller 2016), brought into being in and through these figures and their publications. Moreover, further consideration of the 'presumed intimacy' (Rojek 2015) said to have resulted from the social media reconfiguration of formerly parasocial celebrity/fan interactions would also help thicken this consideration of the social function of celebrity feminism, particularly in its authorial forms.

The latter raises a further point regarding the role of the celebrities who are accumulating this 'attention capital'. That is, there is a need for critics to further explore 'the perspectives of celebrities themselves', asking questions such as 'What are the qualities and characteristics of their lived experiences as celebrities?' and 'How do they see their own celebrity?' (Ferriss 2010, p. 394). Within the parameters of my chosen methodology I have attempted to flesh out answers to these questions, but, where possible, empirical work centring on the 'lived experiences' of these women qua celebrities would further work to destabilize the focus on either industry or audience discussed earlier (York 2013), perhaps illuminating why and how particular self-representational strategies have been deployed over others. Studies attending to celebrity feminism as *lived* would add another layer to our understanding of this complicated phenomenon.

It is also necessary to acknowledge that what I have been mapping are very specific Western forms of celebrity feminism and feminist identity building. There is, as noted, a need to maintain geographical differentiation (Ohlsson et al 2014) when it comes to attempts to come to terms with the impact of individual celebrities. As Olivier Driessens (2013, p. 643) argues, 'every culture or nation has its own heroes, stars and celebrities. Most people's fame does not reach beyond cultural or national boundaries, which makes celebrity culture essentially a plural and heterogeneous phenomenon.' Shifting the focus to other cultural contexts would undoubtedly complicate this picture of Anglo-American celebrity feminism, and more work on transnational celebrity feminism could also provide some insights into how shifting contexts of reception alter the forms of feminism that circulate in the wake of such books, and how celebrities operate in different contexts. Is the feminist blockbuster a key way of celebrifying women in other locations? If so, what kinds of feminisms are offered through such texts and authors? What is the key mode of feminist public subjectivity in Europe, Africa, or Asia? Has digital feminism produced micro-celebrities who are working to change the public conversations around feminism in these spaces? Work based on such questions would help further underline the cultural specificity of celebrity feminism.

As I have argued, there are now a number of ways in which feminism and celebrity can be seen to explicitly intersect—most obviously through feminists who have been celebrified and, more recently, through celebrities who come to identify as feminist at some stage during their career, and use their public persona to articulate political positions broadly consistent with feminism. There are, too, increasing numbers of 'ordinary' or 'micro'-celebrities who seek to intervene in these debates over the meanings of feminism through various forms of social media, garnering high public visibility and illustrating that the yoking of celebrity and feminism continues to evolve. Although markedly different, these modes of feminist celebrity help to shape the kinds of feminism circulating publicly—perhaps in different ways to their counterparts in the publishing sphere.

Despite this, it is still necessary, I would argue, to refuse the conflation of celebrities who choose to identify with feminism (*celebrity* feminists) and those who are famous *because* of their feminism and its public articulation (celebrity *feminists*).[10] This has nothing to do with authenticity or the feminist border policing that I have problematized here—it is simply to acknowledge those whose feminism follows their stardom and those whose fame is a product of their feminism, a point that has a bearing on their representations and self-representations, as well as on the kinds of affective investments audiences make in them and their feminisms. Maintaining this distinction, therefore, recognizes that the media—and consumers—have a different relation to these blockbuster celebrity feminists than to celebrities who come to identify as feminist. Both forms, however, contribute significantly to public understandings of feminism, and thereby require further critical interrogation.

Celebrity feminism, and the bestselling feminist non-fiction from which it has largely emerged, have both changed little and changed markedly since the first blockbuster studied here was published. Here I have shown that, despite now being augmented by various forms of new media, the feminist blockbuster remains a viable commodity, and still represents a key means through which particular forms of feminism come to circulate and, subsequently, come to be debated and contested. And it continues to act as an important vehicle in the process of feminist celebrification. As a form of 'performative practice', blockbuster celebrity feminism now seems to rely on even more media platforms. But it also appears to encompass various kinds of feminist activism and campaigning, through which celebrities work to establish their feminist credentials and secure their feminist 'brand'—itself not inevitably problematic. This does mean, however, that the terrain of celebrity feminism is becoming ever more complicated, requiring a nuanced critical vocabulary to help us come to terms with the ideological and cultural work it is doing. The intersections of feminism and contemporary culture only seem to be intensifying, in ways that we perhaps could not have imagined in the mid-twentieth century when the earlier blockbusters were produced. The 'celebrity zone', as Wicke (1994, p. 776) so persuasively argued a few decades ago, is one to which feminists must 'pay heed'; this zone, as my analysis has shown, is rapidly transforming, raising a number of political, critical, and practical issues that feminist media and cultural studies needs to address.

Notes

1. Some celebrity men have received much coverage on the basis of their public identification with feminism, including in magazines like *Marie Claire* (see Thorp 2015). Prominent male 'feminists' include Gordon Levitt, Matt McGlorry, and, more controversially, Aziz Ansari. Like their female counterparts, the feminism they espouse is more often than not the liberal variety, with 'equality' discourses being mobilized as the basis of their affiliation. See Ziesler (2014) and Cobb (2015) for critiques of the celebration of such figures.
2. Problematically, though, as Michelle Smith (2014) argues, even her delivery, so-called 'feminine appearance', and her heterosexuality were heavily scrutinized.

3. Indeed, within celebrity studies, Watson has not been subject to critical attention, despite audience investment in her and her feminism (Mendick et al. 2015, p. 375).
4. Most recently, in September 2015 Watson received intense criticism after provocatively suggesting 'some of the best feminists I have encountered are men' (in Day et al. 2015).
5. See: https://www.youtube.com/watch?v=6wx-Qh4Vczc
6. However, much of this commentary about the politics of celebrity identification with feminism, coming as it does from feminists such as Jessica Valenti in her regular *Guardian* columns, reveals the extent to which feminists are not simply 'misrepresented' but actually have become the media. Women like Valenti also point to another area of under-examined celebrity: the celebrity feminist journalist, women whose journalistic capital is predicated largely on their feminism and their intervention into various public debates through a patently feminist lens. Others may include Hadley Freeman in the UK and Clementine Ford in Australia.
7. For example, the *Everyday Sexism Project* is one of the more successful, well-known online campaigns; originally begun as a website and a Twitter hashtag, the initiative encouraged women to post their everyday experiences of sexism online as a way of repudiating claims about the demise of sexism. Not insignificantly, in terms of my argument regarding the ongoing pull of non-fictional feminist literary texts, these stories were collated by the project's initiator, Laura Bates, in 2014 and published in book form. Similarly, Australia's online *Destroy the Joint* Facebook group, established 'for people who are sick of the sexism dished out to women in Australia, whether they be our first female Prime Minister or any other woman', published a series of essays in 2013 (Caro 2013).
8. For my purposes, it was interesting that Beyoncé and Emma Watson (along with other women such as Kim Kardashian and Kate Middleton) were among those invoked by Mendick et al.'s participants as being most significant (Mendick et al. 2015, p. 375). This example buttresses Mendick et al.'s claim that, through simply performing textual analyses of those 'we assume to be culturally significant,' we miss the opportunity to capture 'how people use [celebrity] culture in their everyday meaning-making practices'.
9. This lack of attention to fandom is partly due to my attempts—following York—to problematize the critical focus on industry/pro-

duction and consumption over agentic celebrities themselves. Nonetheless, there is important work that still needs to be done around celebrity feminism and audiences, including consumers of blockbusters.
10. In addition to celebrities who later add 'feminism' to their brand, there have also recently been other high-profile feminist activists such as Russia's Pussy Riot and Femen, and some consideration of their role as celebrities is also worthy of further critical engagement.

References

(2013) '10 Celebrities Who Say They Aren't Feminists', 17 December, *Huffington Post*, accessed via: http://www.huffingtonpost.com/2013/12/17/feminist-celebrities_n_4460416.html

Ahmed, S. (2000) 'Boundaries and Connections: Introduction', in S. Ahmed, J. Kilby, C. Lurie, M. McNeil & B. Skeggs eds. *Transformations: Thinking Through Feminism*, London: Routledge, pp. 111–118

Aran, I. (2014) 'Cosmo, Ms Foundation Name Emma Watson Celebrity Feminist of 2014', 20 December, *Jezebel*, accessed via http://jezebel.com/cosmo-ms-foundation-name-emma-watson-feminist-celebr-1673601657

Arquette, R. (2015) 'Best Supporting Actress 2015 Oscar Speech', YouTube, accessed via https://www.youtube.com/watch?v=6wx-Qh4Vczc

Baer, H. (2015) 'Redoing Feminism: Digital Activism, Body Politics, and Neoliberalism', *Feminist Media Studies*, DOI: 10.1080/14680777.2015.1093070

Banet-Weiser, S. (2015) 'Popular Misogyny: A Ziegiest', 15 January, accessed via http://culturedigitally.org/2015/01/popular-misogyny-a-zeitgeist/

Bates, L. (2014) *Everyday Sexism*, London: Simon & Schuster

Berlant, L. (2004) 'Introduction: Compassion (and Withholding)', in L. Berlant, ed. *Compassion: The Culture and Politics of an Emotion*, New York: Routledge, pp. 1–13

boyd, d. (2013) *It's Complicated: The Social Lives of Networked Teens*, New Haven: Yale University Press

Brady, A. (2016) 'Taking Time Between G-String Changes to Educate Ourselves: Sinead O'Connor, Miley Cyrus, and Celebrity Feminism', *Feminist Media Studies*, accessed via DOI: 10.1080/14680777.2015.1137960

Bratich, J. (2007) 'Programming Reality: Control Societies, New Subjects, Powers of Transformation', in D. Heller ed. *Makeover Television: Realities Remodelled*, London: IB Tauris

Brown, W. (1995) *States of Injury: Power and Freedom in Late Modernity*, Princeton: Princeton University Press

Brunsdon, C. (1997) *Screen Tastes*, London: Routledge

Budgeon, S. (2001) 'Emergent Feminist (?) Identities: Young Women and The Practice of Micropolitics', *European Journal of Women's Studies*, 8.1: 7–28

Butler, J. (1990) *Gender Trouble*, New York: Routledge

Caro, J. ed. (2013) *Destroying the Joint: Why Women Have to Change the World*, Sydney: Penguin

Casey, S. (2015) *Australian Feminist Approaches to Mass Awareness Campaigns: Celanthropy, Celebrity Feminism and Online Activism*, unpublished doctoral thesis, Griffith University, Australia

Cobb, S. (2015) 'Is This What a Feminist Looks Like? Male Celebrity Feminists and the Postfeminist Politics of "Equality"', *Celebrity Studies*, 6.1: 136–139

Couldry, N. & Markham, T. (2007) 'Celebrity Culture and Public Connection: Bridge or Chasm?' *International Journal of Cultural Studies*, 10.4: 403–421

Day, E., Hoggard, L., & Bromwich, K. (2015) '99% of women working in the film and TV industries have experienced sexism', 27 September, The Guardian, accessed via https://www.theguardian.com/film/2015/sep/27/sexism-film-industry-stories

de Leon, A. (2015) 'The Trouble with Celebrity Feminism', 24 April, *Bitch Media*, accessed via https://bitchmedia.org/post/the-trouble-with-celebrity-feminismpatricia-arquette-oscars-emma-watson

Destroy the Joint (2012) https://www.facebook.com/DestroyTheJoint/

Douglas, S. (1994) *Where the Girls: Growing Up Female with the Mass Media*, London: Penguin

Dow, B. (1996) *Prime Time Feminism: Television, Media Culture and the Women's Movement Since 1970s*, Philadelphia: University of Pennsylvania Press

Drake, P. & Miah, A. (2010) 'The Cultural Politics of Celebrity', *Cultural Politics*, 6.1: 49–64

Driessens, O. (2013) 'The Celebritization of Society and Culture: Understanding the Structural Dynamics of Celebrity Culture', *International Journal of Cultural Studies*, 16.6: 641–657

Eberly, R. (2000) *Citizen Critics: Literary Public Spheres*, Chicago: University of Illinois Press

Everyday Sexism Project, accessed via http://everydaysexism.com/

Ferriss, K.O. (2010) 'The Next Big Thing: Local Celebrity', *Society*, 47.5: 392–395

Fuqua, J.V. (2011) 'Brand Pitt: Celebrity Activism and the Make It Right Foundation in Post-Katrina New Orleans', *Celebrity Studies*, 2:2, 192–208

Gamson, J. (2011) 'The Unwatched Life Is Not Worth Living: The Elevation of the Ordinary in Celebrity Culture', *PMLA*, 126.4: 1061–1069

Gay, R. (2014a) *Bad Feminist: Essays*, New York: Harper

——— (@rgay) 'The idea that queers & POC have had their time in the struggle spotlight long enough. Eek. Ma'am. Congrats on yr Oscar tho. You are talented', 22 February 2015. Tweet

——— (2014b) 'Lena Dunham, a Generation's Gutsy Ambitious Voice', 24 September, *Time*, accessed via http://time.com/3425759/lena-dunham-a-generations-gutsy-ambitious-voice/

——— (2014c) 'Emma Watson? Jennifer Lawrence? These Aren't the Feminists You Are Looking For', 10 October, *The Guardian*, http://www.theguardian.com/commentisfree/2014/oct/10/-sp-jennifer-lawrence-emma-watson-feminists-celebrity

George, K. (2014) 'Emma Watson's #HeForShe UN Speech Inspires Taylor Swift and Five Other Amazing Reactions', 30 September, *Bustle*, accessed via http://www.bustle.com/articles/41889-emma-watsons-heforshe-un-speech-inspires-taylor-swift-and-5-other-amazing-reactions

Gill, R. (2007) 'Postfeminist Media Culture: Elements of A Sensibility', *European Journal of Cultural Studies*, 10.2: 147–66

Griffin, P. (2015) *Popular Culture, Political Economy and The Death of Feminism*, London: Routledge

Hamad, H. & Taylor, A. (2015) 'Feminism and Contemporary Celebrity Culture', *Celebrity Studies*, 6.1: 124–127

Hasinhoff, A. (2014) 'Contradictions of Participation: Critical Feminist Interventions in New Media Studies', *Communication and Critical/Cultural Studies*, 11.3: 270–272

Henderson, M. (2006) *Marking Feminist Times: Remembering the Longest Revolution in Australia*, Bern: Peter Lang

Hills, R. (2015) *The Sex Myth: The Gap Between Our Fantasies and Reality*, New York: Simon & Schuster

Hindman, M. (2009) *The Myth of Digital Democracy*, New York: Princeton University Press

hooks, b. (1994) *Outlaw Culture*, New York: Routledge

Hopkins, S. (2016) 'Bow Down Bitches: When Celebrity Feminism Goes Wrong', *The Conversation*, 25 February, accessed via https://theconversation.com/bow-down-bitches-when-celebrity-feminism-goes-wrong-55033

Jane, E. (2014a) '"You're a Ugly, Whorish, Slut": Understanding E-bile', *Feminist Media Studies*, 14.4: 531–546

Keller, J. (2012) 'Virtual Feminisms: Girls' Blogging Communities, Feminist Activism and Participatory Politics', *Information, Technology and Society*, 15.3: 429–447

——— (2015) 'Girl Power's Last Chance? Tavi Gevinson, Feminism and Popular Media Culture', *Continuum*, 29.2: 274–285

——— (2016) *Girls Feminist Blogging in a Postfeminist Age*, New York: Routledge

Keller, J. & Ringrose, J. (2015) '"But then Feminism Goes Out the Window!": Exploring Teenage Girls' Critical Response to Celebrity Feminism', *Celebrity Studies*, 6.1: 132–135

Kilpatrick, A. (2015) 'The Problem with Making Celebrities the Faces of Feminism', 3 April, *Newsweek*, accessed via http://www.newsweek.com/problem-making-celebrities-face-feminism-319430

Mackenzie, M. (2015) 'Why I'm Not Really Here For Emma Watson's Feminism Speech At the U.N.', 24 September, *BlackGirlDangerous*, accessed via http://www.blackgirldangerous.org/2014/09/im-really-emma-watsons-feminism-speech-u-n/

Marshall, P.D. (1997) *Celebrity and Power*, Minneapolis: University of Minnesota Press

Marwick, A. & boyd, d. (2011) 'To See and Be Seen: Celebrity Practice on Twitter', *Convergence*, 17.2: 139–158

McDonald, S.N. (2015) 'Are Celebrity Feminists Glamorous Hypocrites?', 3 April, *Sydney Morning Herald*, accessed via http://www.smh.com.au/comment/are-celebrity-feminists-glamorous-hypocrites-20150401-1md9fy.html

McNay, L. (2010) 'Feminism and Post-Identity Politics: The Problem of Agency'. *Constellations*, 17.4: 512–525

McRobbie, A. (2004) 'Notes on Postfeminism and Popular Culture: Bridget Jones and the New Gender Regime', in A. Harris ed. *All About the Girl*, London: Routledge, pp. 3–14

——— (2009) *The Aftermath of Feminism*, London: Sage

Mendick, H., Allen, K. & Harvey, L. (2015) 'Turning to the Empirical Audience: The Desired but Denied Object of Celebrity Studies?', *Celebrity Studies*, 6.3: 374–377

Moran, R. (2015) '#EndViolenceAgainstWomen: Thousands Join Social Media Campaign to Name the Men Who Troll Them Online', 4 December, *Daily Life*, accessed via http://www.dailylife.com.au/dl-people/endviolenceagainstwomen-thousands-of-women-join-social-media-campaign-to-name-the-men-who-troll-them-online-20151204-glfffm.html

Negra, D. (2009) *What a Girl Wants: Fantasizing the Reclamation of Self in Postfeminism*, London: Routledge

——— (2014) 'Claiming Feminism: Commentary, Autobiography and Advice Literature for Women in the Recession', *Journal of Gender Studies*, 23.3: 275–286

Ohlsson, A., Forslid, T. & Steiner, A. (2014) 'Literary Celebrity Reconsidered', *Celebrity Studies*, 5.1–2: 32–44

Page, R. (2012) 'The Linguistics of Self-Branding and Micro-Celebrity in Twitter: The Role of Hashtags', *Discourse and Communication*, 6.2: 181–201

Pearce, L. (2004) *The Rhetorics of Feminism*, London: Routledge

Penny, L. (2015) *Unspeakable Things: Sex, Lies and Revolution*, London: Bloomsbury

Redmond, S. (2016) 'Introduction: The Publics of Celebrity', in P.D. Marshall & S. Redmond eds. *A Companion to Celebrity*, London: Wiley Blackwell, pp. 79–82

Reger, J. (2012) *Everywhere and Nowhere: Contemporary Feminism in the United States*, New York: Oxford University Press

Rein, I., Kotler, P. & Stoller, M. (1997). *High Visibility: The Making and Marketing of Professionals into Celebrities*, New York: NTC

Rojek, C. (2015) *Presumed Intimacy: Parasocial Interaction in Media, Society and Celebrity Culture*, London: Polity

Romano, T. (2014) 'Laverne Cox: "I Absolutely Consider Myself a Feminist"', *Dame Magazine*, accessed via http://www.damemagazine.com/2014/06/01/laverne-cox-i-absolutely-consider-myself-feminist#sthash.xNdmwepz.dpuf

Saad, N. (2015) 'Kaley Cuoco-Sweeting Explains Why She's Not a Feminist', 30 December, *Los Angeles Times*, accessed via http://www.latimes.com/entertainment/gossip/la-et-mg-kaley-cuoco-redbook-feminism-breast-implants-sinus-surgery-20141230-story.html

Scharff, C. (2011) *Repudiating Feminism: Young Women in a Neoliberal World*, Farham: Ashgate

Shaw, F. (2013) 'Blogging and the Women's Movement', in S. Maddison & M. Sawer eds., *The Women's Movement in Protest, Institutions and the Internet: Australia in Transnational Perspective*, Oxford: Routledge, pp. 118–131

Slaughter, A. (2015) *Unfinished Business: Women, Men, Work and Family*, New York: Random House

Simic, Z. (2010) 'Door Bitches of Club Feminism: Academia and Feminist Competency', *Feminist Review*, 95: 75–91

Smith, M. (2014) 'Emma Watson's UN Speech: What Our Reaction Tells Us About Feminism', 29 September, *The Conversation*, accessed via http://theconversation.com/emma-watsons-un-speech-what-our-reaction-says-about-feminism-32024

Sollee, K. (2015) '6 Things to Know About Fourth Wave Feminism', 31 October, *Bustle*, accessed via http://www.bustle.com/articles/119524-6-things-to-know-about-4th-wave-feminism

Steinem, G. (2015) *My Life on the Road*, London: Oneworld

Taylor, A. (2008) *Mediating Australian Feminism: Rereading the First Stone Media Event*, Oxford: Peter Lang

────── (2011) 'Blogging Solo: New Media, 'Old' Politics', *Feminist Review* 99: 79–97

────── (2012) *Single Women in Popular Culture: The Limits of Postfeminism*, Basingstoke: Palgrave Macmillan

Thorp, C. (2015) '8 Male Celebrities Who Are Proud to Be Feminists', 25 March, *Marie Claire*, accessed via http://www.marieclaire.co.uk/blogs/548739/8-male-celebrities-who-are-proud-to-be-feminists.html

Turner, G. (2006) 'The Mass Production of Celebrity: 'Celetoids,' Reality TV and the 'Demotic Turn'', *International Journal of Cultural Studies*, 9.2:153–165

────── (2010) *Ordinary People in the Media: The Demotic Turn*, London: Sage

────── (2014) *Understanding Celebrity*, London: Sage

────── (2016a) *Re-inventing the Media*, London: Routledge

——— (2016b) 'Celebrity, Participation, and the Public', in P.D. Marshall & S. Redmond eds. *A Companion to Celebrity*, London: Wiley Blackwell, pp. 83–97

Valenti, J. (2014a) 'Beyoncé's Flawless Feminist Act at the VMAs Leads the Way for Other Women', 26 August, *The Guardian*, http://www.theguardian.com/commentisfree/2014/aug/25/beyonce-flawless-feminist-vmas

——— (2014b) 'When Everyone Is a Feminist, Is Anyone?', 24 November, *The Guardian*, http://www.theguardian.com/commentisfree/2014/nov/24/when-everyone-is-a-feminist

——— (2015) 'Feminism Isn't Just a Fad – And That's Why So Many Anti-feminists Are Angry', 30 December, *The Guardian*, accessed via http://www.theguardian.com/commentisfree/2015/dec/30/feminism-not-just-a-fad-anti-feminists-are-angry?CMP=fb_gu

Vernon, H. (2015) *Hot Feminist: Modern Feminism With Style, Without Judgement*, London: Hodder & Stoughton

Watson, E. (2014) 'Gender Equality Is Your Issue Too', 20 September, UNWomen, accessed via http://www.unwomen.org/en/news/stories/2014/9/emma-watson-gender-equality-is-your-issue-too

Weidhase, N. (2015) 'Beyonce Feminism and the Contestation of the Black Feminist Body', *Celebrity Studies*, 6.1: 128–131

Wicke, J. (1994) 'Celebrity Material: Materialist Feminism and the Culture of Celebrity', *South Atlantic Quarterly*, 93.4: 751–778

York, L. (2013) 'Star Turn: The Challenges of Theorizing Celebrity Agency', *The Journal of Popular Culture*, 46.6: 1330–1347

Ziesler, A. (2014) 'Let's Not Fawn Over Male Celebrity Feminists: Making Stars Weigh in on Women's Rights Is Hurting the Cause', 21 August, *Salon*, accessed via http://www.salon.com/2014/08/20/lets_not_fawn_over_male_celebrity_feminists_making_stars_weigh_in_on_womens_rights_is_hurting_the_cause/

Erratum to: Celebrity and the Feminist Blockbuster

Anthea Taylor

Erratum to:
A. Taylor, *Celebrity and the Feminist Blockbuster*,
DOI 10.1057/978-1-137-37334-2

This book was inadvertently published without updating the following corrections:

Abbreviations:
p. = page

Corrections:

Introduction
p.3 "well-knowness" has been changed to "well-knownness"
p.14 'different ways – ' has been changed to 'different ways–'
p.19 'intersections' has been changed to 'intersection'

The updated online version of this book can be found at
https://doi.org/10.1057/978-1-137-37334-2

Introduction to Part I

p.59 'second-wave' has been changed to 'second wave'
p.60 'their own, and thus feminism's visibility' has been changed to 'their own, and thus feminism's, visibility'

Chapter 3

p.63 'feminist, Lena Dunham' has been changed to 'feminist Lena Dunham'
p.64 'an homogenous' has been changed to 'a homogeneous'
p.70 'as wide as audience' has been changed to 'as wide an audience'
p.77 'indeed a goal' has been changed to 'indeed was a goal'
p.79 'toll,' has been changed to 'toll'

Chapter 4

p.95 'its author's' has been changed to 'their author's'
p.103 'Her she recruits' has been changed to 'Here she recruits'
p.104 'It is not just journalists making such claims but Friedan herself, who is' has been changed to 'It was not just journalists making such claims but Friedan herself, who was'
p.104 'describes Friedan' has been changed to 'described Friedan'
p.106 'thereby seeking' has been changed to 'thereby seeks'
p.115 'feminist' pasts' has been changed to 'feminist pasts'
p.115 'kinds' has been changed to 'kind'

Chapter 5

p. 127 'USA texts and journalists' has been changed to 'American media'
p. 128 'more recent attempts to adapt' has been changed to 'attempts to adapt'
p. 130 'USA $25,000' has been changed to '$25,000 (USD)'
p. 131 'as well to' has been changed to 'as well as to'
p. 141 'celebrity game, and quiz' has been changed to 'celebrity game and quiz'
p. 145 'situate in itself' has been changed to 'situate itself'
p. 148 'critique' has been changed to 'critique,' and '*The Whole Woman,*' has been changed to '*The Whole Woman*'
p. 148 'thus the feminism' has been changed to 'thus to the feminism'
p. 150 'let alone analysis of,' has been changed to 'let alone analysis, of'

Introduction to Part II
p. 161 'selves has' has been changed to 'selves have'
p. 161 'predecessors is not' has been changed to 'predecessors not'

Chapter 6
p. 172 'imbrication' has been changed to 'implication'
p. 174 ', with the headline' has been changed to '; with the headline'
p. 182 'as for other' has been changed to 'as other'
p. 185 'could up take up' has been changed to 'could take up'

Chapter 7
p. 198 'forms of celebrity,' has been changed to 'forms of celebrity'
p. 200 'rather advocating' has been changed to 'rather than advocating'
p. 204 'mother,' has been changed to 'mother'
p. 207 'branding to' has been changed to 'branding in'
p. 211 'Roxanne' has been changed to 'Roxane'
p. 213 'the grounds of privileging of' has been changed to 'the grounds of privileging'
p. 214 'she takes up in further' has been changed to 'she takes up further'
p. 220 'via such as platforms as Twitter' has been changed to 'via platforms such as Twitter'
p. 223 'Sandberg' has been changed to 'Sandberg's'

Chapter 8
p. 238 'Poehler' has been changed to 'Poehler's'
p. 248 'of maintaining' has been changed to 'as maintaining'
p. 250 'has been to seen' has been changed to 'has been seen'
p. 260 'attempt exercise' has been changed to 'attempt to exercise'
p. 254 'thus reaffirming' has been changed to 'reaffirming'
p. 260 'notoriety' has been changed to 'fame'

Chapter 9
p. 272 'school girl, Hermoine Grainger' has been changed to 'school girl, Hermione Granger,'
p. 272 'UN Women's' has been changed to 'UN Women'
p. 279 'of different tenor' has been changed to 'of a different tenor'
p. 284 'attempts to the silence' has been changed to 'attempts to silence'

ERRATUM TO: CELEBRITY AND THE FEMINIST BLOCKBUSTER

p. 287 'new environment' has been changed to 'new media environment'
p. 290 'social function of celebrity feminists' has been changed to 'social function of celebrity feminism'
p. 291 'chose' has been changed to 'choose'
p. 292 'come terms' has been changed to 'come to terms'
p. 292 'is one of which' has been changed to 'is one to which'
p. 293 footnote 6: 'reveal' has been changed to 'reveals'

INDEX

A
activism, digital, 235–63, 282–6
activism, discursive, 33–4, 212, 258, 283
advertising, 72, 75, 98, 130, 172, 209, 253, 258
affective investments, 11, 39, 45, 80, 83, 86n5, 99, 103, 105, 132, 185, 188, 212, 253, 288, 289, 291
agency, 2, 5, 6, 12, 19n5, 43–8, 63–85, 99, 101, 110, 113, 131, 139, 143, 152n18, 167, 179, 183, 245, 247
ageing, and celebrity, 15, 138–41, 147–8
Ahmed, Sara, 145, 148, 285
Amy Poehler's Smart Girls, 242–8
archives, 10, 14, 46–7, 52n8, 63, 71, 129, 132, 289
Ask Amy, 243, 245–7, 253
audiences, 2, 11, 13–16, 18–19, 27, 33, 35, 39, 41, 44, 45, 60, 65, 70, 73, 75, 82, 83, 95, 98, 103, 106, 113, 128, 129, 132, 138, 141–2, 144, 146–7, 149–50, 180, 182, 184–5, 188, 202, 203, 208, 210, 212–13, 216, 217, 223, 236, 238, 243, 245–6, 257, 259, 273, 278, 282–4, 287–91
authenticity, 5, 14, 27, 31–2, 70, 95, 109, 112, 139, 179–80, 187, 218, 221, 238, 243, 247, 248, 251, 253, 255, 261, 278–80, 288, 291
authorial profiles, 10, 14, 37, 82, 94, 101–7, 133–4, 176, 201, 221
autobiography, 10, 18, 40, 47, 66, 97, 101, 103, 106, 109–16, 212, 236–8, 250–2, 288

B
Bad Feminist, 17, 197, 211–22, 257, 279–80
Bakhtin, Mikhail, 128
'Ban Bossy', 208–10

Note: Page numbers followed by "n" refers to notes.

Banet-Weiser, Sarah, 48, 162, 199, 200, 203, 207, 209, 214, 219, 222, 242, 243, 246, 247, 254, 260, 274, 283, 284
Barker-Plummer, Bernadette, 5, 29–31, 129
Barthes, Roland, 35, 38, 40–1, 107
Beauty Myth, The, 16, 98, 165–73, 175–7
Beyonce, 3, 209, 271–3, 275, 280, 281, 289, 293n8
biography, 37, 40, 47, 76, 94, 97, 102, 109, 112, 139, 168, 176, 209
blockbuster, definition of, 2, 35–6
blogging, 222, 241, 274, 278, 282, 283, 285, 286, 289
book covers, 37, 83, 169, 175, 187, 199, 201, 253
Bourdieu, Pierre, 11, 36, 37, 71
boyd, dannah, 3, 6, 44, 46, 128, 179, 181–2, 184, 186, 187, 220, 235, 246, 253, 260, 280, 290
branding (incl self), 7, 17, 38, 48–9, 64, 69, 71, 73, 81, 85, 93, 103, 140, 144, 161–2, 178–86, 197, 203, 205–10, 211, 214–16, 220–3, 236, 242, 243, 245, 246, 248, 249, 257, 278, 281, 282, 287, 292
Brown, Helen Gurley, 2, 14, 61, 63–92, 98, 251
Butler, Judith, 105, 128, 221, 251, 273

C

capital, celebrity, 2, 7, 9, 14, 17, 18, 38, 59, 60, 80, 82, 100, 113, 118n5, 129, 138, 139, 150n5, 162, 165, 167, 169, 173, 177, 178, 186, 203, 206, 207, 209, 210, 217, 223, 224n9, 242, 244, 249, 255–7, 259–61, 272, 290, 293n6
celanthropy, 207, 208, 254

celebrity, academic, 220–3
celebrity, literary, 19, 31, 34, 39, 41, 44, 46, 52
celebrity, micro, 179, 189n6, 205, 211, 216–18, 245, 253
celebrity studies, 4, 5, 12, 37, 41, 44, 45, 74, 288, 293n3
choice, 108, 209, 241, 247, 248
class, 31, 32, 43, 49, 98, 209, 212, 278, 279, 282
Clinton, Hillary, 204, 239, 244, 257
comedy, 128, 141–7, 237, 239, 248
consciousness-raising, 51n4, 75, 97, 132, 195, 207, 213, 215, 261, 273
consumption, 16, 44–5, 68, 71, 77, 81, 82, 180, 183, 185, 201, 204, 209, 220, 245, 246, 291
convergence culture, 16, 71, 224
Cosmopolitan, 64, 66, 70, 73, 81–2, 153n20, 258, 272
Cottin, Letty, 68, 71–7, 87
cultural intermediaries, 2, 11, 14, 37, 60, 63, 71, 77, 81, 84, 101, 176, 220
cultural memory, 13, 25, 49, 94, 105, 111, 115, 140

D

democratization, 187, 271, 284, 285, 287
Denfeld, Rene, 8, 167, 172–5
digital optimism, 285
Dunham, Lena, 2, 17–18, 63, 81, 162, 219, 235–63, 283, 284, 287, 288
Dow, Bonnie, 3, 11, 20, 29, 30, 51, 167, 276
Douglas, Susan, 65, 100, 161, 167, 276, 281
Dworkin, Andrea, 45, 116, 118n4, 133
Dyer, Richard, 10, 11, 26, 37, 94, 102, 110

E

empowerment, 63, 64, 80, 183, 199, 207–9, 236, 242, 243, 245, 248, 256, 273, 285
epitextuality, 37, 76, 99, 102, 183, 202, 253, 254

F

Facebook, 140, 199, 203, 210, 218, 223, 242, 243, 282, 286, 293n7
Faludi, Susan, 28, 98, 109, 119n16, 167, 200, 203, 224n6
fandom, 45, 238, 243, 293–4n9
Felski, Rita, 28, 35, 36, 51, 110
Female Eunuch, The, 10, 13, 15, 27, 51, 96, 127–8, 129–41, 146, 151n10
Feminine Mystique, The, 13, 14, 51, 61, 64, 85, 94–101, 103–4, 105, 106, 112–14, 116, 118, 164, 168, 190, 276
feminism, critiques of celebrity, 5, 27–31, 275–80
feminism, commodification of, 1, 3, 30, 48, 80
feminist, critiques of the wave model, 49–51, 171, 258–9, 283
feminism, fourth wave, 18, 247, 282, 283
feminism, generationalism within, 13, 50, 93, 212
feminism, liberal, 8, 15, 29, 94, 107, 109, 115, 131, 165, 201, 204, 241, 276, 280, 281, 289, 294
feminism, popular, 14, 27–30, 65, 91, 172, 177, 198, 211–14, 247
feminism, radical, 29, 36, 45, 66, 67, 82, 100, 116–17, 118, 130, 131, 133, 143, 150, 276, 281
feminism, second wave, 1, 8, 12–15, 19, 27, 29, 30, 49–51, 59, 64, 66, 84, 94–6, 98, 100, 101, 104–6, 111, 113–17, 130, 132, 134, 143, 150, 168, 172, 174, 185, 207, 212, 213, 257, 273
feminism, third wave, 8, 16, 82, 165, 167–74, 212, 215, 256, 257
Fey, Tina, 146, 238–41, 261, 262n1, 272
Fire with Fire, 16, 165, 166, 168, 172–5, 189n4
Foucault, Michel, 35, 40, 76, 217
Friedan, Betty, 2, 7, 8, 13–17, 26, 29, 46, 52, 63, 93–126, 130–2, 136, 138, 161

G

Gamson, Joshua, 10, 44, 71, 73, 76, 79, 144, 217, 284
Gay, Roxane, 2, 17, 36, 42, 47, 117, 162, 197–25
Geis, Bernard, 69–81, 86n2
Genette, Gerard, 12, 37, 76, 183, 202
Gill, Rosalind, 3, 197, 209, 222, 248, 273
Girls, 237, 248–2, 254, 256, 263n9
girls, 48, 162, 198, 199, 207–11, 242–48, 261, 289
Greer, Germaine, 1–2, 7, 8, 11, 13, 15–17, 26, 27, 45, 46, 59, 69, 80, 83, 85, 93–6, 98, 99, 117, 119n16, 127–53, 166, 167, 169, 172, 176–8, 185, 189n11, 214, 237, 261, 286, 288, 289

H

hashtag feminism, 219, 283
Having it All, 66, 107, 251
Hemmings, Clare, 4, 10, 111, 201, 211
Henderson, Margaret, 2, 11, 26, 30, 31, 35, 36, 94, 111–16, 201, 276
Henry, Astrid, 33, 50, 82, 93, 105, 168, 171, 173, 180, 198, 212, 215, 257

heterosexuality, 31, 98, 133–4, 212, 292n2
hooks, bell, 5, 30, 31, 98, 200, 205, 210, 213, 225n13, 279

I
individualism, 17, 48, 63, 199, 200, 211, 223, 274
industry, celebrity, 44–5, 48, 60, 99, 177, 293–4n9
identity, feminist, 6, 102, 145, 148, 212, 235, 236, 239, 256, 257, 260, 271, 275, 276, 278, 282, 286, 290
identity politics, critiques of, 32, 275
Instagram, 242, 254, 255, 262n8, 283
intersectionality, 17, 32, 213–15, 217, 223
intimacy, 41, 99, 107, 179, 180, 182, 184–6, 218, 220, 238, 246, 250, 256, 258, 288, 290

L
labour, 2, 5, 11–12, 14, 16, 19n6, 41, 44–8, 70, 77, 78, 80, 81, 95, 99, 138, 144, 162, 166, 182, 186, 187, 211, 220–2, 253, 283, 287
Lean In, 17, 67, 117, 197, 199–206, 209, 210
Lenny, 18, 248, 249, 256–60
Life So Far, 15, 95, 101, 110–14, 119n10
life writing, 15, 97, 100, 110–2, 110–12, 176, 250, 252, 261

M
McRobbie, Angela, 4, 5, 7, 30, 48, 145, 199, 200, 207, 239, 246, 252, 273, 274, 280, 282

Marshall, P.D., 5, 10, 19n5, 26, 44, 46, 142, 144, 179, 180, 217, 218, 221, 222, 275, 288
Marwick, Alice, 3, 6, 16, 44, 46, 48, 52n7, 79, 128, 179–82, 184, 186, 187, 218–20, 235, 245, 246, 253, 260, 280
Millett, Kate, 27, 29, 59, 96, 133–4, 151–2n14, 161
misogyny, online, 162, 254, 255, 283, 284
Moran, Joe, 5, 6, 34, 39, 60, 79, 102, 110, 112, 135, 137, 221, 253, 255, 284
Ms magazine, 29, 60, 75, 241
Murray, Simone, 2, 12, 27, 33, 35, 36, 80, 100, 119n9, 130, 133, 168, 172, 180, 181, 187, 202, 252

N
Negra, Diane, 4, 5, 48, 108, 148, 199, 201, 203, 204, 223, 236, 254, 273, 287
neoliberalism, 16, 17, 48, 84, 143, 162, 197–201, 207–11, 220, 223, 224n2, 237, 241, 243, 247, 248, 277
Norton, W.W., 96, 99, 118n5, 119n12
Not That Kind of Girl, 18, 235, 238, 246, 248, 250–4
National Organisation for Women (NOW), 93, 100, 117n1

O
obituaries, 83–4, 101, 104, 105

P
parasociality, 181, 290
paratextuality, 12, 33, 37, 40, 77, 83, 151n12, 169, 201, 204

Paglia, Camille, 8, 167, 173
Parks and Recreation, 237–40
Pearce, Lynne, 24, 36, 40, 66, 95, 131, 182, 288
planned parenthood, 253, 254
Poehler, Amy, 2, 17–18, 146, 162, 235–63, 287, 288
politics, celebritization of, 41–2
postfeminism, 12, 30, 49, 51n1, 145, 147–8, 162, 200, 211, 239, 243, 251, 257, 274
'post-race', 17, 198, 200, 213
promotion, book, 4, 36–7, 39, 46, 63, 70–80, 84, 86n10, 87n22, 99, 101–3, 118n5, 119n12, 129, 133, 137–8, 144, 152n18, 161, 180, 183, 185–7, 189n8, 201, 202, 248, 252–4, 259
publishing, 1–2, 19n1, 27, 35, 51n3, 60, 71, 73, 80, 82, 87n21, 119n9, 169, 213, 217, 242, 258, 287, 291

R
race, 32, 198, 201, 211, 223, 260, 278
reviews, 10, 37, 69, 98, 102, 175, 176, 178, 183, 204, 205, 215, 216, 218, 252, 262n3, 289
Rich, Adrienne, 168, 213, 257
Roiphe, Katie, 8, 167–8, 172–7
Rojek, Chris, 3, 9, 11, 26, 71, 79, 81, 88, 102, 107, 110, 112, 127, 137, 182, 207, 217, 255, 258, 290
Rowe, Kathleen, 128, 141, 147

S
Sandberg, Sheryl, 2, 17, 67, 97, 117, 150, 162, 197–225, 242, 243, 262n5, 288

Scanlon, Jennifer, 14, 63–71, 73–5, 77, 78, 80, 82, 85, 87n18, 87n22, 87n23, 98
Schumer, Amy, 146, 237
Second Stage, The, 95, 108, 166
serialization, 72–3, 96
Sex and the Single Girl, 13, 14, 51, 63–84, 96
Sex and the Office, 67, 79, 83, 86n2
Sex and the City, 13, 51n1, 63, 83, 87n23, 249
social media, 6, 17, 45, 140, 162, 178–88, 201, 203, 216, 222, 239, 242, 244, 254, 255, 277, 278, 282–5, 287, 290, 291
Steinem, Gloria, 19–20n8, 29, 66, 86n1, 87n16, 99–101, 130, 134, 166, 168, 169, 204, 257, 288

T
TED talks, 201–203, 215, 224n3
television, 7, 10, 15, 19–20n8, 40–2, 45, 47, 51n1, 52n9, 63, 66, 67, 72–3, 80, 82, 86n10, 99–100, 118n3, 128–30, 132, 135, 139, 141–9, 152n17, 153n25, 177, 182, 201, 211, 222, 235, 239, 242, 245, 247–9, 260, 261
transgender, 137, 153n22, 215, 280
Turner, Graeme, 5, 6, 9, 19n7, 34–5, 37–8, 40, 44, 48, 60, 70, 71, 76, 78, 80, 99, 103, 107, 136, 144, 179, 182, 183, 187, 188, 236, 245, 253, 259, 282, 284, 285, 288
Twitter, 17, 42, 48, 162, 165–90, 166, 179–88, 189n9, 207, 218–23, 225n17, 239, 242, 244, 254–6, 277, 283, 285, 290, 293n7

V

Vagina, 17, 165–6, 175–8, 181–8
Valenti, Jessica, 205, 224n9, 274, 281, 282, 293n6

W

Watson, Emma, 3, 237, 249, 272, 273, 276–8, 279, 289, 293n3
Weber, Brenda, 5, 6, 42–3, 47–8, 94
whiteness, 31, 197, 198, 209, 211, 213, 225n12, 250, 257, 277
Whole Woman, The, 129, 146, 148, 152n15
Wicke, Jennifer, 5, 11, 12, 25, 26, 31, 51n2, 110, 165, 174–5, 178, 225n11, 260, 261, 271, 278, 280, 292
Wolf, Naomi, 2, 7, 8, 16–17, 42, 47, 97, 98, 162, 165–90
Woolf, Virginia, 33, 43

Y

Yes, Please, 18, 235, 238, 240–2, 246
YouTube, 202, 239, 242, 245–7, 253, 262n4
York, Lorraine, 6, 9, 19n6, 44–6, 137, 140, 180–1, 255, 290, 293–4n9

The manufacturer's authorised representative in the EU is Springer Nature Customer Service Centre GmbH, Europaplatz 3, 69115 Heidelberg, Germany. If you have any concerns regarding our products, please contact ProductSafety@springernature.com

Printed and bound by CPI Group (UK) Ltd, Croydon, CR0 4YY

23/03/2026

02076459-0004